The Autobiography of John C. Van Dyke

The Autobiography of

A Personal

Narrative of

American Life

1861–1931

Edited by

Peter Wild

Foreword by

Philip L. Strong

University of Utah Press
Salt Lake City

John C. Van Dyke

709.2
V 2884 r

Title page photo: John C. Van Dyke in 1898, near the time of his desert travels. *(Special Collections and Archives, Rutgers University Libraries)*

Library of Congress Cataloging-in-Publication Data

Van Dyke, John Charles, 1856–1932.
    The autobiography of John C. Van Dyke : a personal narrative of
  American life, 1861–1931 / edited with an introduction by Peter
Wild   ;   foreword by Philip L. Strong.
        p.   cm.
    Includes bibliographical references (p.   ) and index.
    ISBN 0-87480-392-6
    1. Van Dyke, John Charles, 1856–1932. 2. Art historians—United
States—Biography. I. Wild, Peter, 1940–   . II. Title.
    N7483.V34A3   1993
    709′.2—dc20
    [B]   93-15742

Contents

Foreword

The accomplishments of John C. Van Dyke, 1856–1932, continue to have influence as I write. Surely, his stirring-up of the first controversial discussion about the works attributed to Rembrandt, great seventeenth-century Dutch painter, is one of his greatest influences. It happened in the 1920s.

A lengthy article which mentioned Van Dyke a few years ago in the *New Yorker* magazine, an exhibit at Harvard University in 1989, another exhibit in Berlin in the summer of 1991, and an article in the *Wall Street Journal* on October 3, 1991, all concern this controversy. It will not go away; we are now almost seventy years removed from the time when Van Dyke started it!

Van Dyke's part in stirring it up and the reasons for his conclusions all are related herein. The controversy led me to write to William W. Robinson, a curator at the Fogg Art Museum at Harvard. I asked him whether there had been controversy over paintings—almost eight hundred in number—attributed to Rembrandt prior to the time when John C. Van Dyke challenged the authenticity of many of them. He replied:

> Your question about disputes over Rembrandt attributions before the 1920s is difficult to answer. The first catalogue of Rembrandt's paintings, published by John Smith in 1836, listed 614 paintings. By the 1920s the number grew to almost 800. The trend was definitely to expand. That there were disputes about individual pictures and private doubts about the status of others is very likely. However, in the nineteenth century, the issue of the authenticity of Rembrandt and Rembrandtesque paintings was overshadowed by the prevailing idea of genius. Rembrandt was a genius and only a genius could be Rembrandt-like. Therefore, if a painting looked Rembrandtesque, it was regarded as a Rembrandt. The development of scientific connoisseurship—the application of observable criteria of style and technique to discriminate between the works of various artists or schools—was a product of Van Dyke's time, and it was this new idea that sparked the controversies over attribution. Berenson and his antagonists carried on over Italian paintings in much the same way and at the same moment as did Van Dyke and his detractors. It was to Van Dyke's

credit that he introduced some of the same critical thinking into Rembrandt studies and that he overcame the obstacle of Rembrandt's genius and tried to give the Rembrandt pupils their due.

I knew the author, John Charles Van Dyke, my first cousin once removed. In the 1920s and in the very early 1930s, he was an occasional dinner guest at "Stronghold," my family's Victorian home on Hamilton Street in New Brunswick, New Jersey. I was a boy then and the youngest of eight children. All of my generation of Strongs called him by an honorary title, "Uncle Jack," although we knew very well that he was not in fact an uncle to us. My father, incidentally, addressed him as "Jackie."

The kinship between the Van Dyke and the Strong families includes common descent from Professor Theodore Strong, 1790–1869, a long-time standout as a mathematics professor and for several years also vice-president of Rutgers College in New Brunswick. His daughter, Mary Dix Strong, married the father of John C. Van Dyke.

When John C. Van Dyke was young, his family resided right next to the residence of Professor Strong. Two of my uncles, Edward W. Strong and Alan H. Strong, as well as my father, Theodore Strong, Sr., were boyhood friends and playmates of their first cousin, John C. Van Dyke. Alan H. Strong, born the same year as John C. Van Dyke, also was his classmate at Rutgers College, and Van Dyke lived at my grandfather's residence— "Stronghold"—while attending Rutgers College.

John Charles Van Dyke was an exceptionally handsome and well-dressed gentleman; you need only look at a photograph of him in this book in order to reach that conclusion. My recollections of him include his sitting erect in his chair in his later years with an ever-present cane in front of him. He placed the cane straight up from the floor and always held it in place with both hands at the top.

The Van Dyke family of John Charles Van Dyke's generation was unfortunate in losing children who died young. Records show that four of nine children succumbed while less than two years of age, and two of those had been named "John Van Dyke." The parents of John Charles Van Dyke desperately wanted a child named John, it appears.

We can guess at the influence of John C. Van Dyke's father, John Van Dyke, on his son's career, and I shall relate some of the senior Van Dyke's life history. John Honeyman, grandfather of the senior Van Dyke, was George Washington's trusted and effective spy who furnished information for the success of the Battle of Trenton.

Born in 1807 and raised on a farm at Lamington in Somerset County, New Jersey, the senior Van Dyke—known by the nickname "Black Hawk"—moved to New Brunswick in Middlesex County, New Jersey, and there began his law career in the office of one James Schureman. Formerly a brave young Revolutionary soldier who had captured British Colonel Simcoe, commander of Simcoe's Raiders, Schureman also had represented New Jersey in the United States Senate.

Working from this good starting point, the elder Van Dyke was elected mayor of New Brunswick in 1830, at which time he could have been considered a "boy wonder." He was re-elected twice, and subsequently served as prosecutor of Middlesex County, New Jersey, congressman from a district in central New Jersey, first president of the former National Bank of New Jersey at New Brunswick, and a judge on New Jersey's highest court. In short, the "boy wonder" became "Mr. Everything," to my way of thinking.

His "finest hour" in politics and in public service, as I see it, came during the formation of the Republican party in central New Jersey. But first, let me refresh your memory from our history books.

The Whig political party failed to function as an effective national political force in the 1850s. Not long thereafter, with slavery as the main point of disagreement, the national Democratic party also sputtered and faltered; and by running two candidates for president in 1860, its adherents were left to observe politically shrewd Abraham Lincoln beat them both. He had united in the Republican party that year many former Whigs and "Free Soilers" as well as voters from other and smaller political parties. Among Lincoln's supporters was the senior Van Dyke.

In the Central New Jersey area there was ferment and disagreement about slavery in the 1850s, even though New Jersey was a state in which slave ownership was not widespread. After a prominent professional citizen of New Brunswick had written a defense of slavery in 1855, the senior Van Dyke came out with a refutation. Published in sixteen blistering pages in 1856, *"Slaveholding Not Sinful": A Reply* helped to keep the senior Van Dyke in the forefront politically in the 1850s and into the 1860s in Central New Jersey.

Given present culture, and our moral standards emphatically in favor of freedom, Van Dyke's 1856 tract is readily acceptable and sensible now. But in 1856, I firmly believe, it was a radical declaration and a bold step, even for New Jersey.

Consider that Rodman Price, governor of New Jersey from 1854 through 1857, openly advocated slavery as an acceptable institution. (In 1861, Price was in favor of secession from the union as an action to be taken by the State of New Jersey!)

That the senior Van Dyke wrote against proslavery sentiments of persons high-placed is a way to measure the radicalism of his writing in 1856. That slavery was legal in those days should not be overlooked. And this was eight years before Lincoln's wartime Emancipation Proclamation, and also his Gettysburg Address, in which he advocated equality.

A family anecdote of my generation of Strongs concerns the service of the senior Van Dyke as a judge. At some point after he had been elevated to the state's supreme court, he became a dissenter and voted steadily in opposition—and often alone in opposition—to the majority of the court. Mercer Beasley, the chief justice, was sufficiently concerned that he contacted my grandfather, the late Woodbridge Strong, who was a brother-in-law of the senior Van Dyke and also a judge. Whether Beasley's concern was addressed successfully or not, I do not know.

After his political power had waned, and when he was sixty-one years old, the senior Van Dyke left New Jersey for good and settled with his wife and youngest children in Wabasha, Minnesota. He served for a time as a judge in a high court in Minnesota thereafter. But what interests me most about Wabasha was the friendship that the senior Van Dyke struck up with an Indian chief. The friendship led to the younger Van Dyke—John C.—participating as a boy in his teens in hunting trips with Indians. Not many of his contemporaries from the East had that experience.

Political and governmental activity, some of both having been related in the foregoing paragraphs, by the senior Van Dyke must have made him controversial as well as prominent to varying degrees in New Jersey between 1830 and 1868. And both the prominence and the controversies inevitably did not affect the senior Van Dyke only. In other words, after his birth in 1856, John C. Van Dyke adjusted to an existence in which prominence and also conflict surrounding the father also affected the son, as well as other family members.

There occurred an example of this prominence early in 1861 when Lincoln was traveling by train to his first inauguration. When the train stopped at New Brunswick, who introduced the president-elect to the crowd? The senior Van Dyke.

And now, finally, "the secret" will be revealed herein. It is a "secret" that in fact was known to many people in New Brunswick in the lifetime of John C. Van Dyke, and a few, old residents who knew it are around to this day. Although he never married, John C. Van Dyke was the father of a daughter, Clare. Her mother was the wife of a Rutgers College faculty member.

John C. Van Dyke was devoted to Clare. Never did he think of disowning her. He raised her, and in his later years frequently visited her and her husband, Professor Harry Parr of the Columbia University School of Engineering. Van Dyke described Clare as his "godchild" and "namesake" in his will, and he bequeathed to her almost his entire estate after his death. Clare Van Dyke Parr, incidentally, was a very beautiful woman.

Professor and Mrs. Harry Parr had no children. Hence no one now living will be embarrassed by this revelation of parenthood.

Finally, John C. Van Dyke lies buried in my family's plot in Elmwood Cemetery, New Brunswick. The graves of two of his childhood chums and playmates—Alan H. Strong and Theodore Strong, Sr.—are close by.

I hope that you enjoy this book as much as my wife and I did.

Cranbury, New Jersey   PHILIP L. STRONG
June 15, 1992

Acknowledgments

Thanking people for their help is more than a matter of form to me.

Renée S. House, who holds Van Dyke's former position as director of the Gardner A. Sage Library, and John W. Beardslee III, Professor Emeritus of Church History, both at the New Brunswick Theological Seminary, generously gave of their knowledge during my trips to New Brunswick. Mr. Milton Nieuwsma, Vice-President for Development and Seminary Relations, helped in smoothing out some of this book's final details. Also in New Brunswick, attorney Philip L. Strong, Esq., Van Dyke's first cousin once removed, not only preserved the manuscript of the following text through the years, he also took time from his law practice to help me piece together the specifics of Van Dyke's life. Without Mr. Strong's guidance and generosity with photographs, our knowledge of one of our century's foremost art connoisseurs and desert travelers would be slim in several important areas. And I should add that at Rutgers University a patient Ed Skipworth steered me toward Van Dyke material in the archives of the Alexander Library, then he followed through by providing photographs from the library's archives. Because of such people, I remember my visits to New Brunswick with special warmth.

At the University of Arizona Library, Lawrence Clark Powell, Professor, Residence Emeritus, listened to my research problems and urged me on despite their intractability. Month after month, Lois Olsrud, Roger Myers, Bruce Parsil, Charles Peters, Edith Ferrell, María Hoopes, Peter Steere, Christine Leischow, Linda Dols, and many other members of the faculty and staff responded to my questions. Their grace and patience convinced me once again that there's a special place in heaven for librarians.

Among my colleagues in the Department of English at the University of Arizona, Richard Shelton first introduced me to Van Dyke; Carl Berkhout helped me through bibliographical mare's nests; Larry Evers offered valued perspectives on Western American literature; and Duane Roen, also my neighbor, listened over the back fence to my Van Dyke stories. It was a pleasure to work with Zita Ingham on her fine dissertation analyzing the rhetoric of Van Dyke's prose. In the process, she suggested several new concepts, and the result of our happy wrangling was the publication of two coauthored articles on Van Dyke. I thank both Ron Steffens and Me Linda Johnson for cheering me through the cryptic ways of computers.

With the buoyant spirit for which she is known, Inga Kohn of the Department of French guided me through French Decadence, and before it was published she read my article on the "French Connection" in Van Dyke's life, Pierre Loti's possible influence on his prose. Robert M. Quinn, Professor Emeritus of Art, pointed me toward books in his field that otherwise likely would have remained unopened by me.

Quite by accident, I discovered that one of my undergraduate students, Linda Bayless, not only grew up across the Raritan River from New Brunswick, she was part of Van Dyke's Dutch subculture. Through many evenings of discussion, she shed light on Van Dyke's background, and she offered encouragement through a personally difficult time.

The trail of Van Dyke leads the researcher beyond his accustomed circles, out into new fields and toward new acquaintances. They range from the conscientious people in the library of a large medical school to desert naturalists and the admirably dedicated volunteers of local historical societies. At my first knock, Mr. E. Davis Gaillard, historian of the Onteora Club, where Van Dyke had a summer home in the Catskills, opened the door to materials not accessible through normal channels. I thank archivist/librarian Nancy Johnson of the American Academy and Institute of Arts and Letters for her faithful correspondence and assistance in obtaining photographs of Van Dyke. Some years ago, Professor James H. Maguire, coeditor of the Western Writers Series at Boise State University, heartened me to write a monograph on Van Dyke. Since then, Jim has continued with support that has turned an editor-author relationship into a friendship. Drawing on her work in the field, anthropologist Marilyn Saul spent patient hours helping me piece together several aspects of Van Dyke's life, particularly those regarding his Western forays. A gentle and thorough genealogist, Professor William C. Kleese, confirmed details of the Van Dyke family. My veterinarian, Dr. Drew Stern, revealed the water and nutritional needs of Van Dyke's little desert party of man, dog, and horse. Yet for all my desire to discover Van Dyke's dog, Cappy, in scattered photographs, Drew remained the professional. Despite my enthusiasm, he refused to identify what obviously was a border collie or a cocker spaniel as a fox terrier.

While working on a long project such as this one, any scholar acquires obligations he never can discharge. For their information and in cases their good help with photographs, I thank the people at the following institutions: the Arizona Historical Society; the San Diego Historical Society; the

San Bernardino Public Library; the San Bernardino County Museum; and the Wabasha Public Library. I particularly thank G. L. Moon of the Mojave River Valley Museum, Dorothea Simonson of the Montana Historical Society, Alan R. Woolworth of the Minnesota Historical Society, and Beryl Bell of the Daggett Historical Society.

One research issue deserves separate mention. A number of art specialists helped in establishing the possible connection between Van Dyke and the fine Stewart painting *On the Yacht* Namouna, *Venice*, 1890. I name them in the order in which they guided me along the trail: Barbara Kittle, Librarian, Museum of Art, the University of Arizona; Nancy Rivard Shaw, Curator of American Art, the Detroit Institute of Arts; Elizabeth R. McClintock, Assistant Curator, American Paintings, Sculpture and Drawings, the Wadsworth Atheneum; Linda Bantel, Edna S. Tuttleman Director of the Museum, Pennsylvania Academy of the Fine Arts; Annette Blaugrund, Andrew W. Mellon Senior Curator of Paintings, Drawings and Sculpture, the New-York Historical Society; and D. Dodge Thompson, Chief of Exhibitions, the National Gallery of Art. Raymond Petke of the Wadsworth Atheneum helped in obtaining the photograph of the Stewart painting reproduced below.

A sabbatical leave and grants from the University of Arizona eased the progress of the research.

I thank Don Bufkin for providing the map. Naturalists Hal Coss, David E. Brown, Neil Carmony, and other desert specialists urged me toward the new evaluation of Van Dyke's outdoor writings appearing below. I enjoyed the professionalism of such scientists. I also benefited from the comments of art historian Professor Sheldon Reich, who reviewed the entire manuscript.

The good ideas of David Teague, a graduate student at the University of Virginia, show the promise of a new generation of Van Dyke scholars.

Finally, I thank Peggy Flyntz. For well over a decade now, she has brought good cheer and sound advice to assembling such manuscripts as this one.

Much of the material in the following notes was pieced together over months and, in some cases, over years. On occasion, as with the possible appearance of Van Dyke in the Stewart painting, doubt continues to cloud the issue, and my method is to outline the circumstances and present the gathered evidence. In such efforts, many generous people, both named and not named, often lent their special knowledge, yet the responsibility for any errors in the editing and annotating of Van Dyke's text is entirely my own.

Editor's Introduction

We are about to open a long-closed door. Writer, desert traveler, and art connoisseur John C. Van Dyke was the friend of such richly varied figures as Mark Twain, John Muir, Andrew Carnegie, James McNeill Whistler, and others in the galaxy of bright personalities swirling about the century's turn. Yet most immediately, the compelling aspect of Van Dyke's life is not the glitter of a career burnished by adventures on the Western frontier, genuine intellectual depth, and nearly fifty books. Rather, the Van Dyke we first see was created by a public projecting its own yearnings on a popular but unusually private person. In this, one side of Van Dyke cooperated with his enthusiastic readers, for at times he lent his own, similar yearnings to shape his image. This hardly was the familiar case of a writer fashioning a public personality to bolster his publishing career. Van Dyke himself embodied many of the longings of the romantic though troubled late Victorians, and in this regard he reflects the national psyche of the period. Thus, our job is to explore this aspect while not losing sight of the quite different private man that the writer kept hidden from his readers. A good place to begin Van Dyke's story, then, is with an ardent public perception that took on its own reality.

The image of the lone horseman turning his back on civilization and, pistol strapped to his side, riding off into the pristine unknown strikes a deep chord in Americans. It wasn't always favorable. To the first settlers of Plymouth Colony, the surrounding forest struck fear in their hearts. It was an endless "howling wilderness" they faced, an unknown place of wolves, lurking Indians, and, some early pioneers believed, prowling devils. But as the decades passed and the first toeholds of Europeans grew into cities, ideas about the wild lands changed. With James Fenimore Cooper's nineteenth-century frontier hero, Natty Bumppo, serving as early evidence, attitudes slowly shifted into a more benevolent focus. Wilderness was not only a reservoir of untapped wealth in lumber, furs, and minerals, it could fulfill people's spiritual longings. In the ferny depths of the forest, far from the grime of cities, a person could enjoy his God-given freedoms. Better than that, by living "close to nature," living with the rhythms of the earth, he could find peace and self-fulfillment. Or so it was increasingly believed as the nation became more urbanized. As the painful realities of life in the wilds receded from daily experience, an appealing romanticism took its place. Fear had turned into desire.[1]

The changes helped make John C. Van Dyke a favorite of the reading public, a public, we should remember, in large part living on the crowded Eastern seaboard. When the writer of *The Desert* (1901) invited his readers to abandon the crowd and ride with him "beyond the wire fence of civilization," to ride out where there were no trails, readers stirred at the heady prospects. Out in the wilds, Van Dyke promised, they'd behold rainstorms rearing up in showers of gold and at evening watch peaks glowing like hot iron in the sunset. Then, as the gloom settled around them into the notches of the unexplored hills, they would feel the immensity of the universe. Living like that, their senses alive, they'd discover "the great truths" at "the source," wild nature (viii). Admittedly, for all the vividness of his observations, Van Dyke said precious little about himself, instead keeping the focus on the panoramas unfolding about him, as if he were describing huge, natural canvases. However, people reading between the lines to fill in their author's image could imagine their wilderness explorer traveling alone but perfectly at his ease with nature. How else could it be as they watched him scaling a precipice or crawling through the brush to observe the lithe ways of a mountain lion? Van Dyke's words were just what a nation too much in city pent wanted to hear.

That is not to say that Van Dyke suckled his readers on cliché. Quite the opposite. It was one thing to gain the public's sympathy for the secrets of New England's gentle hills, as Thoreau had done, or to have readers thrilling along with John Muir as he explored California's soaring, light-filled Sierra. Van Dyke staked out a far more difficult territory. In fact, he flew in the face of the nation's prejudices. That is, he took on the writer's greatest task, to change his readers' beliefs and to make them see the world with new eyes.

For up until Van Dyke's time, the country all but universally despised the deserts of America as wastelands. To a practical nation bent on wresting gold, timber, and other riches from the land, the Southwestern deserts of bare rock and endless cactus sweeps seemed useless places, and certainly they were not pleasant to look upon. Before them, nineteenth-century travelers eager to reach California's riches balked, pausing in awe at the unmapped, sandy regions. There, it was rumored, bandits lay in wait, renegade Indians thirsted for wayfarers' scalps, and human skeletons circled dry water holes. So people wondered over such feared and useless expanses, dubbing them, depending on one's preference for imagery, "The Devil's

Domain" or "God's Mistake" in the otherwise bountiful world He'd created for human usufruct.

Challenging such deep-seated prejudices directly, Van Dyke changed the nation's mind with the sheer force and beauty of his language. This he wisely combined with the revolutionary's ploy of turning the common wisdom upside down. To Van Dyke, the desert was a far safer place than the streets of crime-infested cities thousands of miles away. And it was a beautiful place. Just look at the sand dunes, drifting in patterns "as graceful as the lines of running water" (53). And it wasn't at all a dull place. How could it be when we see toads that bleed from the eyes and chromatic storms boiling across the endless landscapes? History favored his unusual approach. Just when the nation that recently had conquered the continent began to worry about losing both its contact with nature and its robust pioneer spirit, Van Dyke invitingly stretched his arm toward the great, arid, long-ignored vastness of the Southwest. Out there, the very air was colored with a "lilac-blue veiling" (81), the wolves still howled, and nature offered the city-weary individual new chances for fulfillment in a wild land, in a wilderness of mystery and superlatives. As Van Dyke hails it, the desert is "the most decorative landscape in the world, a landscape all color, a dream landscape" (56). In this sense, yes, Van Dyke told the public what it wanted to hear, but he spoke from the heart, in an unexpected way and about an unexpected subject. And, as we shall see, he also was writing the words that *he* wanted to hear.

In any case, largely through *The Desert* the nation "discovered" the Southwest, its Indians, strange plants, and exotic animals. Discovered, too, the first and still the best book to praise the arid lands. After nearly a century Van Dyke remains the grandfather of almost all American desert writers since, from Mary Austin to Joseph Wood Krutch and on down to today's Edward Abbey (Powell, *Southwest Classics* 315). But *The Desert* was not merely a literary coup. The shift it helped effect from utilitarian values to delicate appreciation of a "wasteland" led to action on the national level, to public outcries for creation of Joshua Tree, Saguaro, Mesa Verde, and the other national parks and monuments we now enjoy as major parts of our Southwestern heritage. And bearing further testimony to his lasting impact, as Van Dyke dazzled his generation, so he dazzles our own "ecological age," for—a remarkable accomplishment in itself—*The Desert* remains in print nearly a hundred years after its first appearance.

For all that, a writer can become lost in the bright light of his most famous work. Year after year, readers bought *The Desert* without paying much attention to the reality of its author. Buoyed by what they wanted him to be, Van Dyke devotees imagined him a romantic "desert rat" who preferred his rocky haunts to the grind of office and the grime of factories (Banham 158; Baylor). A few admirers, however, began to wonder how a man could possess, at once, the toughness and frontier skills to survive desert treks through 110-degree heat in a nearly waterless land and yet shrug off hardships to produce a book penned with the delicacy of the art connoisseur's refinement. Here the long string of ironies surrounding America's foremost desert writer begins to unfold. Chief among them is that the answer, at least the hint of one, was available all along, in reference books and in Van Dyke's own writings, waiting on library shelves, though even with them he remains a somewhat shadowy figure. Secondly, a point now verified by the publication of his autobiography, Van Dyke turns out to be not at all the man people imagined he was. He was hardly a frontiersman but, of all things, a professor of art history at prestigious Rutgers College (now University). He was not a ragtag wanderer but a habitué of the East Coast's most fashionable salons. And now the ironies begin to turn and turn on themselves. For the autobiography shows Van Dyke as a frontiersman, and, indeed, as something of a ragtag wanderer to boot. Such things reflect the richness of the figure we're about to meet, and perhaps at this point it would be helpful to give a brief outline of the elusive writer's life.[2]

John C. Van Dyke (1856–1932) was born at Green Oaks, a country mansion on the outskirts of New Brunswick, New Jersey. His was a prosperous, educated, and well-positioned family. The Van Dykes were proud of their long Dutch heritage going back to the settlement of New Amsterdam in the seventeenth century. They were well aware of the Revolutionary War heroes, public officials, and scholars in their lineage. Van Dyke's father, John Van Dyke, was at turns an attorney, bank president, congressman, friend of President Abraham Lincoln, and a member of the New Jersey Supreme Court. Van Dyke's maternal grandfather, Theodore Strong, was a noted mathematician and a professor at Rutgers. In brief, the Van Dykes were eupatrid folk, members of the country's unofficial aristocracy, but they allowed little room for affectation. Rather, mental and physical toughness, love of the outdoors, and public service were the family's watchwords. It was expected that the five Van Dyke boys would prosper, and they didn't disappoint their elders. Four of them became lawyers, one a medical doctor. But with that we have far more than yet another admirable but somewhat ho-hum American success story.

For the scene shifts from the idyllic college town of Van Dyke's early boyhood, with its ivied towers surrounded by gentle, green hills, to a Mississippi River steamer a few years later. We're in the freewheeling days of the opening West. Up in the pilot house the captain hears a disturbance on the deck and sends his tenderfoot clerk, little more than "a thin, whey-faced boy," down to stop the ruckus. In a few seconds, the boy confronts a drunken man trying to bash in a barrel of whiskey with an iron poker. The boy orders him to stop. The drunk turns, scoffs at the clerk, and supposes he'll run this mere stripling through with his poker.

What does the boy do? "Instantly I whipped out a small pearl-handled revolver and brought it to bear straight between his eyes." Allowing that he's no longer interested in whiskey, the man drops his poker and slinks off (*The Open Spaces* 175).

Of course, the pistol-wielding boy is our young John C. Van Dyke, and the incident shows the dual nature running through his character, whether in matters of art, religion, or society. In the variety of places he traveled or the people he met, Van Dyke presents himself as a study in contrasts. He was equally at home camped out alone on the bandit-infested U.S.-Mexican border or arguing the fine points of esthetics in a fashionable London bistro with expatriate artist James McNeill Whistler. For though Van Dyke grew up to take his place as a well-known academic and popular writer, in the process there were twists and turns in his life and a natural bent that gave his later work an extraordinary shape.

In 1868, for reasons still not entirely clear, Van Dyke's father moved the family from the East Coast to sparsely settled Minnesota. Reared to be independent, the Van Dyke boys had romped and hunted in the tame woods surrounding their mansion in New Brunswick. Now they were turned loose in a real wilderness. Van Dyke recounts how he made friends in a nearby settlement of Indians. The youth spent his days hunting and fishing with his new Sioux companions and idling about their tepees. In turn, the Indians liked the boy, so much so that one summer they invited him on a months-long, bone-jolting hunt after buffalo. It was an adventure with far more thrills than the usual dangers of stampeding buffalo pursued by galloping riders, for the little band boldly swung out into hunting grounds jealously guarded by tribes that were traditional enemies of the Sioux. But the party survived, traveling many hundreds of miles and ranging far out across the unsettled Great Plains, clear to the Rocky Mountains in present-day Montana. His appetite whetted for adventure, Van Dyke later went back to the area and lived the rough-and-tumble life of a cowboy.

In a word, Van Dyke saw himself as a child of the frontier. There he learned the outdoor skills that would serve him in adult forays into the American wilderness. When in later decades a respiratory ailment drove him to seek a cure in the dry air of the American Southwest, he didn't huddle in a hotel for invalids but struck off on his own into the much-feared deserts, wearing moccasins and finding his way by the stars. He was determined either to die in the wilderness or to come back to civilization cured. When confronted by five horse thieves with murder in their hearts, he brought his rifle into play and sent them slouching off.

Thus in Van Dyke we have the fortuitous blend of the frontiersman and the gentleman. Toughened to hardship, out in the wilds Van Dyke handled the everyday struggles of survival as a matter of course. This freed him to concentrate on his real interest, viewing nature as an art connoisseur would, describing the scenes before him as vast, natural canvases. As literary historian Lawrence Clark Powell states in *Southwest Classics*, frontiersman and art scholar Van Dyke developed into a superb outdoorsman as well as a superb "indoorsman" (319). Perhaps no one else in the nation was so well equipped to write his series of nature-travel books crowned by his esthetic masterpiece, *The Desert*. The dual qualities, then, served Van Dyke throughout his years. Steady with a gun, sharp of wit, the gentleman was not a person to be trifled with, either in a physical face-off or in the swordcraft of criticism.

However tempted he was by the wilds, the youth wanted more than the thrill of midnight stampedes and the freedom to throw down his bedroll wherever he pleased. He also felt the tug from the family's tradition of learning. In 1876, at the age of twenty, he returned to the East. There he attended Columbia Law School, and in 1877 he was admitted to the bar. But Van Dyke never practiced. After a *Wanderjahr*, he settled permanently in hometown New Brunswick, taking a position as an assistant in the Gardner A. Sage Library of the New Brunswick Theological Seminary. A pivotal period followed. Attracted to art, the young librarian became an admirer of impressionist paintings and a devotee of Art for Art's Sake. The airy movement held that the appreciation of beauty, especially the beauty of wild nature, is life's highest good. Thus we have the link between art and nature that informs the rest of Van Dyke's life. Getting his esthetic legs under him, he began publishing articles and books on art and started traveling across the Atlantic to visit Europe's treasure-troves of art.

In the meantime, he had become head librarian at the Sage, and his appointment in 1891 to the Rutgers faculty as its first professor of art history, a position he held concurrently with his library work, indicates his early publishing success. Thereafter, though his life is busy, the pattern is set. Using New Brunswick as his home base, the professor traveled often and widely, to every continent except Antarctica. And he also traveled in the "best" of social, literary, and artistic circles. In chapter 7, for example, the young esthete attends what he calls "beauty dinners." Here, the guests were chosen for their good looks, and Van Dyke tells of one such function "where all the women wore red tulle and diamonds, and the center of the round table was a great mass of poinsettias, with red ribbons leading up to the chandelier." But he was too much the aloof Calvinist not to look a bit askance at the bold display of extravagance, though, of course, as a fine fellow, he *did* attend. More importantly, when his career as a writer and art critic brightened nationally, he became an art advisor to millionaire industrialist Andrew Carnegie. He hobnobbed with Mark Twain and found the popular magazines of his day seeking out his work. In later years, his *Rembrandt and His School* caused an uproar in the art world and marked him as America's preeminent scholar of the old master.

At times in all this busyness, there seems hardly a president, actor, writer, painter, or millionaire outside Van Dyke's orbit. Yet as often happens with Van Dyke, one characteristic complements its opposite. The frequenter of fashionable dinner parties was also a loner, a man who periodically escaped glittering society and plunged off into the wilderness where he contended with dark thoughts and doubts about civilization's future. But Van Dyke was no self-absorbed, romantic fool. He realized that if out in the wilds he found solace and esthetic pleasure, brutal competition underlay the lovely appearances of nature. Human civilization, for all its ills, was a radical reply to the vast, heartless, Darwinian mechanism of the universe. So he swung back and forth, torn by the combined appeal and ugliness of two opposing systems. On this he remarks in chapter 21 of his autobiography: "I had always fought off the weariness of the one with the freshness of the other." And if the meaninglessness of it all sometimes dogged him, he drew on his staunch Dutch heritage: work was the antidote, the human mind wrestling with chaos. Thus Van Dyke kept coming out of the woods to write more books. When he died in 1932, he had nearly fifty titles on nature, travel, and art to his credit. He had become a popular author of his day. One might go on at some length reciting the accepted version of a life full of bright, contrasting swings, of ecstatic flights and morose self-doubts, of outer steeliness and inner sensitivity, of refined conversations and frontier adventures. But since we now have his autobiography, we can let Van Dyke tell his own story.

Or so it would seem reasonable to assume. Yet at the outset the book takes a curious turn. In its very first paragraph, the writer boasts that he's "kept the door barred" on his private life and has "no notion now of opening it." That's a curious opener for an autobiography, but it is not as inconsistent as it first may seem. As an aristocrat, all his life Van Dyke disdained people who enjoyed seeing "their doings . . . flung abroad in the morning's newspaper" (*The Raritan* 19). To him, the behavior is lowbrow, smacking of trivialized lives. In contrast, Van Dyke wishes to give the best of himself, and in keeping the focus on issues larger than mere personality, he's complimenting his readers for their refinement. Yet, noble as the stand is, to our good fortune he doesn't always take his own advice. Time and again throughout his autobiography, the aloof professor lets the door fly open—on our heroic desert wanderer confessing that he's glad to be done with the desert, on the well-off traveler coming close to facing a firing squad in Bulgaria—and his readers are made the wealthier by his personal revelations. Particularly so for two reasons: first because his life is so well worth revealing, and second because his personal papers that might otherwise fill in the details have disappeared.[3]

Yet the many glimpses of Van Dyke in the following chapters form only one part of the autobiography's value. As we have stated, Van Dyke sees his task as larger than personal glimpses. His preface makes the broader purpose clear. He wants to correct a historical record distorted by younger writers taking glee in attacking his era. Such writers twist what Van Dyke sees as the grace and worthy ideals of his day into "grotesqueries" and sensational exposés of their elders' imagined shortcomings. Though he's "out in protest" against such mistaken notions, as a gentleman Van Dyke doesn't name the critics, and, if anything, he understates the savagery of their assaults.

It is a commonplace to observe that each generation questions the values of its elders, casting doubt on the old ways and often deeming them unworkable in new times. Van Dyke moved in exclusive circles of educated and refined Northeasterners, a small and privileged group thinking itself the "culture bearers" of what was best in America. In many cases, such people had wealth and/or position to shore up their sanguine concepts of themselves. At the Seminary of Van Dyke's day, for example, with its large, Victorian houses, servants, and tinkling crystal, faculty members could think themselves on a pinnacle of intellectual accomplishment manifested by gracious campus life.

Whatever might be remarked of the stuffiness that can accompany tightly structured societies, surely all the ills of civilization cannot be heaped at the doorstep of one group, in this case, the late, upper-class Victorians. If they dealt with problems of social intercourse by expecting certain behavior, to an admirable degree they had eased the issue of "getting along" with one another. And their social structure allowed them far more freedom—and psychic comfort—than the popular imagination of today may suppose. When Van Dyke blunders onto the grounds of Thomas A. Edison's estate, he knows how to tip his hat, "make his manners," as he puts it, and by thus identifying himself as a gentleman, gains immediate entree with Mrs. Edison. Off the coast of Italy, Van Dyke lounges on the *Namouna*, the most sumptuous private yacht of its time. He's at ease in the company of bons vivants who, if well-mannered, hardly could be described as repressed. Yet he could question his own subculture's values and be admired for the effort. If anything, people of Van Dyke's class occupied enviable positions. Through the accidents of history, they at least knew, or could pretend to know, who they were—as far more "liberated" but agonized generations after them often have not. People in Van Dyke's circles could feel secure in their positions.

But they didn't remain secure. Immigrants not sharing their values were flooding into the Republic by the millions. The nation, with attendant social wrenchings, was shifting from a rural to a bleak industrial landscape in which the new masses felt no allegiance to their "betters." Darwinism and Marxism shook the old, comfortable edifices of religious and cultural faith.

The neoteric younger generation, espousing egalitarianism and open sexual freedoms, mocked its elders as frauds. Young critics scoffed the privileged society of fine-minded thinkers, branding them hypocrites who stood on the backs of the poor. And the young intellectuals soon had their "proof." The gore of World War I—the Great War that was supposed to bring lasting peace to the planet—showed instead that the old *modus operandi*, the gentlemanly alliances, did not work. With a malice born of disillusionment, iconoclasts savaged their elders with a viciousness rarely seen in America. Critic Van Wyck Brooks damned "inherited culture" because it "utterly failed to meet the exigencies of our life" (118). His attack seems tame, however, by comparison to that of H. L. Mencken, who bludgeoned the gentlemanly art of creating literature because it produced only "amiable hollowness" and "timorous flaccidity" (15).

The time-honored rules had changed, or, rather, now there were few rules. Graciousness was out; vindictiveness carried the day. Van Dyke was stung, all the more so because such sneering writers didn't hesitate to name names. Mencken, for instance, dismissed Van Dyke's friends William Dean Howells, William C. Brownell (19), and Van Dyke's own poet cousin, Henry, as "old maids" (22). Piled on top of that, tastes in art had changed. Once offering the excitements of a new way of seeing, Van Dyke's beloved impressionism had won acceptance, only to fall out of fashion. By the early decades of this century, impressionism was considered passé by many up-

and-coming artists and critics, the treacly sweet fare for enervated frequenters of tearooms (Boyle 20). By the time Van Dyke reached his later years, cubism, surrealism, and a number of other robust movements had crowded impressionism aside—movements the professor dealt with, incredibly enough, by all but ignoring them in his books.

There was no way that aging Van Dyke could undo the damage he perceived, but he could present the case that people of his heritage were not jejune Yahoos in pleasant disguise. Wisely, Van Dyke didn't apologize or overstate his position. Humanity continues pretty much the same throughout the ages, he observes, despite changes in appearances and successive generations of carping youth. Yet each age also makes its special contributions, and his generation, he argues, was particularly commendable for its graciousness and intellectual generosity.

Thus we have a unique autobiography. In it we see aspects of a private life never before revealed. But Van Dyke also emphasizes the context in which his life takes place, a lively context of writers, cowboys, painters, pioneers, and captains of industry who valued the life of the intellect. In large part, my notations, then, intend to bridge the gap when Van Dyke's personal life and its context become separated. When Van Dyke praises his editor at Scribner's as a refined critic but neglects to mention the profound impact of the man on Van Dyke's own writing, an explanatory note appears on what Van Dyke left out. When the wanderer reminisces about his cowboy days in Montana, I identify the ranch where he worked and note further material elsewhere in his writing on the subject. My main concern here is to keep bringing a sometimes reluctant Van Dyke back on the stage of his own creation so that readers may gain the larger picture of him as a man and a writer.

As to other editorial decisions, primarily I wish to present a reliable text that is accessible to readers. Most of the necessary changes consist of fairly slight adjustments. I have regularized Van Dyke's punctuation, occasionally added or edited out a minor word or two to smooth out his grammar, and corrected inconsistencies in spelling. For instance, at times Van Dyke writes "grey," at others "gray," and I have chosen the latter spelling, more often used in the United States. Sometimes Van Dyke's rendering of names of people and places is doubtful, but when not sure of the specific people and places involved, I have let his spellings stand. In a very few cases, two I believe, an awkward sentence creeps into Van Dyke's typescript. When this occurs, I have rewritten the sentence in order to rescue its meaning from opacity, but Van Dyke's original wording appears in an accompanying note. Most of the pages of Van Dyke's typescript bear penned corrections, but typically they make only slight adjustments to the text. Van Dyke corrected the spelling errors of his typist, occurring most often in the names of people and places. Here and there he tones down a passage somewhat or cuts back on wordiness. In several places, a revised word or two floats in the margin, illegible and sometimes without indication of placement, and such instances could not be incorporated into the text. However, since elsewhere Van Dyke almost never alters the essential thrust of a passage, I am confident that the text presented here closely mirrors his intentions.

Van Dyke wrote his autobiography in his closing years, and some of the dates he supplies can be questionable. At times he gives no date or fails to pass on other information on major people and issues that would be helpful to readers. Furthermore, though in general the autobiography proceeds chronologically, it does not always hew to the strict sequence of events as they occurred. To help the reader in such places, I occasionally provide dates or other brief information in brackets. When a larger matter arises, I supplement the text with a note. Van Dyke included seventeen footnotes, most of them occurring early on in his manuscript. These I have numbered along with my own commentaries and identified with brackets as Van Dyke's notes. The summary of chapter 26 and part of that of chapter 35 were missing from the original table of contents. These I supplied.

Other changes I approached with greater caution. Lacking a page number and typed in a different face than the rest of the text, a list of twenty-six people appears in the typescript after Van Dyke's table of contents. This is Van Dyke's choice of photographs, and it creates several problems. For one, Van Dyke accompanies a number of the entries with notes indicating that he favors a certain likeness, but he is not specific enough to identify the particular photograph. In other cases, as with Mark Twain, Van Dyke simply states a name, giving no hint of what he has in mind from the many photographic choices possible. In any event, locating photographs for a number of the more obscure people quite likely would be impossible. With little chance of following through on Van Dyke's intentions on the matter, I have relegated his list to a note.[4] To the left appears Van Dyke's list, to the right my few words identifying the person. This gives a quick synopsis of the especially valued people in Van Dyke's life. Beyond honoring his parents and President Lincoln by placing them early in the list, there seems no reason for the order of the other names following. Finally, Van Dyke denotes his own photograph as the frontispiece, and though, again, he doesn't specify which photograph he prefers, the one reproduced here was used in his time as the frontispiece in some of his own editions. The portfolio appearing in these pages is gleaned from a number of archives and Van

Dyke relatives, and many of the photographs are printed for the first time. Wherever possible, I have dated the photographs and identified their figures; otherwise, to avoid repetition, I remain silent.

For similar reasons as pertain to the handling of Van Dyke's list of photographs, and to avoid an endless clutter of notes, I have not elaborated on every reference in the myriad of people, places, and events Van Dyke mentions. Rather, in the editing I have kept one question constantly before me: What additional information would be most helpful to readers? They will find a good number of examples from several Van Dyke volumes illustrating the statements in his autobiography. To give a sense of Van Dyke's breadth and depth, I've drawn from a variety of Van Dyke's works, though a large share of the illustrations come from *The Desert*. Reissued many times over the decades, widely found in libraries, and still in print, it likely is the Van Dyke book most available to readers.

As discussed above, one of Van Dyke's main concerns was justification of his era. In line with this, he emblazons his autobiography with the title *My Golden Age: A Personal Narrative of American Life from 1861 to 1931.* For fear that his main title would be misunderstood by modern readers as an excess of sentiment, I have opted for clarity over confusion, making the main title descriptive and keeping Van Dyke's subtitle. Lastly, to jump from the title of the autobiography to the bibliography at its end, the selected bibliography includes some, but by no means all, of the dozens upon dozens of books Van Dyke mentions. To cite them all would salve my sense of completeness, but such a list would be of little service to most people. Rather, the bibliography points readers toward resources further revealing the wealth, along with some of the blemishes, of the man and his contribution.

Van Dyke wrote his autobiography in longhand on twenty-two notebooks, preserved in the archives of the Gardner A. Sage Library of the New Brunswick Theological Seminary. As noted, a typist worked from the holograph manuscript to prepare the autobiography for publication (see chapter 15, note 1). I do not know why the manuscript wasn't published. Completed in the last year or so of his life, it simply may have fallen by the wayside as Van Dyke's health deteriorated. However, the history of the manuscript provides an opportunity to set the record straight on another matter. As Mr. Strong points out in his foreword, though Van Dyke was a bachelor, he had a daughter, Clare, who married Harry L. Parr, a professor of engineering at Columbia University. After Van Dyke's death in 1932, the typescript went to Mrs. Parr. She in turn gave the manuscript to Cornelia Strong, sister of Philip L. Strong, Esq. The latter, Van Dyke's first cousin once removed, preserved the manuscript through the years. During one of my research visits to the New Brunswick area, Mr. Strong graciously invited me to dinner with his family at his home in rural Cranbury, New Jersey. There, during the after-dinner talk in his fine old Victorian farmhouse, Mr. Strong suggested he had something that might be of interest to me. He disappeared into his attic. A few minutes later, he came down the stairs with Van Dyke's typescript. It was one of those moments scholars dream of.

The autobiography answers many questions, both about a time that gave birth to our own and about one of the late Victorians' most prolific and popular writers. Gracious, urbane, and humorous, Van Dyke's writing offers lively portraits of the Revolutionary War heroes in his family and of Gilded Age high society, vignettes of Abraham Lincoln and Mark Twain, of frontier ruffians and millionaire railroad magnates, of flamboyant painter James McNeill Whistler and of a good number of other turn-of-the-century artists, publishers, and writers. And here the seasoned Van Dyke keenly applies a number of devices—irony, foreshadowing, and use of dialogue— to enliven his autobiography and make it no mere rundown of a life but a complex piece of literature in itself. Perhaps most importantly for the study of literature, we finally learn Van Dyke's surprising version of how he wrote *The Desert*, the best and most influential book about America's deserts. The autobiography reveals Van Dyke's victories as well as his disappointments and in the process shows a man of unusual strength and surprising personal vulnerability. Both in detail and in broad brush, Van Dyke's chapters capture the late Victorians, and his portrait has a haunting familiarity about it, for here we see our ancestors struggling, as we do, with issues of overpopulation, religious doubt, and social justice.

For all the autobiography tells us, much calls for further exploration. A thorough evaluation of Van Dyke's art criticism, especially his detective work on Rembrandt, would throw further light on a major aspect of his career. It would be good to know more about Van Dyke's teaching methods at Rutgers, rumored to have been ahead of his time. Though with the autobiography the general overview of Van Dyke's life and many of its details now come clear, uncertainty continues to shroud some of his activities. At times we don't know where he was, when, and with whom. The gaps become particularly nettlesome in chapters 19 and 20, covering Van Dyke's desert travel, the most graphic period in the professor's life as he presents it. On this score, we'd like to believe that the manuscript of Van Dyke's one novel, *The Jaws of the Desert*, in which, he says, he at last tells the "truth" about his famed desert travels, awaits discovery where the aging professor left it, "in a table drawer." Compounding such puzzles for researchers, Van Dyke's writings often are the sole accounts of the events he mentions.

For the most part, the foregoing expands on the accepted notions of Van Dyke. But up until now, no one has explored a major aspect of the man. The basic outline of Van Dyke's life as he tells it here holds true. There is no doubt that he spent part of his youth in Minnesota, was the librarian at the New Brunswick Theological Seminary, and visited his brother's ranch in Southern California. Photographs and other records bear this out, and testifying to his output, his fine books are available in libraries and book-stores. But caution lights begin flashing upon the discovery of a photograph of the Van Dyke family house in the early days of Minnesota. The photo reveals a lavish, three-story affair, in the midst of what Van Dyke represents in his autobiography as "a rather wild country." Is it possible to believe his account that close to the nearby town, complete with its Ladies Circulating Library and high school, there are "wild" Indians in tepees, who romp off for hundreds of miles on a buffalo hunt clear to the Rocky Mountains? An anthropologist who is an authority on Minnesota Indians labeled the sce-nario "fanciful" (see chapter 5, notes 3 and 4). And one shakes his head when Van Dyke later claims he slaked his thirst on desert treks by drinking cactus juice—in fact, nasty, sickening stuff, hardly a remedy for thirst—or recalls shooting wolves in Southern California, where scientists tell us there were no wolves.

After many hours of discussing such features of the autobiography with historians and naturalists, I can't avoid the conclusion that, though a superb "indoorsman," when Van Dyke deals with his Western forays he sometimes leaves the realm of the factual and begins spinning tales. In chapters 5, 8, 18, 19, 20, 24, and 28—wherever Van Dyke speaks of wolves, Indians, grizzly bears, cowboys, the Sun Dance, the background of *The Desert* or *The Grand Canyon*, and other of his outdoor exploits—the reader should be highly skeptical, for Van Dyke tends to slip from reality into the world of his fantasies. Neil Carmony, a desert-born naturalist with decades of experience in the arid lands, declared in one of our discussions that Van Dyke's desert chapters here are "fabulous" and "patently untrue." Mr. Carmony believes that Van Dyke never spent a night sleeping out among the cactuses and coyotes of the Southwest but preferred the ameni-ties of civilization to the hard ground.

Certainly, Van Dyke's chapters here raise such doubts, as does a close look at his other adventures in the wilds. Buoyed over the decades on Van Dyke's rich prose, both scholars and the reading public have hailed the *The Desert* as the account of one man's lone and sometimes dangerous tramps through the Southwestern wilderness. However, it now seems clear that the most influential volume ever written about America's desert sweeps likely was derivative and based on Van Dyke's limited experiences, mostly in Southern California. Mr. Carmony builds his case precisely:

> Last night I read my copy of *The Desert* in some detail, particularly the wildlife and vegetation chapters, with Sonora, Mexico, in mind. It is clear to me now that the detailed wildlife summary in *The Desert* is told from a Southern California perspective. Mule deer, pronghorn, mountain sheep, grizzlies, mountain lions, wildcats, and coyotes are among the large mammals discussed (along with some fictitious gray wolves). These animals (except the wolves) were found in Southern California and were described reasonably well, given the fact that John Van Dyke was a visitor to the Southwest and not a trained naturalist.
>
> However, the information he gives about white-tailed deer (an animal not found in California) is vague and garbled. He states that whitetails are found in Sonora "along river-beds," and that a "dwarf" deer also lives in Sonora. Whitetails are found throughout most of Sonora, from the desert foothills up into the Sierra Madre. Evidently, Van Dyke did not know that whitetails were also to be found in southern Arizona. The "dwarf" deer is an old southwestern myth. It should be noted that such a characteristic Sonoran animal as the javelina is not even mentioned.

The inconsistencies lead Mr. Carmony to conclude:

> I am convinced that the best explanation for this apparent Southern California bias in the wildlife discussions in *The Desert* is that John Van Dyke obtained most of his wildlife information through talking with his brother Theodore, an outdoorsman and long-time California resident. Presumably, Theodore knew much more about California wildlife than that of Arizona or Sonora, and this is reflected in his brother's book. This could also explain such errors as John Van Dyke's assertion that saguaro cacti have purple flowers (they are white). Saguaros are mostly found in Arizona and Sonora, and none are found near Theodore's ranch at Daggett, California. Thus, Theodore Van Dyke would have known little about this plant and could not have helped his brother with accurate information about it.

This is not a case of isolated faux pas. In *The Grand Canyon*, Van Dyke advises hikers: "As for food and water, any athlete or Indian will tell you that you can travel better without them. They are good things at the end of the trip but not at the beginning" (110).

That is about the most wrongheaded advice anyone could offer. In the Grand Canyon, water is not *a* limiting factor but the *chief* limiting factor. It's a subject constantly on hikers' minds, athletes and Indians not excluded. It's all but inconceivable that anyone who has walked more than a mile or two in the Canyon's heat-stoked labyrinths, in summer, as Van Dyke claims he did, would make the preposterous suggestion. Based on such evidence, one comes to the conclusion that Van Dyke greatly exaggerated his physical prowess in the wilds and, for example, found the material for his Canyon book—lovely as it is—not far beyond sight of the elegant El Tovar Hotel or while motoring blithely along the Rim. But enough. The upshot is that we have a pattern in Van Dyke of fabulous constructions.

As a poet, I can understand the appeal of the fabulous. But I am not a psychologist and won't attempt to explain the urge in Van Dyke when he describes the events of his life, other than to note his considerable admiration for his elder brother Theodore, a bona fide outdoorsman with real adventures to his credit. I cannot prove all of what Van Dyke did or did not do in the outdoors. However, I can point out that Van Dyke's impulse to fabricate is often and incontrovertibly there, here in his autobiography and also in his earlier work, as the following notes will discuss in some detail.

To be generous and place the examples from Van Dyke's earlier work aside, it could be argued that the professor wrote his autobiography in his latter days, when he was ill, and many years after the events he describes. Understandably, the aging traveler might misremember what actually happened. Yet some of the incidents, such as drinking cactus juice or feeding his horse cholla, strike the ear as the recitations of popular but factually false desert folklore rather than the product of a faulty memory. And on similar points, Van Dyke, a writer who can be wonderfully detailed elsewhere, suddenly turns suspiciously vague in passages containing questionable information. For instance, chapter 19 claims that he traveled across the desert "for weeks without seeing a soul," all but an impossibility, as note 1 to that chapter explains.

Having said that, I add that it would be silly for the many readers and writers who have considered Van Dyke an early desert traveler of heroic proportions to lapse into depression, or, worse, anger, at the prospect of being hoodwinked. As is true of many writers, especially writers about the American West, at times Van Dyke blew his share of literary smoke. He was a romantic fabulist, and he was a talented one. The dichotomy in his personality does not diminish the accomplishments of his volumes, and it makes him all the more fascinating as a literary figure. As regards the esthetic quality of his writing, it should make little or no difference whether Van Dyke wrote *The Desert* while roughing it alone with dog and horse, as he claims, or, more probably, while gazing out the windows of trains and hotels and sitting on the porch of his brother's ranch. Though Van Dyke was not a wonderful doer when in the wilds, he was an artistic seer of natural landscapes. The central truth is that the professor wrote very fine books that people rightly find inspiring. As an evenhanded Carmony adds about *The Desert*, Van Dyke "undoubtedly experienced the desert in a very ordinary way and wrote a very extraordinary book." For me, the latter is the issue that counts.

As to other uncertainties, reconstructing a life is at best a chancy business, but it is a risk the biographer has to take or remain silent. In our pursuit of a person it is easy to make too much of some things, too little of others. This is especially true of a man as elusive and various as Van Dyke. For instance, while helping me with the manuscript, a secretary who once herself suffered from the condition commented that Van Dyke's representation of the brand of his cousin's ranch in Montana as 70L instead of ⌐O⌡ (see chapter 8, note 7) was just the sort of reversal a dyslexic person would make. It was a sharp observation on her part. But swamped by details as I was at that point, my first impulse was to dismiss the idea, a dangerous state of mind for a researcher. However, the suggestion began working on me.

What if Van Dyke *were* dyslexic? The implications could be immense. After all, dyslexia was not described until 1896, and one can assume its diagnosis and treatment were not well understood in Van Dyke's day. The condition might go some distance in explaining Van Dyke's bouts of anger, especially his frustration over all the reading he had to do, as expressed in the pages ahead. It also might have something to do with his unusual way of seeing the world. Such things, I understand, are typical of dyslexia sufferers. Wouldn't the malady, in other words, be a key to Van Dyke's character and in turn have a bearing on his writing?

But I am hardly an authority on learning disabilities, and then, too, further evidence for rushing to such a conclusion is decidedly slim. The holograph manuscript of the autobiography names the ranch as the 70L— so the problem was not created by the typist—yet there is no profusion of reversed words and letters in Van Dyke's handwriting, as one supposes would hold true for the dyslexic. Chances are good that Van Dyke simply misremembered the brand from the distance of forty years or more, a perfectly human thing to do. When a boy, I also worked on a ranch, but after weeks of effort, I have been unable to dredge up our brand, though at the time it was daily all around me on the rumps of our cattle. So I tip my hat to Van Dyke for coming as close as he did. In any case, one remains tantalized but cautious about such things.

The business of research is far more akin to happy drudgery than a long but thrilling roller-coaster ride, though sometimes one experiences unexpected jolts. Not long before I completed this manuscript, an innocent-looking letter postmarked in California turned up in my office mailbox. Idly flipping it over, I was shocked to see "John C. Van Dyke" nicely embossed in blue on the back. Could it be that the old gentleman might be alive? For one electric instant I was a believer. Of course, the writer was not *my* John C. Van Dyke but a namesake relative who had heard of my researches, though I was glad for the correspondence nonetheless. Such are the ups and downs of scholarship.

Those may be extreme, if perhaps fantastic, examples, but along similar lines, I have not said everything that might be said about other matters surrounding a sometimes mysterious Van Dyke. Rather, I have tried to restrict my notes to what can be found, or at least is reasonably suggested, from the documented record. In the latter case, when doubts surround an issue, I do not hesitate to say so.

Whatever was going on in the professor's life that continues to puzzle and intrigue us, the important thing remains the wonder of Van Dyke's prose, the volumes the writer left behind that far surpass the personal circumstances lying behind their creation. However, it is hoped that filling in the details of Van Dyke's life might add other dimensions to understanding his books. And in this I think the old professor would agree.

It would be easy to shrug off Van Dyke's mysteries as beyond our reach, their solutions lost forever. However, after living with a writer for several years, one develops—at least, thinks he develops—a sense for his ways. Van Dyke was a wily man and a wily writer. At times, his trail suddenly fades, but if his tracker is dogged enough, he sometimes finds that it picks up again in unexpected places. Then, when looking back, he sees that he's found the way again by clues Van Dyke himself dropped. One suspects the professor was having his little laugh, playing the elusive litterateur but finally wishing to be followed. It's that trail that we now begin to follow.

Chronology

1652	Thomasse Janse Van Dyke arrives in New Amsterdam from the Netherlands.
1856	John C. Van Dyke born on April 21, 1856, at Green Oaks, a mansion on the outskirts of New Brunswick, New Jersey.
1868	Van Dyke's father moves the family to pioneer Minnesota. Young Van Dyke begins his Western adventures.
1876–1877	Returns to the East, attends Columbia Law School, and is admitted to the bar.
1878	Settles permanently in hometown New Brunswick. Becomes assistant librarian at the Gardner A. Sage Library of the New Brunswick Theological Seminary.
1883(?)	First of many trips to Europe initiates Van Dyke's world travels.
1886	Appointed head librarian of the Sage.
1889	Begins lecturing on art at Rutgers College.
1891	Appointed professor of the history of art at Rutgers, a position he holds concurrently with his librarianship of the Sage.
1893	*Art for Art's Sake*.
1898	*Nature for Its Own Sake* begins his "natural appearances" series.
	With cousin Theodore Strong, travels to Montana, visiting old cowboy haunts.
1899–1901	First explores Southwestern deserts.
1901	*The Desert* becomes the first book to praise the beauty of America's arid sweeps.
1908	Elected member of the National Institute of Arts and Letters.
1911–1924	Serves on the New Jersey State Board of Education.
1914	Narrowly escapes the German advance at the outbreak of World War I.
1915	*The Raritan*, a history of the Van Dyke family.
1916	*The Mountain*.

1920   Edits the *Autobiography of Andrew Carnegie*.
        The Grand Canyon.
1922   *The Open Spaces* celebrates Van Dyke's life in the outdoors.
1923   *Rembrandt and His School* causes a storm in the art world.
        Elected member of the American Academy of Arts and Let-
            ters.
1926   *The Meadows*, Van Dyke's praise of the gentle countryside
            surrounding hometown New Brunswick.
1931   *In Egypt*.
        Completes his autobiography.
1932   *In the West Indies*.
        Dies on December 5, 1932, at St. Luke's Hospital in New
            York City at age seventy-six, following an operation.

The Autobiography of John C. Van Dyke

A Personal Narrative of American Life, 1861–1931

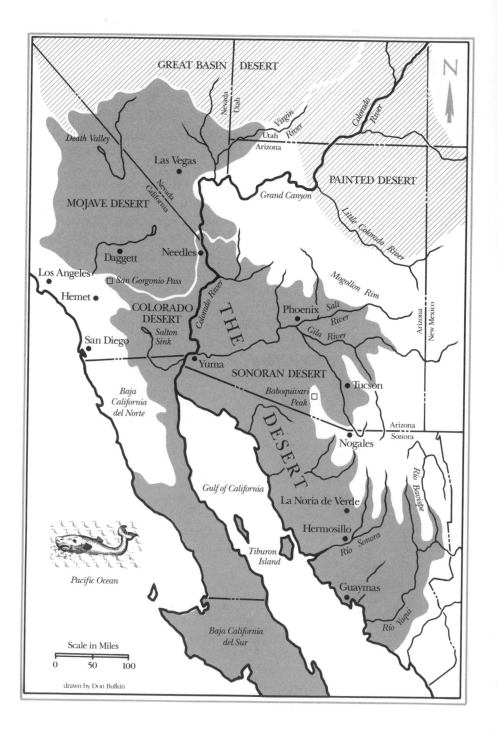

GREAT BASIN   DESERT

Death Valley

Las Vegas

Nevada
Utah

Virgin River

Utah
Arizona

Colorado River

PAINTED DESERT

Grand Canyon

Little Colorado River

MOJAVE DESERT

Nevada
California

Daggett

Needles

Los Angeles

San Gorgonio Pass

Hemet

COLORADO
DESERT

Colorado River

THE

Mogollon Rim

Phoenix   Salt River

Gila River

Arizona
New Mexico

San Diego

Salton
Sink

Yuma

SONORAN DESERT

Tucson

Baja
California
del Norte

Baboquivari
Peak

DESERT

Arizona
Sonora

Nogales

Gulf of California

La Noria de Verde

Río Bavispe

Hermosillo

Tiburon
Island

Río Sonora

Pacific Ocean

Guaymas

Scale in Miles

0   50   100

Baja California
del Sur

Río Yaqui

drawn by Don Bufkin

Preface

I have not written these memoirs in response to a popular demand. I am neither a celebrity nor a notoriety, at least not one the world yearns to know in private life. My public appearance has been in books and lectures, and beyond that I have kept the door barred. I have no notion now of opening it and stepping into the spotlight, except by way of introducing the play in which I have had a small speaking part. It is the play—the men and events of my own time—that I am putting forward rather than the genius of any leading man. In these days, everyone knows the genius as he knows the dunce, and it is often difficult to say which is the bigger bore. They are a part of the play, and so I shall have to speak of them, but they are not to be unduly prominent. The play is the thing, with all the actors great and small cast upon the background of their times.

I have seen the history of my own time written so abominably that I am out in protest. Young historians who have gathered their facts from sensational newspaper headlines, dramatists who have dressed their characters out of books of costume, novelists who have portrayed American life out of their imagination have so bedevilled the Sixties, Seventies, Eighties, and Nineties that one who has lived through those decades cannot recognize them. Poets, painters, and sculptors have distorted Lincoln, made a Jupiter Amon of Cleveland, and an Ariel-like idealist out of Wilson.[1] As for their backgrounds, the grotesqueries and absurdities have been so "featured" that the reality has been lost in the shuffle.[2] Their times were not essentially different from ours, but the modern presentation of them makes them out very primitive, very crude, very dull. In Lincoln's day there were no automobiles, or jazz bands, or smart barbers; therefore, Washington in the Sixties was merely a gathering place for longhaired old fossils. Youth has always viewed its forebears with assured complacency, and it is not until youth becomes age that it realizes the difference between Jack and his grandfather has been largely a matter of road vehicles, dance music, and hair cut.

Inevitably my story has taken the form of a personal narrative. I myself am perhaps typical of many others in American life who have carried on from Lincoln's day. At least I know my own story, and in telling that I hope to present a truthful picture of the decades through which I have lived. It is in measure social history (if the reader will so regard it), and the autobiography of it is merely the form in which it is cast.

Sage Library   JOHN C. VAN DYKE
October 1930[3]

Contents

Chapter 1

Lincoln in 1861

The grandfather had great faith in prayer. He prayed with his family about him twice a day, asking each evening that we might be taken to that land where "the wicked cease from troubling and the weary are at rest" and giving thanks each morning that we had been spared to see the light of another day. The little inconsistency in the prayer never seemed to disturb him. We, his small grandchildren, were dragged up to his house at the evening session, if not always in the morning. We did not like it. The oak floor was hard, our childish knees were thin, and the prayers were long.

One evening there was an unusual gathering. All the uncles, aunts, and cousins were there. Something had happened. The grownups talked excitedly in groups. The youngsters tried to break in but were waved away. There was pounding of clenched fists, angry shaking of heads, and when the grandfather led in prayer his voice trembled and broke with emotion. Three times he repeated one sentence: "Oh, Arm Almighty, stretch out and save us!"

It was a long prayer but did not oil the troubled waters. I was taken off home, down the cedar lane that connected our house with the grandfather's, and, holding my mother's hand, I asked her what had happened, and why Uncle The was so angry, and why grandfather called on an Arm to save us. She said I was just a little boy and would not understand, but that there had been a great battle, our army had been defeated, and war to free the slaves had begun in earnest.

But would not the Tall Man make them stop?

She seemed to gather comfort from the thought. Yes, the Tall Man would make them stop.

That was the night the news came of the Battle of Bull Run. The grandfather was praying for the Union cause. And Uncle The was going to the war.[1]

I had had before this a memory of a Tall Man and had been told that he could do things. I had gone down to the little railway station of my native town (New Brunswick, New Jersey) in the family carriage, seated beside William the coachman with my mother and aunt[2] on the back seat. A great crowd had gathered at the station, and a band was playing some lively music. We waited in the middle of the crowd. Presently, a shrill whistle came from the covered wooden bridge across the Raritan, and a little locomotive and train, bedecked with flags, streamers, and rosettes, came over the bridge. It drew through the crowd and came to a stop. There was a great shout and then a pause. Two men came out upon the platform of the last car. One of them I recognized. Instantly, I was upon my feet, standing on the cushioned seat and shouting in a boyish treble:

"There's Daddy! Oh, there's Daddy!"

For a moment I attracted considerable attention. Half the crowd turned around, looked at me, and then laughed. But I was quickly pulled down from behind and told to "keep quiet." I sat there and watched the two men. My father was nearly six feet in height—a boy's father is always a big man to the boy—but there beside him was a man who was taller. That evidently excited my wonder and sharpened my attention. I can see him very plainly to this day in his long, black broadcloth coat, his narrow-brimmed silk hat, and his round stovepipe trousers, standing there a little awkwardly, smiling a little sadly perhaps, and bowing to the plaudits of the crowd. I do not remember that he made any speech, though the *New York World* of February 22, 1861, reported that he "was welcomed in a speech by Judge Van Dyke and made a speech in response."

In a few minutes, the train drew out and disappeared around a bend in the track. My mother told me afterwards that the Tall Man was Mr. Lincoln and he was on his way to Washington to be inaugurated President of the United States. But that meant little to me at that time. I was impressed only by his personality and by the fact that he was taller than my father.[3]

I learned later why my father was on the train with Lincoln. He was escorting him across the State of New Jersey. They had been friends for some years. In 1847, when Lincoln, then quite unknown to the East, was elected to Congress and came on to Washington to take his seat, he happened to take that seat beside my father who was then representing the Third Congressional District of New Jersey. They became friends immediately. The father was quick enough to see great possibilities in Lincoln. He admired his broad humanity, his unerring sense of right and wrong, his shrewdness of resource, his persuasive speech.

Lincoln served only one term in Congress, retiring in 1849, but he was not forgotten. In 1856 when the first Republican convention was held in Philadelphia and General Frémont was chosen for the presidency, the name of Lincoln came up for the vice-presidency and received 110 votes on the first ballot. There must have been tradition even in those early days of the vice-presidency leading to political oblivion, for my father, who was heading the New Jersey delegation at the Convention, was instantly upon his feet in opposition to Lincoln's nomination. He made a long and strong speech for Lincoln, insisting that he was not the man for the vice-presidency but was the man for the future.[4] He insisted upon the nomination of William L. Dayton of New Jersey. Dayton was nominated, and Lincoln was not displeased by it. His letter to my father (still in family possession) reads:

> Springfield, Ill.
> June 27, 1856
>
> Hon. John Van Dyke
> My dear Sir: Allow me to thank you for your kind notice of me in the Philadelphia convention. When you meet Judge Dayton present my respects and tell him I think him a far better man than I for the position he is in, and that I shall support both him and Colonel Fremont most cordially. Present my best respects to Mrs. V. and believe me
>
> Yours truly
> A. Lincoln[5]

Lincoln's political friend and adviser, W. B. Archer, wrote to him from Philadelphia about the convention and the nominations, and in the letter he says:

> Mr. Van Dyke of New Jersey had served with you in Congress. He paid you a high compliment and at some length. It was well done and I regret that his remarks in full as to yourself were not published. He did you great credit.[6]

I do not know how well or how intimately my parents knew the Lincolns. They never said. They were very reticent people, and they died before I was old enough to be inquisitive about their acquaintance. Shortly thereafter the family correspondence went up in fire. A Lincoln letter turned up in later years with an older brother in California, and I at twenty in New Brunswick, New Jersey, had in possession a copy of the first edition of Poe's *Raven*, published in yellow paper covers in 1845 and bearing on the cover in ink the inscription:

> Mrs. Van Dyke with the regards of
> A. Lincoln
> Washington 1847

I shudder now to think how stupidly careless I was with that publication. Even in 1876 I regarded it more for the poem than the Lincoln inscription.

It knocked about my rooms at New Brunswick. College students read it, and one of them finally had the audacity to part the cover from the book and make away with the inscription. Once it was lost, I began to realize its worth. It has never appeared in any autograph collection and I presume is now lost beyond any recovery. I am referring to it here not to establish any family intimacy but to suggest the possible falsity of some current notions about Lincoln.

The impression that Lincoln looked like a boor[7] has always gone on all fours with the complementary impression that he was a man of very limited education. No one knows just what he read, but the inference has been that in his western country he could have no books except the Bible, some schoolbooks, and a dog-eared copy of Blackstone. These he read lying on his stomach before a wood fire. Everyone has seen that picture of Lincoln lying before the fire or seated on a wooden bench reading Blackstone by the light of a tallow dip. Like his rail splitting, it looks and sounds romantic. And both were no doubt effective material in political campaigning—too effective for denial. But how much truth was there in either of them? And how much truth in Lincoln's ignorance of books? Because a thing is not matter of record, does it follow that it never happened? Where did Lincoln get the remarkable style of his letters and speeches? Do they read like the utterances of an uneducated man? Try them over again for their rhythm and cadences, and you will begin to think Lincoln must have been a reader of poetry. I am offering the suggestion at least.

In 1847 Lincoln was quite unknown to the East. He was thirty-eight, and the greater part of his career was before him. He had not gone through the Douglas debates and must have known less about books than in 1860, and yet there in Washington in 1847 he was keen enough to pick up the first important poem of a new poet. Poe was practically unknown to the public until the appearance of *The Raven*. Lincoln no doubt read and admired the poem. How otherwise account for his sending a copy of it to my mother?[8] And why should he not have been a reader of books? The West in Lincoln's day was not a bookless wilderness. That he had copies of Gibbon and other English writers is matter of belief. I shall later on bear testimony to the books in a small Minnesota town in 1868 which was quite as wild then as Illinois in Lincoln's day. He is said to have been fond of the poem "Oh, Why Should the Spirit of Mortal Be Proud?" and to have known the poems in the back of Kirkham's *Elocution*, but I am disposed to believe that his knowledge went beyond that and beyond Poe's *Raven*.[9]

I did not see Lincoln again, but I heard much talk about him as the war developed. There were prayers and there were curses, but people went on living, waiting for news from the front, biding their time as best they could, angry and yet anxious. Distinctly I remember driving across New Jersey from Trenton with my father in an old-fashioned end-spring buggy behind Jerry the sorrel, riding to some city where my father was to hold court. I cannot place the date, but possibly it was 1862 or 1863. I well remember how every village, crossroad, and farm held us up to inquire about the war. Everyone seemed to know my father, and it was Judge here and Judge there and what about the war? Would the Union hold? Would we win? And to everyone almost the same answer. We could not fail to win with Lincoln at the helm. He was sure of Lincoln's judgment, of his calmness and patience, of his adroitness and skill in maneuver, of his honesty, earnestness, and tremendous sincerity. Davis and Alexander Stevens and the southern leaders would be beaten at their own game. Our army would win, the Union would stand, and slavery would go. Again and again he told the farmers and villagers that he was so confident of Lincoln that he had put every dollar he had in the world into government bonds and had advised all his friends and clients to do the same thing. Of course, the advice was given to uphold the finances of the government, but he believed it, and he carried conviction to others. At that time he was seated on the Supreme Court bench of New Jersey and had just given up the presidency of the Bank of New Jersey. He was well-known throughout the state, and no doubt his words were heartening.

All day we jounced and bounced over the dirt roads in the end-spring buggy, and at night came to Lamington where my uncle, Richard Vliet, lived. He was the proprietor of Vliet's Mills, the general store at Lamington, and owned I know not how many acres of land. He was a great man to me because he owned all the water in the mill pond and even had a proprietary right in the sunfish and shiners that dwelt therein. We stopped at his big house opposite the mills, and before we had finished supper the neighbors began to pour in. Word of my father's arrival had spread quickly. That was his birthplace, and everyone knew him. They came in to get the war news. I left them talking through clouds of tobacco smoke and was taken upstairs to see Aunt Charity. She was a very old lady, in bed and wearing a white, lace cap and gold-rimmed spectacles. At that time she was about ninety and I think was bedridden, or at least did not leave her bed. She looked me over curiously and remarked to my Aunt Ida that I was a "substantial-looking boy." I remember afterwards asking my mother what "substantial" meant but was given no flattering interpretation. It was long afterward, after Aunt Charity died in 1872, that I learned she had been born during the Revolution and as a child had helped her mother hold

the farm and feed the family while her father was at the war. But of that
further on.

I was taken off to bed and was soon lost in sleep, with the moonlight on
the white counterpane and the sound of the rushing mill water in my ears.
The water still runs in the Lamington, but the pond and the mills and the
store have gone, and even the big house has been so changed by a recent
owner that no one can recognize it. The Vliet's Mills of my childhood has
passed away, and the very name of the mills has perished.[10] My uncle's name
was borne up to a few years ago by a very distinguished New Jersey lawyer,
Richard Vliet Lindabury, but what his relation to the family was, if any, I
never knew.

Chapter 2

The Family in the Revolution

Almost every autobiographer is prayed by friends and publisher to "cut out the family." Genealogy is not wanted by the reading public. But one has to say a little something about his origin. He cannot leave the reader to imagine he was "born and bred in a brier patch," like Br'er Rabbit. Besides, sometimes one's family makes up a good story or hands down contemporary history in a very convincing manner. I am not sure that my ancestors are not herein my best asset. At any rate, I shall not cut them out, though the reader may if he so chooses.[1]

My father [John Van Dyke, 1807–1878] was bred out of the Spartan kind. He had been reared to face any kind of music, and he did it without flinching. Both of his grandfathers, with two great-uncles and others of family connection, fought through the Revolution, and his great-grandfather had been killed at the Battle of Monmouth. The war had cast the family in heroic mold, and when he was born in 1807 the echoes of it were still reverberating among the New Jersey hills. Naturally, he grew up a serious-minded, determined person who feared God and did the right thing, regardless of consequences. Perhaps the Dutch blood in him inclined him that way at the start. Tenacity, endurance, self-reliance, fearlessness were marked traits in his character.

He was of the eighth generation in this country, the family having come over from Amsterdam to New York in 1652. The first ancestor, Thomasse Janse Van Dyke, must have brought some wealth with him, for he owned larger property in Breukelen (Brooklyn), and the boweries [farms] of his sons and grandsons extended down the Bay shore and even included Con-eyn Eylandt (Concy Island). Three generations lived on Long Island farms, held municipal offices, became magistrates, captains in the Dutch Army, and probably stowed away money after the Dutch manner. But when Jan of the fourth generation came along, he found New York and Long Island too much "settled up" to suit his fancy. He loved the wild and probably had the Old World hankering for land.[2] At any rate, in 1711 he crossed Staten Island and came up the Raritan to Inian's Ferry (afterwards New Brunswick).[3] He lived there for some time, for his name appears on the roster of Colonel Harmer's militia in 1715 and on the first board of aldermen of the City of

New Brunswick in 1730. Then he went back on the highway between New Brunswick and Trenton and came into possession of 2,135 acres of land near Maplewood and along the bank of the Millstone River.

How he came by all that land is now a forgotten story, but evidently there was large wealth at Jan the Fourth's disposal. In addition to the land, he owned many slaves and operated great farms at a profit. His will, still on file at Trenton, gave farms to his sons and money in £500 sums to his daughters. And they in turn became well-off. Jan the Fifth's wife left each of her daughters a black girl to act as a personal servant, and the sons were left the black field hands. I have always been a little curious as to what became of that wealth, because very little of it came down to my father's time. It seems to have been dissipated by the Revolution with the flaying of New Jersey by the raiding British.

For the Revolution came on in earnest during Jan the Fifth's time. All the family took a hand in it. Jan's brother, Ruloff, was a deputy to the Provincial Congress and also a member of the Committee of Safety. Abraham, another brother, was a lieutenant of grenadiers. Jan's own son, Abraham the Younger, was a private in the ranks. His cousins, nephews, and relatives by marriage were all in arms against the King and for the country. Jan himself was one of the company of Minutemen organized by Hillsborough Township (adjoining Harlingen) the 3rd of May 1775 to be ready at a minute's notice "to march in defence of the liberty of our country." He was in Captain Vroom's company, 2nd Battalion, Somerset County Militia. Abraham Quick was the Colonel of the regiment. On the 16th day of May 1775, the officers of the militia and Committee of Observation appointed three members "to provide ammunition for said company and arms for those who are not able to buy for themselves, and the aforesaid gentlemen are desired to take £40 Proc. in money, on the credit of the Township, to buy 140 pounds of powder, 420 pounds of lead and 120 flints," etc.

Jan the Fifth was then an old man but madly patriotic for the country and against the British. Unhappily, his patriotism met a stubborn barrier in the person of his eldest son. That son at the time of the outbreak of the Revolution was a Colonel in the British Army and wore the King's uniform. He was a Tory, against his will perhaps, yet still a Tory. Always he was known in the family as Colonel John the Tory. When driven to the wall by his father, he made a good plea for himself, declaring that he had sworn an oath to uphold the King and had taken his bounty and would not now violate his oath. He would not fight the British, neither would he fight his own people. He asked to be relieved and was transferred to the British Navy, where he had only a small part in the war.

But his irascible father would listen to no pleas. He insisted that Colonel John deed back a farm that he had given him, and this was done on condition that his wife should have it in case he were killed in the war. Then the two parted and never spoke, never saw each other again. The family quarrel was never healed. Colonel John and his faithful wife died outside of the family pale, ostracized and cut to the last. And his angry father, incensed beyond endurance, an old man in his seventieth year, threw himself into the American line and was killed at the Battle of Monmouth.

This was my father's great-grandfather, but the Revolution came down a generation further. His grandfather, Abraham the Sixth, youngest son of Jan the Fifth, was also in the American line. He was in the second company of the second regiment, the first battalion of the Somerset Brigade. He evidently went out quietly, without blare of trumpets, and came back as he went, as though he were merely doing his duty and no more. After many months of absence, he returned from Morristown at night to his home, so ragged, bearded, and dirty that his wife did not recognize him and would not let him in the house. The story, as told to me when a child, was rather awesome.

There was the sound of hoofbeats on the road that drew nearer and nearer and then stopped in front of the house, followed by steps on the walk and a loud knock at the door. It was not opened. His heroic wife—Ida Stryker, may her name endure!—stood behind the door, flintlock in hand, with two children crouched behind her on the floor. She had fought off marauding Hessians before and could do it again. Of course, that stress lasted for only a few minutes, but the bravery of it was often commented on in the family. Nothing was ever told about the final recognition and the joy of the reunited family. That was mere sentiment, of which the family had a plenty but never cared to talk about it. Down to my own time, sentiment in the family was tabooed as savoring of weakness or effeminacy.

Now, the girl of seven who crouched behind her mother in the dark was the Aunt Charity whom I saw at Lamington, old and bedridden, many years later. That projects the shadow of the Revolution down into my own times, and, of course, in my father's time that shadow must have been all around him. It was not only his grandfather Van Dyke and his wife Ida Stryker who fought through the war, but his maternal grandfather, John Honeyman, and his even more heroic wife, Mary Henry, were in it, too. John Honeyman, the spy of Washington, is now a matter of New Jersey history.[4] Novelists have written his adventures (notably Frank Stockton), and high-school boys are still writing compositions and essays about him, but perhaps I can add a few new details. My father was much with him in his later years, and he had fragments of the story from the spy's own lips, but the spy was never very communicative. He held his tongue and shook his head. I stood by and saw my father write down the Battle of Trenton story, as he had heard it, but much of the spy's other activities were never told, not even to his faithful wife.

John Honeyman was a Scotch-Irish covenanter, who, in 1758, as a conscript, a young soldier of fortune, came over the Atlantic with Colonel (afterward General) Wolfe. He was attached to Wolfe's bodyguard, fought with him on the Plains of Abraham [1759], and when Wolfe was mortally wounded carried him from the field of battle, walking, as he afterward expressed it, "most of the way in blood." After the close of that war [French and Indian Wars], Honeyman went to Philadelphia and there married Mary Henry, a young woman of his own faith and race. When the Revolution broke out, by means of letters, his relations with Wolfe, and his discharge papers, he sought and obtained an interview with Washington. No one of the family ever knew exactly what passed between them, but the understanding was very definite that Honeyman should play the spy for Washington in New Jersey, where he was well-acquainted with the land and the people. He went over to the British forces as a Tory, acted for them as a buyer of horses and cattle, and was branded everywhere through New Jersey as a notorious Tory giving aid and comfort to the enemy. His family was then living at Griggstown, near Princeton, and so indignant were the neighbors over Honeyman's Toryism that one night, suspecting that Honeyman had returned to his family under cover of darkness, a mob surrounded the house and demanded that the Tory come out. But only Mary Henry and her three children came to the door. Old Major Baird, who was leading the mob, was for searching the house, but she called him to her and handed him a paper, which read:

American Camp, Nov. A.D. 1776

To the good people of New Jersey and all others whom it may concern:

It is hereby ordered that the wife and children of John Honeyman of Griggstown, the notorious tory [*sic*] now within the British lines and probably acting the part of a spy, shall be and hereby are protected from all harm and annoyance from every quarter until further orders. But this furnishes no protection to Honeyman himself.

George Washington
Com - in - Chief

That letter was a dash of cold water to the mob. It slipped away some-what mystified but satisfied that Honeyman was not there. As a matter of fact, he was with the British Army at Trenton, carefully noting out of the tail of his eye the lax discipline and riotous living of the British. He had news to impart regarding roads and camps and arms and sentinels. Accord-ing to plan, he ventured beyond the British lines, ostensibly looking for cattle and horses to purchase but in reality seeking an opportunity to be captured by American troopers. The opportunity came. Two American cavalrymen spied him, gave chase, and when Honeyman slipped on a scrap of ice, they caught him. He protested he was only a poor cattle dealer, but they recognized him as a Tory who had been long in the seeking.

Now, Washington had given strict orders that if Honeyman, the notori-ous Tory spy, were caught, he was to be brought at once to his headquarters, and under no circumstances was he to be harmed. This was carried out to the letter. He was taken to headquarters. The two were closeted for an hour. Then Honeyman was placed in a guardhouse with sentinels before the door. In the middle of the night, a fire broke out in the camp, the sentinels rushed to put it out, and when, after a short time, they returned to their post, the guardhouse door was open and Honeyman was missing. Three days later, Washington recrossed the Delaware and won the battle of Tren-ton. Honeyman was directly responsible for it. The battle was crucial. It was the turning point in the war. The army was heartened and the country was saved.

Honeyman made his way back to the defeated British, telling a doleful tale of his capture, ill-treatment, and escape and was severely reprimanded for his carelessness. But, nevertheless, he was received back into the camp. He was cursed in both camps but went on to the end of the war getting information for Washington, aiding the American cause and holding his tongue. Even after the war ended and Honeyman went back to his family at Griggstown where the neighbors cut him, he still maintained his silence. And then one day there came to visit him Washington and several of his staff. That brought the story out, and the ban was lifted. But still Honey-man said little. Not even to his grandson, my father, did he more than hint at things. He never wanted the British to know that he had fooled them.

His later years were spent on a farm at Lamington, where he lived to be over ninety. He had always been considered a poor man, and his neighbors were much surprised when he died leaving about twelve thousand dollars. That was a large sum in those days, and there is no way that Honeyman could have come by it save through Washington. But once more he was silent even with his own family. He and Mary Henry, with Abraham the

Sixth and Ida Stryker and their relatives, are buried in the Lamington churchyard, and ivy wraps their headstones, but their deeds are living after them and are now being considered rather heroic.

My father's mother was Sarah Honeyman, daughter of the spy and child of the Revolution. Having known the hardships and dangers of the war, she naturally trained her son in fortitude and courage. She also instilled him with the idea of playing a part in the world—ambition, something his [Dutch] ancestors had always despised. He was the boy orator of the Lamington countryside and soon left the ancestral home, going down to New Brunswick to study law with Judge James Schureman Nevius, the grandfather of my lifelong friend, Dr. W. H. S. Demarest, former president of Rutgers. He was the first to break away from the big farms. For seven generations in America the family had been sufficient unto itself, living its own life, ordering its own affairs, caring little for towns and governments, and nothing at all for place, position, or power. It had no ambition beyond leading a quiet, God-fearing life in the open air, upholding its own traditions and passing away quickly when the time came. But a change came with Sarah and her son.[5]

Admitted to the New Jersey bar, the young lawyer sprang into prominence almost at once, as prosecutor in the then-celebrated Suydam-Robinson murder trial. He rose rapidly, becoming in succession prosecutor of the pleas, mayor of the city, congressman from his district, first president of the Bank of New Jersey, now the National Bank of New Jersey, a judge of the New Jersey Supreme Court, judge of the Third Judicial District in Minnesota, and a member of the Minnesota Senate. He held many positions of honor and trust, was considered an excellent trial lawyer and judge, and all told had a successful career. I have every reason to be proud of him, and no mock modesty about the family shall prevent my saying so. His portrait appears herewith and suggests the quality of the man better than words. He was a Spartan in the virtues and yet withal one of the kindliest of men.

My mother's portrait appears here also. I never had cause to blush for her appearance, her intelligence, or her social graces. She was a brilliant, well-educated, high-strung Puritan, with nerves, principles, and convictions to her fingertips. That was her heritage from nine generations of New England ancestors. She was Mary Dix Strong [Van Dyke, 1819–1875], a daughter of Doctor Theodore Strong, professor of mathematics at Yale, Hamilton, and finally for over thirty years at Rutgers—a man who ranked with Bowditch of Harvard and Robert Adrain at Columbia as one of the great mathematicians of our middle period. He was directly descended from Elder John Strong of Dorchester, Massachusetts, who settled there in

1630. The family had carried on through generations of teachers, preachers, colonial governors, and Revolutionary officers and was connected by marriage with almost all of the prominent families of New England. My grandmother Strong was Lucy Dix and from her side brought in more Puritanism, nerves, and ministerial, professorial ancestry. But I shall not enlarge upon the Strong family, because Benjamin Dwight wrote two volumes about it. Its descendants still maintain its traditions with honor, but it is not the tale I have set myself to tell. My story deals with New Jersey, where my father's family lived for so many years.

Chapter 3

Green Oaks

After so much parade of family history, it would be quite useless for me to pretend to any log-cabin origin or very humble birth. When I was born, my father was president of the Bank of New Jersey, a prominent lawyer, considered well-off, and lived in a larger and better house than I have ever been able to afford during my lifetime. The house is still standing on Hamilton Street, across the Mile Run and just outside the city limits of New Brunswick. It now belongs to Mrs. John Ross Rowland and is precisely as it was built by my father in 1851. It was a Swiss chalet type of house set back in a grove of oaks and was called Green Oaks.[1] There I was born in 1856, the birth year of the Republican Party. I do not know if the first presidential candidate of that party, Colonel John C. Frémont, was a very close personal friend of my father, but at any rate I was given his name.

Green Oaks was a country place of a dozen or more acres and adjoined my Grandfather Strong's one hundred and twenty-five acres where there were great fields of clover, barley, and corn.[2] A wood road through a grove of cedars led from one house to the other, and it was along that road we traveled every evening to family prayers. There was an extensive lawn under the oaks, a garden at the back, and stables where William Mason curry-combed the horses, milked the cows, fed the chickens and guinea hens.

The guinea hens, half a dozen or more, had my childish wonder and admiration from the start. They could not only run but fly like the wild, an accomplishment vouchsafed to the chickens only in very moderate degree. They had something of the forest about them that the chickens had completely lost. And that call of the ones behind to those ahead, "Come back! Come back!" was always a puzzle to me as a child.[3]

The garden was a large one, with hollyhocks, sunflowers, and yellow roses against the white picket fence and many beds of sweet williams, violets, pansies, carnations. Around it was an oak wood and down at the side ran the brook. It was a famous place for birds, and I often sat there under the rustic grape arbor watching the orioles, firebirds, blackbirds, catbirds, and robins, or at evening waited for the wood thrush with her young (with spotted breasts) to appear or the little bats to come out of the wood and dart for flies and mosquitoes. One day I remember bursting out with violent rage at William because he had shot a catbird for stealing the strawberries. When my oldest brother came home on vacation from Princeton and went hunting, I always had a wail over the dead birds in his game bag. I thought then that the shooting of birds was outrageous, though later on I did perhaps more than my share of it.

But my tenderheartedness did not extend to the fishes. The Mile Run was the division line of our property, as it was also the boundary line between Middlesex and Somerset counties, and there I spent whole days wading the shallow brook, turning over stones in pursuit of crayfish and small eels. There was a swimming hole in the brook where my brothers must have taught me to swim. I became later a very strong swimmer, but I have no recollection of where or how I learned the art.[4]

Back of the garden in the woods was DeRussy's Gully where a small stream ran, and there my father often took me for a walk on Sunday afternoons. The shallow pools were full of small fishes, but I was never allowed to disturb them, though the destructive instinct was large in me from the start. I stoned the goats and the geese of the Irish and "chunked" stray chickens and cows in the road whenever opportunity offered. Livestock had more liberty of range then than now, and between our house and the city there was an Irish town that was very partial to predatory goats and geese.

There were only some eight or ten large houses west of the Camden and Amboy Railroad in New Brunswick at that time. The old Queen's building at Rutgers stood on the hill overlooking the Raritan, Old Hertzog was built on a neighboring hill in 1856, and beyond that was the Scott place (now Buccleuch Park) near the Landing. The Bishop houses were built about this time, the Miles Smith and Dayton houses on Easton Avenue were standing, also the Gordon, Kinney, Adrain houses. In between these places and the city there were smaller houses and shanties that were the cause of much caustic comment because the larger householders had to pass by them on the way to the city. I can remember my mother's indignation at the people who used to throw their wash water in the street and cause bad smells. The streets were then receptacles of all sorts of refuse. They were unpaved and uncared for by the street-cleaning department, if there was such a thing at the time.

In a few of the streets there were cobblestone pavements, but they quickly ran off into dirt roads that in winter were almost impassable. In the country the narrow-tired wagons cut through the red mud up to the hubs, and walking during the winter months was usually accomplished by wearing heavy rubber galoshes. My grandfather walked to college every morning for exercise, going down first to the steamboat dock, where he would strike a large tree with his cane, and then back to his classroom, but my father often went to town on horseback to avoid the mud. There was a small wooden bridge over the Mile Run, but most of the creeks and brooks on the way to Trenton were forded. All bridges at that time were built of wood. The railroad and the Landing bridges over the Raritan were covered—the first disappearing in fire in 1877, the second being replaced by steel some years later.

Among my earliest memories was that of the long music room at Green Oaks, with my mother seated at a blue-and-red-piped organ singing "Long, Long Ago." I can see myself seated on the floor playing with toys, the room darkened to keep out the heat, and my mother dressed in white. There was a large glass chandelier hanging from the ceiling, and a stray sunbeam striking the prisms threw a halo of color about her head. I have always remembered that picture and the sadness of "Long, Long Ago" and "Gaily the Troubadour," which she sang out of a large music book.

It was a romantic time, and sentiment was in the air. Much poetry was read, with Mrs. Norton, Mrs. Hemans, and Mrs. Browning as the favorites among the women poets. At five, I was stood on a drawing-room ottoman to recite "Bingen on the Rhine" for visitors. The father, too, was not above a lofty admiration for Walter Scott and Byron, reading to me "The Lady of the Lake" long before I was old enough to understand it. He liked the heroic in Byron, but the mother clove to the sentiment. Some years later while living in Trenton, she found Mrs. Ellen Clementine Howarth, who wrote "The Wind Harp," "Rufus the Red," and other poems, living in dire distress. She raised money for her through lectures by such women as Elizabeth Oakes Smith, built her a house, and put her on her feet financially. I have a volume of her poems beside me as I write, dedicated to my mother, and with an excellent introduction signed R. W. G. Many years later I asked Richard Watson Gilder if he had written that introduction. He said he had, that it was one of his first literary efforts done when he was a cub reporter on the *Newark Daily Advertiser*.

There was much reading in the family. Even William out in the stable read Shakespeare and threatened to write a tragedy about Mark Antony. And not a little fiction was absorbed. *Harper's Monthly* was eagerly awaited for new installments of Dickens' novels. Cooper and Washington Irving and Brockden Brown, with Walter Scott, were in the library. I doubt the existence there of the Brontës or Jane Austen or Fielding or Richardson, but Mrs. Rowe's *Charlotte Temple* was hidden away behind other books on an upper shelf. There was much weeping over the story of Charlotte Temple.

It was not a severely critical age, not a period of fine art. Painting and sculpture were largely a matter of portraiture, and not very good portraiture at that. People went to see Powers' *Greek Slave* with a shudder and Thomas Cole's *Voyage of Life* with a wonder. As for opera, it was unknown. There were tales told of Jenny Lind's singing and the elder Booth's acting, but the stage was rather tabooed in the family. The church was against it.

At that time, the church was a very active factor in the community. Rutgers College and the Theological Seminary were the center of the Reformed Dutch Church [now, the Reformed Church in America]. Theologians like Doctors Cannon, Ludlow, Van Vranken, Milledoler, and Berg made pronouncements that no one questioned. Everyone attended church, and if there were doubters they sat in the square pews, smothered their doubts, and bowed their heads. Aside from Sunday service, almost all of the social life was interwoven with the church and church work. People were not then dining out and going to the theater or a dance afterward. Dining was a midday affair, and balls or evening parties were not frequently indulged in. The families came together on holidays and feasted at weddings and birthdays, but aside from that, social life was largely a matter of "calling" or visiting. Relatives came and stayed on as long as they pleased, and clergymen were continually dropping in overnight. There was always a spare room and a parlor opened on these occasions. The clergy sat about in white stocks and solemn black, talking with a pulpit intonation, and the laymen, in black stocks and broadcloth, listened with deference.

Almost all of the men wore long hair and were disfigured by heathenish beards. Barbers in those days were almost unknown, and the wife cut the husband's and children's hair, with sometimes startling results. In the early Sixties I remember seeing the seven judges of the New Jersey Supreme Court coming out of the State House at Trenton and thinking at the time that they were the most villainous-looking lot of men I had ever seen. In reality they were fine of feature, but hair and beards had done for them. In those days Frederick T. Freylinghuysen, the United States Senator from New Jersey, was considered the handsomest man in the state, probably because he was smooth-shaven and wore his hair neatly trimmed.

The hoop skirt was then in vogue, but I never remember my mother, nor anyone in the family, wearing one. I recall the poke bonnet worn about the house and grounds, but I cannot remember that it was worn in the street. The women dressed simply, in black silk or white muslin, with silk mitts, lace, and ribbons. When with "company," they said little, but when making social calls they were not at a loss for language. My mother was always spoken of as "a good conversationalist," which meant probably that she could fill in holes in a dinner-table talk with considerable skill.

There was a prodigious lot of talk, Bible readings, prayers, and grace-saying when any of the clergy came to the house. I think my brothers and I counted the clergy rather slow, but we were not allowed to publicly express ourselves on that point. We had the Bible read to us and on Sunday were taken to Sunday school and afterward to church to sit in the great tank pew. In the afternoon we were not allowed to go off the grounds except with father. We could read the American Tract Society books and the *Christian Intelligencer* if we liked. Naturally, we grew up to hate the *Christian Intelligencer*, the *New York Observer*, and all the tract literature without exception.

The restraint of those days argues no more lack of intelligence than the liberty of the present times. Indeed, a talk then, over cigars, often resulted in some worthwhile conclusion, where a cocktail party of today ends frequently in mere muddleheadedness. Intelligence did not concern itself then with so many subjects, but those that were discussed were serious and worth while. The hop-skip-and-jump talk of today is different but not necessarily better; and the mind of today, spread out thin over many themes, is not necessarily more acute. You can line up any three contemporary writers against Hawthorne, Emerson, and Lowell, any three statesman against Lincoln, Seward, and Stanton, any three military men against McClellan, Grant, and Lee, any three orators against Webster, Clay, and Calhoun, any three of any calling in the Fifties and Sixties against any three of the same calling in the 1930s, and the difference will be one of time and circumstance rather than of mentality. It is the same quality of mind at work, but the problem it is working upon has shifted to something different.

Of course, the sphere of mental action was necessarily smaller in diameter than it is today. The era of transportation had not begun. People were concerned with problems of their own immediate bailiwicks, Europe was a long way off, and China and Japan were only color spots on the map. Only the exceptional ones went overseas. My uncle, Woodbridge Strong, went to California with the Argonauts in '49, but my father's farthest west was the Mississippi, his farthest north Canada, his farthest south Florida. During the Civil War he went through the Union lines into Virginia on some unknown mission. I have his pass signed by Drake de Kay, aide-de-camp of General Mansfield—signed with large black letters that the pickets could read at night. But these journeyings were considered Sinbad voyages in those days. Eight generations of the family had lived on without going out of the country, but the ninth generation wandered over the entire face of the earth. There has been great change of circumstance, but I am insisting no great change in mentality. Kant never ventured but thirteen miles from Königsberg in his life, yet he wrote the *Critique of Pure Reason* while thousands of the brainless were chasing each other around Europe in aimless pursuits.

Green Oaks was an ideal child's paradise. There was the brook where I fished, the garden where I was taught the names of birds, and the forest where my father told me the names of the trees. Lying farther out were the great fields of my grandfather's farm, the hayricks and barns and horses and cattle. With my two brothers I soon began wandering afield, coming home at night with the guinea hens and bringing with me perhaps the measles or some other picked-up trouble. When we were all washed and put to bed, my mother must have been weary. But all of us loved Green Oaks. It was a romantic home in the woods, more romantic than we ever guessed until we had left it.

For in 1862 we all took sudden flight like a flock of wild fowl. Green Oaks was sold, and we moved to Trenton. It was a city more convenient to my father's judicial circuit.

Chapter 4

Trenton

For some weeks we lived at the Trenton House, then presided over by the redoubtable Peter Katzenbach, but a large double house was being built for us on West State Street, a short step from the State House, and there we were presently domiciled in one of the houses, while Pliny Fisk, the banker, moved into the other. Evidently, this house was not large enough, had not enough ground about it, for it was presently sold to Barker Gummere, a well-known lawyer, father of the present Chief Justice of New Jersey, and we moved into a brick house on State Street opposite the A. G. Richey place. A half dozen acres had been bought on Greenwood Avenue, and there a house as large as a small summer hotel was put up for us. One's social standing in those days was somewhat determined by the size of the house he lived in and his surrounding acreage.

Trenton in the early Sixties had more distinction than it has today. It was more spacious. The square houses on State Street and elsewhere were set back in extensive grounds, and there were trees and lawns and boxes and flowers, with an air of dignity and individual taste about each place. Even the side streets with their rows of brick houses and marble steps (after the Philadelphia pattern) were substantial and well ordered, never so monotonous as the corresponding rows of brownstone fronts in the side streets of New York.

There was display of horses and carriages, a good deal of entertainment, with official receptions and a dressing to correspond. Young dandies paraded State Street in the afternoons, wearing cape coats, silk hats, close-fitting gloves and boots, and carrying switch canes. The elders wore broadcloth and the women lace cloaks and voluminous silk skirts. They all took themselves rather seriously, especially the dandies.

Trenton was the capital of New Jersey, and its official life gave it social prestige. Sooner or later, everyone of prominence in the state drifted in there. That meant little to me, but even as a boy I began to recognize and place the prominent people. Governor Vroom in top hat and overcoat, small, old, hugging himself with the cold, coming down State Street to the State House, Chancellor Green, wearing a shawl around his shoulders, shuffling home from his chambers, the handsome John P. Stockton, with the dashing Mrs. Stockton rattling down the street behind a spanking team, the Richard Stocktons living next door to us on State Street. The Cooks living opposite, the Richeys, the Gummeres, the Strykers, the Samuel K. Wilsons, the John A. Roeblings, the Scudders, the Hewitts were familiar figures. The children in those families were schoolmates and playmates of mine. The Model School, next to the Normal School on Clinton Street, had just been built, and there most of the Trenton youngsters got their early schooling, and I with them. It was the practice school of the Normal School, then as now, but I cannot recall any foreign element in it. It was all American then.

Foreigners were few and far between in Trenton in 1860. Charlie Jay, who was the newspaper free lance of the day, was continually poking fun at Naar of the *True American*, calling him the venerable Rabbi Naar, and Colonel Freeze of the *State Gazette*, calling him Jerusalem Freeze, because he was a Jew and had been to Jerusalem. But these were merely newspaper fisticuffs and meant no large Jewish population. Another foreigner, not in public life, was a source of some wonder to me. This was a Greek gentleman, Ion Perdicaris, who lived in a romantic castellated sort of house where State Street debouched into Clinton Street. I used to pass the house on the way to school and suggest to my schoolmates that the ivy-mantled tower was haunted. The old gentleman, short and round, we occasionally saw on the street, usually with a book under his arm, from which probably grew the story that he was a great scholar. Also the tale ran that he was a political refugee. Some tyrant had tried to shoot him or hang him. He had to flee for his life. He had come out of Greece and was a countryman of Alexander the Great, about whom we had some misinformation in *Peter Parley's History of the World*. He had come across the great ocean to Trenton. It was all very impressive to me then. Today, with I know not how many hundreds or thousands of Greeks in my native town, I am once more impressed but not in the same way.

Schooling at the Model School under Doctor Webb and Mr. Lippincott was probably not very different from what it is today, but two brothers and I naturally thought it rather tiresome. But we carried on through the forms, played baseball, and occasionally played hookey like other schoolboys. We all got our elementary education there, I up to my twelfth year. During the better part of this time, the Civil War was dragging on. News of battles came to us and were discussed violently on the ball field. McClellan had his partisans, and others of us were always ready to stand for Lincoln. This became more violent when the second Lincoln campaign came in 1864 and McClellan was the opposing Democratic candidate. We wore round, tin pins with portraits of McClellan or Lincoln, and this led occasionally to fisticuffs and bloody noses. None of us knew what we were fighting about, but we fought.

Then months later there came a morning when entering the breakfast room I found my father standing at a window with tears in his gray eyes. I had never seen that before and knew instantly that something terrible had happened. Lincoln had been shot. And the father was standing there looking out of the window, looking through tears, but saying never a word.

It was a time of great stress. People were in a profoundly sorrowful mood. The streets were heavy with crape and draped flags, bands with muffled drums came and went, bells tolled, and crowds lined the pavements. It was a silent crowd, but under the silence was a current of anger all the stronger because there was no outlet for it. There were curses not loud but deep. That day the North would have torn the South to pieces had there been anything left to tear.

The train bearing the dead Lincoln, already a martyr, passed through to New York and out into the West, the whole North and West wept, and even the South realized it had lost its best friend. But the sun came up each day as usual, and presently life resumed its normal rounds, with people going about their affairs thankful at least for one thing—the war was ended.

New Jersey soldiers, train after train of them, came into the Trenton station, were detrained, and camped, awaiting their discharges. The ladies of Trenton—my mother in the van—had built a large soldiers' rest on Clinton Street, and there for days I carried coffee and food down the long tables of waiting, hungry soldiers. Their blue caps and cloaks were faded and ragged, they were bearded and grimed and thin-looking, but they cheered themselves hoarse with delight at their reception and in their gladness at being once more back home in New Jersey. Cavalry rode up the street. Ranks and ranks of horses—I had never seen so many horses. And at the rear of the troop, within a hollow square, handcuffed and riding led horses, were half a dozen shaved-head deserters. After they had passed, a furiously driven carriage, a helpless soldier on the back seat with a companion holding an umbrella over his head, dashed through the town looking for a doctor's office. The unfortunate had been riding on the top of the cars and in passing through the Trenton tunnel had been hit by the arch of the tunnel, killed within sight of home and peace after four years of war.

Gradually, the drums and fifes died out in the distance, the soldiers melted away, the lookers-on went back to work. Trenton resumed its everyday life, and we tripped back and forth to school as usual. Once more, during a vacation, I drove with my father across New Jersey up to

Lamington. The farmers left their teams standing in the furrows to come to the fences for a moment's talk. They all began with the same question:

"Well, Judge, what are they going to do with Jeff Davis, hang him?"

And always the same answer:

"Oh, no. That would not help matters. It would be counted against the North as mere revenge. Better let him go."

With always the same reply:

"Well, I dunno."

They wanted to hang him for Libby and Andersonville, but above all for the assassination of Lincoln. They knew Davis was not personally responsible for that dire disaster, but they were still angry and wanted a victim.

My reading at this time was desultory to say the least—at home everything of natural history, travel, and adventure that I could lay my hands on and at the State Library everything of exciting fiction. *Kenilworth* and *Rob Roy* to be sure, but the *Deerslayer* and the *Last of the Mohicans* preferred, with the *Red Rover* and *Jack Tier* as good seconds. Marryat's novels with lives of Boone and Simon Girty and tales of Frémont and Kit Carson also claimed my warmest admiration. And surreptitiously, read in the stable or the woods, Beadle and Munro's dime novels of Indian life. Squint-eyed Bob and the way he shot Indians put me in the mood of shooting a few on my own account. I had already equipped myself with a hickory bow, and I could drive my feathered arrows into a pine tree at thirty yards with considerable accuracy. George Onderdonk had a single-barreled gun which I occasionally borrowed on Saturdays and, munitioned with powder and shot in bottles, a liberal supply of hornet's nest for wadding, and a box of G.D. caps, I went forth to the slaughter. The blackbirds in the pines were assaulted, an occasional snipe along the river fell a victim, but gray squirrels as large as grizzly bears and muskrats along the canal as large as South American tapirs were my chief quarry. No Cooper Indian could have beaten my masterful stalking and killing of a half-grown muskrat in a puddle by the canal. It was superb.

The parents were never told about these big hunts. They had always been teaching me self-reliance. At Green Oaks I had been sent to bed each night in the dark. If I met a bear on the stairs landing, I was to fight him off. In the big Trenton house, when called upstairs one evening about dusk and before the lamps were lighted, I bawled back that I couldn't see. The mother's soft voice replied:

"Well, feel."

That was the Puritan of it. If I could not do a thing one way, then do it another way, and under no circumstances lean on anyone. They made me a swimmer before I could remember and put me on Jerry's bare back with nothing to hold by to keep me from slipping over his tail. And now, profiting by the lessons in self-reliance, I was doing a little hunting on my own initiative. There would have been a fit in the family had my hunting been known, but George Onderdonk got the contents of the game bag and kept silence.[1]

One day in spring, gun in hand, seeking what cave bear or lion I could slaughter, I was startled by a call coming out of the blue sky. It was the honk of wild geese. High overhead, flying in wedge formation and honking as they flew, were ten or a dozen of them. They were flying to the northwest, beating back the wind, going on a long flight to the prairie pools of Dakota or the far lakes of British America. Oh! What a thrill was mine! This was the real thing. Hunting muskrats along the canal and Assanpink Creek was mere child's play. I would follow the wild geese into the unknown wilderness, toward the prairies with the buffaloes and the Indians, trail the great forests and lakes beyond the farthest West of any Natty Bumppo! I stood there and watched that moving wedge of geese until it faded out against the blue. I have never forgotten the look of it.[2]

A few nights after that experience, my father, in a playful mood, asked me what I wanted to do in life. When I grew up, would I be a lawyer, doctor, preacher, or merchant? No. I would none of them. When I became a man I was going West to be a mighty hunter. It was many moons before the smiles of the family over that remark passed away. But I cherished the dream. On the walls of my bedroom were two steel engravings, one called *Still Hunting on the Susquehanna* and the other *The Hunter's Last Shot*—this latter being decidedly dramatic. I used to look at them night and morning and sigh over my enforced confinement at the Model School, at living in Trenton. Even the whole of New Jersey was too small for me. The United States government report of the Frémont expedition to the West, seeking a pass through the Rockies to California, contained engravings of buffalo hunts and Indian raids, and one of them showed the camp fire at night, with Indian heads peering around boles of the pines. That was it! Long live the life of adventure!

And this is the reality that came out of the dream. My oldest brother was at that time something of a hunter and already a famous shot.[3] He went through Princeton College "with a dog and a gun," as my father said, and to this day there lives at Princeton the tradition of his wonderful shooting with a dueling pistol, with bullfrogs as targets. "A Van Dyke shot" was synonymous with a bull's-eye. He himself declared that he had learned nothing at Princeton, but, as often happens, once he had graduated he turned about and became a student. All his life he was a reader and a thinker. My fifty years' association with university and college men has not lessened my respect for his knowledge and ability.

But study undermined his health. After Princeton he read law with James Wilson in Trenton, and after admission to the bar he went West, joining a cousin at Henry, Illinois. There he first shot the pinnated grouse of the prairies and the wild fowl of the Mississippi Valley.[4] Minnesota was a lure. It was a new land. He went up there by Mississippi steamer and stopped at Wabasha. From there, glowing letters came back home. The father was induced to go out and join him. Some weeks later, the father returned, and at the breakfast table the next morning we were told that he had bought hundreds of acres of land in Minnesota and that we were all going there in the spring. There was great rejoicing on the part of my brothers and me. The Sioux and the buffalo were already in sight.[5]

We started in April 1868. Almost all of our bridges were burned behind us. Probably much valuable correspondence was then destroyed, books and furniture were sold, pictures were left behind, law libraries were turned over to relatives. It was a long journey, and we were to travel with little impedimenta. By some it was considered perilous. Our William Mason would not go with us for fear of the Indians, but his cousin, Edward Mason, volunteered.

There were disagreeable leave-takings and, for me, several wet-eyed farewells at parting from as many blue-eyed young misses whom I would never, no never, forget. But in spite of tears, we got away to Pittsburgh by what is now the Pennsylvania Railroad and from there to Chicago by the Pittsburgh, Fort Wayne, and Chicago road. The railways were but iron ribbons stretching through a very sparsely settled country, and we noticed the increasing wildness as we passed on farther west. There were few restaurant stations, and we were living out of hampers of food brought with us. At Fort Wayne we got our first "square meal." The close approach to Chicago was across great marshes and shallow lakes in which were thousands of geese and ducks. Oh! if that train would only stop for half an hour! My second brother had a single-barreled gun with which I could have potshot a dozen ducks fired in almost any direction. But the smoky, spark-spitting little train moved on, and the ducks continued to rise and wheel in clouds.

At Chicago we transferred to the Chicago and Milwaukee road and rattled on across Wisconsin to the Mississippi at La Crosse. That was then the jumping-off place. There were no railroads along the upper Mississippi.

The Milwaukee and St. Paul came some years later. At La Crosse we took the *Annie Johnson*, a little stern-wheeler plying on the upper river. It was cold, with flurries of snow, a strong wind was blowing down the river, and the *Annie Johnson*, flat-bottomed and with her upper decks high out of water, had difficulty in making headway. It took several days to reach Wabasha, and during those days the wild fowl, turned back south by the cold, were coming down the river in strings, battalions, and clouds. I have never since seen such a rain and hail and blizzard of ducks. Of course, I was as mad as a hatter over it. The prospect of mighty hunting loomed large.

Chapter 5

Minnesota in 1868

Minnesota in the spring of 1868 was a rather wild country. There were small towns along the Mississippi and some others in the interior, but there were ten thousand unknown lakes at the north and a thousand miles of prairies at the west that very few had as yet traveled. The river towns depended for existence on river traffic. They were small, hastily built of wood, but each one of them had a tremendous future ahead of it. Wabasha was typical of them. It had railways coming into it from all points of the compass, it had prairie wheat from the west, great timber shipments from the Chippewa River at the northeast, and great flour and furniture mills in prospect. It would outrun Lake City, St. Paul, and St. Anthony, and as for Minneapolis it was then practically unknown and not in the running. But Wabasha today has about the same number of inhabitants that it had in 1868. It has hardly put out a new building or street or park in sixty years. A pretty little place of a thousand people that promised well but never fulfilled.[1]

The country was magnificent. The river basin was five miles across, with bluffs five hundred feet in height on either side, the tops of which were the level of the great prairies. From the high prairie level we could see the Mississippi lying down below and stretching away like a band of silver through the dark bottom timber. The river at that time, with the forests for the greater part still untouched, ran a full stream almost the entire summer, three-decker sidewheel steamers ran to St. Paul, and great rafts of sawed timber, put up in "cribs" and held together in long "strings," went drifting down to St. Louis. There was activity along the river, but back from the river's edge began the heavily timbered bottoms, and beyond the bluffs began the prairies where men and their doings made little impression. The sun shone bright, and the wind blew free over a new country. Humanity counted for little.

A small house had been prepared for us, while a larger one on a high bank of the river was building. Once more the father built a house three times too large. For some years that house was pointed out from the decks of the steamers as the largest dwelling between St. Louis and St. Paul. It was huge only by contrast with the other buildings along the river. But for the time being we were very content with a much smaller house on a lower bank of the river. The first day of our arrival, a brother and I spied a birch canoe coming across the river, with the heads of two Indians showing above the gunwales. Down to the shore we went to meet that canoe. It was loaded within a few inches of the water with muskrats, minks, and beaver. The Sioux were half buried in muskrats and steel traps. The muskrats seemed twice the size of my New Jersey breed, and the beavers had tails as broad as the blades of the Sioux paddles. Our eyes popped out of our heads. Great heavens! But the Sioux did not even look at us.

Within a week we had guns, two dogs, a birch bark, and a dugout canoe. There were plenty of Indians and half-breeds in the country—it was just after the big Sioux massacre[2]— and we had no difficulty in meeting the Indian boys from an encampment just across the river. They could speak English in a queer way, and we soon picked up a little Sioux. They took us into the bottoms to the big rice lakes where the ducks and geese came in at nightfall. And so we began our western shooting. The elder brother knew all the waterways, and with him and his gun we generally came home with great strings of wild fowl, but we liked the pothunting and sneaking with the Indians. We liked hanging about the Indian tepees, and we quickly dropped into Indian paddling, trailing, exploring, spearing fish by torch-light, and catching them by line in the river eddies.[3]

I was just twelve years old. We had been some months in Minnesota, but I had not yet realized my dream of becoming a mighty hunter. I had no desire to shoot my good-natured Indian companions. We got on very well together. Nor had I shot any elk or grizzlies as yet. We shot more prairie chickens, pheasants, woodcock, sandhill cranes, ducks. The dream was flattening out a bit. But the quantity of game and fish in that Mississippi valley kept my pulse beating rather strongly. The great flight of wild pigeons that went up the valley about 1870 would of itself have driven most boys out of their wits. Later on I was to cross Minnesota and Dakota to the northern buffalo range to see the great herds and to meet the plains Indians face to face. But that flattened out my dream still flatter. Mighty hunting was not quite what I imagined it. There was much bareback riding of wild mustangs, too much eating of burnt meat from the end of a stick, too much sleeping under a bush like a jack rabbit. I think all that put a heavy crimp in my wings. At any rate, the dream began to fade and the ambition to falter.[4]

The great cribs of lumber coming in strings out of the Chippewa were coupled up in great square rafts almost in front of our door. We fished from these rafts and naturally enough came in contact with the raftsmen. As a body, they were somewhat like the later cowboy of Montana, a ne'er-do-well, semi-criminal element that had dropped into the valley to avoid the clutch of the law but with boundless good nature and some praiseworthy characteristics. The Chippewa Jacks, the Indian Bills, the Bat Rocques, and Bill Drews all had gambling and shooting records, but they were very good company, very generous, very good-hearted. We adored them, hung about the rafts with them, ate "horse pie" (dried apple pie) with them in the cook shanties, and listened with avidity to their tales of the lower river. Finally, I persuaded the family to let me go with Chaska, a Sioux Indian, down the river to St. Louis on one of the big rafts. That and the return up the river on the lower deck of the *Dubuque* took weeks. It was an adventure in which I saw gambling aplenty, daily fights and accidents, with one man shot and another one of the crew drowned. But I never batted an eye over it, persuading myself that that was life and had to be faced.

Later on, I again went down the river but this time as the clerk of the *Chapman*, a small stern-wheeler pushing ahead of it a twenty-string raft. I kept the books, paid the men, delivered the strings of lumber, and shipped the twenty-four men of the crew back up the river. As a third early adventure, I took the clerkship of the *Ida Campbell* running on the Mississippi and the *Chippewa*, carrying freight, passengers, mails, and express.[5] I was merely a thin lath of a boy, but I carried a pearl-handled Smith and Wesson revolver and let it be known that I would not be bullied or robbed by any raftsman or raft crew. I was carrying the United States mails, and I would shoot.

I never had a chance. Only once did I have trouble, and that with a red-shirted, steel-corked raftsman who had been drinking. He started to break in a barrel of whiskey being carried as freight on the lower deck. He had gotten a ten-foot poker from under the boilers and was driving at the barrel head. I had to interfere. He raised the poker at me, but I whipped out the revolver and gave him a chance to look down the muzzle of it. I had to tell him that if he didn't drop that poker I would shoot. He sneered and smiled and said he guessed I wouldn't, but he nevertheless turned away to talk with another raftsman, lowered the poker, and the incident was closed. In about five minutes I began to feel very weak in the knees and got away to the engine room where I sat down on a bunk. It was my first serious coming to grips with anyone, and I felt rather shaky. But that encounter, witnessed by a dozen raftsman, gave me a reputation on the *Chippewa* for being a fire-eating young daredevil not to be trifled with. And overnight I got to be a dead shot with the revolver. Reputations then, as now, were built up on very slight foundations.[6] But all this hunting, fishing, rafting, steamboating were carried on during the summer months. In the winter the river was frozen over, the boats stopped running, the wild fowl went south, and a great mantle of snow spread over the Northwest. The bobsled mail stages came crying in over the snow, with the horses bearded with frost and the drivers smothered in buffalo coats and robes. Ugh! how cold! The ice froze three feet thick, the mercury sometimes went down forty below zero, the sun came up with white sundogs on either side of it. The air was filled with hoarfrost that glittered like an atmosphere of diamonds.

We put on moccasins and deerskin jackets and speared pickerel and muskellunge through the ice, we put on Norwegian snowshoes and hunted deer in the big pineries of Wisconsin, but most of our time was put in at a very good high school in the village. I exhausted the resources of the school and then, not knowing what else to do, became assistant postmaster of the town. My elder brother soon dragged me out of that position, insisting that I should go on with my studies under him. That I did for four years to my great profit.

At first I qualified for West Point, had the promise of the appointment from our congressman, but finally declined it. I took up with the brother German, French, English literature, philosophy, history, law. I read incessantly, talked much with my preceptor, and was determined to find out all that I could in books. And I can now testify, *contra* general opinion, to the books attainable in that small Minnesota town from 1868 and on. It should suggest that Illinois in the 1830s and 1840s was not so barren of books that a man like Abraham Lincoln had to put up with a school rhetoric and the Bible. I believe that notion is quite unfounded. Lincoln talked and wrote like a well-read man for his time. Why not? Did not the settlers in Illinois come from the East, as the later settlers in Minnesota? And did they not bring books with them?

The Ladies Circulating Library of Wabasha had much travel, biography, poetry, all the older and some of the contemporary novelists—the romantic Scott, the elegant Disraeli, the flamboyant Bulwer, the very intelligent Charles Reade, Dickens, of course, but neither Thackeray nor Jane Austen. I never grew up to Jane Austen and never more than half liked Thackeray. I was then in the romantic stage and in our home library read and reread Byron, Scott, Tom Moore, Shelley, Leigh Hunt. The force of Byron blinded me to his rather poor craftsmanship. At that time I did not appreciate the fine accomplishment of Keats nor the breadth of beam of Wordsworth, nor the culture of Landor. The more obvious wit of Pope, the thunderous quality of Milton, caught my admiration, but all of them put together had not the great drag of Shakespeare. I read and reread the plays and sonnets and at one time could recite *Hamlet* and *Macbeth* almost verbatim.

But my prose reading was considered more worth while. I got from a family newly come from Brooklyn a volume of Carlyle's *Sartor Resartus* and his *French Revolution*. They were books that ran on all fours with Macaulay, Jeffrey, Dr. John Wilson, and—of all books on the Mississippi in 1871—Ruskin's *Modern Painters*. I did not then at all comprehend the art theories of Ruskin, but I read him for his vehemence of style and scathing denunciation. It was a carry-on of the Macaulay tradition. Everyone in those days seemed "so confoundedly cocksure, you know."

From St. Paul came a copy of Taine's *English Literature*. Here was a man who saw the light and piled up evidence without heat. He was not seeking to put anyone in the wrong but trying to get at the truth. The difference between the Gallic and the British mind came out in sharp relief and was something of a revelation to me. From St. Paul again came Lewes' *History of Philosophy*, Hamilton's *Metaphysics*, McCosh's *Logic*, and Sir Charles Lyell's *Principles of Geology*. I had to reread them in later years with many other heavy volumes that I hawked at in my impetuous youth. Goethe's *Faust* and Hugo's *Les Orientales* quite floored me. Even in later years I found Bayard Taylor's translation of *Faust* an excellent substitute for the original.[7]

Some bright people from the East, cronies of my father and college chums of my eldest brother, came out to visit us. The brother had been elected to the state legislature and there met many of the state political leaders. One who came to visit us was Cushman K. Davis, afterward governor and United States senator from Minnesota. He was very bright, quick-witted, talked well. I liked to hear him talk against Alexander Ramsay, then the state boss, or Ignatius Donelly, who was stirring up the farm vote. His law firm was then Davis, O'Brien, and Wilson. Much later came his two famous partners, Cordenio Severance, whom I knew intimately for many years, and Frank Kellogg, formerly secretary of state, whom I last saw in Innsbruck about 1912.

Wabasha was the county seat, and the court of the Third Judicial District was embraced in its circuit. Members of the bar came from all over the state. Judge Waterman, the presiding judge whom everyone admired, died suddenly, and Governor Austin appointed my father to fill out his unexpired term. The father had retired from active practice but nevertheless accepted the appointment. I was then studying law and attended court sessions, admiring this lawyer's presentation of his witnesses, that one's cross-examination, the other one's summing up. Judge Wilson, then living at Winona, was the leader easily first and the object of everyone's esteem and regard. I thought him quite wonderful. Many years afterward, when he was an old man and I was stopping for a few days with Cordenio Severance at Cottage Grove, he called me on the telephone from St. Paul to say he had remembered me as a boy and had followed me in my books with pride and pleasure. That was one of the compliments of my life that I never forgot. I remember going back into the drawing room with a lump in my throat. The brilliant Wilson of my youth had remembered me. I could have cried over it.

Court week always brought an influx of strangers, and there were social activities about the Riverside, the half private hotel of the town. Girls came down from St. Paul or up from Winona or St. Louis, and there were dances, occasionally a fancy dress ball, or a lawn tea for charity. There was nothing very startling about this, nor was there anything very wild or woolly. It was not a dance-hall town. People then and there lived very much as they do now in the small towns of New York and New Jersey. There were church "sociables" that were tiresome, subscription dances during the winter that were lively, and summer picnics that were as full of ants and bugs as those of today. But the pretty girl then wearing long skirts was the same pretty girl who now wears short skirts. The fashions changed there as here. Just so with the men. More than one blooming dandy in the town ordered garments from St. Paul and wore a top hat on the boardwalks of Wabasha. Everlasting youth is much the same in all times and places. Doubtless, there has been a change with the native-born who have grown up in Wabasha. I am speaking of the early Seventies, when people from the East first moved out to Minnesota.

It was a fine country but intensely cold in winter. The cold, a large law practice, and much study, began again to undermine the health of my eldest brother. The winter of 1875 he had to go to Southern California.[8] The unexpected happened with those at home. My mother died. There were no sisters to hold the family together. It began to disintegrate. The father went to Florida, returning to die in Minnesota three years later. The eldest brother had gone back to California, and I had gone East. In two or three years the remaining brothers had gone West. "Minnevista," the big house at Wabasha, sold for a Catholic hospital and was immediately remodeled out of recognition, the huge farms were sold for so many songs, and the family fortune disappeared in taxes and worthless mortgages.[9]

The Minnesota episode was finished. Fifty years after, I could find only two people in Wabasha who knew my name or had even heard of my family. We had faded out and been forgotten.[10]

Chapter 6

New York in 1876

I had been taken to New York when a child, but the only things that impressed me there at the time were a barrel-organ museum on the corner of Ann Street, presumably Barnum's, and the gray granite mass of the Astor House on Broadway. When next I saw the city, I was coming up Chambers Street from the Pavonia Ferry, skipping over skids placed across the sidewalk and dodging heavy trucks on the greasy stone pavements. New York was not very impressive then, not even to a youth who had just finished seven years in a small Minnesota town. It was dirty, noisy with the clatter of iron-tired trucks, and uneasy with sidewalk throngs that trod on each others' heels. Trinity Church was the high point in the lower city, and St. Paul's Chapel was not lost on Broadway, as today. But the pretentious post office had disturbed the whole angle of Park Row and Broadway and put the beautiful city hall out of countenance. The buildings on Broadway and the immediate side streets were of brick or granite, with a few in marble, but the "iron clad" had appeared and was feeling its way. Of course, none of them was of the huge proportions of today. The towers of the Brooklyn Bridge, with the cables not yet in place, rose high over both New York and Brooklyn.[1]

The horse cars on the West Side ran uptown through Church and Greene Streets, but uptown was not far off. The Broadway center was about 11th Street, around the St. Denis Hotel and Taylor's Restaurant, but it was pushing up into Union Square. Tiffany's, the Everett House, and the Clarendon were within the Square. I remember being held up in the Square by Brown's equestrian statue of Washington. I knew nothing of sculpture then, but that struck me as a very large and grand affair. I have not to this day changed that early impression and still think it the finest equestrian statue in America. I walked about it, examining the surface and wondering how it was cast, not knowing that its final triumph was its casting and that Brown, with the help of Quincy Ward, both of them inexperienced, had hit it at the first attempt. A few years later I met Quincy Ward but had not the gumption to ask him about that statue. Everyone has read Benvenuto Cellini's account of the casting of his *Medusa*, but I wonder if the story of

Brown and Ward and their venture with the Washington has ever been adequately told.

The Fifth Avenue Hotel was in Madison Square, and swelldom lived on the Avenue, but fashionable living was still below 23rd Street, reaching down to Washington Square. Broadway had not ceased to be the great promenade. More people went up Broadway by the Gilsey House than up Fifth Avenue by the Brunswick. Still, Fifth Avenue was taking the lead with the smart and the moneyed folk. A. T. Stewart's marble palace on the corner of 34th Street was a white beacon that beckoned them on. At 42nd Street was the Reservoir, and that was about the end of the promenade, though carriages and horses with silver-mounted harnesses dashed up to the Central Park, and riders from Dickel's Riding Academy followed the park bridle paths, and four-in-hands were tooled out to New Rochelle and Pelham Bay to the winding of coaching horns. My cousins, the Hoffman Rogers family, living on 42nd Street opposite Bryant Park, thought themselves on the suburban edge, but some other cousins, the Jeremiah Lamberts, living in a brownstone front on West 52nd Street, were persuaded they were quite within the fashionable belt. New York socially, as well as geographically, was in a transition stage.

I did not stay long in the city but went to my aunt, Mrs. Ferdon, living in a large home at Piermont, on the Hudson River.[2] There I soon became great friends with my cousin William Ferdon, a year my senior. He was bright, attractive, intelligent, and at that time much devoted to society. In fact, the whole family had very positive ideas about "the best people" and "nice" people and who constituted society and who did not. I heard quite a little about "correct form" and right social procedure and the atrocities of conduct proceeding from the newly rich. Young as I was, I think I was able to smile occasionally over this, but I did not argue the matter. I went along and accepted what came. There was a smart set in New York then, as there is now, the hem of whose garment I was permitted to touch. I went almost every night somewhere, usually with Ferdon, dined out much, met many people, and made many acquaintances.

Dining as a social function preliminary to a ball had come into vogue. Cotillions were led, and the Boston was danced, and the corkscrew waltz passed away and was forgotten. But the long skirt lingered. Women wore furbelows, ribbons, trains, and I know not what else, and the men went in evening dress. In the afternoon promenade on the avenue, the men wore Prince Alberts with light trousers and derby or top hats. The dressing then was quite as good as today, the difference being merely a matter of tweedledum and tweedledee. A lower shirt collar, less crease in the trousers, more derby hat for the men; more headgear and less footgear for the women, and there you have it in substance.

There was more difference in the interior of the houses. It was the brownstone-front, black-walnut period. The city houses were lighted from windows, fore and aft, and were gloomy in the middle. This gloom was enhanced by dark wallpapers, dark furniture, dark-red curtains, with occasionally a ray of light from a gilded ceiling, a gold-striped chair, a red, satin sofa, or an inlaid piano. The pictures on the wall were Sartain engravings after Landseer or Wilkie, with an occasional landscape by Kensett or Mount, or bootblacks by J. G. Brown, with a flimsy piece of marble, representing Faith or Hope, pushed into the space between the front windows. It was not quite so bad as it sounds, though bad enough. At least there were chairs to sit upon, which is not always the case in the modern drawing room, with its resemblance to an antique shop gone astray.[3]

I decided that winter to attend lectures at Columbia College Law School. Ferdon had already attended one year. Professor Theodore W. Dwight, then the head of the school, was cousin to our mothers, and we were well received. The school was located on Great Jones Street, near the Astor Library. We commuted on the Erie, coming in every morning from Piermont to Chambers Street and riding uptown on the horse cars. Some winter days, with even four horses, the horse cars could not get through for the snow. The bottom of the car was filled with straw, for there was no heat. It was not good going, but there was no appeal from it, except to the much worse Broadway buses.

We sat on the same bench with Howard Ford, Frank Tracy (son of General Benjamin F. Tracy), Harry Oelrichs, and John H. Euston. Nearby sat Walker Blaine, very bright in answer and much admired by the class. We occasionally applauded his answers, but most of our enthusiasm went out to Professor Dwight. He was always very happy in exposition, very popular with his pupils. Professor George Chase, who was second in command, was greatly respected but voted rather "dry." Half of my class was made up of sons of rich men who were there for entertainment as well as a little information. I was there to get something, but my success in getting it was very moderate. I had already been over the ground covered by the Law School lectures.

Professor Dwight gave me letters of introduction to J. Carson Brevoort and Frederick Saunders of the Astor Library, to Judge C. P. Daly of the Geographical Society, to the librarian of the New-York Historical Society. Law School lectures were over at one o'clock, and I put in my afternoons sometimes with lectures at Columbia College but more often at the Astor

Library. I ran at first to the old English dramatists, Marlowe, Johnson, Beaumont, and Fletcher. I read much in dramatic literature, saw a good many plays and some famous players—Booth, Davenport, McCulloch, Bangs, Barrett, Adelaide Neilson, Agnes Booth, Wallack, Charles R. Thorne, Boucicault—and projected a play of my own, which I fortunately never finished. Through Judge Daly I met Augustin Daly, then having great success with society drama at his Fifth Avenue Theater. I had a little talk with him about plays and play writing but was too callow to appreciate his practical stage point of view. I was up in the air with dramatic literature of the Shakespeare-Marlowe kind; he was on the stage with a working Sardou melodrama. It seems a very human failing to see things at first either out of value or out of proportion; at least it was one of my failings. Later on I got some comfort out of Ruskin's despondency over his blunderings. The idiosyncrasies of the great have always been the consolation of the dunces—a remark of Disraeli's, if I remember rightly.

At the New-York Historical Society, I blundered about the Bryan Collection, looking at the pictures but more impressed by the Egyptian and Assyrian antiquities. I went back to the Astor Library to read Wilkinson's *Ancient Egyptians*, to study the large plates of Lepsius, to follow up Champollion and Mariette, and to dip into Herodotus and Strabo. The Assyrian reliefs at the Historical Society sent me to Victor Place's great folios, to Layard, Botta, and Flandin. Again I was wrong in my sense of values. I was interested in the romantic history of these lost empires, and the massive modeling of the Egyptian heads, the superb outlines of the Assyrian figures, were not seen. Art was a sealed book to me.

Even when I took up with the pictures in the Bryan Collection (with Richard Grant White's catalog), it was for what they meant rather than what they looked. The *Continence of Scipio* by Eeckhout, the very good *Tobias and the Angel* by Bol, the *St. John Weeping*, a Leonardo school piece, the *Samson* by Reubens were all so much illustrated Scripture to me and valuable merely because of their illustrative quality. I had scarcely a glimmer of such a thing as the decorative quality in painting. The Italian Primitives had fine depths of color, and the robes of the Saints showed rich patterns, but the idea of painting for the sake of pattern and color was still a long way out on my horizon. As for doubts about the genuineness of the pictures as attributed, I had merely a natural suspicion and skepticism not based on any knowledge. Cavalcaselle had written his *History of Italian Painting*, but I did not know the work, and Morelli had begun to write under the name of Ivan Lermolieff, but I had not heard of him. I was pottering alone lackadaisically with Messrs. Jameson, Ruskin, and Lübke.[4]

I had been for a week at Philadelphia attending the Centennial exhibition and had devoted most of my time to the pictures, but they seemed a mad medley in which I found merely confusion. Aside from a few family portraits, I had known very few pictures before coming to New York, and the Centennial exhibition was a swift plunge into unfathomed waters. The size of some of the pictures, the subjects of others, the blaring colors of still others attracted or repelled me, but I could not have told why. I had no criterion or standard and was going about in circles like a homing pigeon trying to orient myself. A huge canvas of Lincoln liberating the slaves I felt *sure* was bad, but the picture of a physician seated beside a dead girl on a slab rather struck me as good. Again, I could not have given any reason for my belief. A head of the *Dreaming Iolanthe*, modeled in cold butter and kept on ice under glass, caused only a smile. The material provoked it. But as for its workmanship, there were a score of heads there in marble and bronze that were just as stupid, just as silly, and yet I knew it not. The Centennial was confusing, but then perhaps it is proper to add the exhibition itself was confusion. Anything and everything was admitted, and standards were nonexistent. I look back upon it as a sort of nightmare.

But this was my blunder year. I blundered about in law, literature, history, art, reading in a feverish way, with heaps of books piled up around me, irritated that I could not read faster, knowing that I never could read all, and yet undecided as to what part I should choose for special study.[5] I had no one to guide me and probably would not have taken advice had it been offered. I was never very fond of advice, and the experience of others seemed to profit me little. I had to bang my head against stone walls to realize they were there.

In May 1877, at the spring session of the supreme court at Poughkeepsie, both Ferdon and I were admitted to the New York bar, I by special dispensation, because though I had not studied full time in New York, I had three years of study to my credit in Minnesota. I was just turned twenty-one, and the opportunity was given me to open a law office in Nyack and also in New York, but I declined both offers. I did not intend to go on with law, and as a matter of fact I dropped it the day I was admitted to the bar.

There followed on that blunder year a wander year that was another blunder. I shall say little about it because it had no sequence, led nowhere, and was a vain attempt at getting my bearings. I did not know what to do, so prowled about, imagining perhaps that I was some incipient Byron doing romantic stunts. Of course, I came back like the average prodigal, with most of my illusions shattered, that being about the only resemblance between myself and Byron. At twenty-two I was once more in New Brunswick, somewhat the wiser perhaps but still hesitating about the future. I could have taken up law anew, but I had too many notions about literature. I had, unwittingly perhaps, determined to follow writing, to be a writer. But my field was still indefinite.

Then one day an unexpected offer came to me. Would I take temporarily the acting librarianship of the Sage Library? I went to see it. The library building was the gift of Colonel Gardner A. Sage of New York to the Seminary of the Reformed Church in America at New Brunswick. It had been built only about five years and then held about 30,000 volumes. It was a scholar's library in many languages and was especially strong in theology, philosophy, philology, history, biography, art, English literature, Greek and Latin classics, manuscripts, original sources, rare editions. Scholars from without the state came to it to consult books not obtainable elsewhere, but the general public did not bother it. It was not for the public but for the seminary students, biblical scholars, and others engaged in research work. The duties of administration were not too exacting nor the salary too high. I should have leisure for my own work and several months each summer to go to Europe if I chose.

I said "Yes" without hesitation, and to myself under my breath: "This shall be the resting place for the sole of my foot." And so it has proved. Many offers of larger office from libraries, universities, editors, and publishers have come to me, but I have declined them all, and today, after fifty-three years, I am still the librarian of the Sage, though the active management has been in younger hands for a half dozen years.

But this is not a story of library management. It has to do with what went on without the library rather than within it. It has always been my home base, but from it I have been wandering afield for many years.[6]

Chapter 7

Reading

I went to live at the home of my uncle, Judge Woodbridge Strong, and took up the management of the Library immediately. Some preliminary measures, some extensive cataloging and rearranging were necessary, but I had leisure to prowl, investigate, and read. For the first three or four years I read in many departments. I reread all the poets, including much that was not poetry, in Voltaire, Camoens, Ariosto, Pulci, Bojardo. I slaved over Rousseau, Racine, Corneille, Molière, Herder, Lessing, Goethe, dabbled in Hebrew poetry, worried with the poetry of the Greeks and Latins—Homer, Sappho, Pindar, Theocritus, Virgil, Horace, Ovid. History reading was extensively planned, but not too much was accomplished. I hated Ranke and Grote and never finished Gibbon. I liked Froude and disliked Freeman. More to my taste were Macaulay, Carlyle, Taine, Cardinal Newman. Essays and criticism engaged me. I followed with interest the different methods of presenting argument employed by Hazlitt, Sainte Beuve, Lowell, Newman, Pater. Also I reveled in travel. Marco Polo, Sir John Maundeville, Kaempffer, with Hakluyt (in the English black-letter of 1599) kept me busy checking up on maps and spinning dreams of future wanderings. For night reading I took up Smollett, Fielding, and Swift, *Don Quixote*, Amadis de Gaul, the *Chanson de Roland*, the *Morte d'Arthur*, the *Gesta Romanorum*, the publications of the Early English Text Society.

The library was a storehouse of medieval and Oriental literature, and I ransacked its many corners, turning up the ecclesiastical histories of Eusebius, Sozoman, Theodoret, the Magdeburg Centuries, the great histories of the Church Councils, the collections of Papal Bulls, the folios of the Greek and Latin writers and the Church Fathers, the Talmuds, Torahs, and Mishnas, the Vedas and the Zend Avesta, the Persian and Indian poets, the Chinese classics. This was with no attempt at mastery or comprehension but rather from mere curiosity to find out what was there. The only things I really studied at that time were Italian and Spanish grammars for a reading knowledge in those languages. And I pored over every treatise I could find on prosody and versification, for I was then writing reams of narrative verse and trying to find out how others had written it before me. But mine was so bad that I dropped it into the fire and put the books on versification back

49

on the shelf. I should have to seek immortality by other channels than poetry.

It has always been rather a disappointment with me that my long years of association with books in the Sage never were, never could be, turned to any practical use in my writing. I had books in all languages at my elbow, and what languages I did not understand I could, for purposes of quotation, get from colleagues in seminary and college; but I could not quote. Again and again, I worked in proverbs from the Spanish or fables from the Norse or bright sentences from Cicero, or figures from the Bible or Homer; but they were all cut out in revision as inept or lugged in by the ears or too pedantic. Lowell could conjure with metaphor and show his immense knowledge of old French, and Macaulay could work in his recent reading as half forgotten memories of early browsings, but with thousands of books about me all my life through, I could not "lift" anything from them. I had to set down what thoughts I possessed in my own way and so simply that I thought them childish or foolish. My first two publications contained some quotation and allusion to books, and perhaps that was their undoing. At any rate, they were short-lived, and after them all my writing was at least my own.[1]

Of course, all this early reading, to which might be added hundreds of volumes of biography, archaeology, geology, and natural history, was taken up in a haphazard fashion. It was not reading with a definite purpose. Curiosity led me on. I knew that this was a wrong method of reading, and with natural perversity I started writing down for others the defects of the method and a possible suggestion of something better. This writing expanded into chapters and became a small book which I had originally designed for the use of seminary students in the library, but it was published in New York for the general public in 1882 [1883] under the title *Books and How to Use Them*. It was a clear case of the blind leading the blind, but the book was well received, well reviewed, and sold well. I did not expect to awake and find myself famous the morning after its publication, and I was not disappointed. Fortunately, it has been long out of print and does not worry me.[2]

At the time I first took charge of the Sage Library, a distinguished-looking young lady came there often to read and borrow books. This was Mrs. Schuyler Van Rensselaer, then but a few years married and living with her husband and small son in New Brunswick. We became very good friends and happily remain so to this day. She was a great reader, had lived for some time in Dresden, was much interested in art, and, like myself, was just beginning to write. Her experience had been much broader than mine, she knew about many things in Europe and the world of art that were not even nebulous to me, and naturally I looked up to her. With an attractive personality she drew about her a small group of congenial people who gathered at her house for nine o'clock tea. I was always there before the tea, and it was there from Mrs. Van Rensselaer that I got my first real fancy for art.[3]

But at first it was little more than a fancy. I had, with misgivings, shown her the manuscript of *Books and How to Use Them*, and she had graciously praised it. In turn I had read some of her stories. Then she began writing in the *New York World*, under W. H. Hurlbut's editorship, articles on current art exhibitions. These I followed with interest, but at that time I was not too keen about art criticism.[4] What finally aroused a lasting interest in art was a trip to Europe and some months in European galleries.[5]

With all my burrowing into books at the Library, my official duties, and my early writing, I found time to travel and to do some burrowing into nature. During 1880 and 1881, I had made excursions into New England and Canada, spent a summer in the Adirondacks, made a journey to New Orleans and up the Mississippi to Kansas and Minnesota to settle some matters of my father's estate. Wherever I went I studied natural appearances not only in trees and lakes and rivers but in skies and lights and atmospheres.[6] Everything interested me. I was eager about all life and took up nature, art, books, society, human nature, the world at large with avidity. I met many people, went to many functions. I was young and very strong.

Let no one abuse the early Eighties. It was a period of awakening. People were prospering, travel was expanding, life was broadening, art was in the air. City life was gay with dinners, theaters, and operas; country life had become modish and even brilliant with house parties. Perhaps society was taken up in some quarters with too much enthusiasm or extravagance, and these exceptional happenings are the things that the young writers of today choose to make merry over. For example, there were beauty dinners given occasionally, for which the guests were selected for their good looks. I recall one where all the women wore red tulle and diamonds, and the center of the round table was a great mass of poinsettias, with red ribbons leading up to the chandelier. And another where the women were dressed in purple velvet and pearls, with purple pansies for the table decorations. But these were avowed extravagances like a fancy dress ball. All the dinners were not of this kind, nor did they last until midnight, nor did the guests become intoxicated. Should you believe the tale of the Eighties as told by the social historians of the 1930s, every doorjamb of every house was decorated with

Japanese fans, every woman wore a chip hat over her nose and flew ribbons from every garment, and every man wore a silk hat with trousers bagged at the knees and smoked his cigar on The Avenue. But such was not the fact.

With development of the East and the expansion of the West, with increased commerce and transportation, there came about a corresponding intellectual and artistic activity. Colleges grew into universities, the metropolitan dailies doubled and quadrupled their pages, and the magazines came out with the beautiful wood engravings of a new American school. Gilder, Johnson, Alden, Burlingame were editing, and Howells, James, Crawford, Mark Twain, Bret Harte, John Hay, and others were writing. The Centennial at Philadelphia had set many young men adreaming about art. Almost immediately thereafter, a contingent left for Munich and Paris to get a technical education in painting, sculpture, and architecture. In the early Eighties they came home and with enthusiasm founded the Society of American Artists. La Farge, Homer, Inness, Wyant, and Martin were already in the National Academy and lending force to it, but the young men brought home a new and much needed technical skill. The Metropolitan Museum and many other art institutions had come into being. John Sargent was painting Carmencita dancing in Chase's studio down on 10th Street. Colonel Mapleson's opera troupe at the old 14th Street Academy of Music went out before the New Metropolitan Opera House with Wagnerian opera, the De Reszkes, and Lilli Lehmann. New York was lifting into the sky intellectually, artistically, even architecturally. It was the beginning. It was the very best of times in the very best of lands. Everyone believed it the dawn of a new era. And it was.

I went alone to Europe in a small Florio-Rubbatino steamer carrying sails. There were two other passengers, a Greek and a Spaniard, and, with the Italian captain, we were four at table, not one understanding the other's language. But we got on famously, except for the fleas under the table. We were fourteen days to Gibraltar and three or four more to Marseilles. There I disembarked and went to Monte Carlo. A few days later I got down at Genoa and was presently brought face to face with the Brignole Palace Van Dycks as practically my first old masters. I was decidedly impressed. The portraits had that air of sublimated elegance that made nobility more noble than reality. The posing was Olympian, the garmenting magnificent, the color splendid, not to say blazing. No wonder Sir Anthony was acclaimed the first of portrait painters. I thought so at the time and was a little sorry he had left no male children through whom I might claim descent.

At Florence I was bowled over by the obvious things—the Strozzi, Riccardi, Pitti palaces, the Duomo, the Campanile, the Loggia. Like other novices, I could rise to the gloom and might of Michelangelo in the Medici Chapel, but I did not then see his modeled surfaces, his command of form, his statuesque composition, his light and shade. In the Uffizi and Pitti I was confused by many pictures and out of the confusion drew disappointment in Raphael. His Madonnas were too pretty. Titian was heavy-handed, Leonardo and Georgione were too scrappy, Coreggio was merely a handkerchief-box painter. Andrea del Sarto went beyond expectation. I spent a long time before the *Descent* and the *Madonna del Arpie*, repeating to myself *Andrea senza erorri* [Andrea without faults]. And several times I went back to see Bonozzo's fresco in the Riccardi palace. Oh! What a wonderful story! And what a superb decoration! At last I began to see that the picture helped beautify the room and was beautiful color in itself.[7]

But there were so many painters and pictures that I had never heard of, so many things of art history that I did not know! And I formed and fashioned so many judgments that had to be reversed in future years. Occasionally I got a glimmering of the truth—just enough to lead me on. The line and composition of Raphael in the Vatican, the coloring and gilding of the Pinturicchios at Siena and in the Borgia Apartments, the charming narrative style of the Carpaccios at Venice, the splendid ceilings of Paolo Veronese, the lofty creations of Tintoretto in the Scuola San Rocco appealed to me as to almost everyone. And rightly enough. But at the north in Germany, France, Holland, and England, I was much disturbed by the Rembrandts. I could not understand how any one painter could see and paint in so many different ways. All the other great masters painted in only one way, in one light, with one palette of color, one model, but Rembrandt made a new problem with almost every picture. It never occurred to me then that perhaps many of the works set down to him were by pupils and followers—falsely attributed to him through ignorance or for commercial purposes. But I noted the variation in handling color and light even at that early day when connoisseurship was in swaddling clothes and I had not even heard the word.

In Switzerland, I joined the family of Captain Frank H. Mason, the American consul at Marseilles. We had met at Piermont [New York] in 1877, became friends and remained such throughout his many years of service as consul general at Frankfurt, Berlin, and Paris. We spent some weeks in the Bernese Oberland, and I then went on to Paris and London. I had letters of introduction from President Barnard of Columbia to that rare soul, Richard Garnett of the British Museum, and also to Dr. Samuel Birch, Keeper of the Egyptian Antiquities in the museum. I had questions to ask Dr. Birch about one of his own articles, in which he had left certain meanings a little obscure. I have forgotten now the exact point raised, but I remember his caressing a wen on the top of his head and asking me what I knew about that question. Of course, I eagerly told him what little I knew, but he offered me no information by way of correction. From one question he asked, I gathered that he knew less about that subject than his questioner. That was a knockdown blow to me. He was then the greatest of English Egyptologists, and yet he failed me on his own ground. It weakened my faith in authority, though Dr. Garnett told me afterwards that Dr. Birch gave out little information and was rather jealous of the younger men, particularly those in the museum.

Garnett willingly gave me much information about library economy and spent much time showing me the rare books and manuscripts in the museum. One day (I cannot remember the year) while I was talking to him, a messenger brought him a note. He read it and handed it to me. It was from Dr. Spurgeon saying he was preaching the following Sunday on the Fall and could Dr. Garnett get him material on the apple tree? Garnett explained that Dr. Spurgeon was a very busy man, and he with his assistants in the museum often gathered material for the sermons of the celebrated preacher. That explains Garnett. He was always giving time and intelligence to others. As for Spurgeon, I did not hear him preach that sermon but listened to many of his Exeter Hall sermons to young men. With others, I often paid a shilling to sit on the platform back of him that I might watch his audience. He could and did turn that audience white with handkerchiefs many times. He was a common enough looking man and talked leaning awkwardly over a railing, but he was a very persuasive talker, a rare personality.

London in the early Eighties was not, of course, the London of today. It was squatter, grimier, dingier, and, if anything, noisier, with its iron-tired trucks and omnibuses, but attractive, comfortable, the most livable city in Europe. I took lodgings in Jermyn Street near my friend Dr. Alfred Kellogg, then studying Egyptology in the British Museum, and from my top-story bedroom I could hear all night long the roar of London. Every large city in Europe had a dull sleepy roar about it in the Eighties. The electric shock and rapid-transit grind of steel had not yet come in. Everything moved slowly. Life was less hurried, perhaps more earnest, certainly less complicated. Travel was ideal. Everyone was hospitable, and the Americans were received with a smile and an open hand as travelers from some bright Hesperian garden overseas. It was very different from today, with the envy and hatred of Europe turned against us and travel there barred to the ultrasensitive. Even London, with its dinner-table protests about ties of blood and kinship of language, receives us now largely for our money.[8]

London was not so ungenerous in the Eighties. It patronized us—it always has done that— but it was glad to see us, opened its houses, showed us about, played the gracious host. I have never fared anywhere in the world so well as in England. And that, too, without formality of introductions or social "pulls." There were National Galleries, Westminster Abbeys, Houses of Parliament, Inns of Court to see, and like a true tourist I saw them, but there were private collections of the Queen, the Duke of Westminster, Captain Holford, which I also saw merely by asking to see them. The same kindness was shown me at Cambridge and Oxford. The librarians there did not know or care that I was a very humble citizen of the Great Republic. I was a fellow librarian and that was enough. I was taken in hand, introduced to professors and dignitaries, given luncheons and teas, until I almost came to believe myself of some importance.

Eventually, I gathered up my traps and went on to Newstead Abbey.[9] I think it was the first and last pilgrimage I ever made to a literary shrine. At that age I could cut out Shakespeare for Byron, and when I got to Newstead I found I could cut out Byron for the Abbey, so very attractive were the buildings and grounds which Colonel Wildman had restored and preserved. That Newstead journey has always remained a pleasant memory, though I regret to say that Byron with me long ago fell off his pedestal.

And so on to Liverpool and home in October.

Chapter 8

Art and Artists

In 1883, Franz Lent had started in New York a small artist's weekly, called *The Studio*,[1] for which Elihu Vedder designed a handsome cover. Lent himself was painter and architect and was regarded by the New York painters as a coming man, a man of ability. He had their support for his publication, which carried announcements of exhibitions, studio items, gallery notices, and a miscellany of art news and criticism. It came out once a week, a rather thin affair of eight pages, started on a shoestring and without financial backing of any importance. When I returned from Europe, Lent, whom I knew as a graduate of Rutgers, asked me to help him with the little sheet by writing for it. In a few weeks I had assumed the editorship of it, expanded it to sixteen pages, and started out to make it the mouthpiece of the younger American painters.

It was an audacious performance, considering the slimness of the treasury and the vastness of my ignorance about art. Carroll Beckwith prophetically told me that it would not pay but advised going ahead with it. I had already made up my mind to jump overboard and swim, even if I had to be dragged in by the heels. Immediately I got in touch with the painters, met both the young and the old, got the promise of their support and help, not only with art news, but with articles of a more serious nature. I wrote all the editorials on such themes as "Art and the Tariff," "Art in American Life," "Mural Art," and all the exhibition notices. At first, Mrs. Van Rensselaer helped me with the notices, and I got from the painters at exhibition openings many practical suggestions. Bruce Crane, William Anderson Coffin, Carroll Beckwith, William M. Chase, Robert Blum, Kenyon Cox, Frank Millet, Alden Weir, John H. Twachtman, John La Farge, George Inness—each one of them explained art from his standpoint, discussed pictures with me, and talked shop with avidity and great good sense.[2]

I muddled on. Presently, I began to glimpse a point of view. It had to do primarily with material and technical conditions. First of all, was the picture well made, that is, rightly placed on the canvas, well drawn, properly lighted, easily handled, well held together? Was it a good piece of form and color? Was it decorative? The subject did not matter. Story telling was "literary." Sentiment or patriotism was an extraneous snivel. Vollon's *Pump-*

kin and Black Pot was sufficient subject, and Manet's *Boy with a Sword* was greater as fine painting than Raphael's *Sistine Madonna* walking on the clouds.

Now this was art from the practicing, producing artist's point of view, art looked at in the light of the producer's intention. Surely the man who makes a work of any kind, picture, sculpture, book, or opera, should know what he intended to do, what he sought to set forth, and for any outsider to read other meanings into his work might be reckoned as little short of impertinence. And the insistence that the grammar of art should take precedence of its prosody, that good workmanship should go ahead of high thinking, fine feeling, or pictorial poetry, was essentially sound. No great work of art was ever carried through to completion without great craftsmanship at the back of it. The painters were right in stickling for technical proficiency. That the vast majority of them never got beyond their technique is unfortunately true. And out of that has come a painter's insistence that there is nothing beyond. But that is the extravagance that accompanies almost every theory or practice in the arts.

This painter's point of view did not come to me overnight. And it was not accepted in toto. I was gathering much of value by contact with artists, but I was also reading day and night in art history and criticism, in theories of aesthetics. Lessing, Schiller, Hegel, Diderot, Théophile Gautier, Lötze, Eugène Véron, Bosanquet, Ruskin, Hamerton, Pater, with dozens of others, were ransacked. Deference to authority influenced me somewhat. I was trying to get at the truth but was confused by many voices, each one telling a different tale. All this no doubt showed in my utterances in *The Studio*, but as I have never read them since their writing, I cannot now say how feeble they really were.

The little magazine went on and for some weeks made not a bad showing. I started a series of articles called "Technical Methods of American Artists," written by different painters. William M. Chase did the "Oil Painting," Hopkinson Smith the "Water Color," Robert Blum "Painting in Pastel," Kenyon Cox "Drawing and Composition," William A. Coffin "Materials," and so on. It was a first attempt in America to bring the painter to the fore as his own spokesman. If the public were to be rightly informed, it should be by the producer himself rather than by the middleman, the critic. But I found out later that the artist was not necessarily a good writer, that painters, like John La Farge and Kenyon Cox, who could write, came only once in a generation, and after all there was need for the critic with his facile pen.

Recognition came to *The Studio*. It was spoken of as the organ of the artists. Its articles were reprinted, its editorials quoted, and its circulation was increased. It was moving, but it had not wind enough or legs enough to reach the top of the hill. Its finances gave out. The editor and the writers could be put off, but the printer was inexorable. The little weekly collapsed. Some weeks later, Clarence Cook took it up and issued a few sporadic numbers, and then it collapsed again. There was not sufficient demand at that time for such a paper. The dailies wrote nice obituaries, and the incident was coffined and properly buried.

But the virus of art had gotten under my skin. I was now thoroughly interested, was learning something, and did not propose to forgo an interesting subject because *The Studio* had failed. I went on visiting the studios, studying pictures, studying nature, drawing and painting a little for knowledge of form, and reading everything on art obtainable. I wrote some articles for the *Continent*, the *American Architect*, the *Evening Post*. Later on, George Forbes Kelly started to publish a handsome monthly, the *Art Review*. He asked me to write the editorials and critical notices. I discouraged him by predicting failure but nevertheless wrote for his review for several months. I had seen two famous picture collections in Paris, the Stewart Collection, with its many Fortunys, and the Secretan Collection, with Millet's *Angelus* as its *pièce de résistance*. I wrote about them. But the circulation of the *Art Review* was very feeble, and its bank account decidedly weak. It, too, collapsed.

I went back to my Sage Library (which I had never left for a day or a night)[3] and began writing my first art book [*Principles of Art*, 1887]. As might have been expected, it was cut out to settle all art questions out of hand and to lay down for all time a proper philosophy of art, superior at any rate to Taine's or Véron's. When I had finished it, I felt the need of a vacation in the fresh air.[4]

My cousin William Ferdon had gone out on the Powder River in Custer County, Montana, where, with Spencer Biddle, he had a large ranch and 40,000 head of cattle. It was in the bad old days of ranching, when the flesh was run off the cattle and the legs off the horses by swearing, howling cowboys, when rustlers were stealing livestock, and wolves were getting the calves and colts, and cold winters were doing the rest. It was difficult to say where the ranchers stood, whether they were living on their capital or their income. Would I come out, spend the summer, and try to figure out a balance sheet? Yes, I would. I needed just such a change. And I longed to get back in the open air, on the buffalo range, in what was still a no man's land.

I went to Miles City, rode out eighty-four miles to the Big Powder, and joined the outfit. There were about twenty cowboys and no ranch house except a corral and a log hut where provisions were stored. Everyone slept on the ground and ate over a camp fire or from the tailboard of a grub wagon. The cattle were running over several hundred miles of territory and were being periodically rounded up for branding of calves, gathering of beef animals for shipment, and the main herd turned back toward the home camp. The nearest town was Miles City, with nothing in between except open country.

I went along with the outfit and fared just as the others. We were up at daylight and down in our blankets again at dusk. I had thirteen horses assigned to me for my riding, and I sometimes rode out three or four of them a day, going perhaps seventy or eighty miles. It was the hardest kind of riding in a half badland country, but I swung into it easily. My earlier experiences stood me in good stead. When my cowboy companions found I could sit a saddle and not be pulled out of it by a steer on the end of a rope, that I could outshoot them with their own six-shooters, and (from Ferdon) that I had ridden that country with the Sioux before cowboys ever saw Montana, they began to think I was not such a tenderfoot after all. But I cared little about what they thought. I had seen their type years before in the raftsmen of the Mississippi Valley. After the lumber days, the raftsman went West and became a cowboy because it was a riding job.[5]

It was a great joy to be back in the open, under the blue sky, riding into the unknown. I often left the outfit and rode off on a twenty or thirty mile half circle just to be alone and to feel for a time that I was the only human on the globe. Occasionally, I met a small band of Crows off their reservation and hunting. We made signs to each other and passed on. And occasionally I shot a gray wolf, but I let the deer, the antelope, and the elk go unshot at.[6] On still rarer occasions, I would find hidden in a swale among thick bushes an old buffalo bull, the last of some great herd eking out a lonely existence in concealment. But the great joy was the open, the huge tablelands, the buttes and long divides, the far vistas, the sunlight, and the silence. Here was nature in her pristine glory still. This was her realm, with no limits to her sway.

There was always more or less excitement about the camp, the corrals, and the roundups. Accidents were of frequent occurrence. We swam rivers and had horses roll over on us, were knocked down by lightning, run over by stampeded beef herds, and flung from the saddle by unbroken horses. On one occasion I set a broken leg with nothing but splints made from a cracker box. I wound the splints with strips from an old shirt. At another time, I nearly killed one of the boys by dosing him with crude castor oil for appendicitis. The name and the disease were then unknown, but in any pain below the ribs castor oil was indicated. Besides, that was the only remedy in camp—crude castor oil used for dosing horses with bellyache. It was a rawhide outfit, the 70L,[7] but no one complained. In fact, everyone rather enjoyed the wildness, the closeness to the ground, and the adventure that came each day as regularly as the sun.

One night a cowboy from an upriver outfit came riding into camp wildly proclaiming that the Indians were on the warpath and coming down the Big Powder. No one paid any attention to him.[8] The foreman finally told him he had better get some coffee and beans from the grub wagon. In an hour we were all curled up in our blankets and sleeping. He was the only messenger that came through that summer, but in September two cowboys from the opposite direction came drifting into camp. They had come up from some ranch on the Little Missouri. After they had swallowed their beef and coffee, one of them began to talk of Theodore Roosevelt, who had taken up a ranch down there.[9] He asked me did I know him.

Yes, I had met him.

Well, what did I think he did the first day he got to the ranch?

I could not guess.

Well, he borrowed a gun from Henry Stoats and went out and shot George Brown's tame buffalo that had a bell around its neck.

And what did I think of that?

I said that Mr. Roosevelt wore glasses, was nearsighted, and probably did not see the bell.

To which he merely grunted.

After Roosevelt became president [1901–1909], and even his political friends admitted his faculty for shooting tame buffaloes and finding out afterward that they were belled, I told this story to Hermann Hagedorn, suggesting that he might add it to his Rooseveltiana. But he did not seem to think it would help Mr. Roosevelt's fame or would be acceptable material for the Roosevelt Memorial Association.

Probably not.[10]

Chapter 9

Authors and Painters

My initial book on art took form and was published under the title of *Principles of Art*. It was well reviewed in the press by writers who knew as little about art as I did, but the moment I saw it in print I wished it had never been born. Then W. J. Stillman, in the *Evening Post*, told me that it would have been better had it never seen the light. He said that art principles and theories were things that old men talked about hesitatingly and that young men should not talk about them at all. This was Ruskinian frankness from an old Ruskin pupil, which I did not particularly enjoy, but it confirmed my own opinion. I was already out of conceit of the book. Impetuously I suppressed it after the first printing had been sold. When a stray copy now turns up in a bookseller's catalog, it is labeled "rare" or "very scarce."

And yet the book held some good material. The main defect of it was too much deference to other people's theories. I had read, collated, and digested almost all of the aesthetic theories and tried to reconcile them all with artistic practice and a theory of my own. It was neither flesh, fowl, nor good red herring. I might better have ignored the wisdom of the ages and written down my own limited experience.

But some good came out of the publication. It was reviewed in Germany and France, and some letters from artists and college professors came to me about it. One of the most comforting of these was from Frank Millet, the painter, who years afterward went down on the *Titanic*. Millet was the most genial of souls and, even as a young man, one of the best loved among the painters. Everyone liked him, admired his versatility and skill, and took counsel with him about important matters in the art world. He had read my *Principles of Art* and with that as a basis offered to propose me for membership in the Authors Club. That was a new turn of the tide. Laurence Hutton seconded me, and in due course I was formally elected.

The Authors Club was brought into being by Charles De Kay. It was organized at 103 East 15th Street, but I do not remember drinking beer and eating green-bean salad and sandwiches at that address. When I joined the club, it had rooms in West 28th Street and the chef in charge was a fencing master whom De Kay had brought in from the Fencers Club. At the 28th Street rooms, there were gatherings of members and guests every fortnight. Pipes and beer and talk were in order, and some interesting people filled the chairs. The corporate members of the club had been Charles De Kay, Brander Matthews, Edmund Clarence Stedman, Laurence Hutton, Richard Watson Gilder, Edward Eggleston, and Noah Brooks.[1]

Besides these there were in the membership such men as H. C. Bunner, Frank Dempster Sherman, Henry M. Alden, Nicholas Murray Butler, Mark Twain, Moncure Conway, George William Curtis, Eugene Field, Laurence Godkin, Park Godwin, John Hay, W. J. Henderson, W. D. Howells, Henry James, Hamilton Mabie, S. Weir Mitchell, Noah Porter, James Whitcomb Riley, Theodore Roosevelt, Josiah Royce, Hopkinson Smith, Richard Henry Stoddard, Henry van Dyke, Charles Dudley Warner. The membership of the Authors Club in the Eighties was rather distinguished, and at its fortnightly meetings celebrated guests from a distance or from abroad added an extra flavor.

In the course of a few years, I had met at the Authors Club almost every man of literary prominence in the country, but I do not remember any very wise or serious discussions of literary matters, any profound criticisms of current books or articles, any philosophic or literary or aesthetic theories being propounded there. I sat beside Lowell one night for an hour while members came up and talked to him, but he did not scintillate. The truth is that it was a social club made up of writers who came together to drink a glass of beer, smoke a pipe, laugh, and have a good time without effort. Small talk went the round. Here is a sample neither better nor worse than the average thrust and counter. I stood in the group and heard it.

The talk had lagged for a moment. Edward Eggleston was rolling under-foot a piece of paper on the floor. Presently, he stooped and picked it up, unrolled it, and exhibited it to everyone's astonishment. A twenty dollar bill!

"Good Gracious!" he exclaimed, "No author ever had so much money as that. It must have been dropped by a publisher."

And he handed the bill to Charles Scribner.

"No," said Scribner, "as a result of publishing books by members of the Authors Club I haven't seen twenty dollars in a month. The money must have been lost by a railroad president."

He offered the money to Chauncey Depew, who shook his head, declining:

"No," he said, "when I come to a place like this I always leave my money at home."

Of course, there were nights when Mark Twain, leaning forward with his head in his hands, told very funny stories, and Brander Matthews turned witty phrases, and Noah Brooks talked about Lincoln, and Edward Eggleston with his great leonine shock of hair spoke with the voice of his own circuit rider. Gilder with his dark velvet eyes, Laurence Hutton with his major's moustache and happy smile, the handsome De Kay, and the sadfaced Ripley Hitchcock were in the circle. It was an interesting circle, not a very large one but rather far-reaching in its contacts. And through it I had my first meeting with the literary New York of the Eighties and came to know a wide circle of writers, editors, and publishers.[2]

Again I went to Europe in pursuit of an art education, chasing the old masters through galleries and palaces, meeting directors, critics, painters, and dealers, taking reams of notes, gathering hundreds of photographs, and buying many books for my Sage Library. I went to see Millet, then living at Broadway, England, met Sargent, E. A. Abbey, E. J. Poynter, Charles Holroyd, Sidney Colvin, R. A. M. Stevenson, and was duly lunched and slated for a good time socially. But I backed out before I got in very far. I had study ahead of me and could not afford to spend time socially, much as I liked meeting interesting people.

I went to Paris and there became interested in Fortuny's work. William H. Stewart, then living in a fine house on the Avenue d'Jena, had a gallery full of Fortuny's, which I had seen and now had the opportunity to study closely. I often went to the house for Sunday luncheon and met there frequently Madrazo, on one occasion the grave academic Gérôme, on another the bright Martin Rico. Art and artists were almost always discussed, and very intelligently, from different points of view.

But these painters did not care to discuss the then popular Fontainebleau-Barbizon painters. Gérôme and Madrazo would shrug their shoulders over Jean François Millet and say they did not understand him, which meant more than met the ear. Rousseau and Dupre and Díaz also called for shrugs, but they liked Corot, who really never belonged to the group. It seems that time has rather justified their preference for Corot, their indifference to Rousseau and Dupre, but not their positive dislike for Manet. But it was all very interesting discussion to me. I held my tongue and listened. Julius Stewart, a son of the house, a pupil of Madrazo and a very good painter, threshed out the schools with me later in the afternoon in his Rue Copernic studio.

Some years after, and for several summers at Venice, we threshed them over again with Rico, Charles Theriat, and Franklin Grist. Venice (in the old Capello Nero or taking coffee in front of the Quadri) was a great place for art talk. Painters almost talked the four horses of San Marco off their footings with their admiration of this and their detestation of that. It served *pour passer le temps* [to pass the time], but no one was ever convinced or converted. We dragged back to our quarters down the Twenty-Second-of-March Street after midnight, with no drop of gall abated nor any drop of wisdom acquired.

That summer in the galleries greatly clarified the history of painting for me. I had arranged, like a hand at whist, all the different schools of painting and almost all of the different painters. I had begun to note not only the different qualities of the painters within the schools but their peculiar characteristics, their repetitions, their mannerisms. In Italy, Botticelli, Filippino, Andrea del Sarto, Mantegna, Bellini, Lotto, Tintoretto, Tiepolo were the first to protrude. Almost immediately men like Velásquez, Goya, Rubens, Rembrandt, and Holbein arranged themselves in their schools and periods. Then the second rank of painters took form. Before I went home, I often amused myself in some new gallery by standing in the middle of a room and guessing at the painters of the pictures on the wall. I was pleased to find that I could hit them about three times out of five. I felt that I was coming to know the painters through their work, but I did not know then what a lifelong study this was to be.

Back in my Sage Library, I found out, from a source I cannot now recall, that the Chautauqua Reading Circle was looking for a small book on art to introduce in their reading course that winter. The membership of Chautauqua was then very large, and a book listed in their courses was sure of selling at least 25,000 copies. I coveted that market, thought of the great missionary effort involved, and sat down to write that book. In three weeks I had it finished, named it *How to Judge of a Picture* [1888], and sent it to the Methodist Book Concern, the publishing agents of Chautauqua. In due time I received word that Bishop Vincent, acting for Chautauqua, would like to see me about it. I went in. He liked the book, thought it would answer well for Chautauqua, and they would take it if we could come to an agreement about the price. I did not want to sell outright, but they would not take it on royalty terms. Finally, a thousand dollars was offered for it, and I let it go at that.[3]

Going home on the train, I rather felicitated myself on doing a good stroke of business. The market was theirs, and I could not expect them to pay on that. The book was good enough for Chautauqua. It would do for a winter's reading and then go its way into the ash can. But I lived to regret my satisfaction, and several times in the following years I offered the Methodist Book Concern to return their thousand dollars for the copyright. I wanted to suppress the book. But it had sold many thousands of copies outside of Chautauqua, and the publishers were well satisfied with their bargain. It is still selling, and I am today sometimes confronted with it by some reader who has just read it and thinks I wrote it yesterday. That proves somewhat embarrassing.

The book was, I believe, the first of the How books. In a few months there were volumes out on How to Judge a Horse, How to Tell the Birds, and How to Know Wild Flowers. Mine was breezy and beautifully superficial, rightly enough planned for the then existing Chautauqua, but not the kind of a book to be broadcasted as a final presentation of one's views on pictures. I was ashamed of it before the year was out, and when commendatory letters about it came to me from people of intelligence, I was amazed.

But I made friends through it. One of the first letters about it came from William Crary Brownell. In agreement with Brownell's other friends, I have always regarded him as the most intelligent critic since Lowell. He had the widest vision, the keenest analysis, the most profound synthesis. That his writings reached no large audience argues that very point. They required some thinking in their reading, and the majority of readers do not like to think. But among writers, Brownell's books were carefully read, pondered, and accepted, just as he, with his shy personality and keen wit, was warmly welcomed by those few who were fortunate enough to know him. I was one of the fortunates and knew him well for forty years. Only a few months ago (1928) he passed on, admired to the last and in his death greatly regretted.[4]

When Brownell wrote me about the Chautauqua book, he was the literary adviser of Charles Scribner's Sons, a position he held up to the last year of his life. Did I have anything else of the kind in preparation that I would care to offer the Scribners? Could I drop in and talk it over some day? I did, at the Scribner headquarters below 23rd Street on Fifth Avenue. I met Brownell and also Charles and Arthur Scribner. Nothing developed at that time because I had nothing ready, but I promised to submit my next manuscript to them. Since that day, Scribner's has published some thirty books of mine. I could not have had better friends and publishers.[5]

A few blocks below the Scribners on Fifth Avenue was a well-known firm of decorators and picture dealers, Daniel Cottier and Co. The firm had high standing among artists because it knew good pictures, bought them, and brought them into America, apparently with a reckless disregard of whether they would sell or not. Cottier was among the first to bring in Corot, Courbet, Millet, Monticelli, Manet, Matthew Maris, and many old masters. Brownell dropped in there frequently to see pictures, to chat with Cottier and his younger partner James S. Inglis, to meet Olin Warner, the sculptor, Gedney Bunce, Alden Weir, Albert Ryder, William M. Chase.

The gallery was a common meeting ground for picture folk and painter people during the Eighties and Nineties, and there (first drawn by a nice letter from James S. Inglis about my Chautauqua book) I went and became a friend of the house, especially of Inglis, whom I came to know well and greatly liked.

Cottier and Inglis were both remarkable for their fine feeling for things artistic. Rugs, tapestries, glass, furniture, pictures, and bronzes were all of a piece with them. Some things they bought and would not sell. The big *Orpheus* by Corot hung in the galleries for years. Cottier would not let it go. Manet's *Dead Toreador*, on the contrary, went begging for a purchaser. No one wanted "the deid mon," as Cottier put it, and he kept it. The same fate was meted out to four great Delacroix and a large Courbet. No one regretted that these works would not sell, least of all the picture lovers who dropped in at the galleries. I was among them and continued a friend of the house until both Cottier and Inglis died. Walter Fearon was a boy with them in their lower Fifth Avenue house, and today I call at Fearon's galleries on 54th Street, because he continues to carry on the art traditions and the fine courtesy of Cottier and Inglis.

Chapter 10

Lecturing in 1890

An invitation came from the Rembrandt Club of Brooklyn to address that body on some phase of American art. This was a new opening and caused some perturbation of spirit. Should I? All writers, missionaries, and uplifters eventually mounted the platform. There were the outstanding examples of Ruskin, Norton, and Lowell. They considered it an opportunity. Why should I balk at it? Still, I did not like being stared at on the platform for an hour at a time, like a wild beast in a cage. Besides, I had inherited a wretched voice and a worse set of nerves. So it was with reluctance that I agreed to go and talk on "Serious Art in America" before the Rembrandt Club.[1]

Carroll Beckwith went with me to the house of a Mr. Lyall in Brooklyn, where in a large picture gallery two hundred or more art lovers were assembled. I was scared almost out of my wits but managed to pull through somehow. Everyone offered congratulations. A lecture audience is usually made up of cheerful liars, but I tried to look appreciative. A motion had been put and carried to have the lecture published for the club members, and from that I could suppose its contents were not so bad. Beckwith abused my voice and said I would have to train it, for from that time forward I would never get off the platform. I laughed. But Beckwith always was wise beyond his artist generation, and he came near the truth in that last prediction.

Professor Raymond of Princeton asked me if I would deliver a course of Saturday morning lectures open to the whole university. I answered in the affirmative, and having gotten myself into that trouble I proceeded to get myself out of it by preparing "Art for Art's Sake: Seven University Lectures on the Technical Beauties of Painting." I prepared the lectures with care, used the simplest language, and drew on my own experience for my material. For one of them I got together some lantern-slide illustrations, but the others were merely hour talks. Of course, I was nervous about possible results. Allen Marquand and A. L. Frothingham, Jr., were then professors of art and archaeology at Princeton and had their department well organized. I was invading their territory. But they were very gracious about it, gave me a reception at their house, and came to hear me. That again was the beginning of lifelong friendships.

President Patton introduced me to a small audience in the old chapel of Nassau Hall. Princeton at that time was by no means the magnificent grouping of Gothic buildings that one sees today, and Nassau Hall was not then a mere curiosity of the past. Its chapel was large enough to hold all who cared to hear me. I began and worried along for seven weeks, with my audience slightly increased at the end. I did not count the course a success, but I realized that other Saturday morning lectures were not crowded to the doors, not more of a success than mine. University lectures even then were voted a bore. But before I had ended my Princeton course, I was asked to repeat it at Rutgers and Columbia.

That proved another story so far as Rutgers was concerned. Everyone in New Brunswick knew me, and the Rutgers chapel was crowded to the doors by people who wanted to see how I would perform. It was a sympathetic audience, and I responded with an improved voice and a greater confidence. But the lectures did not set me up in my own esteem. I knew too well how a lecture should be delivered, and I could not live up to that standard. I worried about it off the platform more than on and eventually got myself into a senseless panic about it.

Still, the audience did not know about my worries, and Rutgers evidently did not care, for it asked me to take a permanent lectureship in the college. It had already adopted me by giving me the honorary degree of Doctor of Letters, and the following year it made me a full professor and asked me to establish a department of art and archaeology in the college.[2] I accepted this program, and after forty years my name is still at the head of the department, though for several years I have been on leave of absence.[3]

The Columbia lectures were given in the winter of 1890, at Hamilton Hall, on Park Avenue where the college was then located. Dr. Drisler introduced me. There was a goodly audience that increased from lecture to lecture, and as Columbia asked me to lecture for several succeeding years at the Metropolitan Museum, I can assume that the courses were reasonably successful.

But worry had me in its grip, and I buzzed like a fly in a spider web. I was obsessed with the idea that I would break down, forget my theme, and make a donkey of myself. I could not get rid of that haunting fear. My dear old friend, Dr. John De Witt, one of our most eloquent preachers, tried to console me by saying that he had never entered the pulpit without similar feelings, and Laurence Hutton said if I broke down there would be twice as many people at the next lecture. But Edwin Booth had spoiled the little comfort of that by telling me that he had never felt nervous on the stage but once.[4] He added, however, that on that occasion he realized that he had played better than ever before or after. I clung to that final straw. Perhaps I was playing better than I knew. But I knew that the whole panic was caused by inordinate self-consciousness and was angry because I could not control it.

Many invitations now came to me from colleges, art societies, and museums. I had to limit acceptances to educational institutions. I would not talk for pink-tea audiences nor in town halls with tickets being sold at the door. I went to Drexel Institute in Philadelphia, to Ogontz School, to the Pittsburgh Art Club, to Smith College, to the University of Chicago, the Buffalo Art Institute, Baltimore, Washington, Providence, Amherst, Harvard. I had to decline many college engagements for lack of time. The demand was greater than I could supply. But, again I may say, I was not the least bit elated by this apparent success. I never for a moment failed to hold myself strictly accountable for a forgotten paragraph, an argument that did not carry home, a mispronounced word, or even a false accent. I was too severely critical ever to get in conceit of myself as a lecturer.

With all the nervous strain and mental worry of lecturing, there was compensation in the meeting of clever people and sometimes in interested audiences. At Smith College I was taken by President Seelye into the chapel and up the steps of a platform high enough for Haman's gallows. From that height I looked out upon a thousand girls, all wearing leg-of-mutton sleeves, sitting in long rows that seemed made up of alternate heads and sleeves, and all eager, bright-eyed, and attentive. It was inspiring. After the course was finished, I stood under a chandelier and the thousand came by in line to shake hands and say something complimentary. That did not bore me. I have heard lecturers recount the hardships of their dinners, receptions, and social entertainments, but I rather liked having a fuss made over me, at least at that time.

I had no such audience at Harvard as at Smith. University lectures were even less of a novelty at Cambridge than at Princeton, and my audience was not above the average in size. President Eliot introduced me and sat in the front row, and I had not been talking two minutes before I picked out Charles Eliot Norton sitting on a back seat. I was starting a course of six lectures on Italian painting, which was Professor Norton's field! That gave me the shivers. But everyone was very polite. The president gave me a luncheon, over which he presided with his usual fine courtesy, and after the first lecture Professor Norton came forward to ask me to his house to dinner.

That dinner I remember as one out of many. There were present only Professor Norton, his two daughters, and Professor Moore, of the Harvard Art Department, but the house with its books, its pictures, its literary and intellectual associations, had an air, a tang, a tone about it. And the simple· dinner with its talk and personalities was an event to me. Many still living, who sat under Norton's Fine Arts 4, will bear testimony to the charm of the professor, and Ruskin has written most enthusiastically of the charm of the man. He has not been overpraised, nor his service to art and letters overstated. He stood for noble things and was a well-timed apostle of the fine arts in America.

The Columbia lectures at the Metropolitan Museum were given Saturday mornings before large and very mixed audiences. Nearly half the schoolteachers of New York were there, besides wandering wraiths who had the lecture habit and went to every free talk in the town. I gave courses there on the meaning of pictures, on Italian and French art, on figure, portrait, and landscape painting, and I have forgotten what else. President Marquand of the Metropolitan usually introduced me. The audience grew so large that one year I had to get on the platform by crawling in a window back of it. The entrance and aisles were choked with men and women.

A lecture audience is always a problem to the man on the platform. He never gets to the end of its mental vagaries. I could drop out the very heart of a lecture through lack of time, but the audience would not notice it, would not know that there had ever been a heart. I could present an illustration and feel the audience following me, but the moment I tried to apply it in the argument the audience would let go and fall back. A tone of voice or an inclination of the head would give a wrong meaning to some simple statement, and an emphatic adjective would be exaggerated into unlimited praise or blame. And then the blank expression on the rows of faces, signifying that the wearers were not following me at all but were stargazing.

One always had to compromise. If too intellectual or academic or technical, you shot over the heads of half the audience; if too popular, you shocked the sensibilities of the other half. You had your choice of a full house or empty benches, and in the end you perhaps weakly compromised and fell down between two stools.

And whatever your material or manner of talk, there were always intelligent-looking people who came to you after the lecture to say something complimentary and in saying it, by word or inference, revealed the fact that they had no notion of what you were talking about. They had missed the point from start to finish.

Well, all this was rather depressing to a person who thought he had a gospel of art to preach. Even the most zealous missionary has his periods of discouragement in which he sadly wonders if his efforts are really worth while. I began to count the cost of lecturing in mental strain and nervous tension. Then I found out, by the reading of memoirs, that almost all of the academic and collegiate uplifters—Lowell, Norton, Ruskin, et al.—had counted the cost before me and after a few years had retired from the platform. Years after, Howells in Paris told me of his great dislike of the public appearance, and I find in his published letters the comment: "I look back on my lecturing with terror. What a hideous trade!"[5]

I followed example, and after half a dozen years of hard talking, I served notice that I was through and would talk no more outside of my classroom. Occasionally since then I have read a paper at a conference or a congress but have let the general public alone.

But with the lecturing came an experience, an adventure in psychology, which I have never regretted. It was more than the psychology of the mob; it was a look-in at the human mind in its many workings and manifestations. The varieties of opinion, the points of view, the predilections and obsessions were all different reflections of gray matter. And this meeting with thousands of minds, this contact with thousands of personalities, this mental and social intercourse with thousands of one's fellows, modifies and liberalizes. You cannot be adamant in such circumstances. You receive impressions and abrasions but also some polished surfaces. The experience comes as near to a liberal education as we ever receive. A four-year course in college is merely this in little.[6] Perhaps no one ever becomes educated, as Henry Adams suggested, but mental and social contact with your fellow man puts you on the way.

From my lecturing also came acquaintance with many bright minds in the academic, artistic, and literary world. And some much-valued friendships. After my first lecture at the Metropolitan Museum, a little lady came out of the audience to say that I knew her aunt, Mrs. Wilmerding, and her cousin, Miss Armide de Saulles, and that she was Mrs. McClellan—Mrs. George B. McClellan. That was the beginning of a close, lifelong friendship with Colonel and Mrs. McClellan. During his two terms of office as mayor of New York, and many times since, we have traveled together in Europe, "expertized" gallery pictures from Rome to St. Petersburg, taken teas with the Berensons in Florence, taken flight from Austria into Italy with the mobilization of 1914, taken counsel together about many things of artistic, literary, or social moment. They have been dear friends and still remain so.[7]

I do not count my friendships as of slight importance. They are about the best assets one can hold. I am not now merely thinking of friends among the great or the near-great. The great are often too much puffed up with their own importance to consider a friendship seriously. Nor am I thinking of those boyhood friends, most of whom grew up and became mere pie-faced sellers of shoes and shirts. There is a friendship of the intelligent, the forceful, the sympathetic, of the brave, the true, the devoted, of those who possess charm or character or camaraderie. It is founded in mutual respect and affection, which go beyond admiration, distinction, or greatness. So I shall not apologize for introducing in the succeeding chapters people who are less talked about than the stars of the movies—people who have never wished to be in the limelight. They are the ones whose intelligence and guidance mold the mass, they are the ones who make a social decade and round an epoch, rather than the occasional eccentric—charlatan or genius—who goes up in fire and comes down in darkness.

Chapter 11

Friendships

I gladly dropped lecturing. It had been only a worry and a bother. With the certainty that I would never again use the Art for Art's Sake series as lectures, I took them to Brownell, and they were published by the Scribners under their original title [*Art for Art's Sake*, 1893]. The book was a success in almost every way. It sold well, was reviewed well in both Europe and America, was accepted by reading circles, and introduced as a textbook in art schools. The painter people liked it, and that pleased me greatly. Many of them recommended it to their pupils. Kenyon Cox reviewed it at length in the *Evening Post*, pronouncing it the best American book on the technique of painting. Even the critic-baiting Whistler became my friend because of it. I had spoken highly of his work at a time when the world was laughing at him, and perhaps that warped his judgment in my favor.[1]

But Whistler was not the only friend come by through that book. It was dedicated to Laurence Hutton.[2] We had become very close friends through a summer together in Paris. Perhaps it was through him that I first came to know Frank Thomson. But Thomson had read *Art for Art's Sake*, had disagreed with parts of it, and wanted to talk to me about it. He wrote me to that effect. Would I join him on such a day at luncheon in New York? He was coming over from Philadelphia and would stop the train for me at New Brunswick.

He welcomed me in his private car—a strong though rather slight-built man, dressed in the best English style, extremely well-spoken, very courteous, very charming, in fact as far removed as possible from the first vice-president of the Pennsylvania Railroad (afterward president) that I had expected to meet. I have always remembered him as he came forward that day with outstretched hand and an inquiring look on his fine face, as though he expected to meet someone with new ideas about art and life. He was always expectant, always eager, always reaching out toward new men and movements, meeting them halfway, anticipating them. He had my interest instantly, and I became his friend then and there.

In New York we met Henry C. Frick and after luncheon went together to see pictures at Durand-Ruels.[3] Frick was then just beginning with pictures, but Thomson was already a connoisseur and a collector. His house at

Merion, Pennsylvania, had rooms full of pictures by Manet, Monet, Pissaro, Sisley, and others of the Impressionists—at that time considered the most ultra of painters. He had bought them when other picture lovers would not look at them. That day at Durand-Ruels he induced Frick to buy a small Monet. I do not think he cared for the picture at that time, but he had confidence in Thomson. Almost everyone had. For Thomson was emphatically a leader. That Monet picture was the first picture, the beginning of the Frick collection, now housed in the fine gallery on Fifth Avenue and eventually to be a gallery for the public of New York.

After that day, I went often to Corkerhill, the Thomson house at Merion. For ten years I went there for weekends to be with Thomson, his family, and his friends. It was a fascinating place, presided over by his daughter, Miss Anne Thomson, and to it came all classes and conditions of humanity—poets, painters, writers, architects, lawyers, musicians, politicians, bankers, foreign ministers, society people. Thomson was the diplomat of the Pennsylvania and often asked friends and foes of the railroad out to Merion as a respite from the office. He knew about music, art, books, sport, travel, society, in fact, almost everything, and had the leaders in every walk of life at his dinners and house parties. John G. Johnson, John Cadwalader, Wayne McVeagh, Charles McKim, Charles Eliot Norton, Senator Hanna, Weir Mitchell, Frank Millet, Miss Thomas of Bryn Mawr, Mrs. Philip Schuyler, Mrs. Robert Lesley, Mrs. Burton Stevenson, wives of cabinet officers and Supreme Court judges, and scores of others came and went. Thomson was as eager socially as artistically or commercially. His energy was enormous. It wore out everyone with whom he came in contact. Illness could not stop him. With an earache that would have put most men to bed, he was walking up and down the floor, holding by someone's arm, discussing Wagner's *Siegfried* or Monet's scheme of light. When George B. Roberts died and Thomson was asked to succeed him as president of the Pennsylvania, he hesitated. He was in his fifties, and much work had left its mark upon him. But he accepted, and in a few years was gone, dying in 1900 [1899]. He was the best friend I ever had, the noblest man I ever knew.

But I must not leave the reader with the impression that Thomson was merely a smooth diplomat. He was a man of action and power. During the Civil War, Thomas Scott, then president of the Pennsylvania but acting for the War Department, put Thomson, a young man of twenty-two, in charge of all the railways around Washington. A cabinet question arose of what could or could not be done in the movement of troops into Virginia. Who could say? No one but Frank Thomson. Send for him.

When he arrived, Lincoln and his cabinet were holding a meeting around the sickbed of Stanton [Edwin McMasters Stanton, Secretary of War, 1862–1868]. When Thomson entered the room, Stanton rolled over in his blankets to look at him and exclaimed:

"Good God! Have we been waiting three days for the opinion of that redheaded boy?"

But they took the opinion of that boy.

A half hour after the flood at Johnstown had swept out all the Pennsylvania's bridges and tracks, Thomson, the general manager, was on the way there from Philadelphia. On the spot he took complete control, took it away from the engineers and under officers, and had new bridges up and tracks down in a few days. He was not frightened by rushing waters or stampeded by death and dire disaster.[4]

And he could say positive things to his best friends. One morning in the breakfast room at Merion while we were smoking over the coffee cups, Weir Mitchell came in. He had just published *Hugh Wynne* and talked about its reception by public and press as though it were the event of his life. He apparently cared little about his reputation as a physician but thought his novels and poems would keep his name alive. Thomson was somewhat disgusted and at last turned around, saying quietly but impressively and severely:

"Mitchell, when we were on the Restigouche [river in New Brunswick, Canada] last summer, you told me that you thought you could locate the passions in the brain and by the use of anesthetics could control them. Mitchell, if you write that down in a fifty-page pamphlet it would be worth all the d—— *Hugh Wynne*s ever written."

Mitchell argued the case, but Thomson was not convinced. He scoffed at Mitchell as a public entertainer but looked up to him as a great physician.

Thomson was the first man I met, aside from painters, who looked at nature from a painter's point of view. He saw the picturesque about him on every side—in light and air, clouds and sunbeams, trees and flowers, water and reeds and meadow grasses. Sitting in a blind at Graces Quarter, waiting for ducks to come in to the decoys, he would be studying the lilac shadows of the little waves, or the golden yellows of the autumn flags, or the orange stain of the salt sea grasses, or the flying shadows of clouds moving across the marshes. His knowledge of pictorial nature (which I thought was my own little bag of tricks) quite bowled me over. And yet it was a bond of sympathy between us even stronger than the fellow feeling for art. At the time I met him, I had partly written a book on nature from the painter's point of view, but I was writing it slowly, at odd moments, and was in no hurry to publish it. It was designed as a companion volume to *Art for Art's Sake*, and it was finally brought out in 1898 under the title of *Nature for Its Own Sake*. Of course, I dedicated it to Thomson as one "who knew and loved Nature."[5]

That book was a success, too, though widely misunderstood. The reviewers talked about it as a happy attempt to popularize science, and some readers regarded it as a book of physics, but its secondary title was *First Studies in Natural Appearances*, which should have been sufficiently explanatory. It was an attempt to point out the beauties of nature as seen by a landscape painter—beauties that all could see if they would—but I do not think that idea ever got through to the public. Half a dozen volumes followed, on the desert, the sea, the mountain, the plains, the meadows, all with the same objective, but even in the public libraries the books were shelved under "Science" rather than "Nature." Most of the science in them was the result of my own observations and was introduced merely by way of illustrating beauty. But I found that any explanation was quite useless. A book audience can misunderstand as readily and as persistently as a lecture audience. And if you are fortunate or unfortunate enough to make any sort of success with a first book, you are at once regarded as a specialist in that field and know nothing about any other field. My little *How to Judge of a Picture* made me an art critic (Heaven knows how or why), and I have never since been able to convince anyone that I knew a hawk from a handsaw about anything else.[6]

Before I met Frank Thomson, I knew and had become friendly with Andrew Carnegie.[7] They had been young men together on the Pennsylvania Railroad under Thomas Scott and had in later years run counter to each other in various railway dealings. This had excited some feeling with Thomson but none with Carnegie. I was the frequent bearer of messages of good will and friendliness from Carnegie to Thomson, which the latter always received politely but with a little reserved smile that meant something. It was the day of big deals and combinations and rebates, and it is not to be wondered at that the dealers were often at swords' points. Thomson was a remarkable energy but so was Carnegie. It was a case of Greek meeting Greek and a tug of war.

My meeting with Carnegie came about through interest in art, not steel. He was well-disposed to help American artists and would have done something substantial for the Society of American Artists had not some of the leaders alienated him by brusque comment. There was a good deal of cockiness and self-sufficiency among the younger men in the society, which took the form of abuse of the public, especially of the western millionaires. It was unnecessary and ill-advised. Mr. Carnegie drew back, and quite properly, but he was willing to help individuals. He had bought many pictures from the older painters (most of them pretty bad) at prices which he had never questioned. One day in his 5 West 51st Street house, he took me about and showed me these pictures. With youthful candor I told him they were poor truck and that I could buy better American pictures for a hundred and fifty dollars apiece.

"Can you? Well, let's see you do it."

He walked into his library, dashed off a check for $1,000 and handed it to me, saying:

"Go ahead and buy them. Perhaps the painters need the money. Pay what they ask. Don't beat them down."

I protested that I was writing on art, not buying and selling it, and that I could not be interested in it commercially. But then I *did* know painters who needed the money, and, besides, perhaps I could make Mr. Carnegie see the light by putting a few good pictures in his house. An uplifter should work with any means that comes to hand.[8] So I took the check, bought some small pictures from the current exhibition of the Society of American Artists, went to the studios of deserving but neglected men, and bought others there. I sent up to the Carnegie house half a dozen pictures. He liked them but gave most of them to Frick, with whom he had at that time no differences, and sent me another check for, I think, $5,000 to buy more pictures. I bought better and more expensive pictures by E. E. Simmons, Irving Wiles, and others. Then I stopped because I came to realize that Mr. Carnegie really did not care about paintings as such and was merely buying them through goodness of heart, a wish to help others. He was naturally a generous man. There was never a time during his later life that I had not carte blanche to buy any work of any painter, at practically any price I saw fit to offer. But only a few times did I avail myself of this generosity, and those were cases of dire distress with the painters. Carnegie never knew, never asked the circumstances, never questioned the price. But his interest was to help the painters, not accumulate pictures. The art he really loved was music, with poetry as a side product.

To his generosity, enthusiasm, and tremendous energy Mr. Carnegie added a very quick and active mind, a wide experience in many fields, and a rare power of expression with both tongue and pen. He talked and wrote well, analyzed facts keenly, and could put a question of manufacturing, transportation, politics, or sociology in as concise a form as any college professor of economics. Very few of the American millionaires were in his class either intellectually or socially. No doubt some people sought him out because of his money, but there were others both in Europe and America who came to his dinners and house parties because he was a stimulus, a virile force, and because they liked the man personally. I can think of no captain of industry of his time who drew about him so many distinguished personalities. This began in the early days with Matthew Arnold and Herbert Spencer and ran on to his latest time with men like John Morley and Lord Haldane.

The first Carnegie dinner I went to in the 51st Street house was a small affair given, I think, to President Schurman of Cornell. There were several college presidents there. I sat next to William Vaughn Moody, the poet, and called his attention to the two men sitting in the chairs opposite to us. Was it not singular that they should be there side by side? One was Burton Harrison, at one time secretary to Jefferson Davis, the other Charles A. Dana, at one time secretary to Abraham Lincoln. Carnegie was the great peacemaker. Had he brought these two together designedly and for a purpose? Lion hunting? No. It was a dinner with some lions present, if you choose. But Carnegie was continually associated with leading men because he was himself a leader. I shall have something to say further on about the people at Cluny and Skibo.[9] The house books of those places, if they were published, would show an astonishing list of names of leaders in every walk of life.

The Nineties have been called "the Mauve Decade," and the late Eighties have been counted a crude and silly period leading up to the Nineties, but the terms have been used largely to describe the social and artistic extravagances of the time and were not generally descriptive even of them. Art and society are usually accepted as the efflorescence of successful commerce. In the Eighties and Nineties, commerce was growing enormously. I was not a part of it in any way, but being in touch with some of the makers of it, I could feel some of its power. Mr. Thomson and Mr. Carnegie were representative of what was being done in transportation and steel, but there were forceful figures in coal, oil, copper, lumber, and a hundred other products. Great combinations were being made, great ventures were being launched, everyone was standing on his tiptoes or riding over his horse's ears with eagerness. Whichever way I turned or to whatever house I went, I could hear the hum of big things, even though they were not the topic of conversation. Even the fine arts developed an unwonted energy. Was not this the time when Burnham was drawing plans for the development of cities—cities as far afield as Manila—and Stanford White was building country houses, and John La Farge, George Inness, Winslow Homer, and Saint-Gaudens were producing their best works? Was this not the time when mural painting began to spread on the walls and domes of state capitols, when sculpture became once more allied with architecture, and the most splendid world's fair of any time came off at Chicago [1893]? Mauve Decade, indeed! The period was gas-blue with energy and flushed red and gold with the promise of beauty.

Chapter 12

Fairs

Everyone was at the Paris Exposition of 1889. There was a famous retrospective showing of French art, and dealers, collectors, painters, writers swarmed to Paris to see it. The Frank Masons came over from Frankfurt and took an apartment near the Arc de Triomphe for the summer. I crowded in with them and settled down for a long study of the paintings in the exhibition. Besides the retrospective French, there was a great showing of contemporary European art. It was worth long study to me.

Every day some newly arrived painter came up and over my horizon— Jacques Galland, W. T. Dannat, Gari Melchers, Chase, Pennell, Henry Moore of London. I had abundant opportunity for discussion and comparison of opinions. And there were new men and movements to be equated. For example, the Scandinavians Lilyfors, Bjorck, Thegerstrom, Larsson, Pederson, and others were having their European hearing. I was much impressed with their schemes of high light and bright color. Art discussion about the Scandinavians and others raged over the luncheons at the Chateaubriand and the Abbaye de Thélème or over the dinners at Foyot's or the Boeuf à la Mode. Every important painter and picture in the Exposition was raked over the coals. Reputations were built up or torn down over bottles of very *vin ordinaire*. Paris was much alive, or perhaps I should say that we were all of us more or less jumpy.

The younger men and art students were just then making much ado about Besnard. Kenneth Frazier, then an art student in Paris, took me down to the little Mairie near St. Germain L'Auxerrois, opposite the main façade of the Louvre, to see some Besnard frescoes there that I thought very fine. I afterwards went to the École de Pharmacie to see others of his ceiling pieces. I was so much impressed by Besnard's work that some time later, when Mr. Thomson asked me who could paint pictures for two spaces beside the mantle in the Corkerhill dining room, I unhesitatingly said Besnard. A year or so later in Paris I went with Carroll Beckwith to Besnard's studio, stayed the morning with him, and left the commission for the two pictures for Mr. Thomson, which he executed with great success.

I went, I think this same summer, but it may have been later, with my friend William H. Fuller (at first a collector of old English pictures but latterly an admirer of Monet) to Givernay and saw Monet in his garden. He was then doing beautiful pictures of the Seine and the French wheat fields but, if I remember rightly, had not yet started his fine decorative panels of the lily pool in his garden. Years after, when Fuller died, he left a very fine group of Monets, one that he had worked over and weeded out until only the choicest examples remained. I proposed to his executor, George J. Peet, Esq., that half a dozen of these Monets be presented to the Metropolitan Museum as a Fuller memorial, but on inquiry at the Metropolitan we were informed that Monet would not be acceptable to the museum authorities. Both Fuller and Thomson were ahead of their time in appreciation of Monet.

Of course, we made excursions to Barbizon and Fontainebleau, the sketch ground of the then famous Fontainebleau-Barbizon group of paint- ers. Millet, Rousseau, Díaz, Dupré, and Troyon had about reached their apogee. Millet's *Angelus* had brought $125,000 at auction, and everyone was stupefied by that high price. Fuller had bought Rousseau's *Charcoal Burner's Hut* at $15,000 and thought he had paid too much for it, though a few years later it sold for $65,000; and Corot's *Biblis*, in the retrospective exhibition and afterward in the collection of James J. Hill at St. Paul, was thought to be worth a hundred times its weight in gold. It is a little aston- ishing, in the light of later years, to find how exaggerated were these values artistically as well as commercially. I had seen the *Angelus* in the collection of M. Secretan and had thought it slight, but Rousseau's great landscape impressed me with its power. I overlooked its want of color, its lack of light. Years afterward, when Louis Hill showed me the *Biblis* in his father's house at St. Paul, I could scarcely believe it the same picture. It had blackened and become woolly in texture. Almost all the pictures of that once-famous school have darkened with time and now look hard and colorless. But in 1889 they were much in vogue.

When modern art palled, I sneaked away to the Louvre and spent days in the long gallery with the Italians and Dutch and heard thin, wheyfaced students abuse "those big bad pictures by Rubens" or grow enthusiastic over the stodgy pictures given to Rembrandt and Velásquez that I felt sure were by their pupils. Between chatter of that kind and tourist parties "doing" the old masters, I made notes on the pictures, putting down their paternity and present condition, with their good and bad features, quite regardless of what authorities had said about them. I was cultivating some arrogance of opinion at this time because I had found the opinions of others so very unsatisfactory. They had not studied the pictures and were rhapsodizing from insufficient premises. Many years later, I published my notes on the European galleries and deliberately retained the arrogance.[1]

John G. Moore, head of the then powerful Wall Street firm of Moore and Schley, whom I had known intimately in his family life for some years, was in Paris in 1889. He had not come for the Exposition and cared little about art. In fact, he jeered a little at my interest in it. In his rooms at the Vendôme, he was engaged by day in cutting out plans for corporate combinations and by night dining at the Pied du Mouton, the Tour d'Argent, or some other smelly old Paris restaurant known to John Munroe or Edward Tuck. I went along with them very often and heard discussion of another sort, which in its way was quite as interesting as that of art and artists. Then occasionally I went to dinner at places like the H——s in the Rue des Petits Champs and heard Mrs. H—— tear into ribbons the diplomatic and consular life of Paris, or went to the D——s on the Champs Élysée to hear the Fauborg St. Germain set sneered at, or the young flash nobility of Europe ripped up the back and hung on hooks. All Paris was talking that summer, and everyone was in either a praising or a carping mood.

Then there was music at the opera, where *Aïda*, *Faust*, *Il Trovatore*, and all the old barrel-organ operas were being given,[2] and the play at the Comédie Française where Mounet-Sully was tearing *Ruy Blas* to shreds and patches. And finally, failing everything else, there was Buffalo Bill outside the walls, beyond the Arc de Triomphe, giving a Wild West show, which Parisians believed a typical representation of American life. There were all kinds of shows and sideshows in Paris that summer. It was a wonderful summer, but even the then wonderful Eiffel Tower finally grew tiresome. I went away to Venice to join Fuller, and we, in the autumn heat, went up the Brenta to Padua to see Mantegna's frescoes, to Castelfranco to see the Giorgione Madonna, to Verona to see Bonsignori and Liberale, to Brescia to see Moretto, to Bergamo to see Lotto. We were out for a study of the North Italians.

After that, we went home.

At the World's Fair at Chicago in 1893, I stopped for a week with James W. Ellsworth. He had a fine collection of pictures by Inness, the famous Vollon *Yellow Pumpkin*, an excellent early Rembrandt, many fine Chinese porcelains, and a quite perfect copy of the Gutenberg Bible. He was an omnivorous collector and gathered in almost anything that was rare and curious. He finally gathered in the famous Villa Palmieri at Florence, where Boccaccio is supposed to have located the audience of the *Decameron*, and there he died only a few years ago. When I first met him, he was a leading businessman of Chicago, making money in coal operations, and in 1893 one of the directors of the World's Fair.

He was in touch with art and artists, much interested in the mural work the American painters were doing in and about the exhibition buildings, and very active in gathering together the fine loan exhibition shown at the Fair. In 1890 I found in Venice a portrait that I thought represented Christopher Columbus. I believed it painted by Lorenzo Lotto and was more interested at the time in the painter than in the painted, but Captain Frank Mason was with me in Venice that year, and he made out that the Columbus end of it was the drawing card because the World's Fair was Columbian, in honor of the four-hundredth anniversary of the discovery of America. He wrote to Ellsworth that the portrait should be shown at Chicago. There was no official money available, but Mr. Ellsworth bought the picture and loaned it to the Fair, Mason handling for him the financial part of the transaction.

I wrote a long article about the portrait, giving the reasons for believing it Columbus and painted by Lotto, for the *Century Magazine*. It stirred up a row. There were forty other Columbus portraits in the field, each one authentic to the fingertips and each one a different personality and giving the lie to all the others. There was much newspaper controversy over it, and I had to stand up and be shot at by people who knew neither Columbus nor art. But in the end my Columbus won out. It was pronounced the officially recognized portrait of the great discoverer and in reproduction was put on all the tickets, diplomas, medals, and coins of the Fair. That was my introduction to Ellsworth.[3]

Handsomely housed at Ellsworth's, put up at clubs, introduced to everyone, I saw the Fair pleasantly and leisurely over ten days or more. The first day Ellsworth took me to see the fine loan collection. I stopped him before Manet's *Dead Toreador*, which was holding a place of honor in one of the rooms, and urged him to buy it. It belonged to Cottier, and I knew he could get it for $5,000. It was the finest piece of painting since Velásquez. It was a masterpiece going for a song. Buy it! But he shook his head. He did not like the "deid mon"—just as Cottier had predicted. The picture today, if put up at auction, would fetch more than $100,000. A similar advance in value with other pictures in the loan collection could be foreseen, but none of them had the unique painter's value of that picture by Manet. I wanted Ellsworth to have it, but collectors have their own ideas about pictures, just as philanthropists their own schemes for distributing their surplus wealth.

Making money by buying pictures and holding them for an advance did not seem to me then (nor now) a very risky performance. Had I been so inclined, I am sure I could have grown rich by dealing in pictures, but I was interested in art only as art and never had anything to do with buying or selling. But I liked to pick out work of technical value and insist upon its purchase by notable collectors. It meant recognition of art as art rather than as a commercial commodity. However, I never had much success in this. Many of the Scandinavian pictures shown in the Paris exposition were here at Chicago, and they seemed to me not only a new point of view but a new technique, yet the picture buyers shied at them and at my recommendations.[4] A few months later, I had a chance to say my say about the Scandinavians in the *Century Magazine*, Gilder having asked me to write an article about the pictures at the Fair. But no tangible results followed.

Fuller came out from New York and joined me at Chicago. He was a person of fine taste and good judgment in art matters, and we went over the pictures day by day, he looking at them for general excellence and I for technical proficiency. I think we praised or condemned every picture in the exhibition, for our own relief and not to any painter's knowledge or loss. At the end, we thought it a remarkable collection of pictures and predicted all sorts of educational influences radiating from it, but whether that prediction was realized or not I have never been able to determine.

When weary of the inside of buildings, we wandered about the grounds and saw the outside show. The beautiful domes of the White City, the parkways, the waterways, and bridges were all very attractive, especially at night when a romantic glamour seemed to envelop them. But this dream was always being shaken by the people who surged by in crowds and platoons and companies. We had never thought for a moment that the American people as a whole could look like that. The rank and file were thin and yellow, as though raised on hog and hominy or suffering from malaria, bent over and dragged down as though malformed by heavy labor, scrawny, hatchet-faced, ill-proportioned, badly set up, as though cast in some misshapen mold. Where did all these ill-favored, ill-dressed, formless, and mannerless people come from? Was this the output of the great Mississippi basin? At noon we went to the New York building for lunch and to see some normal-looking, properly dressed people.[5]

Happily, there has been a change for the better in the Midwest type in the last thirty years. It is now better fed, has lost its sallowness, has intermarried with newer types, and has become rather moon-faced, full in girth, jovial in disposition, noisy in conduct. Here is a condition and a change that the historians who have so beautifully damned the Eighties and Nineties might have argued with effectively, but so far as my reading goes they have not even noticed it. They have watched the change of hats and ribbons in the little smart society of the East but have not reckoned with the shift of skirt and shirt in the great Midwest.

The St. Louis Fair [1904] was not as important as that at Chicago. I went out with a paper to read at the congress. Professor Munsterberg of Harvard had taken the congress by the collar and assigned to different people papers on every subject under the sun, including art, about which he knew nothing and probably cared less. I slashed at connoisseurship, expertism, and art theories. Professor Furtwängler of Munich was in my audience, and my paper drove straight at his recently put forth theory of the School of Phidias. He took it with a smile, and we came together after the talk for a handshake and a little chat.

At St. Louis I joined Brander Matthews and Professor Lounsbury of Yale. With others we made up a round table for the evening dinner that was rather keen in gibe and comment. Both Matthews and Lounsbury were cunning of fence and could pile up wit with epigram. But my boon companion at that fair was Joseph Pennell. We had become great friends in London, and I was devoted to him. At St. Louis he was on almost all the art committees, and in order that I might attend the meetings he had me appointed official expert advisor to the committees. Needless to say, I gave no advice. I listened to discussions about awards and noted that things other than kissing went by favor. I myself came into possession of several medals, without knowing any reason for their giving. It was probably some of Pennell's doing.[6]

But there was much art discussion at St. Louis. There is always that at every fair. Artists are like volcanoes that erupt and blow their heads off at stated periods. Later on at the Pan Pacific Exhibition at San Francisco [1915], all the art people on the Pacific coast were in a sizzle of excitement that found vent in papers and discussions. They had discovered Frank Duveneck (after forty years), with Chase, Twachtman, Weir, Whistler, and a dozen others who had been accepted and passed on into tradition on the eastern coast. But the exhibition really did much in spreading a knowledge of American art and was a great success.

Chapter 13

The Players

The Players came into existence in 1888 through the generosity of Edwin Booth. He gave the fine clubhouse (remodeled by Stanford White) in Gramercy Park, became president of the club, and had a suite of rooms in the clubhouse, where he lived. Around him in the early days gathered a large number of young and middle-aged men, men who were not players. They were writers, painters, sculptors, architects, editors, lawyers, college professors, with only a few players like Lawrence Barrett, Joe Jefferson, and John Drew. Indeed, it was the standardized joke of the club that people liked the Players because "one never met any d—— actors there."

But everyone was devoted to Booth, his fine gentlemanly qualities, his lovable nature, his distinguished personality. He did not talk a great deal, but he was always the center of an admiring group. His mere presence spread a feeling of content. The groups varied from day to day. If Thomas Bailey Aldrich dropped down from Boston, he would generally be at the Players after luncheon, with perhaps Laurence Hutton, Mark Twain, Richard Watson Gilder, Charles Dudley Warner, E. C. Stedman. The conversation sparkled when Aldrich was in the group. His wit and quickness in reply always astonished me. Often I would get his meaning too late to laugh. Mark Twain was, of course, humorous but much slower in his comebacks, and Hutton, though bright, could not keep up with Aldrich. Booth greatly liked Aldrich and was always down in the main club rooms when Aldrich was in town.

After four o'clock, another group of young men would begin dropping in at the Players. These were men perhaps through with the day's work and out for a walk and a talk—Augustus Saint-Gaudens, Robert Reid, E. E. Simmons from the studios, Brander Matthews, Nicholas Murray Butler, George E. Woodberry from Columbia, Oliver Herford, William Carey, C. C. Buel, Robert Underwood Johnson from the *Century*. There was wit enough, too, among these younger men. Matthews, Herford, and Carey could keep any table on a roar. In fact, there were many young men who sharpened their wits with the intellectual fencing of the Players in those days. Even downstairs in the billiard room there were clever things said that were repeated upstairs. Perhaps I violate club confidence, but I must narrate one bright return in the billiard room, of which I had personal knowledge.

Two men had been playing billiards all the afternoon, Professor Scott and Charles J——. Scott played the better game and was far in the lead, and J——, perhaps by reason of several highballs and some facetiousness, presently began addressing him as "Professor Squat." After several passes, Scott rather resentfully said:

"Don't call me Squat! My name is Scott."

J—— immediately came back with an apology: "Oh, I beg your pardon. The fact is you play such a fine game of billiards that I didn't know but what you spelled your name with a cue."

I must also relate here another story, one about Mark Twain, because Albert Bigelow Paine in his biography of Twain never heard but half of it and failed to get the humor of it and because I am the only surviving party who can tell the story.

One afternoon at the Players, Mark Twain told me that he was writing an introduction to a new edition of his *The Celebrated Jumping Frog of Calaveras County*. It was practically his first story and had made him famous. There had been many comments upon it, amusing and otherwise. He was recounting them to me, and when he had finished I ventured to suppose that he knew the jumping-frog story, like all good stories, was not exactly new. He asked me what I meant by that, and I answered by saying that I thought I had seen a similar story in a Greek anthology. He looked up with surprise saying:

"Why, it was told to me in a mining camp in '49."

Of course, I replied that there was no question of his good faith and originality, but coincidentally had not the story gone the rounds in Greek days and then been forgotten for ages?

He was greatly interested. Would I get him that story? I told him I would try but that the Greek anthology was a large order, and I probably would not be able to locate the story.

The next day in my Sage Library I got down the various editions of the anthology and spent two hours over them but with no success. Later in the day, Professor Cooper of the Greek Department of Rutgers happened in. I told him of my talk with Mark. Did he remember any such story in the Greek? Yes, he did, but he doubted it was in the anthology. Did I have perhaps in the library a copy of Sidgwick's *Greek Prose Composition*? Yes. I got it for him, and after a few minutes he turned to page 116, and there was the jumping-frog story in English translation. It was the same story except that it now told about an Athenian and a Boeotian, instead of two Americans, and the frog was stuffed with pebbles instead of birdshot. It was cast in the form of an exercise to be translated from the English into the Greek by the pupil, and Professor Sidgwick had not given the Greek source, obviously for the reason that had he done so some of his pupils would have gone to the original and "cribbed" it. Professor Cooper thought the story was a free translation from the Greek.

All this, with due reference to book and page, I wrote out and sent to Mark, adding that I could not find the Greek original, but possibly this English was a free translation of that original.

No word came back.

Two or three months later I picked up the current number of the *North American Review* (April 1894) to find an article by Mark Twain on the "Private History of the 'Jumping Frog' Story." I found myself on the first page (with name and address given) in a wholly imaginary conversation with Mark, in which I offered to furnish him with the original Greek of the story, but Greek made him tired, and he preferred Sidgwick's English translation. It was an amusing article, just what one would expect from Mark Twain, and that rather lessened my apprehension. He had not told me that he would use my haphazard findings in print. It is customary to ask permission to print conversation. I did not know then that Mark would use almost anything that answered his immediate need and purpose, whether people liked it or not. But the article would produce a laugh, and that would be the end of it.[1]

Six or eight weeks later in New York, Laurence Hutton hailed me with:

"Have you seen Mark?"

"No."

"Well, he is hunting the town over for you."

"What about?"

"Why, Professor Sidgwick of Rugby has written to the *Saturday Review* to say that both you and Mark are mistaken about that English translation in his *Greek Prose Composition* being taken from the Greek. He says it is his own English adaptation of Mark Twain's story of the jumping frog of Calaveras."

That was a decided climax and left me gasping between surprise and laughter. When I came back I protested:

"He should have told me he intended to use the materials in print, and then I would have looked up the matter more thoroughly. Now what is he going to do about it?"

"Why, he is shooting back at Sidgwick in the *Saturday Review*."

"How?"

"He is going for him for using his jumping-frog story without his permission and without giving him credit for it."

With that second climax, the story ends. At least I stepped out of it, though I was afterward told that Mark and Professor Sidgwick actually did batter each other in print. I never saw their articles.[2]

While I am telling tales out of school about the Players, I may add one about Booth.

When I was young, I more than once read and heard the report that Edwin Booth had never mentioned the name of his brother, John Wilkes, after the assassination of Lincoln. I do not know how true that report, but one day at the Players, Laurence Hutton came in with a small and very early photograph of Edwin, one taken in St. Louis. He had picked it up somewhere and had brought it over to the club to get Edwin's signature upon it. Booth was upstairs in his rooms, and Hutton asked me if I would go up with him. We found him reclining in an easy chair—he was not well in those days—and after ten minutes of general talk, Hutton drew out the photograph and asked him if he would put his signature upon it.

"Certainly."

He put on his glasses and took a preliminary look at the photograph. Almost immediately, and without facial expression of any kind, he said:

"But there is no use of my signing that."

"Why not?" queried Hutton.

"Because that's John."

John's face in the photograph was so much like Edwin's that we had both mistaken it.

Booth's health did not improve. He wanted to cancel engagements and retire from the stage, but Lawrence Barrett had urged him to carry on, thinking that action was better for him than rest. The result was he continued on the stage a year longer than perhaps he should. And then one Saturday afternoon, as I stood on the upper landing of the stairway in the club, in came Booth walking very slowly and leaning heavily on the arm of Evert Jansen Wendell. He had difficulty in mounting the first step, and I went to him at once to help him, taking his free arm. He was breathing hard and evidently was much exhausted. When we reached the upper landing, he paused for breath and then turned to me, saying slowly:

"This is the last time."

He was referring to his playing. He had just come from Brooklyn, where he had played at a matinee in the Academy of Music, and was very weak. True enough, that was his last appearance, April 4, 1891. After that he gradually weakened and suffered from attacks of aphasia. His tongue—

with that wonderful voice and perfect pronunciation that had swayed so many thousands—could not at times articulate. And the splendid dark eyes began to have a weary look. He said little. But I remember one day, when I was inquiring about his health, his saying rather sadly that he would be glad if he could go to sleep and not wake up. He was tired of everything. His life had not been happy, and all that success and fame could give had not made it so. Perhaps he was somewhat comforted by the knowledge that everyone loved him. He must have known that from the devotion of his friends at the Players.

About this time—to be exact, December 20, 1893—a dinner at Sherry's to Brander Matthews came off.³ It was given by his many friends as a testimonial to both the man and the writer. It was a large dinner and represented the literary New York of the early Nineties very well. I still have the menu of the dinner, with the autographs of some of those present, and perhaps it will convey an idea of the company if I transcribe from the menu some of the names: W. D. Howells, Mark Twain, Joseph Jefferson, Laurence Hutton, Nicholas Murray Butler, Parke Godwin, R. W. Gilder, H. C. Bunner, E. C. Stedman, R. U. Johnson, Charles Dudley Warner, William Milligan Sloane, W. C. Brownell, H. H. Boyesen.

There were speeches, of course, and a poem by Bunner, with Mark Twain to make the closing remarks. Mark was at his best in a humorous speech on the enormity and atrocity of Brander Matthews's name. Several times he wandered afield, only to return for a climax on that name. After the fourth return and the getting of tremendous applause, everyone was willing to wager he could not do it again. But he did. He finally ended with the statement that Brander had been given a name that was only fit to swear with, and he had made it a name to conjure with. Immense applause.

The Brander Matthews dinner was a personal tribute, but there were other dinners that were given to forward some public purpose, commemorate some event, such as the Copyright League dinner at Sherry's in 1891 or the tenth anniversary of the Authors Club in 1893. The guests of these dinners were more representative of the country at large, and yet the bulk of those present belonged to the New York literary circle. It was a bright little, tight little circle compared with that which exists today, but in spirit and endeavor not so very different. Writers then worried about their technique and railed at standards, tradition, and precedent, just as they do today. And Bohemia then roared over wine bottles in Bleecker Street, just as it does now in Greenwich Village. One generation is not so different from another generation that common characteristics do not crop out.

Chapter 14

In England and Scotland

Timothy Cole had been sent to Italy in the late Eighties to engrave for the *Century Magazine* a series on old Italian masters. I met him in Florence, at the back end of Gillie Letti's restaurant, near the Loggia del Lanzi, where he was eating macaroni and contemplating empty space. We became friends. His engravings for that series were published in the *Century* with a text by William J. Stillman. Afterwards he did a series called *Old Dutch and Flemish Masters* [1895], for which I was asked to write the text. It was later published in handsome imperial octavo, uniform with the Stillman volume. There was nothing remarkable about my part in it, but I was glad to be associated with Cole and his beautiful wood blocks and to be so handsomely printed by the DeVinne Press of the Century Company.

The *Century* editors then asked me to go to England to select a series on old English masters for Cole to engrave and to write the text for the magazine. When I arrived in London, Cole already was there, and we began at once. I wanted the best and the most famous of the English masters for engraving, but these were scattered through many private collections. I had to secure access to them, for both Cole and myself, as well as permission to engrave them. Sidney Colvin was then in charge of the print room of the British Museum, and I went to him, asking what letters of introduction I should need and how I could get them. To my surprise, he said not to bother with letters of introduction but to write directly to the people whose pictures I wanted to see and perhaps use for engraving.

I began by writing to Mr. Holmes, the Queen's librarian, telling my mission in England, and could I see Her Majesty's pictures at Windsor, with permission perhaps to engrave one or two of them? The answer came back at once. I could see the pictures when I chose and select for engraving what I pleased. That was very handsome and encouraged me to write to Earl Spencer, Lord Rosebery, the Duke of Devonshire, Sir Charles Tennant, and others. They all responded favorably and, when I went to their houses, received me most courteously. I have spoken elsewhere of English courtesy and hospitality and repeat it here because some years later when, on a similar mission for the *Century*, I tried to see pictures in American houses, I met with some difficulties and not a few rebuffs.

I cannot recall my first meeting with Mr. and Mrs. Joseph Pennell. Perhaps it was at the Paris Exposition of 1889. But in London, working on the *Old English Masters* [1902], I went to the Pennells (14 Buckingham Street and later at 3 Adelphi Terrace) almost every night. Whistler, too, was a nightly visitor there, with many others. Almost everyone of artistic or literary London went to the Pennells at one time or another for dinner or for an after-dinner chat or for Thursday evening. It was a famous gathering place. And not the least famous of those in the house was Augustine, Mrs. Pennell's large French *bonne*, who knew everyone on familiar terms, cooked all the dinners, and bossed hosts and guests alike. She was unique but very good-hearted, and everyone liked her.

Whistler chose to occupy the center of the stage, there as elsewhere, but he was not always the hero of the evening. Sometimes he went to sleep at his post, and sometimes the conversation ran away from art and left him lonely. There were a good many bright people who gathered at the Pennells, R. A. M. Stevenson, D. S. McColl, McLure Hamilton, John Galsworthy, Ivan Müller, and Fisher Unwin. Whistler had competitors in wit and wisdom. Besides, he was frequently sidetracked in an argument. I remember one night at a man's dinner of eight or ten the talk turned upon Velásquez's *Las Meninas* and what the painter intended in light by the small portraits of the king and queen in the mirror at the back of the picture. Whistler was insistent upon his own explanation and drew diagrams with a reckless tableknife across one of Mrs. Pennell's best tablecloths to prove his point, but all the company was against him. He could not carry through and rather sulkily collapsed. The amusing thing about it was that of the eight or ten people present he was the only one who had never been to Madrid and had never seen the picture.[1]

Mrs. Pennell was the angel of the house. She sat through all the mad arguments and midnight talks, smiling and undisturbed, comprehending but perhaps not coinciding. Occasionally at a fitting moment she would put in a word of cool comment that really summed up the situation better than Whistler's expletives or Joseph's denunciations. Everyone admired her. She was hostess not only to Americans in London but to French and Italians from the Continent, and yet with all her social engagements she found time to write for the London dailies, turn out criticism for the (American) *Nation* under the initials of N. N., and publish book after book on a variety of subjects. Both she and Joseph were good friends of Whistler when he needed friends most. He was not only in continuous controversies, but, at the time of which I write, he had lost Mrs. Whistler [1896] and was very lonely.

Cole came in one day with some new blocks he had cut of Gainsborough's *Mrs. Siddons* and Hogarth's *Marriage à la Mode*. They were in the old English masters series and were beautifully done. These were the original boxwood blocks, and Cole had a method of temporarily bringing out the values of light and dark by sifting white powder into the lines cut by the graver. It produced an effect similar to an impression on Japanese paper. Cole wanted to show these blocks to Whistler. Would I go along? We went to Whistler's big studio (I have forgotten the street) and found him in. He liked Cole's work and was enthusiastic about the blocks. He, however, carefully dusted out the white powder, preferring the gray face of the boxwood. I recall his lingering long over a block made from a portrait of Hogarth himself at work in his studio. He greatly admired Hogarth and thought him the best of all the old English masters.

After the Cole blocks were sufficiently admired, Whistler brought out many of his own pictures to show us. They were standing in rows facing the wall, and many of them were covered with dust. There were a dozen whole-length portraits in various stages of incompleteness, starts that he perhaps had wearied of or felt were unsatisfactory. He talked about them in a most sober and serious way, saying what he thought was good or bad about them, asking Cole and me what we thought of them, how the models stood, how they were placed on the canvas, what their depth in, what their color scheme, what their backgrounds and surfaces. He was looking at his work in a severely critical way, not talking about it for newspaper publication. Scores of smaller works were brought out. The dissatisfied painter passed them in review with such comment as might have been applied to the inferior work of another. It was by no means the extravagance of the author of *Ten O'Clock* or the wit of the critic-baiter in the *Gentle Art of Making Enemies*. It was the real Whistler, the sensitive, hesitant, apprehensive painter who strove for splendid effects and grieved because he could not always achieve them.

In August the London fashionables went to the country, and I found it convenient to go to Scotland in search of pictures by Raeburn. The Carnegies had asked me to come to Cluny for a visit, and I could thus make a combination tour. The Cluny station wagon met me at Kingussie, and I was driven across country some twenty miles to the rather lonely castle on the Caledonian moors. It was a picturesque stone structure in a beautiful open moorland, a fine, wild moorland that seemed far removed from any breath of civilization or impress of mankind. Cluny had not the proportions or the grandeur of Skibo, Mr. Carnegie's later purchase in Sutherland, but to my fancy it was far more romantic and in keeping with the great Scotch moors.[2]

I entered the drawing room to find a man of middle age and medium height standing with his back to an open peat fire. He came forward with outstretched hand, saying that all the house party had gone out for tea on the moors with the shooters, and he had been deputed to receive me and explain that they would be back shortly. He said he was Mr. Morley.

I looked at him for a moment.

"But you are not Mr. *John* Morley?"

"Why, yes, I suppose I am."

"Well, you surprise me."

"How so?"

"Why, when I was a young man I read your life of Voltaire, and I remember thinking at the time that it must have taken a learned and consequently rather old man to write such a volume, and here I find you looking but little older than I myself.

He laughed and then remarked, "Someone should write a good life of Voltaire."

Tea was brought in, and we sat and talked over the teacups for over an hour. I regret now that I never kept a diary or put down notes of such conversations as this. For Morley was a very good talker and one of those few men of intellectual aplomb peculiar to England who could never be stampeded or driven from a base of common sense. He talked in a calm, leisurely way, with no exaggerated English intonation and no gestures—a plain, simple talker but to the point always and very convincing because of his candor and sincerity. Sir Richard Webster (afterward Lord Alverstone, Lord Chief Justice) was in the house party and came in from the moors later in the afternoon, but he was almost the reverse of Morley in being very positive in criticism, rather mannered in speech, rambling in talk, and by no means so convincing.

I saw Morley for a week and had a number of afternoons with him. He was at his best over the coffee and cigars after dinner, when perhaps some matter of political moment came up. He argued (as he wrote) very simply, and it was great fun watching his approach and development of a theme. Ordinarily he was not scintillating but just bandying, playing with a subject, like the others at the table. He and Carnegie were great friends and remained such to the end, but perhaps they did not always agree. I remember one evening when we were going out to the dining room to the music of the bagpipes that Morley and I came at the end of the procession, and he leaned over to me asking with a little smile:

"What do you think of all that noise?"

And again one day on the moors apropos of nothing: "Your friend Carnegie is a very extraordinary man."

"How so?" I asked.

"Well, he will give you almost anything you don't want."

True enough, Mr. Carnegie did give Morley the library of Lord Acton, which he did not want because he soon passed it on to one of the English universities. But, nevertheless, they were great friends.

I did not see Morley again for twenty-five years. At Cluny, he was plain John Morley, Secretary for Ireland, but when I met him again after the Great War [World War I], he was Lord Morley of Blackburn. In London I had gone up to the Langham Hotel to call upon Mrs. Carnegie and found Morley in the drawing room on a similar mission. He had grown older in looks and was far from well. I recalled my meeting him at Cluny, which he remembered in saying:

"But that was an entirely different man you met up there. I'm not the same person at all."

This was said half in jest and half in earnest, but it was wholly true. He had greatly changed. The War had about done for him.[3]

I have never heard better after-dinner table talk than at Cluny with Morley, Webster, Shaw (then Solicitor General for Scotland, afterward Lord Shaw of Dumfermlin), and Carnegie. They were all of them quick on the trigger, and I was glad to see that Carnegie more than held his own. He talked extremely well and was quite at home on every English or American subject broached. Sometimes at the breakfast table or at afternoon tea he said sharp things to his guests. He never missed a chance to denounce smoking and yet provided cigars and cigarettes for his guests. He disliked anyone using sugar on porridge, insisting that salt was the only thing permissible. And sometimes he could be witty in criticism as well as brusque. Mrs. Burton Harrison was of the house party, and she was one day talking of her morning tub when he broke in with:

"Oh, Mrs. Harrison. You are always talking about tubs and frocks. If you must talk about such things, why don't you say baths and dresses, like other people?"

"Mr. Carnegie, when I was a child in Virginia, we always spoke of tubs and frocks."

He came back instantly with:

"Nonsense! When you were a child in Virginia, there wasn't a tub in the whole state."

Mrs. Harrison's son, Francis Burton Harrison (afterward Governor

General of the Philippines under President Wilson), was with her in the Cluny party. He was then nineteen or twenty and with a young man named Fowler (son of the Viceroy of India) was interested in the Misses Phipps, daughters of Henry Phipps, one of Mr. Carnegie's partners in steel, who were also in the house party. They were given to long trout-fishing excursions, but their catch was not very large. Mr. Carnegie took me with him out to their brook one day, and we caught six or seven times their basket. It was the one sport he was really enthusiastic about, though he was fond of golf. And at that time he was in need of recreation, for though the great strike in the Carnegie steel mills at Pittsburgh had died out, the aftereffect was still visible upon him. He had been put in a false position. He believed that his partner, Henry C. Frick, was too severe with the men on strike, believed had he been there he could have prevented the strike. But Frick was his partner in charge, and he had to stand with him and against the men. That worried him greatly, for he had always been friendly with the men. Now he was regarded by them as an enemy. It cut him to the quick.

What he said to me about his relations with the men was afterward confirmed by McLuckie, the burgomaster of Homestead, who, as burgomaster, tried to arrest the Pinkerton detectives as an armed force invading his bailiwick. That started the riots. McLuckie was afterward indicted for murder, conspiracy, and I know not what else, was wounded, hounded, blacklisted, driven out of the United States into Mexico, and reduced to abject poverty. In 1900 I found him on a Mexican ranch in the mountains of Sonora, where he, a high-class mechanic, was trying to get a peon job at fifty cents a day. He was penniless, hatless, almost shoeless, among strangers, without a word of Spanish to his name. I had gone up there from Guaymas to shoot wolves and had no idea of finding anyone but peons and Yaqui Indians on the ranch. But here was this outlawed American. He was overjoyed to meet someone who could talk his language. He told me all about his troubles and the Homestead riots the day of my arrival. How I tried to help him with money; how I wrote to Mr. Carnegie and got word from him: "Give McLuckie all the money he wants, but don't mention my name"; how McLuckie refused all help; how I got him a job on the Sonora Railroad and he recouped his fortunes; and when a year later I told him it was Mr. Carnegie's money I was offering him, how he replied, "Well, that was damned white of Andy"—all this has been told in Mr. Carnegie's *Autobiography*. After his death, Mrs. Carnegie put the autobiography in my hands to be arranged and edited for publication, and it was brought out by

Houghton, Mifflin & Co. in 1921 [1920]. It contains this McLuckie story
in full.[4]

But the point of it all is that McLuckie quite vindicated Mr. Carnegie,
insisting that: "If Andy had been there, everything would have been all
right."[5]

Chapter 15

Of Many Things

I am putting down my various comings, goings, and doings, not because they are important in themselves, but rather to suggest to the people of today that the Eighties and Nineties were not such leisurely, yawny decades as they have perhaps imagined. Men hustled and bustled then as they do now. And in bookmaking pursuits as well as in selling stocks on Wall Street. My contemporaries were going about each with half a dozen bundles on his back, and I was living and working on trains and steamers, sleeping and eating as I could, trying to keep my nose above water and not neglect my various duties.

I had my library and college work always before me, from 1889 or thereabouts. For half a dozen years thereafter I was the art editor of the *New York Evening Post* and wrote all the art criticisms for that newspaper. I was editing a series of college histories of art for Longmans, Green & Co. I was off with studies of the old masters. Besides this, there was the call of various circles of society to which I listened and which took more time than I could rightly spare.

The work on the *Evening Post* was not entirely satisfactory. My immediate predecessors, Kenyon Cox and William Anderson Coffin, had carried on for a few years and then resigned. If one told the truth about the pictures in the current exhibitions, he often made enemies of the exhibitors, who, for the greater part, were friends and associates. If he did not tell the truth, the notices were spineless and not worth the doing. But there was compensation in the writing. Newspaper work offers the very best of training for the writer. It teaches conciseness, clearness, and crispness. You cannot dawdle mentally and suck the end of a pencil while the printer is waiting for copy. You must think and decide quickly and throw into sequential order as you think. One presently learns to adapt himself to situations, to be pliable, facile, ductile, to turn the theme about and show its various phases, to hand it out in simple and forceful English.[1]

There is today more good literature to be found on the editorial pages of the newspaper press than in the magazines or books. This is not equally true of the news columns. The average newspaper reporter of the present day thinks he must work up his story and put a kick or a purple patch in every paragraph. And that is precisely the trouble with half the novels that are issued. They are too full of kicks to have sobriety and carry conviction. Readers, like other people, get a bit tired of being kicked, and after half an hour of "the telling phrase" in Chesterton or Rose Macaulay, they put the book down and go out for a little fresh air.[2]

But, aside from any style of writing, it was necessary as an art critic to formulate definite opinions about art in general and make them applicable to present-day art if I could. This, I think, was the chief teaching of my *Evening Post* experience. I had to take a stand for a certain point of view or approach to fine art, and, naturally enough, this point of view was that which I had gotten from painters—the painter's point of view. This was nothing more than the examination of the painting for its technical and decorative qualities.[3] What the picture might mean or symbolize or illustrate or emotionally signify was an after-consideration. Written down arbitrarily, the insistence was that every great work of art is primarily based on great craftsmanship, *ergo:* the first inquiry should be as to craftsmanship, and not as to theme or subject or emotional content. In this I have always had the concurrence and support of artists, because it is about the only point of view held in the studios. Painters are craftsmen first and foremost.

They have always been. The old masters, perhaps even more than the new, were people who prided themselves on their skill and were ranked by their fellows according to their proficiency in their craft. The *bottegas* were places where they served long apprenticeships, and when masters and apprentices alike applauded Andrea del Sarto as "the faultless painter," it was not because of his subjects or his sentiment or his beautiful wife-model, but because he was a finished craftsman and knew his métier. So, naturally again, when I took up the study of the old masters, I went at their pictures precisely as I did at the pictures of the moderns. The first question was always as to their drawing and handling, their arrangement, placing, lighting, coloring, their content in skill and decorative pattern, rather than their mentality or pictorial poetry.

Now, I had early discovered, not only in painting, but in sculpture, architecture, poetry, music, and, in short, almost every form of human expression, that genius is not versatile but on the contrary rather singular and prone to repetition. The same idea or theme or pattern recurs, and the artist does it over again, trying to improve upon former attempts. Kenyon Cox said to me one day that sometimes he would start Monday morning with a fresh canvas determined to do something entirely different from anything he had done before, but by Saturday night he would find it was "the same old thing."

That, I think, will explain not only Kenyon Cox but Titian, Raphael, Rembrandt, Velásquez, in fact all the great gods of art, including Shakespeare and Goethe. We know a newly discovered Titian or Velásquez a long way off because we have seen him do that very thing, in that very way, a hundred times before. He is recognized because he repeats himself. Repetition is the chief clew that the art expert follows. It is a very positive blazed trail and leads to very positive identifications.

Now in the process of repetition, not only Michelangelo, Raphael, Titian, Velásquez, but Shakespeare, Milton, Byron, Swinburne, Wagner, Brahms—all the artists—fall into what are called "mannerisms," that is, formal ways of doing things. These among the painters show in methods of drawing or modeling or composing or brushing. Each painter's brush is autographic in the same way as is his pen. Any one of us could sign our name a dozen different ways if we chose, but we do not choose; we do not think it worth while. We write in one way from youth to old age, with some slight variation from decade to decade, perhaps, but in substantially the same style or manner. Just so with the painter. He paints in one style, and it is by his one individual style that the expert recognizes him.

I had also discovered among the old masters certain formal ways of doing hands and ears and fingernails, lines and folds of drapery, trees and hills and clouds. The triangular jaw of Botticelli, the elegant hand of Van Dyck, the plastic drapery of Mantegna, the trees and mountains of Perugino, Costa, or Francia, for examples, were too obvious to be overlooked. I was acquiring memories of these earmarks and thought I could perhaps build up from them a little system of expert knowledge all my own, when in the summer of 1890 I happened to meet George Edward Habich.

I had gone up to Cassel from Frankfurt with Captain and Mrs. Mason. We were on a summer *flucht* [flight] and wanted to see again the pictures in the Cassel gallery. Habich owned many of the pictures in that gallery. They were there "on loan" from him. We met him, a very intelligent, middle-aged German, and he took us to his house to tea. There he showed us his drawings and some pictures he had not sent to the gallery. I talked a good deal about his pictures as he brought them out one by one and placed them on a chair before us, talked about where they belonged, aired my knowledge of different schools, called attention to mannerisms and earmarks that belonged to certain painters. Habich heard me patiently, and after I had talked myself to a standstill, he asked:

"Do you know Morelli?"

"Yes, I have heard of him as an authority on Italian painting, but I have never read any of his writings."

"I will give you his books."

And he did.

That was my introduction to Morelli—Morelli who had discovered and recorded the earmarks and mannerisms of the Italian painters some years before I saw Italy. I started to make up for lost time by a close reading and following of Morelli. I checked up on his method and his attributions for several years and with much admiration for his learning and his quick eye. I got a great deal from him and yet finally came to realize that his method was not infallible. It was not a science, as he believed, but just a happy help in connoisseurship. Everyone, except Dr. Bode and the Germans at Munich, accepted it, and, after the quarrel over the attribution of Italian pictures in German galleries had died down, even the Germans acknowledged its truth and force.

It was not until later that I met for the first time Bernard Berenson. The meeting was in the Berlin Gallery. I think he had not been long in Europe, but he was working over the Berlin pictures with the Morellian methods at his fingertips. We went out to lunch and talked Morelli and his attributions. We were both badly bitten by expertism. The fascination of running down an old master in his pictures was greater than any detective hunt of our experience. Since then I have seen Mr. and Mrs. Berenson many times in their Florentine home. They have become the great experts in Italian painting and today know more about it than any others.[4]

So my discoveries of mannerisms and earmarks in Italian painting had for the greater part been discovered before me. Morelli and Berenson have left me only about one thing, and that did not and does not vitally concern Italian painting. I mean the trail of the brush. In Italian painting, the trail, except at Venice, was left by the pencil. The Italians, generally speaking, were draftsmen rather than painters, and, barring Tiepolo, even the Venetians did not understand the manipulation of paint as did Rubens, Rembrandt, and Velásquez. The handling of the brush is the most reliable earmark in latter-day painting, and in determining the authenticity of late Spanish, Dutch, and Flemish pictures it is vital. The copyist cannot imitate it without losing verve, and the restorer cannot replace it when once disturbed. The cleaner can take it off and show thereafter a ruined picture, but no one can put it back again. It is an autographic touch peculiar to each painter and one of the most positive of data at the expert's command.

For more than forty years I have been following this matter of the attribution of pictures, well knowing that it has nothing to do with the picture as a work of art and that the beauty of the picture may be quite apart from name or pedigree; knowing also that most of the false attributions of pictures have come about through the cupidity of dealers and the stupidity of collectors; and that expertism at its best merely returns the picture to the original parent and status. Yet always feeling that the truth of history demanded truthful data, that the pupils should not be robbed of their pictures in the name of the master, that the forger, the fakir, and the reckless restorer should be reckoned with and accounted for. In other words, the record should be clean.

Most of the experts of today are in the employ of dealers or are engaged in certifying pictures that are for sale. My own use of expertism has been almost wholly in affirming or denying the attributions of pictures in public galleries. My series of guidebooks to the European galleries, "New Guides to Old Masters," has much to do with attributions, and my two volumes on the pictures, drawings, and etchings of Rembrandt are entirely devoted to the wrongly attributed work of that master.

Aside from such use, I must confess to a positive joy in the chase as a chase. Nothing in the picture itself is quite so exciting as running down its obscured paternity. A clew that you may pick up in the Hermitage at Leningrad and carry down and apply in the Prado at Madrid—a line, a tone, a color, even a nose, an ear, or a fingernail—is a great deal more subtle than any broken button of Sherlock Holmes. It requires not only a good eye and visual memory but years and years of study and association with pictures. But when at last you arrive, when you can stretch out a forefinger and name the painter with certainty, it is a real triumph.[5]

Chapter 16

Play and Work

Activities in the Eighties and Nineties were not all work. People played then, perhaps not as fast and as furiously as today, because they played with intellectual as well as physical things, but they played. By that I mean that people went to the races, played tennis and football and baseball and polo, rode and canoed and fished and hunted, but they could talk about something else than scores and dances and theaters. They were interested in sport and play, but they did not let it run away with them. Over the teacups and around the dinner tables they discussed every issue of the day, commercial, political, ethical, esthetic. Conversation was upheld by quick wits. People in those decades were still admired for their brains rather than their brawn—or at least the brawn was not such a factor in evidence as at the present day. No, it was not wearisome talk. Often it was highly stimulating, and though one sometimes went to bed with a headache, he occasionally woke up the next morning a wiser man.

I am, of course, thinking of my own immediate circle, but in the early Nineties that circle had become rather wide. It embraced casually, not intimately, a good many sets and groups. It included not only the collegiate and academic, the artistic and literary, but also the commercial, the financial, the political. People overlapped from one set into another and were not content to run on indefinitely in just one groove. Stedman could be both poet and banker, Hay and Lodge were writers as well as statesmen, Cox and Millet wrote, talked, and painted. Out of the West came people of steel, coal, and oil who were mightily interested in music and painting, and the railway men of the country were interested in every phase of human progress.

Everyone at that time was eager for information on almost any subject. The dinner party, which seemed to reach its height in the Eighties, was given to meet Mr. or Mrs. So-and-So, who was here from Europe or the West and was an authority on This or That. You went expecting that the guest would say something about his subject, that there would be discussion, and that perhaps something worthwhile could come out of it. It was an eager age in which I found myself. I was not blind to what was going on before my eyes, but I am afraid I did not appreciate it then as I do now.

Of the many houses to which I was asked at this time, I counted that of
Frank Thomson the most stimulating and, in many ways, the most representative of the general intelligence of the times. Every manner of man,
sooner or later, turned up at the Corkerhill dinner table, asked there as a
matter of social courtesy but rather expected to pay for his dinner by con-
tributing some thought to the evening's entertainment. During the Nineties I spent almost all of my weekends with Thomson and his family. A
locomotive and car 60 was at his command, and the weekend was frequently spent at Graces Quarter near Havre de Grace shooting ducks, or at
Stone Harbor on the Jersey coast fishing, or at the West Island Club fishing
again. At the holidays or on summer vacations, longer runs were made to
Florida or Indiana for quail shooting, or up the New England coast yachting, or out in western Pennsylvania trout fishing. Thomson was the most
expert fisherman I ever met. It was a joy to see him casting for trout
because he did it so easily, so surely, and so effectively. Alas! the trout that
rose to his fly. He was struck before he knew it. His shooting was less
cunning, but he did all things well and could drive a horse as readily as a
locomotive, strike a salmon as easily as a United States senator.

Wherever he went for sport, there were people to be met, some of them
bent on business but others more often on recreation.[1] And these people
came in at the dinner-table talks. For discussion went along with him and
was part of his recreation. He could shoot and fish all day, but the evening
was for some form of entertaining or profitable talk. He was an extremely
good talker, but he could draw out others and bring the shy and the bashful
into the limelight with good results. His tact was as remarkable as his
mental energy.

Thomson asked me one day what American painter could do panels on
either side of the dining-room chimney at Corkerhill—do them so they
would be in harmony with the Monets, Sisleys, and Besnards already in the
room. I suggested Twachtman. He agreed. Would I see Twachtman, ask him
to come over, see the room, and do the panels? I did so. I told Twachtman
what was wanted, that we could go over to Corkerhill and see the room,
that he could paint what he pleased and name his own price. Twachtman
was quite overcome. He said it was the first commission he had ever
received, and he hoped to God he could fulfill. I noticed as he spoke that
his eyes filled with tears.

He and Weir went with me to Corkerhill, and we spent the night there.
They were delighted with Thomson and the table talk, and Twachtman was
enthusiastic over his commission. That summer he went to the Yellowstone
Park and made many pictures of the blue pools in the park. I saw them later

at his house up in Westchester near Greenwich, Connecticut, but Twacht-man did not think any of them quite right for the Corkerhill dining room. He hesitated, could not decide on his subject, listened to Weir's advice, and finally sent two pictures, a flower piece and a landscape that were inadequate. He admitted that he had failed to rise to the occasion.[2]

Mr. Thomson also asked me to name a man to do his portrait for the house and also for the office of the board of directors of the Pennsylvania Railroad. I suggested Wilton Lockwood, and I finally asked Lockwood to undertake the portrait at his own convenience and terms. He accepted, painted the portrait, rubbed it out, did it over again, but never completed it, never presented it, and at last gave it up. He was not satisfied with it.

At a later time, Stephen B. Elkins, Secretary of War [1891–1893], asked me to name a painter to do his portrait for the War Department at Washington. I named Alfred Q. Collins, a very able and well-known painter who had recently done a fine knee-piece portrait[3] of Dr. Rainsford, and I thought Collins would perhaps paint Elkins in a similar style. He accepted the commission, and Elkins sat for three or four different portraits, each one in succession being rubbed out because not satisfactory. Collins finally gave it up, and Elkins afterward told me that he had slaved over the portrait but could not do it, though Elkins thought the likeness very good and would have been content with it.

I have brought these three incidents together, not for reproach but for praise. Twachtman, Lockwood, and Collins were perhaps overly conscientious about their work. But there speaks the true artist. His grasp is never equal to his reach, he never realizes what he sees in his mind's eye, and he is never satisfied. These three were exceptionally sensitive, they were positively unhappy about their work, and it is not too much to say that a noble discontent was largely responsible for the untimely passing of all three of them.

In the Eighties and Nineties there were a number of houses in New York where literary and artistic people gathered for tea or dinner or evening music. None of the hostesses thought of setting up a salon, and yet there was a salon effect at many of the afternoon teas when quiet, serious talk was indulged in by, say, eight or ten people. There never was anything set or formal about these talks, and no one dreamt for a moment of making an impression or creating literary atmosphere or history. It was all good-natured social intercourse solely for the pleasure of it. And each house had its peculiar group of habitués, though all the groups were known to each other and often met on common ground. I mean by that merely that you met a slightly different set at the Gilders from those of the Huttons. At

Mrs. Schuyler Van Rensselaer's afternoon teas you might meet people from Boston and at the Stedmans or Howellses people from England or Italy or almost anywhere.

I knew Stedman very well and Howells slightly, but I cannot remember the insides of their houses. There were many people and places I knew casually but few that I knew intimately. I was always a little shy about committing myself to any one set but very well disposed to have a look-in at any open door.

However, I did know the Huttons intimately and saw a great deal of them during some twenty years or more. Their house on 34th Street was open to everyone, and Laurence was always bringing home someone from the club. He was emphatically a club man and a very popular one at that. Everyone liked him, and, as someone said of him, "He had a genius for friendships." He had many friends, and I was one of them, one whom he frequently took home to dinner from the Players or the Century. Often I was the only guest, but oftener there were others. Several times Edwin Booth was there, and (with Mrs. Hutton) we sat long over the table, talking commonplaces perhaps but in a quiet, comfortable way. None of us wanted to move or say "good night." Booth was one of those people you liked to have near you, though he said little. Hutton, too, was good company whether he joined in the talk or not. Mrs. Hutton and I were the fidgety ones, but even we were calmed down by the quiet presence of the others.

Then there were evenings when Booth would not come, nights when the house was thrown open to all the literary and artistic people in the town, and there was a crush. In the late Eighties, when women wore more clothes and ribbons than today, moving about in a crowded drawing room was difficult, and one often got stuck in a pocket with some sentimental furbelow and perhaps had a bad quarter of an hour. The large reception was not more enjoyable then than now. It has always been an occasion for shouting "hello" at people you see once in ten years and are secretly glad you see no oftener.

Mrs. Hutton was fond of attractive-looking young people and often matched Laurence's group of well-known men with a galaxy of fair ladies. Large dinners of fifteen or twenty were made up in that way, and not infrequently a John Drew or a Dana Gibson would find himself sitting beside some girl of the smart set who had been longing to meet him for years. After dinner there was sometimes a rush for the theater or opera but more often an adjournment to the drawing room where there was music or storytelling.

I remember one night when Henry Irving and Miss Terry were the guests of honor, and many people of note came in to meet them. Everyone was in a pleasant humor after the toasts in champagne, and in the drawing room Irving told several good stories at some length. But Mark Twain, with his head in his hands, sitting on a low stool in front of the fire and talking as though repeating his story to himself, quite beat out the brilliant actor. It was, however, reserved for Kate Douglas Wiggin to go beyond both of them with a made-up adventure in a Bowery restaurant. She was excellent in spite of much trepidation. I happened to be seated beside her and could feel her tremble, and several times she had a "catch in the throat" from nervous excitement, but she carried it off to great applause. A very bright and attractive woman was Mrs. Wiggin.[4]

When hot weather came, many of those who gathered at the Huttons went to Onteora, a club in the Catskills that had been started by Mrs. Candace Wheeler and the Thurbers. Many literary and artistic folk had cottages there or were guests at the Bear and Fox Inn. In the late Eighties and early Nineties, Mark Twain, Brander Matthews, Ruth McEnery Stuart, Mary Mapes Dodge, Maude Adams, the John W. Alexanders, the Carroll Beckwiths, the Ripley Hitchcocks, and many others were guests there. I was a guest of the Williamsons and the Huttons and went along with the social life of the place. Onteora was very attractive in those early days. It is so at the present time. After an absence of many years, I have gone back to it and now pass my summers there in a small cottage with Professor and Mrs. Harry L. Parr and have for neighbors Hamlin Garland on my right and Frank Chapman at my left. Book and painter people still cling to the place, though Mark and Brander and Laurence have passed on.[5]

Chapter 17

More Books

At Onteora I cut out a plan for a series of textbooks on the history of art for use in schools and colleges. I felt the need of some outline history, some elaborated syllabus, that the student could study in connection with lectures by the professor. It should indicate the relative importance of artists and art movements by the amount of space given, it should have critical value, and above all it should have continuity, showing the derivative, as well as the indigenous, quality of art. That it should be suitable for classroom work I determined that the different writers should all be teachers— teachers in the subject of which they were to write. And the title of the series was "College Histories of Art."

I asked Professor A. D. F. Hamlin of Columbia to do the volume on architecture, Professors Allen Marquand and Arthur Frothingham of Princeton to do the sculpture, and I undertook the volume on painting. Brander Matthews came in for consultation, and on his suggestion I took the series to Longman, Green & Co. They at once undertook the publication. The success of the series was immediate, and after thirty-five years still continues. My own volume [*A Text-Book on the History of Painting*, 1894], dealing with the most popular of the arts, had the widest sale, many editions and many thousands of copies having been sold. The sales of the other volumes were only a little less than mine. The whole series from the publisher's, writers', and teachers' standpoints was so satisfactory and put so much conceit in me that I at once planned another volume along similar lines.[1]

The new volume was a book of painters' criticism. It came to me by way of the president of the Century Company, who wanted me to put in book form some beautiful wood engravings (a number by Timothy Cole) of French pictures that appeared in the *Century Magazine*. As planned, the book took the title of *Modern French Masters: A Series of Biographical and Critical Reviews by American Artists* [1896]. So far as possible, I had each master reviewed by one of his pupils or at least by one of his admirers. For example: Carroll Beckwith wrote about his master, Carolus Duran, E. H. Blashfield about Bonnat, G. P. A. Healy about Couture, Will H. Low about Gérôme. The other artists who wrote chapters were Kenyon Cox (Puvis de Chavannes and Paul Baudry), H. W. Watrous (Meissonier), Theodore Robinson (Corot and Claude Monet), W. A. Coffin (Rousseau and Dagnan-Bouveret), Arthur Hoeber (Díaz), W. H. Howe (Troyon), D. W. Tryon (Daubigny), Wyatt Eaton (J. F. Millet), Samuel Isham (Courbet), Alden Weir (Bastien Lepage). There were twenty French masters treated in as many articles by American painters. And the articles were carefully written. The contention had been for many years that only a painter was entitled to talk about pictures and that art critics were a lot of silly-billies who might better be employed on other themes. Here was a chance for the artists to show what they could do. And here was criticism from the artist's point of view—the real thing. I think that every one of the contributors to that volume felt as though he were on trial and had to do his best.

The letters that came to me during the progress of the work were many. Some of them were amusing, some almost pathetic, because the painters had to struggle with writing, a new medium. One from Kenyon Cox I may quote, not for any difficulty with writing, but because of his struggle with himself to do a satisfactory piece of work:

New York
April 19, '96

Dear Van Dyke:

Here is the Baudry article, well on time. I made it about 4,500 words. I couldn't do it shorter and it seems a little brief and bald now to me, though I have tried to jam everything I had to say in the space. Of course, I shall want proofs as I daresay the style would be improved by revision when I see it in print. I don't know how good it is but it must serve.

You have not yet told me what to do about the photos of drawings from the (Art Students) League nor what was settled about portraits. There is one of Guillaume the sculptor that would serve—a late one—which is published by Goupil. The drawings are waiting for word from you and the League has the Guillaume also, if you can't get anything acceptable elsewhere.

Baudry is a harder man to write about than Puvis and I doubt if I have made so much of him. His work is thoroughly good and there is nothing to explain about it. However, I have done my best and shall be glad to know what you think about it. I am usually in a funk about any piece of writing I have just finished. It always seems so ludicrously obvious as not to be worth saying.

Yours very sincerely,
Kenyon Cox

Anyone who has done much writing will quite understand and agree with the last two sentences of the Cox letter. The "funk" over work recently done is common experience. But almost all of the writers in the *Modern French Masters* book were afraid of the work from the start. D. W. Tryon, in writing about his Daubigny article, thought: "It is not up to concert pitch. My slight practice in writing makes it difficult for me to express myself as well as I could wish. I have given it much thought and rewritten it several times and while still conscious of many parts which I feel to be weak I cannot say them any better."

Alden Weir came forward with: "I will gladly do my best but unless you take a hand in it I fear the result. I have a few notes in the country which I will have to gather in. I have the original (Bastien Lepage) sketch for the Joan (of Arc) in charcoal."

He sent in the article on Bastien with this note: "I send you the article which I have been cutting down instead of adding to. I feel it quite concise but do not know if you will care for it. I had Mrs. Weir write it so you could read it. Let me hear what you think of it."

I had asked Swain Gifford to do the article on Díaz, but he begged off and would have none of it, writing that he was afraid to trust himself in print.

Well, the book was beautifully set up and printed by DeVinne and was duly published with a blare of trumpets. But the walls of Jericho did not fall down. It was the book that fell down. It almost fell flat. Neither the reviewers nor the public saw anything unique about it. It was the first book of art criticism by artists in America, or for that matter anywhere else, but no one seemed to know or to care about that, though I had emphasized the fact in my introduction. Perhaps it was not so unique in its point of view as I had fancied. And maybe Kenyon Cox was right in saying to me one day at the Players that he had read the book and that after all it didn't seem different from any other book of art criticism.

I was disappointed that the book was not taken more seriously and understandingly, but I did not abandon hope as an editor. Nor did I entertain any silly notions about editorial work being merely hack work and lacking in originality. It takes quite as much brains (and infinitely more patience) to arrange other people's thoughts as to conjure up thoughts of your own. Young painters sometimes have a way of speaking about portrait painting as being merely potboiling work, apparently unconscious of the fact that the portraits of Titian, Velásquez, and Rembrandt are the great masterpieces of art. I could not think of the Boswells, the Skeats, and the Leslie Stephenses in such exalted terms, but they were high enough in the empyrean for my emulation.

So a few years later I started still another series of books with the Macmillan Company, "A History of American Art." This was ambitious. I planned the gathering up of the materials for the history of all the arts in America and, again, the texts and the criticisms to be written in each volume by a professional practicing in the art of which he should write. I asked Lorado Taft, the sculptor, to do the volume on American sculpture, Samuel Isham, the painter, to do the American painting, Louis Elson, a musician and musical critic of Boston, to do the American music, Joseph Pennell, the illustrator, to do the American illustration and engraving, Clarence Blackall, the architect, to do the American architecture. They all accepted, but Pennell died before his volume was finished and Blackall begged off because of too much professional work. I asked no less than half a dozen architects to do the architecture. They all accepted and signed contracts, and then one by one they failed me. They could not write, or had not time, or fell ill. So out of the large planning there issued only the volumes on music, sculpture, and painting. Even with these there was some friction but never any bad feeling. Isham declared good-naturedly that I had bullied him, Taft had heart failure over my cutting out some of his narrative, and Elson groaned in spirit and almost gave up the ghost over my drastic rearrangement of his sentences.

But the books came out, handsomely printed and illustrated, and were very well received. Out of much travail there came forth something permanent. Isham had written the first comprehensive history of American painting and Taft had done the same for American sculpture. The volumes have not yet been superseded but are continuing on in new editions.[2] No history of American art will be written hereafter without reference to them. They contain original materials that never can be ignored. So with all the worry, the work, and disappointment of an unfulfilled plan, there was, nevertheless, the satisfaction of something valuable having been produced.

But much work, and still more worry, about books and lectures, college and library, study in Europe and society everywhere were beginning to wear upon me. I fell into ill health, lost flesh and spirits, and began to see the sky as a pestilential congregation of vapors. There was too much art and literature, too much civilization, too much talk and not enough fresh air. I began thinking of the sunlight and the air on the Montana uplands, wondering if they were still to be found there, if my buffalo land was still intact. Would it not be a good plan to go back there for a summer outing? Would it not perhaps be the very thing needed for my exhausted condition? I decided that it would.[3]

Chapter 18

Montana

In June of 1898, I started for Colorado with Theodore Strong, a cousin and my junior by half a dozen years, who had never been west of Philadelphia.[1] He was naturally enthusiastic about the trip, and when we got up on the plains of western Nebraska and the unbroken land came into view, I, too, began to pick up an interest. A veil seemed to let down behind me, shutting out the East. I was back to the open country of my boyhood, but alas! that country had lost its charm of wildness. Cattle were running on the ranges where once were buffalo and antelope. Cabins of sod and of cottonwood logs were scattered here and there, cowboys in "chaps" and big hats came down to see the train at the tank-town stations. It was the West, the woolly West, but not the wild West.[2]

We went on to Colorado and then turned northeast to the Black Hills. At Deadwood I bought half a dozen horses, got an old wagon, a driving team, and a cook-driver; bought blankets, saddles, provender, and guns. Then we started across country for the Yellowstone Park.[3] I had planned a riding trip in which the wagon and the cook should be merely the center of gravity at nightfall. But the cousin had never done any riding, and the first day left him so stiff and unhappy that he forthwith abandoned the saddle for a seat beside the cook in the wagon. After that, I had to ride alone, going off each morning in a half circle from the line of travel about twenty miles and coming in to join the wagon in the later afternoon.

There was no road or trail. We went across open country and saw no one for the first week. It was not until we reached the Powder River [in Montana] that any sign of humanity appeared. We ate out of a frying pan, slept on the ground, and fought off mosquitoes, rain, and rattlesnakes as they happened. I enjoyed it, but the cousin was hardly rapturous over the great open spaces. After the first week, he asked if I knew where we were on the map, to which I answered that I did in a general way.

"Why?"

Well, he didn't like the idea of being lost out there.

I assured him there was no danger, as we were following the run of the land by sun and riverbeds and divides. We had crossed the Little Missouri and Box Elder and could not help but strike the Powder River in a few days. Besides, we had enough provender in the wagon to last us six weeks, and it made no difference whether we were lost or found. But he had not so much faith in my guiding as I thought myself entitled to, and he was uneasy until we came to the Powder and finally to the 70L [⌐○⌐] Ranch. We had passed through a country that had reverted to wilderness and had seen bands of antelope, white-tailed deer in the willows of the river bottoms, plenty of coyotes to serenade us as we slept, and occasionally at night an old gray wolf, or a bear, prowling and snuffing about the grub wagon. But again I fear that the cousin did not enjoy it as much as I did.

We went across the Powder, the Mizpah, Pumpkin Creek, and the Tongue, swimming the rivers as we came to them, and reaching up into the Cheyenne Indian Reservation. It was still unbroken land, no roads and practically no trails. We drove and rode across rough country, getting up and down hills, cutbanks, and riverbeds, Heaven only knows how, but succeeding. The horses did not bother us, though one of them was an "outlaw" that fought everyone and had to be double hoppled and picketed every night lest he lead off the other horses on the back trail. The bothersome thing was the wagon. It was more convenient than a pack train and saved an immense amount of packing and diamond-hitching, but it was a new problem at every steep descent. We let it down into creek beds by trailing a tree (top foremost) behind it. We dragged it up the opposite bank with ropes and horses. We floated it across rivers and lifted it out of quicksands with an improvised Spanish windlass.[4] But we went on. Occasionally, we met two or three Cheyennes wandering off the reservation who came into camp out of space and always about the time we were getting a meal. Doubtless, they caught sight of the smoke from our camp fire. They had excellent appetites and sat in around the frying pan as long as anything eatable was in sight. They amused the cousin but worried me, for I feared a night raid on our horses. Night after night I slept with one eye open and both ears set for sounds from that horse bunch. One night I heard voices and went out to explore them, rifle on my arm; but it was merely two Indians riding through the night and talking to each other to keep the devils away. They passed near me without seeing me or our horses. A shot would have sent them scampering.[5]

We rose to higher land in the Rosebud Mountains, where from the lofty peaks I could see to the south a hundred miles away the faint outline of the Big Horn Mountains. The air was thin and clear, the sun was almost white, the sky was like cobalt. Piñons grew on the mountainsides, sego lilies in the grass, wild columbines by the brookside. Occasionally from some swale, two or three deer would plunge out with a bump and a smash, but there was little game just here. The Indians had seen to that. The reservations were almost deserted of wildlife, but it was still a wonderful land lying there so still in that high mountain air. I was riding great half circles morning and afternoon, using up two horses a day, getting far too much exercise and not enough food and rest; but the wonderful air was buoying me up, and the love of the wilderness was leading me on.

We struck north and followed the Little Big Horn up to the Custer Battlefield. Since I had first been through that country,[6] there had been a great fight on the Little Big Horn, and the Sioux had surrounded and shot up the Custer command to a man [1876]. The battlefield was there with its monuments bleaching in the sun. There was no ambush in the common meaning of the word. Custer had been caught, or chose to make a stand, on a round-topped hill. Five thousand Sioux rode around the hill like a whirl-wind, firing as they rode, until there was not a white man left standing. Sitting Bull may have shown great generalship in this; the Sioux have always insisted that he did. I do not know. But it seemed that Custer was merely overwhelmed by vastly superior numbers.

We swam the Big Horn, turned west to the Crow Indian reservation, and stopped at the agency. Some of our horses were much the worse for wear and had to be left there. About the only horse remaining in our outfit that was still sound was the "outlaw." At the agency the first night, he got caught in a wire fence, thrashed about and got tangled up in it, and when we found him the next morning, down on his back under the fence, there was scarcely an inch of him that had not been raked and gashed by that barbed wire. We cut him loose, fried a panful of bacon fat, and coated him with that. The incident never dimmed the glitter in his eyes, never fazed his spirit in the least. In spite of knocks and gashes and beatings-up, he pulled the whole outfit through to the end, and when I finally turned him loose, to be thereafter a free-footed wild horse if he would, he sailed out of camp, head up and tail up, with no whit of energy or wickedness abated. He certainly was a devil.[7]

At the agency we took on half a dozen new horses. They were Indian horses, costing only about five dollars a head, but dear even at that price. They were merely half wild cayuses, brutally broken to bit and rope, but always vicious, disposed to buck at every mounting, and ever watching a chance to roll over in swimming a river or fall backwards upon you with any little pull on the bit. I had to watch them continually while riding and lie awake at night lest they pull their picket pins and make off on the back trail. But still we went on, the "outlaw" doing most of the pulling and I most of the fretting and storming. It was not the serene, carefree trip in the open that I had planned.

The Crows let us pass through their reservation without molestation, and day by day we rode on, crossing Clarke's Fork, the Big and Little Rosebud, the Stillwater, and rising again toward high land as we pushed west. Then we turned south, heading for Gardiner, Montana, the entrance to the Yellowstone National Park. In entering the park we had to give up our rifles, but no objection was made to our taking in our wild band of horses. We moved around the park for ten days, catching heavy, stupid trout, bathing in blue pools of hot water, and "doing" the geysers as we moved. It was not very interesting, or perhaps I was losing my interest, or maybe I was ill. At any rate, I was shortly thereafter very glad to sell our horses and outfit (all except the outlaw, who was freed) and with my cousin creep into a comfortable Pullman on the Northern Pacific and start for New York. I noticed that the cousin took kindly to the softness of the Pullman seat. It was evidently an improvement on the hard board seat he had occupied for some hundreds of miles.

I had not profited physically by the Montana trip because I had ridden too hard and fretted too much. So I came back East and went to the Winter Harbor home of my friend, John G. Moore. There I met Captain Arthur Lee (now Lord Lee of Fareham), who had contracted fever in the Spanish-American War [1898] and, like me, was in need of rest. So we rested with Moore. Lee got better, fell in love with the daughter of the house, Miss Ruth Moore, and shortly thereafter married her. But I was restless and got nothing out of Winter Harbor but a good time. I could not rest.

Back in my library, I resumed my work, but it was taken up halfheartedly. Illness, even though not of major importance, is a great handicap to any form of human endeavor. One cannot see things in true proportions or say things with the necessary restraint. I dawdled with pencil in hand, doing several short articles, but they were lacking in energy. I had written a fairly good introduction for Rossiter Johnson's Edition of Cellini's *Memoirs* and also an essay on Ruskin for Charles Dudley Warner's *Library of the World's Best Literature*.[8] Warner had sent me this handsome note, characteristic of him in its generosity of praise:

> New York   Oct. 23, 1896
>
> My dear Mr. Van Dyke:
>   Your paper on Ruskin is excellent, one of the very best we have from native or foreign writers, so temperate and discriminating, so just. You must allow me to say that it pleases me exceedingly.
>
>   Yours Sincerely
>   Charles Dudley Warner
> The whole is prepared for the press in tip-top shape. I thank you.

Well, why could I not go on and do more things like the Ruskin, since Warner thought it a good piece of work? But I couldn't. I had not lost my grip, but I was perhaps unduly concerned lest I should lose my breath. I could not even grow enthusiastic over the Spanish war, which had broken out during my absence in Montana. It seemed to me an unnecessary, rough handling of a weak old cripple. For saying words to that effect, I got into bad odour with the highly patriotic press, in company with Charles Eliot Norton and others. But it was a very small tempest in a teapot. Norton wrote me that:

> The barkings of Tray, Blanche, and Sweetheart and the rest have not troubled me. At least in any personal respect they have not troubled me, but I have been sorry for them as an expression of a widespread and dangerous disposition to suppress free thought and speech. I believe with you that there is a great body of sober people who think as you and I do concerning the war and its results. But I fear that we are to be overborne.

We were.

But after the mob and the yellow press had yelled themselves black in the face, the country settled down to the conviction that the "victory" was hardly a thing to be proud of.[9]

When the cold of February came on, I decided that I would once more go back to the wild, or at least go to California for an indefinite stay. To clear the way, I wrote out many resignations. I resigned from the Players and the Union League Club but still retained the Authors, the University, and the Century, resigned from college and library, though these resignations were never accepted, resigned from boards, committees, newspapers, and magazines. I wanted to be foot-free for a long run.[10] How long, I did not then know or realize, but when finally I came back and entered my own house, my old housekeeper told me I had been gone two years and four months. I had not planned so long an absence but so it turned out.

Chapter 19

The Desert

I went West[1] with my law-school classmate, Howard Ford, and both of us had been well cared for as regards transportation and letters to railway people by my ever thoughtful friend, Frank Thomson.[2] It was the last I was to see of him, for he died [1899] while I was in the desert. I thought then I should never look upon his like again. And I never have.

In California I immediately joined my brother [Theodore Strong Van Dyke], who was then living in Los Angeles. The city was not much of a city in 1898, though even then afflicted with a boom and growing rapidly. It did not impress me in any way, and in a few days I went out toward the Cahuenga Pass so as to be nearer to the foothills and the wild of the Santa Monica Mountains. An aged woman, with a gift for mothering, took me into her house and supplied me with board and lodging. The place even then was called Hollywood, but there were only a few houses, and the present city of the movies was not dreamt of. Returning there twenty-five years after, I could not recognize one single thing I had known in 1898, so completely changed was the whole face of the land. The movie town had completely covered the region where I shot quail and watched jackrabbits at play.[3]

From the brother I got some buckskin of his own shooting and tanning and immediately made some moccasins after the Sioux pattern, which I had not forgotten. With those on my feet and lightly clad, I began tramping the bare hills and mountains with an eager eye on the birds and animals, the distant Pacific with its great spread of blue, and the light, air, trees, and flowers of the semi-desert valley. But Hollywood soon proved too close to civilization for me, not wild enough, and as spring came on I went up to Hemet at the foot of San Jacinto Mountain. An irrigation district had been started there by some San Francisco capitalists. They had built a pretty little hotel and tried to start a town. The town did not grow, and the hotel did not pay, but while it lasted I was glad enough to stop at it. The district lay in a valley, and the mountains and foothills about it were practically unexplored. The chaparral was dense, and several times I got so well tangled up in it that I had doubts about my ever getting out.

With a fox terrier that I picked up at the hotel, I tramped the Hemet region, scaled all the mountains, thrashed through all the chaparral, and, having exhausted its novelty, began looking about for new fields. Even Hemet was not wild enough for me. I had met one grizzly in the chaparral and had slipped away from him without trouble. I had a very reliable .30-.30 rifle in my hands and was then a good shot, but I did not care to beard Old Ephraim in his chaparral, where he was perfectly at home and I was so much like a fly in a web. I let him alone. I didn't shoot at the deer or the coyotes and sometimes let the rattlesnakes go unscotched, but the gray wolves heard from me several times to their undoing.[4] Still, even that region was too close to civilization. I could hear the distant puff and whistle of a locomotive from the mountaintops, and the hotel brought me back at evening to the daily newspaper and people from the everyday world.

Not far away was the San Gorgonio Pass leading out to the Colorado Desert—the desert that everyone talked about but very few had ever traveled. Tales came in from every quarter about its heat, its drifting sand, its dust storms; about its few springs, and those poisoned by copper, its lost mines and miners, its human skeletons and bleached bones of horses found in the sand; about perils of emigrants, and even Indians, who had perished in the waste coming over from Yuma. It was a place to be avoided. Everyone who went in there eventually got "caught up with." At least that was the warning that came to me when I talked of exploring the region. I would never come out, either alive or dead.[5]

But I was just ill enough not to care much about perils and morbid enough to prefer dying in the sand alone to passing out in a hotel with a room maid weeping at the foot of the bed. I laughed at all the tales and set to work preparing a light outfit for desert travel. This consisted of my .30-.30 rifle for large game and a Chicopee .22 caliber pistol for small game, a camping kit of light blankets, hatchet, small shovel, a few pans and tin cups, a gallon of water in a canvas bottle, and several sacks of condensed food. I made my own condensation by grinding together parched corn, beans, coffee, chocolate, and dried venison. I packed this closely in shot sacks. This was my mainstay in case of disaster. It would last me for weeks without another item of any sort, except water. But, in addition, I took along with me some tablets of chocolate, some flour and bacon, salt, tea, and a small bottle of saccharine. My whole outfit to last me for weeks weighed less than fifty pounds.[6]

I bought a desert-bred horse, half Indian pony, and he and the fox terrier were my chief anxieties. The horse could go for two days without water, but he liked it every day if he could get it, and he could live on the dry grass of the desert valleys, but he preferred the grazing and the browsing high up on the mountainsides. He was something of a nuisance but also a convenience, and in case of emergency, a means of safety. I could ride him fifty miles a day for two or three days and thus get out of the desert quickly if I had to do so. He was tough, used to heat, and knew how to pick his own living, but for the first week I had to hopple him and watch him closely for fear he would take his backtrack and leave me.

The dog was a bravo. He would fight anything except a rattlesnake, live contentedly on a rabbit a day, and stand heat and thirst without much whining. After eight in the morning, the desert sand burned his feet, and he would finally halt under a creosote bush or cactus and howl his ultimatum, to the effect that he would go no farther. I would then lift him on the horse, and he rode behind me, crosswise of the horse and leaning his back against mine. We were an odd combination, but after the first week we pulled together like Kipling's "Ship That Found Herself."

I was astonished to find how quickly both dog and horse came to know what was expected of them and how understandingly each did his part. Being alone, I talked to them a great deal, until finally I came to think they really comprehended most of what I said. After a week, the horse forgot all about his backtrack, and I could turn him loose with only a picket rope trailing. He wandered a bit in search of food but finally got into the habit of coming back to camp once or twice in the night to see if I and the dog were still there. I could hear him coming in with a stumbling step, sniffing and snorting a bit to find out just where we were stretched out. The dog lying on the blankets at my feet would growl at the interruption. He liked the horse but no doubt occasionally thought him a fool and treated him accordingly. In the morning I sent the dog out to bring in the horse, and again I was astonished at the way he would trail that horse, turn him around by biting his heels, and start him toward the camp. It was no part of his heritage or training to herd horses, but he could do it if necessary.

But both animals required more water than I did. After a few days, I had trained myself to take water only at night and morning and not too much of it then. I chewed creosote leaves, or a bit of stick, and fought off thirst that way. But the animals required water, and that was always my chief quest. I was able to locate two water holes—mere drips at the foot of the San Bernardino Mountains—before I had fairly started into the desert. One of these was large enough for my purpose. I camped down there and from that base immediately began scouting for another drip farther on. That was my plan of procedure. I never left one water hole until I found another. If after going twenty miles I found nothing, I turned back. Once or twice I ran pretty dry (it was a year of fierce drought) and had to slash into a bisnaga or saguaro to get at the wet pulp, but, while that sustained me, the dog and the horse would scarcely touch it.[7]

After a week or so on the desert, I grew rather cunning about finding water. The first thing I noticed about a little, open drip of water at the foot of the mountains was the quantity of desert doves that would gather there. They were the only desert birds that would drink at all. In traveling, they would pass over me very often, flying in pairs, and by following the flight of several pairs, I would get a general direction for water. This, as I followed the flight, would lead gradually to the drip itself. More than once I chanced upon a desert spring by following the flight of doves.[8]

Then, as I led the horse up into the mountains every night to find grass or bushes for him to browse upon, I began to notice where sparse vegetation was growing and to reason out the existence there of underground water. In the winter there is considerable rainfall on the mountaintops, rain that never reaches down into the hot valleys. This high rain would run down the mountainsides, cutting stream beds that would perhaps run dry in a few hours. But under ledges of overhanging rock, where the fall of the stream would wear potholes in the rock, there would be catches of water in the basins. This would not be visible because of the accumulated sand and gravel under which the water was hidden. I had to dig several feet for it.

I was quite pleased with my cunning in finding water in drips and potholes under dry waterfalls. And the dog and horse grew cunning about it, too. When I began digging in the gravel, they knew at once that I was after water and would crowd forward with paw and hoof, pushing the gravel into the hole until I had to drive them away with the shovel. They were thirsty and could not disguise the fact. Sometimes I would find several barrels of water lying under the gravel and sometimes not a drop—a crack in the basin having let it all out. Occasionally, I found particles of gold at the bottom (seen through a microscope), but that did not greatly interest me. I was not seeking gold.

The night camp was usually made up in the mountains because of feed, water, and coolness as compared with the valley. Wherever I could find a small mesquite or madroña tree to hang up my camp supplies out of the way of rats, coyotes, and the like, there I stretched my blankets and slept. Nothing ever disturbed me. I daresay the wolves and coyotes and perhaps an occasional bear smelled me over from a distance, but nothing came very close. The dog kept watch. One night the horse came plunging into camp with three gray wolves behind him. I heard him coming and knew there was good cause for his rapid pace. I caught up my rifle and surprised the wolves by crippling one of them. They turned off swiftly and ran down into the valley. But that was the only adventure of importance. The dog some nights would growl and grumble to himself for hours as though there were some enemy in the offing whose evil smell came faintly on the breeze, but we were not molested. The animals had more fear of us than we of them.[9]

Sometimes I would stay a week beside a good water pocket, exploring the country in half circles out from the camp. At other times I went afoot with the dog, leaving the horse picketed; but oftener the three of us went together, with the camp plunder cached in a mesquite out of reach of coyotes. When moving to a new site, we always started before daylight and stopped by nine o'clock. Travel in the heat of the day was unnecessary and hot work. We traveled easily down the San Bernardino Range and out toward the Colorado River near the Mexican border. There I met a few Yuma Indians living along the river. We "howed," and I talked a good deal of sign language about water to the east of the river. After some miles of river surveying, I found a place where we could cross with a little swimming. I made a raft of reeds and driftwood and took all my supplies over on that and then swam back for the horse. The river was very low, but I would not risk my supplies on the horse's back.

The route then lay down toward the mouth of the river and then east along the Arizona boundary line. I had no definite line of travel in mind. I was not an exploring expedition, was making no map, and keeping no journal. I had no thought at first of even writing about the trip. In short, I was just drifting with the wind. But even drifting in southwestern Arizona I found rather difficult. The hills held mighty little water, and the desert valleys stretched out into enormous wastes. More than once I was minded to turn north and make a run for the Southern Pacific Railroad. But we worried on a little farther with short rations of food and water, picking up rabbits and quail and slashing into cactuses for wet pulp. Even the dog finally tackled the astringent pulp, and the horse ate joints of cholla cactus after I had beaten off the spines. But the region was too dry, and in less than a week after leaving the river, I made a push north for the railway. We got there pretty well exhausted, and after following along it for I know not how many miles, we found a siding with some tank cars upon it. We tapped the tanks and camped in the shade of the cars for twenty-four hours. Then we moved on along the line to Casa Grande and Tucson.

At Tucson I rested and restocked.[10] In a week I had gone south to Baboquivari,[11] meeting some Papago [Tohono O'Odham] Indians and some miners on the way. After passing over the [United States–Mexican] border into Sonora, I ran on for weeks without seeing a soul. This was because I traveled southwest, going toward Tiburon Island, a then almost unknown region. I found water and feed, and there were antelope, with much small game, everywhere. So the outfit did not suffer, but I began to weary of the sun, the hot sky, and the lone region. I was studying every phase of the desert, and during the heat of the day, when I could get in the shadow of a rock wall, I was writing some rambling impressions. But I was ill and alone, and the whole outlook was dreary.[12]

If asked why I went in there, I could answer because I was ill, and perhaps some animal instinct urged me to leave the herd and go off by myself. If asked why I went alone, the answer would be, again, because I was ill and wanted to be alone, or perhaps it would be truer to say that I could find no one to go with me. But the course I was taking was not helping me back to health. I was exhausting my strength by unnecessary exertion.

Still I pushed on down toward Tiburon Island and then turned to the east to strike the Sonora Railway. I ran into several Mexican ranches just before coming out on the railway, stopped and recuperated, got my direction, and then went on. Near Hermosillo I left the horse and outfit on a ranch and, taking the dog, went down by the railway to Guaymas. I spent the winter in that little town by the sea with its fine harbor and its desert background. All winter I came and went in that desert region and up in the Yaqui Indian country. I was gaining much knowledge of desert climate, geology, botany, zoology; but it was a rather lonesome study. At first it was a relief to be alone, to be out of sight and sound of civilization, to be able to stop and think, to strike a balance of values and try to find out the real worth of things human. But there came a time when the instinct to get back into the herd asserted itself. I never tired of the beauty of the desert. Its fiery dawns and orange sunsets and opalescent air, with the grim grandeur of its bare mountains, never palled. But I began to long for the sight of familiar faces and the sound of friendly voices. Still, I kept on alone. There seemed no alternative.[13]

Chapter 20

Mexico

In the spring [of 1900], I left Guaymas, left the horse and outfit on the Mexican ranch near Hermosillo for anyone who cared to annex them, and went up to Tucson. Thence to the Grand Canyon for a week or more and over to the Colorado River at the Needles. I made up a smaller outfit, one that I could pack on my back when necessary, and with the dog started along the line of the Santa Fe Railway. I held by the line for its tank stations and water but began making great half circles to the north and south in walking trips. Only the dog went with me. We were in the Mojave desert [of Southern California] and (with side trips up into Death Valley and elsewhere) spent several months there.

The Mojave showed a slightly different face and a somewhat different vegetation from the Colorado. But in light, air, and color the two deserts were practically one. A number of extinct volcanoes, many petrified and cracked lava flows, with desert floors packed with small stones like a mosaic pavement, offered some study. I had been studying the breakdown and pushout of mountains into valleys and plains for many weeks. And I had been writing about that and a number of other things as they came up in the desert. The writing was done under difficulties of heat, wind, dust— done with my back against a rock in a double sense. I was still far from well and suffered greatly from depression. To write cheerfully under the circumstances was not easy.

But the book (*The Desert*, 1901) that finally emerged from these circumstances cheerfully enough was well reviewed, and proved a success. It sold edition after edition and is still (1930) selling.[1] Readers and reviewers told me it was my best work, was "a prose poem," and praised it for its "style." If they had in mind Buffon's definition that style is "the order and movement" of one's sentences, then I suppose I paid some attention to its style; but I take it they meant "fine writing" and an occasional purple patch. What really was of value in the book was the material which I had gathered firsthand. I knew my subject. When one has that, it is not necessary to bother about style. The book tells itself and because of its peculiar knowledge dictates its own style.[2]

In late summer I went up through the San Joaquin Valley to Oregon.

From Grants Pass I went into the Siskiyou forest region with a friend and for three weeks rambled in the big woods, caught rainbow trout, and camped under the great Port Orford cedars. This was a relief after the scorching heat of the desert but not a rest. It seems, as I now look back upon that western wandering, that I never got any rest. I did the wrong thing and persisted in it, month after month, with the result that I grew worse instead of better. Apparently, I was as tough as a gray wolf and could run the mountains day and night. But fever was running with me. That, however, did not give me pause.

I came out of Oregon and started for El Paso. There I entered Mexico by train, went to Chihuahua, thence on to Mexico City, and down to Cuautla. Under the lee of the volcano Popocatepetl, in the delightful climate of a western valley, I stayed for some weeks, with a handful of Mexicans and a great many Indians. It was very attractive, picturesque, almost romantic, but fever had got into my bones. When or what it meant I did not know, but the Mexicans told me it was malaria. I left Cuautla and went down to Oaxaca, three hundred or more miles south of Mexico City. Again I found the picturesque and the attractive in Oaxaca with the most delightful climate in the world, but I could not enjoy it. I went to Mitla to see the [Mayan] ruins there, but the fever must have been very high, for the next week I could remember nothing I had seen there. This went on for several weeks, and then feeling the uselessness of struggling against malaria (or whatever it was), I went north with my dog. I worried around by El Paso and Nogales, finally arriving once more in the old Hotel Almada at Guaymas.

I passed some sorry months of a second winter [1900–1901] there, again in a wonderful climate, with a beautiful bay and some very kind friends, both Spanish and American. Cappy, the terrier, went with me into the hills each morning where we had improvised a sun shelter and put up some boulder seats. There I read Spanish books because there were no others obtainable and each day absorbed an issue of the *New York Sun*. Also I did a little writing that was not very effective, not very energetic in style. I began to think the better plan for me was to go back to my New Brunswick home. I had been roughing it and toughing it a long time but had not been able to throw off whatever was the trouble with me. It was now very apparent that I was not going about it the right way.

I went up to Tucson and from there into the Santa Rita Mountains and finally drifted over through New Mexico to Texas and stopped for some weeks at Del Rio.[3] There I was told by my thirty-fifth doctor that there was nothing much the matter with me, and I would better go home and go to work. I could still walk twenty miles a day and was not howling with pain; therefore, I was doing very well. But perhaps the doctor was right, and, at the least, I could not be worse off in New Jersey. So with Cappy the terrier under my arm, I came home, sat down in my big library, and took up the burden of things where I had dropped them more than two years before.

Strange to say, the civilized agreed with me where the wild had not. I had always believed that "back to nature" was a panacea for all ills, but, lo! it was not.[4] I had overdone everything, walked myself to a shadow like a town postman, chased nature up a tree, and worn "out of doors" to a frazzle. In the end, it turned out that the frazzle was mine, not nature's. I went to the Presbyterian Hospital for diagnosis, and at the end of a week they had cut a perfectly good appendix out of me, and I had developed postoperative pneumonia. The Adirondacks received me for six months. When I came home again, it was with the determination to stick to my work and not go on any more desert or hospital cruises.

I came back to myself, but in a dull, heavy way. After such an illness in middle life, one is never young again. But when I returned to my home town, I went on lecturing to my students, went at another book, went on living as usual. I had already started the series of books on the history of American art, had in hand a series of articles for the *Century Magazine* (the old English masters, of which I have spoken), and had written a booklet, *Italian Painting* [1902], for Elson & Co. at Boston. In addition to these, I began putting into shape *The Meaning of Pictures* [1903], a companion volume to *Art for Art's Sake*, and began writing a series of eight or ten articles for the *Ladies Home Journal* on great painters and great masterpieces.

Besides writing, I had much reading to do. There were three years of accumulated books on art and allied subjects that I had to know about. For weeks and months I sat at my desk with volumes heaped about me. But it was not leisurely, thoughtful reading. It was the same, old, feverish dash— the shooting of glass balls on horseback with perhaps more misses than hits. I had never the gumption to get anything out of reading that I could use in writing. My assimilative powers seemed nil, and always I came back to my own poor stock for selection. And now I seemed thrown back on myself more violently than ever. But I had to know what others were writing and saying, had to keep up with the procession, and so I read—read unendingly and unceasingly.[5]

Once more I am putting down my various activities in the hope that the reader will see them as, in measure, indicative of the times and the people, will see that the close of the nineteenth and the opening of the twentieth century was not the dull backwater that latter-day historians would make it out. I was at that time no doubt popularly supposed to be a university professor, droning to my class by an open window, looking out on great elms and the green lawn of a college campus, or browsing leisurely in my big library by the colored light of a La Farge window. But such was not the case. The Nineties may sound old-fashioned, stupid, or ridiculous, as told to the young people of today, but they were not so to the people who lived through them and knew them.

Not in America alone was the progressive spirit. All Europe was roused to energy. London, Paris, and Vienna were growing almost as rapidly as New York. Trade, commerce, invention, and science were building up new cities like Berlin, or rebuilding old ones like Rome. The Nineties in Europe were years of prosperity. Especially was this true of England. Her trade piled up wealth for her in that period. And there was no falling behind in the professions and the arts. There were as bright men then as now, perhaps brighter. I remember at this time running up to Skibo for a week—Mr. Carnegie's new castle near Dornoch—and meeting there Miss Agnes Irwin, a great-granddaughter of Benjamin Franklin and then dean of Radcliffe College; Mr. Haldane, afterward Lord Haldane; Principal A. M. Fairbairn; Principal Lang; and Yates Thompson. John Morley came the next week. It would be difficult to pick up a more intelligent group of people in the Nineties or in any other decade.

Fairbairn was about the brightest man I ever met. His wit was quite the equal of Haldane's, which is saying much, for Haldane was not only profound but brilliant and very quick of wit. He knew his German philosophy very well, but Fairbairn, with his Scotch theology, often left him with not a leg to stand on. It was a great treat to hear them talk. Haldane was then middle-aged, and Fairbairn was further along, but they both had youthful energy in their movements and swift words on their tongues.

Of course, they were the leaders in conversation, the exceptional ones, and some of the listeners ran no risk of being shot for their brains. Here is an illustration. I came away in the station wagon from the castle at the same time with Miss Irwin and Haldane. I was shortly aware that they were having a joke at my expense on the back seat. I asked them to elucidate. Haldane did so by saying that when I came into the house party an English baronet, who was a house guest, asked him who I was. He answered by saying my name was Van Dyke and that I was greatly interested in art. The second question came at once:

"Oh! Is he the old master?"

We all laughed and Haldane explained further:

"You may think that was his little joke about your white hair, but Sir S—— had no notion of making a joke. He really thought you were Sir Anthony Van Dyck, whose portraits he had seen and heard about in English houses."

A present-day view of Green Oaks, Van Dyke's childhood home near New Brunswick, New Jersey. *(Linda Bayless)*

Theodore Strong Van Dyke, John C. Van Dyke's elder brother, at his ranch near Daggett, California. *(Memoirs of Ed Fletcher)*

Van Dyke's boyhood home on a bluff overlooking the Mississippi River, near Wabasha, Minnesota.

Van Dyke's daughter, Clare Van Dyke Parr.
(Philip L. Strong)

Van Dyke (right) in northern Mexico, possibly at La Noria Verde ranch near Hermosillo. This is the only known photograph of Van Dyke while he was on the travels that led to publication of *The Desert. (Special Collections and Archives, Rutgers University Libraries)*

Front: John C. Van Dyke beside his aunt and uncle, Harriet Anna Hartwell Strong and Honorable Woodbridge Strong. Rear: Theodore Strong, Sr., and Alan H. Strong, two cousins of Van Dyke's. *(Philip L. Strong)*

Van Dyke in 1929 at "Laghet," his summer home in the Catskill Mountains of New York. *(Archives of the American Academy and Institute of Arts and Letters, New York)*

Van Dyke on the west porch of "Stronghold," the mansion of his relatives, the Strongs, in New Brunswick, New Jersey. *(Philip L. Strong)*

Dog-lover Van Dyke with cocker spaniel at the exclusive Onteora Club, 1929. *(Archives of the American Academy and Institute of Arts and letters, New York)*

Van Dyke, about 1930, at his brother Theodore's ranch in the Mojave Desert near Daggett, California. *(Alan Van Dyke Golden)*

A nineteenth-century view of the New Brunswick Theological Seminary. *(Gardner A. Sage Library, New Brunswick Theological Seminary)*

Interior of the Gardner A. Sage Library of the New Brunswick Theological Seminary. *(Gardner A. Sage Library, New Brunswick Theological Seminary)*

Hay-cutting time at the Van Dyke ranch in California's Mojave Desert.
Left to right: John C. Van Dyke, his brother Theodore Strong Van Dyke,
and Theodore's son Dix. *(Alan Van Dyke Golden)*

On the Yacht Namouna, *Venice*, 1890, an oil by Julius L. Stewart. The editor argues that
Van Dyke is seated on the right reading to English beauty Lillie Langtry. *(Wadsworth
Atheneum, Hartford. The Ella Gallup Sumner and Mary Catlin Sumner Collection)*

Daggett, California, 1906. When Van Dyke knew it, Daggett was a wild place, raucous with miners and land speculators. *(Mojave River Valley Museum)*

Chapter 21

Art for the Public

I have found most of the impulses of my life, intellectual and otherwise, explicable largely by a theory of heredity. This, that, or the other thing was born in me. My mother's people, as I already have intimated, were preachers and teachers, Puritans, pietists, and pedagogues who bullied their families and bossed their communities, telling everyone his duty and how to do it—bellwethers leading flocks of sheep without too much knowledge of where they were going or how they would end up. I fell heir to this family slant and readily took up with the teaching and preaching. It seems that most of my endeavors have been of a missionary kind—a telling people something, an advising and admonishing, a guiding and a girding. All my books of whatever name or nature are infused with this spirit, the missionary spirit of carrying the gospel of art and nature to the heathen. Of course, I thought to help my fellow man, to spread the cult of beauty, to make life better worth living for everyone. I suppose we all have good excuses for our actions or at least think the excuses good.[1]

Perhaps the ancestors were not wholly responsible for my didacticism. Ruskin was an influence of my youth, perhaps more of an influence than I reckoned with, and maybe something of his querulousness came to me without my knowing it. And Jeffrey, Macaulay, Carlyle, Arnold, Emerson, Thoreau, Lowell, Norton—all of them scolders and faultfinders but nevertheless leaders who ran people around by the neck—may also have been an influencing force in the environment. Besides, the field invited. In my formative years (the Seventies and Eighties) there was not too much thought, feeling, or knowledge in America about the fine arts. The first stir came from the Centennial at Philadelphia in 1876. With the founding of the Society of American Artists and the Bartholdi Loan Exhibition, there was inducement to go along with those movements. People wanted to know about art. It was a new and open field—a missionary field.

Well, at any rate, I wrote in a dictatorial spirit and have continued to write thus and so, because perhaps the need and the opportunity were at hand and inheritance aided impulse. My new volume, *The Meaning of Pictures* [1903], was made up from lectures that I had delivered for Columbia

University at the Metropolitan Museum. It was addressed to the same kind of audience as the Art for Art's Sake book. Several years later I published *Studies in Pictures* [1907] and *What Is Art?* [1910],[2] addressed to the tourist public in European galleries. They were similar in style and thought to the others. All of them had their day, and some of them still continue to sell. So, I presume, they may be counted as fairly successful. But I never looked upon them with any affection. I had to be comprehended by my audience and had to deal with the simplest problems in the simplest manner. If I had had a philosophy of art, I could not have put it forth in those books. Every lecturer wishes to be considered profound, but lecture audiences do not readily grasp profundities, and they balk at philosophies.

So in the end, one has to talk of things elementary or else talk to empty benches. But no lecturer goes out from the applause of a crowded lecture room with any feeling of elation. He knows just how much of knowledge (or ignorance) lies behind the applause and just how short he has fallen of right accomplishment. In the final summary of his endeavor, he feels that compromise has ruined the result, that he has done what he could rather than what he would, and that in trying to stand on two stools he has perhaps fallen down between them.

But I would not be understood as apologizing for *The Meaning of Pictures* and its companion volumes. Rather am I explaining how they came to be cast in their present form. That one is not satisfied with what he has produced is common experience. Discontent began in the Garden of Eden, or earlier with Lucifer in Heaven.

But the writers of the popular have never had a monopoly of discontent. Those who produced the profound have been unhappy, too, because of their limited audience, and that not always an understanding one. William Crary Brownell was said to be "hard reading," though his criticism was about the clearest and the truest that we have ever had in American letters, and John La Farge with his *Considerations on Painting* was thought "involved," though again he had put forth the most thoughtful book of painter's criticism in our art history. The suggestion that in reading such books the reader "should work his passage" and do some thinking on his own account never fell on other than deaf ears. Readers expect their thinking to be done for them and do not care to pause over a printed page. And writers, though pleased by the appreciation of the discriminating few, never were exactly dismayed by the applause of the many. Besides, there is the publisher to reckon with. He is a seller of books as well as a publisher, and a writer cannot ask him to go on publishing books that will not sell. So there is some discontent for both the popular and the unpopular writer. Both of them perhaps compromise in the end, but neither of them is quite happy about it.

At this very time there was an attempt to establish a monthly magazine, what might be called a "high-class" magazine for thinkers. Frederick A. Richardson of Vermont put it forth under the title of the *International Monthly: A Magazine of Contemporary Thought*. I was asked to edit the art department, and in this task I had the assistance of associate editors, such as George Perrot in Paris, Sir Walter Armstrong in London, and others elsewhere. Many excellent articles were prepared, but only three or four volumes of the magazine were issued. It did not pay. *Contemporary Thought* called for some thinking, and again readers would not give it. The idea had to be abandoned and the publication suspended.

The St. Louis Fair also came off at this time (1904), and some of our educators and uplifters conceived the idea of holding there a Congress of Arts and Sciences—once more a "high-class" symposium of the best thought and thinking. People from Europe came (were subsidized to come) to deliver the latest and most compelling thought of the time. I went out to say the last word on art for America. Professor William Milligan Sloane went with me to deliver a similar message on history. We read each other's papers on the train. That probably was the only serious attention either paper ever received. An audience of several hundred gathered to hear me, and not more than half a dozen in the audience knew what I was talking about. Professor Adolph Furtwängler, as I have already recounted, sat in the front row. Word had gone out that he was to be there, and there was curiosity about his personality, so when my paper began bombarding his discoveries and conclusions in regard to Greek art, everyone looked at him to see how he was taking it. That was the extent of the thinking and the thought. Mr. Rogers afterward brought all the papers together in eight volumes, but I never heard that there was any wild rush to get the volumes. They constituted a "record," as Brander Matthews and Professor Lounsbury informed me, but I have never seen or heard the "record" referred to from that day to this. All of which is deplorable but true.

So, perhaps a little weary of theories and thinkings that were left hanging in midair, I for the moment let go of art and snapped back to nature. I had always fought off the weariness of the one with the freshness of the other, and now I took up my nature studies anew with a volume on the sea, *The Opal Sea: Continued Studies in Impressions and Appearances* [1906].[3] No argument, no hairsplitting distinctions, no subtleties of thought. Just impressions and appearances of the sea, with a wonder for its immensity and a dithyramb for its beauty. Brownell thought it my best book, my "most sustained effort." Perhaps. I do not know. Like other writers, when I have finished with a work, it seems to me mere stuff and nonsense. After twenty years, I can still see the raw spots in it and feel the creaking of the ill-joined parts or, what is worse, pooh-pooh the thinking as juvenile and idiotic. If one trusted wholly his own judgment, perhaps he would never publish at all.

In writing about the sea or the desert, or, for that matter, any subject whatever, I always considered the logical and sequential arrangement of my material and then tried to put it in a decorative pattern that would not only be pleasing but facilitate the exposition. But beyond that I followed no standards or theories, never bothered about whether my view was detached or personal, never worried about the historical method or the analytical method or expression as art, never even followed the theories that I myself had set up. I read largely in criticism and had the greatest admiration for the clearness with which Brownell, for example, had sifted and codified the whole field. His analysis, deduction, and synthesis were acute, convincing, indisputable. I also had profound respect for the opinions of George Woodberry, Paul Elmer More, Irving Babbitt, Stuart Sherman, and other American writers, not to mention Benedetto Croce and the Europeans. But out of all the philosophies of style and aesthetic theories, I could get no practical help in writing my plain prose. That had to be done with my own personal view of the material, set forth in my own personal way, with such effect in the pattern as I could command. One book of a writer may be more interesting than another because of its subject, because of the enthusiasm of the writer, which leads him to do better thinking or express himself more forcefully in that book; but these are mere modifications or expansions of his individual method. Of course, one can make a fetish of method and lose himself in his technique, as Henry James, for example, but the less gifted usually do not take their approach to their subject or their method so seriously.

Chapter 22

Adventures

It would seem that the modern autobiographer is so bent upon telling us when, where, and how he met President Roosevelt or Mussolini or the Prince of Wales that he has forgotten to mention his love affairs and has left "the female" entirely out of his picture. If asked, he would probably tell us that for family reasons, as well as mere, ordinary discretion, it is just as well not to tell your loves out of school. Benvenuto Cellini, Casanova, and a few others did not seem to think so and were greeted with tumultuous applause in consequence. But I am not thinking of following their example.

Another omission of the present-day biographers in which Benvenuto did not concur is personal adventure. It seems that only mental fisticuffs can now be indulged in and that anything strangely happed by land or sea is banal or beside the telling of one's life story. There I shall disagree and record a chapter of unusual happenings. For many summers I had gone to Europe without mishap or adventure, not even a fall downstairs, and then one year everything came at once. The summer was something of a nightmare.[1]

Steamship travel on the North Atlantic in the early Nineties had greatly improved over that of the late Seventies. The wretched little cigar-shaped craft that rolled like a porpoise, had only gravity ventilation, and smelled like a rat trap had been superseded by a larger and more comfortable ship. The older types were not, however, scrapped but rather shunted on to less-used routes, so that when I went to Europe by Gibraltar and Naples I got one of them, willy-nilly. In 1905, in the merry month of June, Captain (now Colonel) Smiley, U.S.A., and I took passage on the *Cretic* for Naples.

The *Cretic* never was a good boat, and age had withered, custom had staled, her infinite variety. She was almost everything that she should not be. Four days out, she developed fire in the hold. Water was poured in, men were sent down through the hatches and were pulled up again by the heels unconscious. The Italians in the steerage lost their heads and came rushing to the upper decks, falling on their knees in the scuppers, beating their breasts, and calling on the Virgin to save them. Even the first cabin looked a little white in the gills. But after forty-eight hours the danger passed, though we smelled smoke for the rest of the voyage.

The next tribulation was intestinal upheaval from bad meat, but that, too, passed. At Naples we were held up by quarantine with seven cases of smallpox on board. We might have remained there for a week,

> As idle as a painted ship
> Upon a painted ocean,[2]

were it not for some *louis d'or*, which the quarantine officers fancied only too well. We got away by night and were joined ashore by George Glaenzer, architect, of New York. We took rail to Taranto, where that night we nearly perished from mosquitoes and other pests of the bedroom. From Brindisi we shipped in a crazy Greek paddle-wheeler for Corfu and Athens. The boat was loaded down with sheep, goats, and nomad Greeks. They were mixed in promiscuous confusion. On the decks in the moonlight, with the Greeks asleep, their petticoats thrown over their heads and their legs sticking out, and the sheep and goats huddled down beside them, the effect was rather more bizarre than picturesque. The ugly feature of the boat was that she was leaking badly and had a heavy list to starboard. But on a smooth sea we somehow got through to the Piraeus and were duly set ashore. A few days later we went on by smaller boat through the Greek islands to Smyrna, where a Russian steamer from Cairo took us up to Constantinople.

The first evening out at sundown, the Russian ship was stopped and swung broadside to the setting sun. The sky was red, and the flat sea about us was like pooled blood—the most striking sea surface I have ever seen. The whole ship's company, including all the crew, several hundred all told, were lined up at the ship's rail facing the sun. The ship's chaplain, a Russian priest in long robe and flowing beard, said prayers and then led the whole company in singing an evening hymn. I have never seen since such an emotion-producing service in such a gorgeous setting of the sea. The three of us standing there were on the brink of tears.

I had a letter to our American minister at Constantinople, Mr. Leishman, a former partner of Andrew Carnegie, from whom my letter came. We were welcomed and told we had arrived at a propitious time, for the next day we could attend the *salemnik* (going to prayers) of the Sultan Abdul Hamid.[3] Mr. Leishman got the permits, made all the arrangements, and the next morning we went in a carriage with the secretary and a dragoman of the legation. Long before we reached the Yildiz Kiosk, we encountered troops. There were rings of them surrounding the kiosk and mosque, and we had to pass through three distinct cordons. Each one of them looked us over, the dragoman on the front seat answering for us with nods and signs. He was vouching for us with his head in a double sense. We entered a square of cavalry and were driven to a small villa beside the driveway and not far from the Yildiz Kiosk, reserved for foreign diplomats and visitors. There we were given seats on the balcony overlooking the roadway and the mosque.

The Sultan's bodyguard was disposed about in full view. There were fifteen hundred Albanians, as many Syrians and Anatolians, with other troops, all dressed in gorgeous native costumes, lined up like automatons, standing on guard like so many squares of machinery. They were perfectly disciplined and moved as a unit. The Sultan was said to have confidence only in this bodyguard.

The bugles blew. Down the road from the Yildiz Kiosk came a span of bays ahead of a basket phaeton. A driver and footman were on the box and on the back seat a lone figure dressed in a plain brown army overcoat and a red fez. No stars or orders or gilt or jewels, just a plain, army-garbed man. The phaeton passed within a few feet of us, and the man on the back seat bowed to our whole party on the balcony with the graceful Mohammedan gesture of touching the heart, lips, and brow. Good gracious! And was that rather handsome, well-poised man of fifty-five or sixty who looked a noble-man the notorious Abdul Hamid of ill-repute in the European press? The tremendous applause going up in one long Oriental cry from the troops said that it was.

The phaeton turned to the left, passed through a great iron-grilled gate, and stopped at the steps of the mosque. The Sultan got down, went up the steps, and disappeared in the mosque. For fifteen minutes we chatted, the troops rested, everyone waited. Then the bugles blew again. The prayers were over, and the Sultan was coming out.

But he did not come. There was some delay. It was only a few minutes, but while everyone waited and looked, a tremendous explosion took place. A great cloud of dust, gravel, and smoke shot up from the grilled gates like a volcano in eruption. In a moment a whole squadron of cavalry seemed to fall onto the ground in writhing confusion. Companies of infantry apparently disappeared. Plunging horses and twisting men were tangled together in a long trench blown in the ground. Shouting officers and riderless horses were dashing about at haphazard.

Everyone knew instantly that a mine, planned to catch the Sultan at the grill, had been exploded. A hot blast of sand and gravel drove across our balcony, dashing out all the windows behind us and covering us with dust. We rubbed our eyes and Captain Smiley said quickly:

"Now let's see what they will do! Now let's see." He was eager to know how the troops would perform under the circumstances. Almost instantly a commanding officer rallied the scattered cavalry and made a swift dash to surround the mosque where the Sultan was still lingering. Captain Smiley thought that very well done and was enthusiastic about it.

But the cordon about the mosque was no more than completed before the Sultan came out upon the platform steps. A number of his councillors, who were waiting for him below, rushed up the steps, begging him by voice and gesture to go back within the mosque. Not a bit of it! He waved them aside with a fine, slow gesture, walked down the steps to his phaeton, and stepped into the driver's seat. It was his custom after prayers to drive himself back to his Yildiz Kiosk, and he now took up the reins, unwound his whip, calmly flicked the ear of the off leader, and came down the lane, through the wrecked gate, over the trench of dead men and horses, never seeing or recognizing such a thing as mine explosion or dire disaster.

Bravo!

It may have been imperial bluff, but it was superbly carried out.

Up the hill with the bays at an easy trot the Sultan came. As he passed our balcony, the Austrian ambassador (I think it was Baron Calice, who at that time was quite close to the Sultan) started a little hand clapping in which we joined half timidly, not knowing how it would be received. The Sultan turned his eyes but not his head and shot a glance at the Austrian ambassador—the glance of an old eagle. A bit of a smile was about the eyes and seemed to say, "Well, they haven't caught me yet." He passed on slowly and leisurely and disappeared about a bend in the road.

So, this was the coward who was always hiding in bombproof cellars! This was the unspeakable Turk who looked like an old vulture and acted like an old spider! But he did not live up to that description. He looked like a gentleman and acted as a monarch should. Oh, yes, it is easy to say it was put on for the occasion. Perhaps it was, but he carried through magnificently.

With the Sultan gone, we turned once more to the disaster before us. A horse's leg was lying in the dust just under us, and torn animals were everywhere. Wounded and dead people were being borne away. An old man in councillor's robe, covered with blood, an officer without his head, soldiers, their red fezes gone and their ghastly faces turned to the sky, were carried past us. We afterward learned that twenty-seven men had been killed outright and over a hundred wounded. No one knew how many horses had been blown up.

And then it suddenly occurred to Captain Smiley and me that we were in a rather uncomfortable position. We were not injured and easily got the

sand and dust out of our eyes and ears, but . . . we had become suspects
with that explosion. No good Mussulman would attempt to blow up the
Sultan, the Commander of the Faithful. Only a foreigner would do that.
We were foreigners. On several similar occasions foreigners had been mas-
sacred in Constantinople. We were already trapped, caged by the cordons of
the Sultan's troops. We might not find getting out of the trap as easy as
getting in.

An officer who seemed to be in command came up on our balcony. I
asked him (in French) if we might go.[4] He slowly waved an uplifted forefinger back and across his decorated bosom. No more. But that was enough.
We understood and sat down. A half hour elapsed. Another officer
appeared, saluted, and said we could go. We stood not upon the order of
going but went at once, picked up our carriage and dragoman, drove slowly
around the dead horses, and passed out as we had entered. Each cordon of
troops stopped and looked us over, talked and made signs that we did not
understand. But we were allowed to go.

Back at our legation, we were told not to attempt to leave Constantinople
by the railways or by steamers, that all the exits would be guarded and that
we would be arrested. We "lay low" for several days. That proving monotonous, we crossed the Marmora and went down to Brusa, the old Osmanlie
capital of Turkey. There we stopped for a week in the most remarkable city
of the Near East and forgot the Constantinople incident in viewing blue
mosques, imperial tombs, precious tiles, and the plunder of the bazaars.
Then we moved north again to Scutari on the Bosporus, caught a Russian
steamer, and went up to Kustendjii on the Black Sea. There we were duly
rounded up on the suspicion of being spies, but a few gold pieces proved an
excellent *laissez-passer*. We went up to Rutschuk on the Danube, where we
were surrounded in our hotel by a troop of Bulgarian cavalry, the colonel of
which wanted to know what in blazes we meant by going up to the Bulgarian summer camp and inspecting the troops without permission. The land-
lord interpreted for us, and we apologized. Smiley had a camera full of
photographs of the camp, which would have had us shot at dawn had they
been discovered.

We went over to Bucharest and were once more rounded up by the police
on suspicion of being something—I have forgotten what. But that was
settled once more by a gold-piece passport. Sinaya in the Carpathians
received us for a week without police or military demonstration. Then we
went up the Danube by steamer to Budapest and were glad to arrive in a
country where we did not have to wear our passports in our hatbands.

At Vienna, Captain Smiley went south to visit someone (probably a female of the species), who relieved him of all the art treasures he had picked up in Constantinople,[5] and I went north to Mannheim, where in the Park Hotel a thief made a midnight call upon me and got thrown out of the window for his indiscretion. My venture resulted in my hasty departure down the Rhine to avoid detention as a witness by the German police. Nothing further happened either to Captain Smiley or me until we got to Liverpool and boarded our homebound steamer, which ran on a mud bank in the Mersey and remained there for twenty-four hours. That ended the incidents and accidents of that eventful summer.

Chapter 23

To and Fro

The year [1906] following the blowup with the Sultan, I started with my friend George Glaenzer to Russia, but we got no farther than Sweden. At Stockholm we were told by our diplomatic representative that there was just then a minor revolution in progress in Finland or somewhere else, and that it was doubtful if we would be admitted to Russia. Reluctantly, we abandoned the idea. I started upon a study of Scandinavian art. I got not very far in that before I was recalled to Geneva by some family matters and finally had to go home earlier than planned.

I cannot now remember what particular depressing phase of business, what drear outlook upon America, what immediate outrage or aggression started me at writing *The Money God* [1908]. It had nothing to do with art or nature but, as its secondary title explained, was merely *Chapters of Heresy and Dissent Concerning Business Methods and Mercenary Ideals in American Life*. I had inherited a love of country, and at stated periods I foamed at the mouth over the wanton destruction of our forests, prairies, rivers, and valleys in the name of "development." It was a flaying of the land, a selling of the furniture out of the house. We were a race of Gadarene swine rushing down a steep place into the sea. Beauty of nature, content of mind, moral growth, and even common, everyday happiness were being bartered away for a mere mess of money. I had to say something in protest.[1]

I am not sorry that I said it. The book was well written and my contention not badly argued. Brownell could not conceal his disgust with it because it was to him a beating of the void with ineffectual wings, something that was futile. And Charles Scribner didn't like it, but he published it. The publication justified their opinion rather than mine. It did not knock a hole in the blue sky. Some of the newspapers featured it and tried to read sensational things into it. Others thought its political economy unorthodox (as though I had put forth a theory of economics instead of a scold!), and still others railed at it because they and their methods had been assailed in the text. Some people in particular were vindictive, and I received many letters from them, the purport of which was that for the reasonable sum of two cents they would cut my throat. Some manufacturers in my native town contented themselves with merely cutting my acquaintance. But the man with the axe, the wrecker, and the money-grubber went their way, blissfully ignorant of both myself and my book. Brownell was right. It did no good. Vultures cannot be driven away by mere scolding.[2]

Brownell I came to regard as always right. His judgment was excellent, and I could recognize its excellence when directed against me as readily as for me. About this time I sent him the manuscript of a desert novel, *The Jaws of the Desert*. He wanted to know at the start why I wished to break into the overpopulated field of fiction when I had a separate patch of my own where I was cultivating a genre of my own quite undisturbed. He read the novel and said it had no "pep"; said further that some publisher who could have more faith in it than the Scribners should publish it. Profuse apologies for the plain talk. He hated to write that letter because he thought it would wound me. But it was only for a moment. I accepted his judgment without question, put the manuscript in a table drawer without trying any other publisher, and there it remains to this day.

The trouble with that novel was that it had too much truth in it for fiction. It was my own experience, which is about the poorest supply the novelist can draw from.[3] Art is always a convention, the novel as well as the opera or the painting, and if one would be a successful novelist, he must recognize and accept the convention. Each day or epoch has its own convention, which is accepted for the time and is eventually superseded by a newer one. Those who came after Sir Walter and Charles Reade and Dickens could hoot at the convention of romanticism, but their own realism was just as conventional in its way. Where now are the excellent, realistic novels of Howells and James and Turgenieff which so effectually killed romanticism? Have they not been superseded, been killed in turn, by the newer realism of Main Street and the sex novel? Each executioner in turn becomes a victim, each new convention becomes an old one and is laid aside.[4] The genius in art is the person who puts forth a new convention.

I had been to Murray Bay, and out of the splendid fields of wild flowers there I half evolved a plan for a book on wild growths. At Lake St. John and on the Saguenay [in Quebec, Canada], I conjured up in my imagination chapters on the beauty of water in canyoned rivers and mountain lakes. Then a following summer in the mountains of California led me to think up a book on mountain beauty. But all these castles in the air were pulled down by Joseph Pennell's arrival from London and his violent insistence that the only castles worth looking at were the skyscrapers of New York. He was already drawing them, putting them on etching plates, and insisting that I should join with him in some eulogy of them. I agreed to write the text for a portfolio of his etchings.

We took the proposition to George Brett, president of the Macmillan Company. Brett liked it but wanted a book on New York City, not a portfolio of etchings. I objected by saying that I could write fifty enthusiastic pages about the skyscrapers, which I had always admired, but did not care to write four hundred pages about New York City. But I was overruled, and the talk ended by my weakly agreeing to write the four hundred pages for *The New New York* [1909] and Pennell to furnish a hundred black-and-white drawings and twenty-five plates in color.

For several months Pennell and I systematically studied New York from the Battery to the Haarlem River, from Brooklyn Bridge to Coney Island. We were in search of the picturesque and found it at every street corner. Neither of us was after the old New York. We cared nothing about its history but were intent only upon its pictorial appearance. The skyscrapers made a new skyline and the canyon streets a new and mighty depth of shadow. These were the most obvious facts, but we allowed little of interest in the smaller things to get away from us. We hunted closely because neither of us were New Yorkers, though we had known the city for many years. Indeed, one reviewer, commenting favorably upon the book, said it had not been put out by bright, breezy young men of New York but by a college professor living over in New Jersey and an illustrator who lived in London.

Colonel McClellan, then mayor of New York, was much interested in the project, took us about to see hidden and unusual things, and placed everything in the city government at our disposal. He had done much for civic beauty in New York, and both Pennell and I agreed that the new book should be dedicated to him. It came out with a flourish of trumpets and met with a quick response from the reviewers. It was a handsome book and sold well. But it had its day. Was it Carlyle who remarked that "everything but asbestos will be burned"? The new book was not asbestos. Twenty years after there is scarcely a mention of it left, but it had not been burned. Perhaps a hundred years hence it may have a renaissance for Pennell's illustrations, which will then look rather antique, and perhaps my text may in that time read like "some quaint and curious volume of forgotten lore."[5]

After publishing *Studies in Pictures* [1907], I again went back to Europe to go over again and again the pictures in European galleries. I never kept any count of the number of times I went to Europe, never any memorandum of the weeks or months or years I spent in the Louvre or the Kaiser Friedrich or the Ufizzi. My legs became like iron from long standing before those pictures, and my accommodating stomach never grumbled when I skipped luncheon that I might have more of the day for study. Often I met friends or made new acquaintances in the galleries—students, painters, writers, gallery directors, society people—but I got away from them as quickly as possible that I might look at the pictures in my own way. The one painter whom I met often in various European galleries was William M. Chase. He was an indefatigable student, knew certain old masters very well, and was always digging up for admiration the technique of some (then) unknown master. Brushwork greatly interested him, and the strong handling of a surface always commanded his applause. A very appreciative critic of painting, old or new, was William M. Chase.[6]

On one of my European trips about this time, I was fortunate enough to have the company of John Sargent.[7] He was bound for Spain and Portugal and I for Italy, so we went along together from New York to Gibraltar. I had written an article about him for the *Outlook*, published just before our sailing, of a more or less critical nature. He must have had his attention called to it. Whether he liked it or not I did not learn. Both of us avoided any mention of it. But at any rate it had not rasped him too harshly, for he was genial and even cordial. We played chess every day, listened to some music of which he was very fond, and occasionally dropped into picture talk. He was a little shy, even with men, and more or less embarrassed by women, but everyone liked him and, of course, everyone admired him for his work.

Sargent's picture talk was limited. I asked him about several exceptional heads by Lawrence that I felt sure he liked. He did admire them but deprecated Lawrence's "shoe-button eyes." I suggested that the Innocent X in the Doria Gallery, Rome, was too hot for Velásquez and, moreover, had not the brush stroke of Velásquez. It had probably been worked up by some Italian from the cool study head in the Hermitage. He would not say about that but agreed that the head in the Hermitage was vastly superior to the one in the Doria. He explained that he had not been to St. Petersburg but knew the Velásquez head in the Hermitage very well through a large Braun photograph. He thought the modeling was superb. Of course, he had a large admiration for Titian, wondered a bit over the uneven pictures attributed to Rembrandt, liked Frans Hals and all the other great gods of painting, but was just then directly interested in El Greco. In fact, he was going to Spain and Portugal to see if he could find more pictures by this man whom he had been so instrumental in resurrecting.

At Gibraltar we went up to the Cecil Hotel and had a large dinner with much English beer. At the end of it, Sargent grew rather loquacious and talked some more about art. I sat up and paid attention, well knowing that he rarely talked about his work and hoping that he might say something of value. But nothing of importance came forth. In theory he seemed to think that the difference between painters was a difference in viewpoint:

"You see that way (motioning to the left), and I see that way (motioning to the right), and that is about all there is to it."

This was substantially Henry James's definition: "Art is a point of view and genius a way of looking at things." James and Sargent were old friends. Whether Sargent got from James or James from Sargent is perhaps of no importance.

Sargent went over to Algeciras and up into Spain, and I went on to Naples.

Chapter 24

Glacier Park and Alaska

Once more, somewhat wearied by the strident hum of the city, the painted canvas and the printed page, I started for the wild, the open, the wilderness of my boyhood. I knew there were untrampled spots still left in the United States if I had but the wit to find them. In Minneapolis I induced a friend of my early Minnesota days, Charles C. Prindle, to join me. We went down to St. Paul to talk with Louis Hill of the Great Northern about the country now known as the Glacier National Park.

Before we got into the talk, Hill took us up to his father's (James J. Hill's) house to see the pictures that had been brought together to form a rather well-known collection.[1] There were many of the Fontainebleau-Barbizon pictures, and I was rather shocked to find how brown and foxy some of them now looked. Had the pictures changed, or was the change with me? I was particularly upset by the large *Biblis* of Corot. I had first seen it in the Paris Exhibition of 1889 and day after day had sat before it with "Billy" Coffin and Jules Stewart, admiring its breadth and light and easy handling. Now it looked woolly, blackish, rather sloppy and uncertain in its brushwork. I could hardly believe it the same picture. Did I see it aright in 1889, or did I see it aright now, twenty years after? I was disappointed, but whether with myself or the pictures I could not then stop to inquire. Perhaps I was too weary for pictures and wanted nothing so much as to get away from art, artists, and:

> The endless clatter of plate and knife,
> The singular mess we agree to call life.

We soon arranged a trip into the Rockies just south of the Canadian line in Montana. The Great Northern train took us to Browning, where we picked up a man with a team and several saddle horses, and before evening we were away across the plain toward St. Mary's Lake. The saddle horses were just Indian cayuses, and the team horses were balky, but I did not worry about them. In forty-eight hours we had disappeared in the timber, were camped by a swift stream, and catching rainbow trout. I had no fault to find with creation, save that our driver-cook wrecked everything eatable with his cooking and sometimes made necessary my taking in hand the frying pan and coffee pot.

We wound along the banks of Swift Current up into higher altitudes. High peaks (some of them 10,000 feet) were in sight. Snow and glaciers were about us. In several places we were turned back by old snowbanks that still held against the summer sun. Iceberg Lake we reached easily and were charmed with its splendid opalescent color, its solitude, and aloofness from the world. Under the drip of slowly receding icecaps sprang into bloom the avalanche lilies and a score of smaller flowers that produced a choke in the throat with their isolated beauty.[2] We went on to the north, leaving our wagon at St. Mary's Lake and going on with a pack train, pausing by streams to catch enough trout for the frying pan and camping by lakes without a name even to our remarkable guide. There were few evidences of anyone having been there before us. The dim trails were evidently left by Blackfeet Indians. The tourist had not yet come this far. Bighorns hung on the mountainsides, watching the slow weave and wind of us in the valley, bear hustled out of our way, and deer jumped from the willows along the brooks. We were back in God's country, the country that was before the Garden of Eden.[3]

After two weeks of this, I caught a severe cold in wading the icy mountain streams casting for trout. Fever came on, and I knew that I had pneumonia but thought in that sunlight and air I could throw it off. We were now far up against the Canadian boundary and were turning east and south on the return. In a few days we came out on the eastern front of the Rockies overlooking the vast plains stretching toward the rising sun. From our height we could see a hundred miles or more across the prairie, which stretched like a mighty carpet of gold, dotted here and there by lakes that looked like pots of dark-blue ink. As we followed down one of the long ridges stretching out into the prairie, we noticed far away moving beads and strings that finally resolved themselves into lines of horsemen. We had small difficulty in guessing they were Indians, Blackfeet Indians coming from the neighboring reservation and moving south. Something was afoot.

We soon noted that other beads and strings were riding down the spokes of a wheel toward a center hub. After an hour or more, we made out the hub and rode toward it, falling in with bands of eight or ten Blackfeet as we rode. Several thousand Blackfeet had gathered on a flat space on the prairie, and a big Sun Dance was under way. A huge tent had been spread, and within it, seated in a circle, were the chiefs and medicine men watching a figure with a reed pipe piping at the sun. We crowded in, though uninvited, and sat down in the circle. No one questioned us or paid any attention to us.[4]

We sat through several performances of incantation, dancing, and tom-tom beating, all of them long and more or less monotonous, and yet decidedly impressive because of their sincerity. This was not a performance prepared for tourists. We were the only whites present, and we were not expected. It was a genuine Sun Dance with a highly religious significance attached to it. No one smiled at it. Perhaps the movement and color appealed to me more than the religion of it, and yet their primitive faith, made manifest in this primitive way, had an appeal and met with quick response. I could not help but entertain a mighty respect for it. And this notwithstanding, there were nonbelieving Blackfeet outside who were trading horses, running races, and gambling after the Indian fashion.

The Blackfeet (with the Crows) are our noblest-looking Indians, and I never saw a finer gathering than that at this Sun Dance. The chiefs had on their beaded buckskins with a great deal of paint and feathers. The circle would have driven a painter out of his mind with its swift movement and bright color under a summer sun on a vast yellow prairie. A Dutch kermess (as seen by Rubens) or a French *fête gallant* (as seen by Watteau) would seem a very dull affair beside their barbaric color and light on these savage figures. I was sick enough to go into a hospital, but I sat up and watched that Sun Dance until the sun went down. Then we crept to cover with the Blackfeet and the next morning pulled out and took our way across the prairie for the railway station at Browning.

That outing was over, but I did not turn back east. On the contrary, we went west to Seattle, where I crept to bed for two days while a doctor puzzled over me. Then I got up and, with Prindle, boarded a coasting steamer for Alaska. I was still running a high fever and could do little more than sit on the hurricane deck, propped up in a chair, and cough the day away. But I kept watching the sea and the shore out of the corner of my eye, and when we got far up among the big glaciers I could even grow enthusiastic over the blue of the ice floating in the water on the glacier front—wonderful patches of peculiar blue that had no exact likeness on land and sea.

Of course, Alaska with its tremendous glaciers (beside which the Swiss Mer de Glace is merely a frozen brook), with its great mountains and forests and tangled undergrowth coming down to the sea, with its huge bays and indented harbors and northern suns sinking into tumbled and tossing waves, was more than impressive. It created the wonder that might attach to a new world. I had never seen anything quite like it, and I was too sick now to see it with any but sick eyes. I sat trussed up in blankets like an infant and like an infant stared and vaguely wondered what it was all about.

But the wonder of its bigness, its splendid color, and its half-arctic sunsets still remains with me.[5]

We came back. I went to Grants Pass in Oregon, where a brother, a physician, lived.[6] He and his fellow physicians in town agreed that I was "a pretty sick cat" because I had a temperature of 103 1/2 F, but none of them knew or could guess what was the matter. Apparently, the pneumonia had abated, but the fever still ran high. After ten days, I started south to California, went to the ranch of my older brother in the Mojave desert, sat down on the ranch house porch, and for weeks watched the wind blowing over the alfalfa. My blood temperature was high, but the air temperature was higher, sometimes up to 110 F. I did not seem to mind it, nor anything else. I just sat tight and waited for a turn of the tide. At Los Angeles, several other doctors went over me and shook their heads. Apparently, I was all right, but that temperature was wrong.

The turn of the tide in my illness came with a three-fingered doctor, who also was a miner and had drifted into the ranch from a desert claim that he was trying to make produce gold where no gold was. He sat on the porch beside me for several days and finally made out that I had a congested liver, an abscessed lung, and an enlarged spleen, with bronchitis and laryngitis thrown in for good measure. He had no medicine chest, and the ranch could supply little beside crude castor oil kept on hand for horses with a bellyache. I had a bellyache, and though I was not a horse, the indications pointed to castor oil or nothing. He gave me a huge dose of that, and I took it. After two months of fever, I would have swallowed rattlesnake oil.

The unexpected happened. The fever left me within twenty-four hours. Perhaps it was getting ready to leave, but that desert doctor with his castor oil certainly accelerated it. I left the porch chair for a saddle and rode the desert for several days. Then I caught a Santa Fe train for Chicago and New York. When I got home and could take account, I found I was able to move about, and that was about all, but I was coming back to myself.[7]

Chapter 25

Happenings

I went over one Sunday morning to Orange, New Jersey, to take luncheon with Mr. and Mrs. L. F. Loree. There were no cabs at the Orange station, perhaps because it was Sunday, and I had to walk and find the house as best I could. The station master said it was about three quarters of a mile from the station and gave me the general direction. I started, and when I had gone what I thought was that distance, I turned in at a massive gate opening upon a wide lawn with trees and an expansive house in the distance. Such a place I thought would be about right for a railway president of Loree's presumed wealth and taste.

I walked up the wide graveled road, and as I approached the house I saw a lady moving about on the flat roof of a wing of the house and evidently talking to someone not seen. The immediate presumption was that she was giving some sort of order about repairs on the roof. She saw me at about the same time that I saw her. Of course, I took off my hat and made my manners. Would she pardon me, but I was looking for Mr. Loree's house. Could she, would she, direct me? She answered from her high balcony:

"Oh, dear me! You are nowhere near it. You go down the road to the left for about twenty minutes and then turn to the right, and it is only a short distance beyond—but you will never find it. Wait a few moments, and I will have my car at the door and send you over."

I gently deprecated the idea. I couldn't put her to so much trouble.

But she came down from the roof to the front door, and the car came up almost immediately. She was a handsome and gracious lady and gently insisted that I could not find the way to Mr. Loree's, and the car was idle, and the chauffeur would take me over in a few minutes. As I entered the car she said:

"And you will remember me to Mrs. Loree, won't you?"

I would be most happy to do so, but I did not know how I could do it unless she would be good enough to give me her name.

"Oh!" she said, "I am Mrs. Edison."

At the Royal Academy in London one early summer, I had gone over three thousand pictures and found little to my taste, when, almost in the last room, I found a three-quarter-length portrait of a man in a black coat with a silk hat in his hand. It was almost like a Manet. Excellent. I enquired at the desk who did it.

"William Orpen, an Irishman."

"Has he a studio in London?"

"Yes, in Bolton Gardens."

The number was given me.

It was a fine day, and I started to walk there. When I had walked enough, I asked a traffic bobby who stood in the street how far it was to Bolton Gardens. He never moved a finger or batted an eye in replying:

"It's a penny ride in an 'orse bus, Sir."

That being a little vague, I called a cab and was taken to my destination. A charwoman came to the gate in response to a ring. We talked a bit. Then a second-floor window in the house at the back was opened, and a man appeared calling:

"Come up! Come up!"

I entered a large studio, and a short man came across to me with extended hand saying:

"Will you dine with me this evening at the Saville Club?"

I protested, amusedly, that the invitation was rather swift, and could we sit down and talk about it for a few minutes?

He showed me many of his pictures, talked interestingly, intelligently, sensibly. I was much impressed with the pictures. He was then a new man to me, but I ventured on what I saw of his work to ask him if he would do a portrait of a Mrs. B—— living in Ireland.

No. He went to Ireland every summer for a vacation but only did landscapes while there.

How much did he ask for a whole-length portrait?

A thousand guineas.

We talked some more and finally adjourned to the Saville Club for dinner, where we met some other painters and talked into the night. Before I left, he had agreed to do the portrait. And he did it very well, making a handsome picture of a handsome woman and her two children.

That was my first and only meeting with Orpen, now Sir William Orpen and a famous painter.[1]

In Spain one year, I, having left the steamer at Gibraltar and crossed over to Algeciras, was on the train bound for Madrid. I was in a first-class compartment, the only occupant until we got to Rondo, where a very well-dressed English-looking man of fifty got in. He sat himself down in a corner and began reading. I, in another corner at the other end of the compartment, did likewise. Finally, I went to sleep for an hour or so. When

I awoke, my fellow passenger was still reading and apparently unaware of my presence or existence. It must have been after five or six hours of silent traveling that he suddenly said, without so much movement as raising his eyes:

"You are Mr. Van Dyke, aren't you?"

The language was very good English, with perhaps just a little accent, but from what other language I could not say, and the voice was pleasant but without any note of wonder or surprise or marked interest. The surprise was mine, for I could not imagine how he knew my name, or knowing it how it could mean anything to him. But I calmly admitted my identity.

"I thought so," he said. "The Spanish minister was on your ship and told me last night that you were coming up to Madrid."

True enough, the Spanish minister to the United States was on the ship, but I had not met him, and I could not guess how he knew about my movements or why either of them should have been enough interested in me to talk me over.

The gentleman said he had heard I was interested in art and was going to Madrid to study the pictures in the Prado.

Yes, I was.

There were many fine pictures there. He knew them very well. He went on to talk about some of them in detail and soon convinced me that he was not boasting. He did know about pictures and talked about them very intelligently. I let him talk and said little more than was necessary to keep the conversation afloat, wondering a little as to whether this stranger was:

> Rich man, poor man, beggar man, thief,
> Doctor, lawyer, merchant, chief.

He talked on and grew a little animated as he talked. He was evidently very clever and, from his clothes and his traveling bags, neither a poor man nor a beggar man.

Presently, he said that he was getting down at the next station and going over to his place in the country. His automobile would be waiting for him. Would I care to go over with him and be his guest over Sunday? That was such a startling proposition, coming from a man whose very name was unknown to me, that it aroused some suspicion. How did I know where that ride in an automobile would take me? Who was he who had developed such sudden interest in a perfect stranger? What was the object of that interest?

I thanked him. But my time was limited, and I had much work to do in Madrid. I hoped he wouldn't mind my declining.

Oh, very well. He thought I might be interested in seeing some of the Spanish country not usually seen by the traveling public. He proceeded to talk about the Spanish country and again talked very intelligently. He knew about crops and cattle and peasants, as well as about pictures.

In less than half an hour the whistle blew, and the train began to slow down. He gathered up his books and papers and again renewed his invitation to go with him to his country place over Sunday. His car would be at the station and would take us there in an hour. But once more I declined. There was something suspicious to me in so much kindness. My life was not so valuable that I suspected any plot, nor my wealth great enough to excite anyone's cupidity, but it was a step off into the dark, something I did not know about.

The train stopped. Out of the car window I saw a handsome automobile with a chauffeur and a footman in livery. He started down the steps of the car, then turned back, and taking out his card case said quite simply:

"Oh, perhaps I had better give you my card."

Then he bade me good day and walked over to his automobile. The footman saluted and opened the door for him. He drove off. Then I looked at the card.

It was that of the Duke of A——, one of the great grandees of Spain and a famous connoisseur of art whose collections I knew very well through photographs. I had missed an opportunity.

One summer in Venice, Jules Stewart was painting a large picture of a yachting party at sea.[2] James Gordon Bennett's yacht, the *Namouna*, was lying off San Marco out of commission, and it was the foredeck of that yacht that furnished the background of the picture. Bennett had given Stewart the run of the yacht, and we practically lived on her, going ashore for luncheon and dinner at the restaurants. Models in Venice at that time were not easy to find, and so I posed for one of the men in the group. Stewart made such an exact portrait of me that it was recognized at once when the picture was exhibited. The other members of his yachting party were rather composite in character. A Venetian girl furnished pretty blonde coloring, but her features were not good. Stewart would paint at her for fifteen minutes and then lay down his brushes and exclaim:

"Great Heavens! How ugly she is!"

Fortunately, the girl did not understand that much English and was pleased with herself in the picture because Stewart had made her both young and attractive.

A monkey on a Brazilian sailing vessel lying alongside of us afforded us much amusement. He ran about the ship, up the ratlines, and out on the yardarms, where he would wrap his long tail about the end of the yardarm and swing free for several minutes with astounding security. One day he ran up the ratlines and at the cross-tree met a sailor seated on a swinging board and greasing the mast. He tried to run past as the sailor, with a greasy hand, made a grab at him. The greasy hand succeeded in catching only the tail, which quickly pulled through. Out on the tip of the yardarm the monkey ran, wrapped his greasy tail about the yardarm and started to swing. But the tail slipped and let go. Down the monkey plunged into the water.

A sailor threw him a rope, which he seized and pulled in on the slack with all the cunning of a drowning human. Up that rope he came, hand over hand in the best monkey fashion. He got up on a hatch and sat in the sun rubbing the water off his arms and legs. For several minutes he sat still and meditated, looking very serious and somewhat perplexed. Then his eyes fell on his delinquent tail. He picked it up and looked it over thoughtfully, as though he were saying to himself, "I wonder what happened to that tail. It never went back on me before." But after that we noticed that the yardarm swinging was suspended.

We went ashore at one for luncheon and usually went to the old Capello Nero where we joined Rico and Carlotta. Carlotta was a very pretty blonde, a girlfriend of Rico's, who looked well and talked Venetian with a pretty accent and intonation. She was not exactly an unkissed Diana, and Stewart and I rather objected to sitting with her in the square at night when the band was playing and the crowd had gathered in front of the cafes, but we liked Rico and at the Capello Nero accepted Carlotta with him. Often after luncheon we went to Rico's apartment to talk or smoke or see his work. I had frequent glimpses there of Rico's sketchbooks and pen drawings than which nothing could be more facile or more beautiful. Those who knew only his later commercial paintings could gain from them no adequate idea of the genius of the man. As a pen draftsman he was superb—more brilliant than Fortuny, more effective than Vierge. I still have in a portfolio a pen drawing of his of the statue *Colleone*, done on the back of a letter, that is a marvel of skill, and I still remember his brilliant sketches of Venetian doors, windows, and chimney pots. He was a genius sacrificed to the money god.

I believe before they parted that Carlotta was minded to sacrifice him with a carving knife as the climax of some lovers' quarrel. She made some suggestion about her willingness to "cut his little Spanish heart out," which was not well received by him. At any rate, they parted at the end of the summer. I did not see Carlotta again until two years later, when one day, crossing the Corso in Rome, I was nearly run over by a magnificent team of bays, with a coachman and footman on the box and a great lady on the back seat. The carriage drew in at the curb, and a white ostrich-feather fan waved at me to come to the step. I did so and found that the great lady in silks, with a poodle beside her, was none other than Carlotta. She had struck it rich with a new lover.[3]

At Florians in the Square, over the after-dinner coffee, there was often much discussion among the painters about painting grounds in Venice, around the lagoons, up the Brenta, over at Murano, down at Chioggio. But the undiscovered country that everyone talked about and no one knew was the Dalmatian Coast. Its wonders were those of the Arabian Nights, but none of the Florian band had seen them. The tales ran of the hardships of the trip, the bad steamers and worse hotels, the black beetles and mosquitoes, the cutthroat inhabitants, the dreadful heat. Everyone wanted to go, but everyone was afraid. I tried to drum up a companion for the trip, but met with no response. And then one morning at daylight, I caught a little green-bottomed steamer in front of the Piazetta, and that evening steamed into the beautiful bay of Fiume. The next morning I picked up another little steamer and was off down the Dalmatian Coast.

The little steamer followed the coast in and out among the islands, stopping at little ports on the way. The water was like glass. The push-out from the shoulder of the boat did not break into foam but rolled in a smooth swell. The color was like lapis lazuli and following us down the coast were the Velebit Mountains hued like old ivory. A more beautiful shore, sea, and islands would be difficult to find. We went ashore at Zara [or Zadar] for dinner while the boat was putting off and taking on cargo and dined in a beautiful air and light, in a rather nice garden, but the dinner was an atrocity. A Polish acquaintance whom I had met on the boat dined with me, and after the feast and the payment of the bill, he called up the proprietor and went over the dinner item by item. I never knew the German language was capable of so much vituperation. The proprietor deprecated the attack, threw up his hands as though to ward it off, and finally fled in terror. And the final shaft the Pole shot after him was:

"Und die Butter stinkt!"

We went on to Sebenico and to Spalato. At the latter place is the enormous Palace of Diocletian, with the houses of the natives built into the great walls—a monument remarkable more for its bulk than its beauty. Farther down the coast I stopped for some time at the beautiful walled town of Ragusa. Built on the shore, with its feet in the sea, it is still a perfect example of a medieval city. Seen from the hill back of it, looking down on the towers and walls and Italian-built public buildings and cathedral, it is a city of romance, the most picturesque spot on the Dalmatian coast. There were no black beetles or deep-dyed assassins, and the hotel at Ragusa, though primitive, was not uncomfortable. I found the people very kindly and quite curious about me because of my stranger's appearance. They talked their language at me, which I did not understand. And I replied in some broken Italian, which they did not understand. But nevertheless we understood each other in a general way.

Ragusa from the back-lying hills is a Ragusa of memory. The impression does not fade. From that height overlooking the walled town, I saw at sunset the most beautiful sea that I had ever seen and, then and there, I wrote the preface and cut out the chapters of my book *The Opal Sea* [1906]. That sea was at once an inspiration and a poet's dream.[4]

In later days, Venice changed little, but my early friends there passed away or never returned to the place. Another group, with Hopkinson Smith as the new spokesman for Venice, came in. A more genial, kindly, right-hearted man than Smith never lived. He was a brilliant raconteur, made very clever watercolors, wrote equally clever short stories, talked well after dinner, built good lighthouses, and was an American success—a typical one as regards versatility and ingenuity. Everyone liked him. But I had formed in my mind a Venice of an earlier day and another group of painters— Robert Blum, Charles F. Ulrich, Jules Stewart, Charles Theriat, Aubrey Hunt, Rico, Favretto, Mariano Fortuny. The new crowd was hardly the old one.

After the war [World War I], when smart society from New York came in to rent the old palaces on the Grand Canal and laugh at the Lido, I was again there, but the artist's Venice had almost entirely disappeared. At a still later date, even the smart society passed out. I walked about the square at night seeing no one whom I knew. And so my last morning there, seated at a table in the Piazetta sipping a glass of vermouth, I wrote on the back of a letter the following lines. Evidently, I was "blue," as the children say.

> THE PIAZETTA
> In pinks and mauves and silver grays,
> In twos and threes they ebb and flow,
> Each graceful grouping swings and sways
> As those of forty years ago.
>
> With softer heel and smoother hair,
> Their short skirts blown against their knees,
> Along the Riva to the Square
> They come and go in twos and threes.

They laugh and chatter as they pass.
Carlotta and her friends did so.
I am not dreaming. That, alas!
Was more than forty years ago.

And Tito, Nono, Rico, where?
With Bella of the Muranese?
Ah! long ago they crossed the Square.
They have gone by in twos and threes.

I walk alone, I am the last.
I know not this new ebb and flow,
But—was that wrinkled hag that passed
The flower girl of long ago?

Good night, my Venice, now unknown!
Poor glimpses of the past are these.
I cross San Marco quite alone.
I should have gone in twos and threes.

Venice, July 25, 1923[5]

Chapter 26

New Undertakings

In 1911 I planned to go with my friend George Peet to India. He was to join me at Trieste in November, and we were to take the Austrian *Lloyd* to Bombay. I stopped on my way for a few days with my friends the McClellans at Frankfurt, and the first piece of news that came to me there was that Woodrow Wilson, then governor of New Jersey, had made up a new State Board of Education consisting of eight members and had appointed me one of the board for a term of seven years. I had known Mr. Wilson for a number of years, and we had been very friendly, but I had from him no intimation whatever of this appointment. I did not care for it and was disposed to decline it, but some letters from New Jersey persuaded me to consider it. There was to be an effort at putting the public school system of New Jersey on a high plane, and I was asked to help.

If I accepted the position, it would not interfere with my collegiate and library work at New Brunswick, but it would effectively block my Indian trip. Governor Wilson cabled me that I could go on to India, and my place on the board would be kept open for me until I returned, but I decided that if I were to take up the board work at all it should be at the beginning, when policies were being established. So I reluctantly cabled an acceptance and sent word to Peet that I could not go to India.[1] But before returning to America, I spent two months or more in Europe starting a series of guidebooks to the old masters in the European galleries.

This was the series I had named "New Guides to Old Masters." It was made up of critical notes upon the pictures of almost every public gallery in Europe. In addition to long study carrying over many years in the European galleries, I now began a close scrutiny of every picture from Madrid to St. Petersburg, writing my comment with the picture directly before me. After revising these notes at home during the following winter, I came back to Europe the following summer with the revision to compare it before the pictures again. This I did, with the exception of St. Petersburg, three different times in three different summers, and after that I felt in a position to say positively just what the material condition of each picture, the amount of injury or restoration it had received, and also its defects and its quality of workmanship.

The close investigation of the individual pictures brought out many surprises. Canvases that I thought good turned out to be mere shreds and patches of overlaid paint, many were wrongly attributed, some were copies, and a few were forgeries. The greater works rose to even greater height, and some of the long-neglected were better than the curators and directors supposed. I grew arbitrary in my utterances about them, and when critics and connoisseurs differed with me about this or that picture, I was disposed to insist that while they had looked at the pictures for years they had never really seen them, that I had gone over them inch by inch and hour by hour, and that if they would read my notes directly before the pictures they would see what I had seen. The note read before the picture itself, not the picture recalled from memory over a cup of tea, was the test to which I submitted and in turn exacted.

Of course, the curators and gallery directors did not like the guides. They told the truth about the pictures, and that is what many gallery directors do not wish told. There are, for instance, five Raphaels in the Louvre, and none of them an outstanding work. But the catalogue (and the gallery tradition) has come down with eighteen Raphaels on its list. What director of that museum would have the hardihood to deny the tradition? The French would hang him. All of the galleries still clung to some wrong attributions, still indulged in some false pretenses, still had some ruined pictures under great names. Of course, they cared as little for my guides as for my later books on Rembrandt. But I was not disappointed about that, for I had anticipated it in my prefaces. It was the unexpected thing that proved the undoing of my series. That was the World War [World War I, 1914–1918].

Some nine or ten of the twelve volumes of the guides had been issued when the war abruptly stopped them. The galleries were shut, American travel to the Continent stopped, and everything collapsed. What was the use of issuing additional volumes with no one to use them or want them? The war dragged on for four years, and after that some of the galleries (notably those at Florence, Milan, and St. Petersburg) held their pictures in the storerooms for further years or brought them out in uncatalogued dribs and drabs. I doubt that the Florentine galleries, the most important in Italy, are even now (1930) free from curatorial tyranny or laziness. A more dilatory handling of an important trust was never exhibited, not even in St. Petersburg.

Of course, the guides collapsed. That was to be expected. But many visitors to Florence collapsed, too, while the directors of the galleries there were smoking cigarettes and wondering what sort of new system or arrangement they should adopt. I can make this criticism without mitigation or apology, because after fifty years of library work and all of that time also in contact with European galleries, I know something about cataloguing and arranging pictures. One energetic man could have done more in a year than those Florentine directors, with a contingent of curators, have done in ten.

The guides never recovered from the war. No gallery in Europe carries them on its guide-and-photograph counter. Every director has banned them or is perhaps unnecessarily ignorant of their existence. A few people here in America still use them, and occasionally I see reference to them or get a letter about them, but practically they are dead. That caused me more annoyance than I have ever before been willing to admit. I spent so much time upon them, prepared them so carefully, and was quite sure they were right. Besides, they contained so much material that no history of art or museum catalogue or talks in a gallery ever so much as suggested. I might better have thrown the manuscripts in the fire, since the books brought me only hatred and my too-good publishers, the Scribners, a heavy loss.[2]

I had gone to Russia in 1913 with my friends the McClellans. We went in by way of Vilna and headed directly for St. Petersburg, where I was to spend some time over the collections in the Hermitage. Mr. Sydney P. Noe (now Secretary of the American Numismatic Society), who had been with me in Europe before and had spent a year at the School of Classical Studies in Athens, was to help me in gathering material. But my first few days in the picture galleries were sadly disappointing. Many things, according to my lights, were so wrongly attributed and thoroughly misunderstood that to try to right them would be a hopeless task. I would not be believed or followed by anyone. I told that to my companions and added that I would give up the St. Petersburg pictures before I began with them. I cited the Rembrandts in the Hermitage as a sample of the difficulties. There were forty three of them in the catalogue, and I did not believe that more than half a dozen of them were Rembrandts. At least thirty-five of them were pupil work or school pieces, and I could name the authors of most of them. But what would be the use of saying that? Europe, with little or no direct knowledge of these pictures, had for years accepted the forty-three. Would it now believe the word or opinion of an American writer to the effect that thirty-five of them were not Rembrandts? It was unthinkable. I might better save my breath and let ignorance prevail until the end of time.

But Colonel McClellan was insistent upon my stating my opinion, regardless of the world against me. The truth would prevail. So I did the volume on St. Petersburg. And nothing prevailed except abuse and hootings from critics and experts who had never seen the pictures and had never read my notes about them. The same thing happened ten years later when I put forth two volumes on Rembrandt. They were condemned without a hearing by dealers, collectors, and gallery directors who were interested in having me suppressed, whether I was right or wrong.

The pictures at St. Petersburg were much better than the city, much less disappointing. In 1913 the city was at the height of its splendor, but its refulgence at that date was not sufficient to knock out anyone's eye. The façade of the Hermitage set one's teeth on edge. The Winter Palace, with its cheap plastered walls painted red, had about as much dignity as a defunct brewery. The Great Square in front of it had once been paved with wooden blocks but was now full of chuckholes. The Nevsky Prospect reminded one of Third Avenue in New York City. There was hardly a building in the city that one could stop and look at from an architectural point of view. As for the people, I suppose those in court circles could talk French and had some veneer of cosmopolitanism about them. I don't know, for I never saw them. The only Russians I met were hotel and gallery officials, with shopmen, carmen, cabmen. They seemed much duller than the same class of people elsewhere in the world.

I went to several princely palaces where I found some good pictures, but the taste of the collectors in furnishing the palaces was something of a surprise. The Tartar showed with very little scratching of the skin. Even the summer palaces of the Czar were a wild wonder in their summer-hotel style of architecture and a shock in their interiors with the way things, good and bad alike, were flung together. The *haut monde* of the Russian civilization—well, perhaps there is more of it in French novels than in Russia. At any rate, I came away a sadder and a wiser man, with no disposition ever to return to St. Petersburg.

I think it was this year that on my way home I stopped in Paris for a few days and called on William Dean Howells at the Hotel Albany. I had met him before but had not seen him for years. He had grown quite old and was showing his years but was as bright and interesting, as full of human sympathy and intellectual curiosity, as ever. I remember our talking along the fringe of socialism without entering upon it and yet going close enough to it to reveal his inclination. He was still interested, but I do not think he had made any endorsement of any system. He was a sympathizer with the downtrodden and oppressed, not a doctrinaire with a theory to enforce. And in that, every disinterested person was with him.

I did not see him again for more than a handshake at meetings of the National Institute or dinners of the American Academy. I think my last glimpse of him was at the three-hundredth anniversary of Molière, when, as president of the Academy, he presided at the dinner. I had always liked his writing, admired his character, and rejoiced in his success. He was a fine type of the self-made literary man, made on a substantial, scholarly model. People who have read his two volumes of published letters telling of his career will realize how he labored and what he accomplished. He was decidedly in the tradition of American letters, a torchbearer and a leader of distinction and prominence.

Chapter 27

Work and War

The work of the State Board of Education of New Jersey proved interesting, and I gave much time to it. My associates were educated people, devoted to the schools of the state, and all of them willing to give service without compensation. Four of the eight were lawyers, which was perhaps the reason why I was called upon to write most of the legal opinions when we sat as a court in school disputes. I was also a member of the advisory committee, vice-president of the board, and, during the later years, acting president. For thirteen years I did wheel-horse work on that board, being reappointed by Governor Edge and finally resigning in 1924 because of ill health.

We were a zealous board and so honest that we often leaned over backwards. As a result, we were disputatious and handed out savage opinions of men and things over the table without preface or apology. I never knew such an outspoken, even denunciatory, commission. For several years we cudgeled Dr. Kendall, the Commissioner of Education and the best commissioner the state ever had. Then we turned on each other, and any measure that got through the board had to be bulletproof against objection.

My chief opponent and best friend on the board was John P. Murray of the law firm of Coudert Brothers in New York. We came to grips again and again but always broke away without enmity. Senator Frelinghuysen, Oscar Jeffery (a partner of my old friend Lawrence Sexton), and Robert Lynn Cox of the Metropolitan Life, all might be foes over the board table but were friends at the lunch table. And out of much dispute finally came good results. We fought with Commissioner Kendall and yet stood behind and for him until he had built up the New Jersey school system to a point of commanding excellence. We built the fine normal school at Glassboro, the group of buildings of the school for the deaf at Trenton, and the industrial school at Bordentown. We established financial systems, building codes, and school codes. We settled school litigation, distributed money, lobbied for legislation, worried the appropriations committee of the legislature, and harried the governor. All told, I think we could point with pride to good work accomplished.

As for myself, the experience was unique and never regretted, while the association with members of the board, with thousands of teachers, and hundreds of legislators, was altogether enjoyable. I think when I left the board I had begun to believe that even the politicians were a decent lot and were disposed to do the right thing if they were let alone.[1]

None of my activities at home interrupted my trips to Europe and my study of pictures in European galleries. For many years I traveled wide and far, studying this, that, or the other thing, taking notes and writing books and articles while on boats and trains, in hotels, restaurants, and galleries. I always carried my work with me, always had an object in view, something concrete to carry out, wherever I went. The great bulk of this work never saw the light of publication. It was a sorting and a codifying for a better understanding of the subject. It irked me at times that I had nine years of weeding for one year of seeding. But I knew that better scholars than I were experiencing the same difficulty. Months of gestation to bring forth something that was, perhaps, stillborn.

The Great War put art upon the shelf in company with all the other graces of civilization. The murder of the Archduke found me in Carlsbad, drinking all sorts of *bitterwasser* under the guidance of the great Doctor Torpfer and in the company of Theodore Shonts of the Interborough Railway, Charles R. Miller of the *New York Times*, and Captain Philip Lydig. I had been walking in the country, and coming home that Sunday afternoon, I noticed a small group of people standing about a chemist's window reading a telegram pasted on the glass. It was the announcement of the assassination of the Archduke. I was surprised that those who read the telegram displayed very little or no interest in it. The Archduke was not popular with the masses. His brother Charles was the favorite. But to me that telegram spelt trouble, and I wondered that the crowd at the window did not see it that way.[2]

The Vienna newspapers immediately began a war propaganda. They apparently cared little about the Archduke, but his assassination provided an opportunity. Now was the time to seize Serbia, take over the railway, and connect up with Enver Pasha at Constantinople. It was the way to the Persian Gulf. The German Emperor was behind them. He was stiffening the backbone of Count Berchtold into sending to Serbia an ultimatum impossible of acceptance. Now was the time to enlarge the power of the monarchy and at the same time open an outlet to the east. The Archduke? Oh, well, there would be no trouble about filling his shoes.

I went up to San Martino to join the McClellans. Colonel McClellan and I sat on a bench near the hotel and day by day discussed every phase of the situation with the aid of dozens of newspapers and maps and figured out that there couldn't be such folly among the nations as to launch a war, with its immense losses, over so slight a cause. I think everything we thought could not happen did happen, and everything we thought possible proved impossible. Everyone shared our errors. Even the brilliant diplomats and clever leader writers guessed wrong. The war came off and with a swiftness entirely unanticipated.

We went down to Karersee. Summer guests were flying in all directions like a flock of quail scattered by a hawk. We took rooms at the big hotel at Karersee and waited. The mobilization was taking place, and the fine peasantry of that mountain country was being hurried, with its horses and wagons, down towards Botzen. No one was being left behind except cripples, women, and children. One afternoon at a hut-restaurant far up on the mountainside, we saw a young woman bidding good-bye to her lover with tears and sobs and he turning and running down the mountainside, not looking back for fear of weakening; and the same evening a man saying good-bye to his wife and children at the door of their cottage. It was all very pitiful. And so useless!

We stopped at the Karersee Hotel until it finally shut down and we had to move. We found an old man with an older, heaved, and spavined team and the oldest barouche in all Austria. The man agreed to take us down to Botzen. Luckily, Botzen was downhill, and the heavy, old barouche pushed the horses ahead of it. Otherwise, we would never have arrived. On the way, every peasant cottage emptied itself of women and children, who waved to us as we passed. They were crying and thoroughly miserable. Halfway to Botzen we stopped at a crossroad cottage to rest our ancient driver and horses. I got out and walking about came upon a little girl and a small boy playing in a corn crib. Was that her little brother? I asked.

It was.

Did her parents live there?

Yes, but her father had gone away.

Where?

To the war.

Was her mother there?

Yes.

She pointed to a small bark hut beside the road.

I went over to the hut, which turned out to be a little booth where there were some picture postcards and a little fruit for sale. A young, good-looking woman of perhaps twenty-five sat on a stool gazing mournfully at the floor.

Was it true that her husband had gone to the war?

Yes. He was a teamster (*Wagenmeister*) and had made a living with his horses. She had helped out by selling postcards and a little fruit out of the garden to tourists who came up into the mountains in the summer season. They had been very happy and contented. But now he had been taken away, and his horses with him, and she was left alone with the two children. She did not know what she should do. She was afraid they would starve to death.

I gave her what little Austrian money I had and went away. What could I do to help her? And she was only one of thousands. The whole mountain region with its women and children had been left to starvation and death.

We drove on down the road and in fifteen minutes overtook two soldiers with an eighteen-year-old boy marching between them. The boy was chewing on a stem of grass and looking serious. The soldiers were looking merely stolid. The story was quite obvious. The boy had tried to slip through the cordon of mobilization. He did not want to go to the front and be shot. And perhaps his mother tried to hide him. She wanted to keep him from being shot. But he had been caught. And now what? Would they shoot him at dawn as a deserter? We looked the other way, and the old barouche rattled on. What could we do? This was war.

At Botzen I went to several bankers looking for money. Every one of them shook his head. No Austrian money was obtainable. But one banker, in response to my inquiry, said he could let me have Italian money. I took a thousand lire. We were going down into Italy, and I could use it. A train crowded with soldiers drew into the station. It was going down the Tyrol. We pushed and squeezed and jammed our way into the train. I had never seen so much confusion and mob madness. I got separated from the McClellans and, in a car full of howling, drinking, swearing soldiers, sat grimly on my baggage and smiled it through.

We got to Verona and went over to Milan. Again, I hunted money at the banks, but all the bankers had run to cover like frightened rabbits, and Milan was full of moneyless tourists. United States gold certificates and letters of credit were of no more worth than Indian wampum. Italian money was not obtainable. I worked the Botzen game once more. Could I get Swiss money? Yes. I took twenty-five hundred francs. With what Italian money I had gotten at Botzen, I was now in affluent circumstances.

A meeting of Americans was called at the Hotel Cavour. Nicholas Murray Butler presided. Everyone made a speech, Colonel McClellan and I included. Telegrams were sent to Washington, bankers were anathematized, and war was deprecated. But nothing came of it. We might as well have sung "Old Dan Tucker" to a hurricane.

A group formed around the proposal to charter the *Principe d'Udine*, an old, small, and uncomfortable Italian steamer, and take all the Americans home directly from Genoa, with a stop at Marseilles. Cabins were taken at large figures. The Butlers, McClellans, Horace Andrews, and others, all of them friends of mine, took passage. I declined, and, in consequence, was duly berated by everyone. I would never get home; it was impossible to get up through Europe; and this was the only chance. I continued to decline, saying I was going up to Geneva to join my relatives, the Parrs, that I would not leave them in Europe, and that we were going home from England together on the *Olympic* as originally planned. Anyway, I was not to be stampeded by mobs, military or otherwise. No one was after my scalp. I saw no cause for fear or even alarm. But everyone looked me over with pity and finally abandoned me as weak in the head. They went away in their chartered ship, and I, having exchanged my Italian money for good Swiss francs at a profit, took my way over the Alps to Geneva.

At Geneva I met L. F. Loree, who was booked to join the *Principe d'Udine* at Marseilles. He had an extra stateroom, which he would give me if I would join him on the steamer. I declined. I went out on the south shore of the lake [Lake Geneva] fifteen miles to the old Chateau Bellerive kept by Mademoiselle de Rovere, where the Parrs were staying. I found everyone at the chateau almost francless. The Geneva banks had been shut down with the rest. I was the only one who had any money. People shook their heads over the war, the financial situation, the grave outlook; but there was no demonstration, no hysteria, no throwing of cat fits. Life went on very much as usual, with people talking, laughing, and eating three meals a day.

Nevertheless, when the Germans kept pushing across Belgium, and Amiens with the Calais-Dover railway became obvious objectives, I thought it time to start if we were to make England at all. We got first-class tickets for Paris, had reserved seats, and took hampers filled with food. We met a mob of panic-stricken people in the Geneva station, who had neither tickets nor food, who were bound to go to Paris on our train, and nothing could stop them. They stormed the train and took possession of it, and we stormed with them to get what seats we could. We squeezed into a second-class car and dragged a lone American girl in with us. We "sat tight," and nothing could induce us to exchange our seats for a prospect of anything better.

Paris at that time was surrounded by military zones, and we had to cross these lines, changing cars at each zone, and going through the scramble for places in the new train. No one except the locomotive engineers seemed in charge of the trains, no one took our tickets, no one at stations could or would answer questions. We all sat still and trusted to luck in the matter of reaching Paris. Our fellow travelers talked and smoked and read, but there was alarm in the air, and everyone was nervous. Peasant, priest, and landed proprietor, as they got in or got out, looked serious and smiled grimly. France had grown very sober overnight.

We found Paris gray, with its whilom fashionable throng departed. The streets seemed empty, desolate, and dreary. At the police department where we went to get a *laissez-passer*, they told us people were dancing on the boulevards, but we did not believe it. The hotels were on a war diet, with black bread to the fore and, again, everyone low-spirited. It was the 24th of August, and the Germans were close to Amiens. Things did not look too promising for Paris.

In a few days we took train for England, passed through Amiens forty-eight hours before the Germans got there, and arrived safely at Calais. The train was crowded, wild stories of treachery passed about among the passengers, and everyone seemed apprehensive of disaster to France. And the individual seemed perhaps unduly apprehensive for his own safety. It seemed to be taken for granted that if the Germans captured our trainload of tourists, we should all have our throats cut. But all that either the Germans or the French desired of us was that we get out of their way. There was no cause for alarm, but there was little use in saying so. When we had crossed the Channel and drew into the dock at Dover, out of the reach of German submarines, there was a "thank God" breathed in silence, but even then the American tourist was not happy. He had the Atlantic to cross with the German submarines "laying" for him.

The Parrs and I did not have to cross that bridge for a month, and we borrowed no trouble in advance. We went up into Devonshire, sat down at the Peacock Inn, and, once more, let the wind blow. The clash of battle was a long way off, and the sun was shining brightly in Derbyshire.³ But over the tea table when the London newspapers had come in and been read, there was much grave talk and no little apprehension. Things were going badly, and Englishmen knew there was a long, stiff fight ahead, but they were confident of winning out. They were grave but determined, apprehensive but not frightened. America was not then involved, and we were only spectators, but we could admire the courage of the English and their determination, even at that early stage, to carry through, no matter what it might cost.

We came home on the *Olympic* as planned, without disaster. We ran through the nights with darkened portholes and no forelights and watched through the days for the enemy. But he did not appear. Halfway across the

Atlantic a cruiser came up over the horizon, and some of the passengers went down on their knees, but it turned out to be an old British cruiser wallowing about in the seas. Once more the ship's passengers assumed the perpendicular. The expected happened. We came into the harbor of New York, on time and none the worse for our war experience.

Chapter 28

Mountain, Desert, and Grand Canyon

With Europe shut off by the war and art a closed book so far as the European galleries and my guides were concerned, there was nothing to do but to turn to nature in the West. I had long been studying the mountains in Europe and America and finally threw into shape a volume in my nature series with the title of *The Mountain* [1916].[1] This work I did at odd hours on my brother's Silver Valley Ranch in the Mojave Desert.[2]

It was a rather good book; at the least I liked it at the time because I kept pushing into it not only quotations from my own unpublished verse, which caused a few inquiries as to their sources,[3] but also I pushed in a good deal of unpublished geology that led two or three geological reviewers to remark the pity of my not knowing my geology better. The fact was that I had early grown skeptical of authorities, scientific or otherwise, and sometimes accepted my own guess as being quite as good as theirs. I had no great faith in my own theories—about mountain forming, for example—but neither had I much belief in the theories set forth by scientists. But the vast impertinence of a layman having any opinion whatever about science! It was in the same category with his supposing that he knew anything about art. Only the cook knows a good broth, and it takes a geologist to tell a mountain from a molehill. But the everlasting changing of opinion about both the broth and the mountain rather shakes confidence.

I think this was the second or third summer that John Muir came to the ranch. He had an invalid daughter who had been living for several years on the ranch, and he made periodic trips to see her. I was, however, much flattered by his saying in his simple Scotch way that he had made this trip, at this time, that he might meet me. He liked my book on the desert, he liked my brother who lived in the desert, and he thought he might like me. Well, at any rate, I liked him. He was Scotch and sterling, an upright, truthful soul if there ever was one. Muir's integrity, knowledge, and homespun simplicity were his great assets, not only socially but scientifically. He was a great botanist who lived and worked outside the college laboratory. What he knew was come by at firsthand, the most vital kind of knowledge. What he didn't know he was quite willing to admit. Again and again on desert walks I asked him about desert plants. I wanted to know their botanical names and classes. But again and again Muir would say:

"I don't know."

He could afford to say that. Many a smaller mind would have dodged the question or sparred for wind, pretending to a knowledge that he did not possess. But Muir was always frank and exactly honest. That is one of the convincing qualities of his books. You feel they are absolutely true.

And he was more than half Brahmin in his aversion to the destruction of life. He, of course, did not hold life sacred in any religious sense, but he disliked wanton destruction. While he was at the ranch that summer, there was an invasion of jackrabbits from the desert that sometimes ate up half a dozen acres of alfalfa in a night. Something had to be done. So every morning at dawn there was a rabbit drive. Sixteen or twenty ranchmen, on horseback and afoot, drove the rabbits into wire corrals and killed as many as five hundred in a morning. More than five thousand rabbits were killed in two weeks. Their decaying carcasses tainted the desert winds. Muir did not like it. He was practical enough to know that it was death to either the rabbits or the ranchers, but he thought the poor rabbits were only following a natural instinct and should not be slaughtered in such a wholesale manner.

I never saw him with a gun and doubt that in later life he ever carried one or shot anything. He used to go into the mountains for days and weeks with only a bag of bread and some tea, sleeping in a bush like a rabbit and enduring rain and cold like a bear. But he had his contradictions like other men. He could not abide bands of sheep. He used to call them four-footed locusts because they destroyed his wild flowers and wrecked his mountain meadows. Had anyone cut the throats of five thousand sheep I doubt that he would have protested.[4]

On the floor of the ranch house, for lack of room elsewhere, were sixteen volumes of Pierre Loti. The brother liked his graceful method and his observation, and I had read *La Galilée* and *Le Désert* with much admiration. His point of view in such a book as *Le Désert* was so radically different from my own that perhaps the attraction was by opposition. He dealt with the human element, and the desert of the Sinai Peninsula was only a background for his Bedouin caravan. I wrote about the uninhabited deserts of our western country, and the human element was reduced to a minimum. But I liked Loti's book better than my own, and in reading those sixteen volumes lying on the ranch house floor, I wished more than once that I had his imagination and grace of manner.

But I have never changed my point of view about that human element. In my thinking, it has no place in wild nature because nature itself is, or should be, the all-absorbing topic. Heaven knows the literature of humanity is large enough without dragging it into such sublime isolations as the desert, the mountains, and the ocean. I wrote something of that to Loti when he was in this country a short time before his death. His answer said that he was very much "touched" by his sixteen volumes on the floor of the ranch house in the Mojave, but I do not remember that he replied to my argument against humanity in desert literature.[5]

The profound ignorance of their antecedents held by the nephews and nieces living on the Pacific coast quite appalled me. They had never been told anything about their ancestry and evidently did not care anything about it. So when I went home that autumn, I wrote for them (and privately published) a hundred-page booklet, *The Raritan: Notes on a River and a Family* [1915].[6] That little publication seemed to be better liked and was more in demand (from people who could not get it) than anything else I ever wrote. That was because it contained the despised human element to start with, and because it contained some unwritten New Jersey history besides. It is now very scarce (what the German booksellers call *sehr selten* [very rare]), and if a copy turns up in a secondhand catalog, it is under "Jerseyana" and commands a large price. What nice little hits we make when we don't try! And what a mess we make of things when we think to do a great masterpiece! "Pressing" in writing is just as fatal as in golf.

The celebration at Rutgers that autumn of the one-hundred-and-fiftieth anniversary of the college brought Frederick Keppel and William Roscoe Thayer to New Brunswick as representatives respectively of Columbia and Harvard.[7] They spent the night at my house, and we talked golf and teed-up literature far into the night. Both were very intelligent, well-versed, and knew how to talk. Had I known then that I should write this autobiography, I would certainly have asked Thayer, our best biographer, how to do it. Perhaps even so I should not have followed instructions. Since I started this, I have read his *Art of Biography*—his University of Virginia lectures—but got no more from it than from reading his *Cavour*. Both volumes were admirable but not to be followed by any other biographer. There is always a personality that defies the imitator, and in the end a person has to be himself, even though he likes someone else better.

I was in California at the desert ranch and in Oregon and Washington the following two years. Both years I stopped for some weeks at the Grand Canyon of the Colorado and looked it over carefully, taking many notes and drawings. It came to me, as to others, as our greatest natural wonder, perhaps the greatest in the world, and grew more wonderful each time I saw it. The Canyon of the Yellowstone, the Yosemite, and Crater Lake were very beautiful but not comparable to the Grand Canyon. It had all their color beauty and more, with a hundred times their bulk and mass. Nothing but a trench in the ground but even so the height of the sublime.[8]

The third summer (1918) I came out early to the Grand Canyon determined to spend some months there. Fortunately, I met at the El Tovar Hotel the well-known painter William Ritschel.[9] He was feeling about in his mind, wondering if he could do any better with the Canyon as a subject than the many painters before him, and I was going around in circles wondering whether I could do any better than the writers before me. We came together in wonder and joined forces. We went east along the Rim some thirty-five miles to Desert View, overlooking the Painted Desert. The El Tovar company had built two cabins out there, and we camped down in one of them for three weeks, doing our own cooking with provisions brought with us.

Ritschel spent his days painting pictures that were scraped off the canvas each night. I thought his work the best attempt at the Canyon I had seen, but he was not in conceit of it, declaring that the Canyon was "too big" and he could not do anything with it. I quite understood that but still thought the portions of sheer wall and shadowed depth that he did were representative of the whole. He made no attempt to do a great perspective view of the Canyon. That would have been a foredoomed failure, a mere panorama of which there had been enough and to spare. But Ritschel was not to be persuaded that he could master the subject, though he kept trying it anew every morning.

I spent my days going down into the Canyon by deer trails, studying the geological strata, fossilizing, botanizing, roaming the lower plateaus, and hanging over precipices. I had moccasins on my feet and could work along ledges and around escarpments without risk. I had the feel of the rock under my feet. The whole summer I felt that rock. I doubt that anyone ever "did" the sixty miles of the Grand Canyon from Rim to river more thoroughly. I was determined to see it in my own way and for my own purposes. Of course, I had a book in mind and was gathering material for a rhapsody on Canyon beauty.

That beauty as seen during those weeks at Desert View was most amazing. Every evening from four until dusk, Ritschel and I sat along the Rim and watched the changing light and color in the Canyon depths, along the great perpendicular walls, and in the western sky. The violet air and light that came at dusk made us rave with meaningless exclamations. Occasionally an automobile with three or four visitors from El Tovar came into camp. We held them until dusk, and they were more mad than we about the color and the light. Then the wildly spectacular appeared unexpectedly in gathering sandstorms and thunderstorms on the Painted Desert, in rainbows and sunshafts and sunsets, in Canyon gloom of the Inner Gorge, and golden glory on the high red walls. Long after dark we sat on the Rim and saw mysterious fields of phosphorescent light gather in the depths, and the great red moon come up to throw still more weird light into the Canyon. This and much more was what Ritschel could not catch with colors nor I with words. He did not have enough palette and I ran short of vocabulary at the very start.

After Ritschel left, I went to the other end of the Canyon, twenty miles west of El Tovar, and made my headquarters with my friend, William Bass, at Bass Canyon.[10] Once more, I went up and down the deer trails, from Rim to river, studying strata, fossils, flora, fauna, with light, air, and color. There are supposed to be only three or four trails to the river, but I found eight or nine ways of getting up and down afoot. And I devised all sorts of ways of reaching so-called "cliff dwellings" on projecting ledges and under escarpments. I felt satisfied that I had thoroughly seen that sixty miles of Canyon and had sufficient information about it, but every attempt to put it into words was more or less of a failure.

Matters of small importance seemed more amenable to language. For example, one day I had walked from sunrise until dusk, with a few sandwiches under a cedar for lunch at noontime. When I got back, Bass asked me where I had been. I told him. He wanted to know immediately if I knew how far I had traveled that day. I said:

"Yes, from the feeling of my legs, about thirty miles."

He thought it more and wondered at my years (I was sixty-three) how I kept my legs in such good trim. That set me figuring on a pine shingle. I was walking in moccasins and with a good yard stride. There were 1,760 yards in a mile and for thirty miles 52,800 strides. That meant that my legs had lifted and carried forward about 160 pounds at least 52,800 times.[11]

How very easily a little item like that tells itself. But try to convey the impression of sunlight through violet air falling upon the red wall, try to give in words the glint and gleam and mica texture of the Archaean rock of the Inner Gorge, try to reveal the splendor of dawn over the Painted Desert, and you will understand how poor a vehicle is language.

But in spite of the many failures before me in both verse and prose, I wrote three hundred pages about the Canyon. The book came out and was no worse than the others. In fact, with many of the Santa Fe Railway's best photographs for illustration, it sold very well and is still selling, but I never was too proud of it. Professor F. L. Ransome of the United States Geological Survey was with me during my August days at the Canyon, and later on he was good enough to read and pass the geological chapters of the book. It was correct enough, but the shaft fell short of the mark.[12]

Chapter 29

Concerning Rembrandt

My studies in the old masters of Europe rather drew me away from contemporary art in America. I wrote little or nothing for the periodical press.
The Outlook asked me to do a series of monographs on prominent American artists, and I did articles on George Inness and John Sargent. I
declined to carry on further. But now that the war was on, and my studies
of the Dutch and Italian schools were interrupted, I turned once more to
our native painters and shaped a book, *American Art and Its Tradition*
[*American Painting and Its Tradition*, 1919]. It was a history of the art movement in America during my own time, as exemplified in nine American
painters: George Inness, A. H. Wyant, Homer Martin, Winslow Homer,
John La Farge, James McNeill Whistler, William M. Chase, John Alexander, and John S. Sargent. I had known all of them, and I wrote about their
methods and their work from considerable personal knowledge. Evidently,
that had much to do with the success of the book. It was accepted as a
contribution to the history of American art, and that, of course, was its
aim.

The war in Europe ended amid great rejoicing, but I did not go back
immediately to my gallery studies. There was so much confusion, distress,
and shortage of food all over Europe that strangers seemed not wanted.[1] It
was not until 1921 that I again went back to Germany—to the north German towns—to continue my intensive study of Rembrandt and his school.
In the meantime, I kept turning out books about people and things American. My long-time friend Andrew Carnegie died [1919]. During his latter
years he had written at odd times chapters of an autobiography. It needed
some editing to establish the continuity and sequence of the narrative. Mrs.
Carnegie put the manuscript in my hands, and I spent some months in
shaping it for publication. Houghton, Mifflin and Co. published it with
great success, selling many thousand copies. School editions of it were
issued, and translations of it were made in German, Japanese, and other
tongues. It was accepted as a remarkable autobiography, the record of a
striking personality and a most interesting period. Burton Hendrick is now
preparing a more elaborate two-volume biography of Mr. Carnegie, and

that will undoubtedly picture the period of industrial development in greater detail. But Carnegie the man is well portrayed in his own words.

Perhaps Carnegie's *Autobiography* [1920] and my recollections of American painters put me in a reminiscent mood, for I began writing another nature book which had to do with my own experiences in the open. I gave it the title *The Open Spaces* [1922], which was explanatory at least, for the book dealt with the prairies, tablelands, mesas, and deserts in America and elsewhere. In my boyhood I would have loved such a book for the bears and wolves and snakes of it, but I fear the boys of today never heard of it. Of course, I was not able to tell my own joy in the open country and the big expanses. I have never read any book that expressed the right feeling for space. But the book chronicled much small beer of adventure and was well enough, if somewhat mistakenly, received.

It, for example, brought me some letters from big-game hunters at home and abroad. But I was not writing a big-game book. Like my desert, sea, and mountain books, it was concerned with the beauty of natural appearances, and yet like them, it was mistaken for a book of travel, or a popularization of science, or something else that I never dreamt of.[2] I seemed to have had a fatal facility in creating misunderstandings, or perhaps I should say for seeing the unexpected or perverse side of things. This was to be demonstrated shortly in my books on Rembrandt. They told too much of the unexpected.

I had been studying Rembrandt in a desultory way for many years, but when, as a result of that study, I decided to say something about him, I began a very precise and direct examination of his pictures and those of his pupils. This carried on for half a dozen years. Some hint of what I was doing got out. Edward Bok, who was editing a series of books for the Scribners on great Dutchmen, asked me to do a volume for his series on Rembrandt, and at the same time the Metropolitan Museum asked me to lecture on the great painter. I made answer to both of them to the effect that I was doing something on Rembrandt, but when they saw it they would be thankful it had not been addressed to their audiences. It would be a protest against accepted ideas and would meet with dissent. I was determined to speak out and tell the truth as I saw it, though the heavens fell about my ears.

Now the study of Rembrandt's handling and brushwork, together with his light, color, composition, his mental and moral attitudes, made me absolutely certain that he never could have painted in all the different styles, in all the different pictures, assigned to him. Great painters are not various in method. They keep on working in one general way, on one favorite theme, trying with each new endeavor to say the thing better and more completely. I became equally certain that many of the Rembrandts were painted by his pupils and sold under the master's name, as was the custom of the times, because I could trace the brushwork and the styles of the pupils as readily as that of the master. Then there were many Rembrandtesque pictures done by followers, imitators, copyists, and forgers that were included in the Rembrandt *oeuvre*. The Dutch, German, and English writers on Rembrandt gave him some 800-odd pictures and to his seventy-two pupils not ten pictures apiece—to some of them not a single picture. The question came up: What happened to their pictures that they had so quietly slipped out of existence? Had they been "signed up" and sold as Rembrandts?

Could Rembrandt paint 800 pictures in his lifetime? Yes, he could. And so could each one of his pupils. But what would be the survival of the 800 after 300 years? Well, in Italy the average survival of the old masters comparable in ability to Rembrandt—the Raphaels, Andrea del Sartos, Giorgiones, Palmas, and Paolo Veroneses—is a little under forty pictures apiece, and only two of them (Titian and Tintoretto) over a hundred. Again I asked, how did it happen that Rembrandt should survive in 800 pictures and that twenty of his pupils should not have a scrap left to their names?

A dozen years ago, what would an Eeckhout, a Maes, a Drost, or a Horst bring in the auction room? Five hundred or a thousand dollars. What the value of a canvas with the name of Rembrandt attached? Why, a hundred or two hundred thousand dollars. Naturally, there was a hunt for Rembrandts, and when not found there was a strong motive to make a picture of a pupil do service for that of the master. The Rembrandt *oeuvre* grew instead of lessening with the years. It is still growing.

Today, the pictures attributed to Rembrandt make up a huge snowball that has gathered to itself hundreds of pictures belonging to the Rembrandt school that are superficially like Rembrandt but are by his pupils, followers, and imitators.

I began taking the snowball to pieces. I found some forty or fifty pictures that I was sure were Rembrandts and represented him in his several periods. They were accepted by everyone as Rembrandts. I put these apart and insisted that they would establish a Rembrandt criterion by which all the pictures in the *oeuvre* might be judged. I did the same thing for Bol, Flink, Eeckhout, Maes, and all of the Rembrandt pupils who had any pictures left under their names. That established some twenty or thirty groups, some of them by name and some of them by number only, each group in itself becoming the criterion of one painter, whether known by name or quite unknown. I took away from Rembrandt several hundred pictures and parceled them out among the group or groups to which (from their style and brushwork) they belonged. I was astonished to find that each group of pictures, when brought together in reproductions, not only fitted together by likeness and analogy but made up and established a definite artistic personality that stood by itself and would not mingle or blend with any of the other groups or personalities. I not only brought this out by notes but by photographic reproductions of the pictures put side by side in "deadly parallel." This argument with much collateral proof was carried through a dozen or more chapters and made up what I thought was a good case.

Of course, I knew the argument would not be accepted by interested parties, that the case would be hotly contested and that I would be severely criticized. I forestalled this by writing in the preface:

> It will be readily understood that such a book as this is not put forth without misgivings. One hesitates about flying in the face of preconceived opinion and inviting denunciation. Writers who have written seriously but mistakenly about Rembrandt (and I am one of them), gallery directors who have catalogued Rembrandt, art authorities, experts, collectors or dealers who have advised about or bought or sold Rembrandts may feel obliged to defend themselves by denouncing my conclusions. I have no wish to discredit anyone's authority or to depreciate the commercial value of anyone's holdings but I cannot be turned aside by such considerations. [*Rembrandt and His School* ix]

I knew that many of my attributions would be attacked and that beyond question I would be found in error here and there. It was not possible for me (or, for that matter, anyone else) to change the attributions of several hundred pictures without making blunders. So I continually wrote in at the end of notes to pictures the words "Attribution tentative." Apparently, no one paid any attention to this. Certainly no one heeded it. But in spite of blunders, I still maintained that my general argument and the bulk of my assignments were correct and that I was merely breaking a rough trail that others hereafter would follow and develop.

Well, the first volume came out in 1923, very handsomely published in a limited edition by the Scribners, and was duly damned from Maine to California, from Paris to Hong Kong, before anyone had time to read it or even see it. Some statement to the effect that it gave only fifty pictures to

Rembrandt instead of 800, that it denied three quarters of the Rembrandts in European galleries and all of the twenty-odd in the Metropolitan Museum, was sent out the day of publication. That was sufficient. A long, loud, and vehement protest went up from dealers, gallery directors, collectors, critics, and art writers. All the interested parties felt themselves aggrieved. They gave interviews, they "wrote to the *Times*," they called me all the names in the calendar. And who was I, anyway?

The sensation of it ran on the front pages of the metropolitan dailies for a week. I was interviewed each day by half a dozen reporters, but my sole insistence was that the book would speak for itself and that I would not retract a line of it. It was the plain, unvarnished truth, and the art world could take it or let it alone, as it pleased. Gallery directors and dealers in London, Paris, and Berlin were cabled for their opinions and denied everything without any knowledge of what they were denying. Wild statements of what the book contained were cabled around the world and found militant echoes in Java and South America. Never an American book was published that received so much abuse.

I suppose some people asked themselves why, if the book was written by an idiot and contained nothing of importance, there was so much fuss made about it. Evidently, some of the interested parties felt that they had been stepped upon, though that was not the aim of the book. The dealers put their heads together and made out that I was shooting at them, though that, again, was not my object. They threatened to sue me but thought better of it, not wishing perhaps for further publicity in the courts. Finally, a long "Shhhh! It will all blow over," went down the line and silence reigned.

After a week or two, long reviews of the book began to appear in the periodical press. With a half dozen exceptions, they might have been written by the snake editor, so far as any comprehension of the book was concerned. They were mere diatribes telling me what Dr. Hofstede de Groot or Dr. Bredius or Dr. Bode said about this picture or that, as though that was the whole law and gospel of art. To the average whippersnapper it seemed incomprehensible that anyone could have an opinion different from that of the Rembrandt doctors. The half dozen exceptions disagreed with me in general, admitting I was right in some particulars. Some others— Professor Allen Marquand, Professor Frank Jewett Mather, Dr. Schmidt-Degener—went a little further and endorsed my general argument. But on the whole, the book was thoroughly cursed out and consigned to everlasting perdition. I had expected dissent but not such wholesale condemnation.

Nothing in the condemnation convinced me that I had not told the truth in a candid, scholarly fashion. No one analyzed my argument or took up my attributions one by one and answered me in kind. For example, I said positively and pointed out in detail over two pages in the *New York Times* that the *Old Woman Cutting Her Nails*, in the Metropolitan Museum, was a repainted picture by Nicolas Maes. No one made answer. I said and pointed out in detail that the principal portrait of Rembrandt in the National Gallery, London, was a flat copy. No answer. I said and pointed out and gave reasons for saying so that a dozen named Rembrandts in the Berlin Gallery were not Rembrandts but works by pupils whom I named. No answer. Hundreds of cases like this appeared in analysis in the book, but no one offered an analytical or critical rejoinder. Pages were given to condemnation, but it was all of a general character, a wholesale, irritable, and contemptuous disapproval.

I could not and would not accept that verdict. Nine tenths of my critics were interested parties. They were dealers who had bought and sold the pictures I denied, experts who had authenticated and certified those pictures for sale, collectors and gallery directors who had bought them at high prices, critics who had written about Rembrandt and were on record about those pictures. I could not be stampeded by such an opposition.³ So I quite calmly went about preparing the second Rembrandt book, *The Rembrandt Drawings and Etchings*. I had promised this second book in the preface of the first, and again I was determined to bring it out no matter what the consequences.

I took four years to the second book, preparing it after the pattern of the first and illustrating it with about 200 drawings and etchings arranged, again, in "deadly parallel." My staunch supporter, Charles Scribner, brought it out in limited edition as a companion volume to the first book. Joseph Pennell was to have written notes about the etchings and drawings and was to have had liberty to say what he pleased, either for or against my views, but unfortunately he died before the book went to press. It was not published until 1927.⁴ It was received with hostility like its predecessor. It ran for a few days in the news columns and was just as ignorantly condemned by dealers and others who never saw it, but it bolstered up the argument of the first book and presently won respectful consideration. The later reviews summarized the whole controversy, some by admitting I had a good case but spoiled it by overemphasis, others that I was about fifty percent right, and others that many of my attributions were correct. What I had really done perhaps was to set people thinking, not only about Rembrandt but about many other old masters. When it is realized that all the pictures by all the old masters of the last 400 years are being sold under less than 250 names, there may be some further thinking.

However, this commercial phase of Rembrandt was not at all my object in writing the Rembrandt monographs. My thought was solely to establish the truth of history, to render to Rembrandt the things that were Rembrandt's and to restore to his pupils the pictures that were theirs.[5] I had no quarrel with dealers. They took up the cudgels against me because I denied their attributions.

Chapter 30

Compensations

There were some honors that came to me about the time of the Rembrandt uproar that were in the nature of consolation prizes. I had long been [since 1908] a member of the National Institute of Arts and Letters and one of its council. In 1922 I became its acting president and later was elected its president [1924–1925]. The Institute was limited to 250 members, and only authors, artists, architects, and composers who had distinguished themselves were eligible for membership. Its roll of members contained the names of the leaders in arts and letters in America. Why should I not feel honored by the vote of confidence of such a body of men?

The 250 members of the Institute form a list from which the American Academy of Arts and Letters elects its members. It is, in short, a waiting list, and when one of the fifty members of the Academy dies, someone from the Institute is elected to fill his chair. When the distinguished painter Elihu Vedder passed out, I was nominated for his chair. The election took place six weeks after the issue of my first Rembrandt book [1923], and I suppose some people regarded it as a bolstering up of my book and its contention—a "crowning" of the work as a rebuke to the clamor against it. If anyone chose to think that thought, I said nothing to undeceive him, though I was in a position to do so. The election had virtually taken place before the book was issued and was in recognition of previous work. More-over, the election was unanimous (as the secretary afterward told me), I receiving the entire thirty-one votes of the section of literature, the section that had to pass on me and hand me up for confirmation by the whole body. Naturally, I was mightily pleased by both the recommendation and the confirmation. To hold a place in an academy where men like Lowell, Mark Twain, Gilder, Thomas Bailey Aldrich, John La Farge, Saint-Gaudens, Theodore Roosevelt, and Woodrow Wilson once sat, and where John S. Sargent, W. C. Brownell, Brander Matthews, George Woodberry, Nicholas Murray Butler, Elihu Root, David Jayne Hill, and Augustus Thomas were still sitting, was a great honor, perhaps the best honor I have ever received.

And a high compliment. One does not care much about the opinion of the man in the street. What the general public thinks of one's rank is not taken seriously by the lawyer, physician, artist, or writer. The lawyer seeks recognition from the bar association, his own professional associates, the physician looks to his medical society, the artist to his brother artists, the writer to his brother writers. Each regards his professional brethren as the best judges of his work, and when they say he is a good lawyer, doctor, artist, or writer it means something. It is an authoritative utterance and constitutes the best compliment he can receive. So I was honored, complimented, and pleased by my election to the Academy, that election having been brought about by the votes of fellow writers.[1]

My own university (Rutgers) stood by me and for me during the Rembrandt row, and at its commencement that year gave me its highest degree, doctor of laws. Again, I knew the conferring of the degree had been determined upon in advance of the Rembrandt book's publication, but its coming at a time "when a fellow needed a friend" was opportune. The commencement audience of some two thousand or more at any rate took it as an endorsement and added its approval by loud and prolonged applause—so much so that all of us on the platform had to stand and wait till the tumult died out. That was the shout of the man in the street. And that time I did not despise it in the least. It was the largest ovation I had ever received, and I grinned over it with delight for several days. Those who applauded wished me well at least, believed I was entitled to that degree, and I never for a moment thought of impugning their judgment. Vanity is at the heart of us all. We are easily flattered. We may know that and yet still be pleased by the wish to flatter.[2]

There were compensations of another kind that came in with 1925. They had to be reckoned with. I fell ill. After a few days in the Presbyterian Hospital, I was told I would have to quit work, give up for some weeks or months. I had been ill for years, struggling to keep my nose above water. I was sixty-nine. It occurred to me instantly that I was old enough to give up permanently so far as routine work was concerned. I went home that night and before going to bed wrote out resignations from the State Board of Education, from the Sage Library, from Rutgers University, from the Century Club directorate—from every board, commission, and committee with which I was connected. Lest I should be smitten with a morning repentance, I went out and put all the letters in the mailbox that night. Both the University and the Library declined to accept my resignations. It was their wish that I be put on leave of absence, and I was likely to remain so for the rest of my days.[3]

In less than twenty-four hours I had made preparations for departure. I went to Asheville, North Carolina, and put myself in the hands of Dr. Charles Miner, who was not only a guide and philosopher but (afterwards) a very good friend. I surrendered unconditionally and agreed to do as I was told—something I had never done before. Dr. Miner was very comforting and told me at once that I was not hard hit and what damage I had received was the direct result of my pernicious vegetable diet. If I would go back to sensible living, stop work, and rest completely, I would be all right in six weeks. I agreed.

At once I began to improve. I sat on the porch and again watched the wind blowing in the trees. I walked in the woods and watched the birds and squirrels. I ate whatever was placed before me and slept in the open air. In six weeks Dr. Miner told me I could go home when I pleased and take up work in moderation if I chose, that so far as he could see I was in excellent shape. But the spring was coming on in North Carolina, southern birds were coming in, and spring flowers were coming up. I wanted to see a Southern spring, and, besides, I liked the place and the people, especially my doctor, and so I stayed on for two months more, listening to the red-bird's "pretty, pretty, pretty" and seeing the robins ganging to go north.

In May I went north, stopped a month at my New Brunswick home, and then went to Onteora Park in the Catskills, where I had taken a house for the summer. Professor and Mrs. Harry Parr went with me. There in the mountain air I once more sat on the porch and looked at the trees against the blue sky. I was taking kindly to the idea that I might look at things and get pleasure therefrom without jotting it down in notes for another book. Letting the world slip was a further idea that began to appeal to me. It would slip anyway. I had not been able to stop it. Why bother about it further? Other people were taking life lightly, and why should I accept it so seriously?[4]

But I was by birth half Puritan, and neither my principles nor my nerves would let me stay idle for long. I began writing another nature book, *The Meadows: Familiar Studies of the Commonplace* [1926]. They were my own meadows lying across the river from my New Brunswick home, the meadows of the Raritan River, which I had walked for more than fifty years and knew by heart. It was a buttercup-and-daisy book, with trees and flags and meadow grasses, with muskrats and field mice and rabbits, with bluebirds and robins, and all the commonplace things of a New Jersey landscape woven into it. Of course, the burden of the lay was the beauty of familiar things, an argument for everyday nature. I even burst into song about it in the chapter headings and nearly burst into tears when I found the songs rated in the (London) *Times* as "average calendar verse." But the *Times* liked the prose, and so did many people living in the Raritan Valley. The book was widely accepted, though perhaps its argument reached only a small audience. People are impressed with a purple-patch description or a sentimental illustration far oftener than by argument.[5]

Before leaving Onteora that autumn of 1925, we bought a cottage in the woods from Mrs. John W. Alexander and became summer residents of Onteora in permanency.[6] My order of living became Onteora in the summer, the tropics in the winter, and New Brunswick in the spring and autumn.

That autumn I went to Jamaica in the West Indies, spending some weeks at Montego Bay and along the north shore, and was much impressed with the deep blue sea and the tropical light. It was here that Winslow Homer had found material for some of his remarkable watercolors. I had no difficulty in recognizing his painting ground, but I was bothered by his light and his palette of color. The palette he had set for himself was the same as that of his Maine Coast marines, and his light was that of the mournful and misty Atlantic. But the Caribbean light is more golden than gray, and its color is rich in reds, lilacs, and oranges, as well as in Homer's silvers, blues, and greens. That is not to question the great beauty of Homer's watercolors but merely an observation about local color. The tropical light is, generally speaking, warm, whereas the temperate zones are gray and the poles white.[7]

I went from Kingston to Panama, passing through the canal and like every other American was properly proud of it, but I did not rave. Joseph Pennell had made etchings and lithographs of it while it was under construction, and I had half agreed to write a text for his drawings. But Rembrandt absorbed my energies at that time, and Pennell unhappily died [1926], and my end of the work came to naught. I stopped at Panama only long enough to catch the steamer *Essequibo* for Valparaiso. We swung out into the Pacific—in a few days the equatorial Pacific—a tremendous expanse of water, smooth and glowing like opalescent glass. I dare say the horizon rim was no farther, no rounder there, than on the North Atlantic, but it appeared far vaster. I had never seen its like before, and I marveled and wondered over it as over the great inverted cup of blue overhead. Balboa, who saw only the water of the Gulf of Panama, had he seen the real Pacific! But he never did.

Chapter 31

South America

I was greatly interested in the Humboldt Current that comes up the west coast of South America. It is the return current of the South Pacific eddy, the main branch of which goes down the coast of Australia and crossing the South Sea flows up the South American coast. Its crossing of the South Sea (with its Antarctic contact) is no doubt responsible for its coldness. The chill of the water in turn accounts for the enormous fish life of it. The small bait fish living in the surface waters frequently cover many acres. The whole surface for a mile or more sometimes fairly seethes with them. Following and feeding upon them are larger fish forms—great mackerels, sea bass, porpoises, blackfish, and whales, with colonies of swift-traveling seals and otters.

The rocky islands of the coast are the roosting and nesting places of many thousands of gannets, cormorants, pelicans, and other birds that follow the chase and live on the fish. The long lines of cormorants patrolling the sea make a dragnet miles in length, and bands of pelicans come and go from island to sea, and from sea to shore, patrolling again and watching for a surface agitation that would indicate a school of fish. The exchange of life for death, and the rapacity of it, is appalling.

Life, and with it rapacity of another sort, appeared in the towns and cities of the west coast where the steamer stopped, but I was not greatly interested in it. Callao and Lima and Antofagasta were neither savage nor civilized but smacking of both. Valparaiso was only a shade better, with some rather good suburbs and a fine harbor. I wished to stay in Chile for more than a week and had to see the police department about it. I had to be photographed, fingerprinted, and put in the police files like a criminal. The chief of police, by way of sweetening this pill, told me that everyone in Chile was fingerprinted and photographed, including the president, commanding officer, and the chief of police himself. This seemed with him a matter of pride in the system, but it struck me as an admission of weakness. A government that has so little confidence in its people cannot be very well based.

The climate of Chile was very like that of Southern California, and going up from Valparaiso to Santiago revealed a country, again, very like

California or Southern Spain. Both were attractive, more so than the towns, though Santiago was interesting, old-fashioned, and half romantic. The clang of the trolleys and the clatter of iron-rimmed cabs made the city almost unbearable. We count New York the noisiest city in the world, but Santiago, and certainly Buenos Aires, are running neck and neck with it. I could get little out of the cathedral or other public buildings at Santiago and nothing of importance out of the museums. The old architecture was bastard Spanish, and the new was violent French. There may have been some respectable sculpture and painting in the city, but I did not see it.

I had met on the steamer coming down the coast a number of Americans. We continued to bump into each other across the Andes and into Buenos Aires, but at Santiago I met the painter E. E. Garnsey, an old acquaintance, who, with his wife, was making the South American tour. We joined forces and together went over the Andes, he making sketches from the car window, and I merely noting that the Andes were new, not old, of soft, not hard, rock, and were continually slipping and sliding into the valleys and the plains. Aconcagua, 23,000 feet high, was an exceptionally hard core. The great bulk of the Andes seemed made up of sedimentary rocks: limestones, sandstones, highly colored shales. That was something of a surprise to me, for I had always imagined the Andes as a range of splintered peaks and schistose pinnacles glittering in the sun. The pictures of Frederick E. Church, seen in my youth, had perhaps created false notions of the heart of the Andes.

Over the divide and into Argentina brought us to the tablelands and the wine-famous city of Mendoza, where we stopped for a day. When we again began the journey across the pampas to Buenos Aires, the interest quickened at once. These great, flat plains, growing tall grass and running on for hundreds of miles, were magnificent. At the little stations where we occasionally stopped, I looked in vain for an inn or a hotel where one could put up. I would have been delighted with any sort of roof overhead and the prospect of riding the pampas for a week on horseback, but nothing potential or possible offered. So I sat still in the train and watched the emeus, flamingoes, geese, and plovers from the car window. All the western side of Argentina seemed tenantless, unbroken, quite wild. For many miles the train ran on through the tall grass, by ponds and lakes filled with wild fowl. My pulse quickened as when a boy I saw similar sights among the Minnesota lakes, and I thought of the glorious days that W. H. Hudson must have known on the pampas fifty years ago.[1]

Buenos Aires proved very modern, expensive, and noisy, but not without some fine streets and parks. A quantity of Paris sculpture decorated the squares and parkways. There was apparent effort to create huge vistas, impressive boulevard effects, and Champs Élysée prospects, not without good results. The influence of Paris and the display of a newly rich country were both in evidence. Not first in natural beauty, for Rio de Janeiro may claim that, but first in commercial importance and economic stability. The energy of it is sure to produce—already has produced—the greatest city south of the equator.

Rio is a natural wonder, an enclosed waterway of magnificent proportions. Its people have improved their heritage by constructing remarkable sea walls and embankments so that today one may say without extravagance that Rio has the most picturesque, and perhaps the most extensive, waterfront of any harbor in the world. The harbor of Sydney, Australia, is the only one comparable to Rio, and even that comparison is somewhat forced. As for the city itself, under the lee of its high mountains and facing its wonderful harbor, it is magnificent in plan and excellent in performance. Its driveways, boulevards, parks, and gardens, its fine streets and commanding public buildings, give it an air that is not Paris or New York but is nearer to Lisbon or Madrid.

An uncredentialed ambassador, sent out from New York by a peace-promoting foundation, kept repeating to me each evening, with some weariness, that there was no future ahead for Rio, that no good could come out of a populace made up of "Portuguese and niggers." The strain was too dank and dark. And I kept throwing back at him what "the Portuguese and niggers" had already done and what the Americans on the other side of the equator had not done. But we got nowhere, and each clung to his belief.

Brazil is an empire of inconceivable resources, with the surface not even known, much less scratched. The whole interior is practically terra incognita so far as development is concerned. When it is opened up with roads and settled with people, a new world power will arise. With Rio the capital feeling the impulse, that city of the "Portuguese and niggers" may rival New York in commercial importance. There is a great future ahead of it, a future which is now held in check by a dictatorial government and an arbitrary rule. A little military clique is now in power, and money, which is always timid, will not venture upon such insecure foundation.[2]

It takes many days of steaming to get around the great shoulder of Brazil which pushes out into the Atlantic. The map gives one small idea of its extent. When you round the turn and head northwest, there are more days of steaming on a flat sea before you come up to Trinidad. The sea is almost like the Pacific and stretches out endlessly flat, still, glowing. All the tropic seas are of this description, save for an occasional typhoon or hurricane.

Perhaps the Caribbean is, all told, the most beautiful of the smaller seas. Its blue water, tinged at times with violet or lilac, its high skies and burning sunsets, its golden green islands lifting mountaintops into the sky, are as near to fairyland as one will ever see on the globe. But I have a book on this sea and its islands lying in my desk, which I may publish some day, and it is perhaps unnecessary to duplicate its descriptions here.[3]

Chapter 32

The West Indies

The passage through the Leeward and Windward Islands proved so attractive, so picturesque and romantic, that I resolved to return to them the following winter. That came about in due course. After a summer at Onteora, I set sail in November for the Virgin Islands and spent the winter going down to Guadeloupe, Martinique, Barbados, and Trinidad, and from there across the top of Venezuela and Colombia to Panama.

At Panama there was much to hold me. At first I went out to the island of Barro Colorado to join Frank Chapman the ornithologist. The island is the top of a low mountain, made an island by the backing up of the water in Gatun Lake. When the great dam was constructed, the water rose eighty-five feet. The valleys were turned into waterways, and all the tapirs, cougars, coatis, agouties, peccaries, and monkeys, with all the birds, snakes, and creeping things, moved up to higher ground. Barro Colorado became a natural-history preserve, was so recognized, and so set apart by the government. Only scientists were allowed there. A small laboratory building was erected, and living accommodations were put in at one end of it. I camped down there with Chapman for some weeks and once more watched the wind in the trees.

But there were also monkeys in the trees—four kinds, including the black howler—with toucans, parrots, trogons, giant orioles. I had merely to sit still on the laboratory steps to watch them. Day after day I sat there, with the trade wind blowing in the palm fronds and the steamers of many nations passing in the canal half a mile away. It was a new scene and a new life for me. The canal was tremendous, but after a few days it became merely so much smooth-working machinery. But every day on the island brought forth a new creation, a new revelation. Nature there was exhaustless, limitless, where man with his canal was merely a thumbscrew turning on or turning off the waters. I could have stopped on at the island indefinitely had I been quite fit physically.

Occasionally, visitors came to the island in a launch from the railway three miles away. One day a four-masted schooner going through the canal swung about and dropped anchor not far from our landing. A boat from it came ashore with Admiral Sir Guy Gaunt and Lady Crewes. They were greatly taken with the island, stopped for dinner, and took away a little red monkey for their ship. They asked us aboard their craft for dinner, and the next day we went out to her. She had prettily planned cabins, a large, empty hold, and a crew of eighteen Chinamen, not one of them speaking English, and we were told that the voyagers had been on a trip around the world. During the serving of a very good Chinese dinner (not one course of which was recognizable), we were told a number of things which were amusing or interesting, and whether or not they were red herring drawn across a trail we neither knew nor cared. We were not trailers. People in the traveling world should be taken at their face value and no questions asked. We did not even ask if the schooner had been employed in smuggling arms into Nicaragua, though we found Panama buzzing with that report a few days later.[1]

The city of Panama is not an antique in a glass case, though so regarded by the swift-moving tourist. Socially, and with the close-lying towns of Ancon and Balboa, it is a bright, even a brilliant, community. I have never seen more interesting people from all quarters of the earth than at the military and diplomatic dinners in Ancon. Panama quite outdoes Suez in the variety of people who stop there. The various birds of passage make up a brilliant assemblage, and each one has a song of his own. I have never heard in Cairo or Singapore or Hong Kong such pretty conversational chatter as in Panama.

Nor have I ever seen in Paris or London or New York such picturesque entertainments, such handsome women, such beautiful dressing, and such graceful dancing as on the terrace of the Union Club at Panama. The marble terrace running out into the bay with its supper tables ranged along the railing, with the moonlight flooding the sea floor and the dancing floor, with brilliantly costumed women and white-clad officers for dancing partners, with soft music, a windless night, and the low hum of voices—ah, what a beautiful and romantic sight! You fall in love with the dark beauty sitting beside you at the table, see visions in flashing gold and silver dresses, and perhaps go home a little wry in the neck, a little twisted in the head, with quite a new idea about our southern neighbors, especially their handsome women.

The military and diplomatic people make up another circle, with a continuous round of dinner entertainments given for prominent people. The Duke and Duchess of York were feted by the British minister, and everyone, consumed with curiosity, turned out to meet them; but I was more interested in the fine, decisive personality of Dwight Davis, our Secretary of War [1925–1929], who came down to Panama on a tour of inspection at this time and was handsomely welcomed. For several days there was the roar of airplanes overhead, and for several nights there was clatter of plate and knife. The Secretary was popular, and Panama put no curb upon its admiration.

Strange to relate that Panama, which came into our keeping as a pest-hole, a land of fatal fevers, is today regarded as a health resort, and many people winter there because of its fine climate. That accounts for another social circle that runs into and blends with the army and diplomatic circles and adds to the remarkable variety of life on the isthmus in the winter. I went there for a few days and stayed on for a few months, and when spring came, instead of going up to California, I took ship for New York with Chapman and Dwight Davis for fellow passengers.[2]

We stopped for twenty-four hours at Port-au-Prince, in Haiti. Colonel Meyers, the commanding officer, gave us a luncheon and sent us about the island in automobiles to see what the United States occupation had done for the people. Aside from new roads, public buildings, schools, markets, and the sanitary cleanup, I was impressed with the agricultural experiment station near Port-au-Prince, where demonstration of what Haitian soil could produce in food for Haitian people was being carried out. Forty substations or schools, radiating out from this center to every part of Haiti, were teaching the black people how to raise different food crops in their back yards. Here was teaching not by precept but by example, the very thing most needed in the West Indies. For it should be understood that the black people of the islands do not as a rule have back yards, do not know how to grow vegetables, and do not get enough to eat. On the miserable wage of from twenty to forty cents a day they cannot supply a family adequately. As a result, the black people keep dying prematurely of measles, alastrim, malaria, and tuberculosis. Thank Heaven! The United States is doing something about it, trying to stop the misery and loss of life. It *has* done something about it. Anyone who goes to Haiti today can see the educational, economic, social, and hygienic benefits. Haiti and its people have become prosperous almost overnight. Of course, the United States is losing money on the project. But what of it?[3]

William Beebe's schooner, from which he was carrying on research work on the life of tropical waters, was lying at anchor alongshore near Port-au-Prince. We went out to her. The Secretary, being in an inquisitive mood, went down in one of Beebe's diving suits and walked about the undersea ledges looking for devilfish and octopi, but Chapman and I were content to sit on the deck and see the pretty watercolor drawings of tropical fishes or study the originals in tanks. Beebe, worn to a frazzle with nervous exhaustion, was as enthusiastic as usual and talked as entertainingly as he writes. But we had to leave him and his schooner for the steamer *Ancon*, bound for New York.[4]

That summer I again went with Professor and Mrs. Parr to the cottage at Onteora in the Catskills, spending the days at golf or reading proofs of my *Rembrandt Drawings and Etchings* or sitting on the porch talking to Hamlin Garland, and at night perhaps listening to the wind in the beeches. A quiet and restful summer, thank God.

Chapter 33

Malay Archipelago

But it seems that my quiet summers always have presaged a restless winter or vice versa. The year of 1927 I started in November for California, went to the ranch in the desert for a week, then to Los Angeles, where some of my former pupils were holding office.[1] For several days I was taken about and shown the wonders of the new city, up in the mountains to see the new reservoir, and finally driven down to the port of Los Angeles, where I crept aboard a large steamer for Honolulu.

I had letters of introduction to people in Honolulu, which resulted in my being given a very elaborate Hawaiian dinner, in being driven about the city and its suburbs, properly introduced to the governor general and others in authority, and, in short, being treated very handsomely by Mr. and Mrs. Frear. They had been many years on the islands and knew exactly what to do with a wayfarer. But on the third day I had to take a southbound steamer or remain over for two weeks, so I caught the *Sierra*, bound for Samoa.

One gets a rather small idea of the globe traveling from west to east, or east to west, in the temperate zone. The time changes but not the apparent position of the sun. When you go south across the equator, the sun keeps moving to the north. You notice this at sunrise and perhaps oftener at sunset. The northern stars and their constellations recede to the north, and some of them disappear, while the southern stars come up over the southern horizon. The clouds heap higher, the air grows warmer, the dawns are golden, the dusks are smoldering red, the night sky is blue and glitters with stars, and the moon is an orange or red bowl when reflected in the flat sea. The only sound is the churn and wash of the steamer. The black smoke from the funnels rises straight toward the zenith.

But the great silent wonder of all is the flat sea. The equator is the top of the world, if there is a top. At any rate, it seems the high point of the world, and from it, around it in an enormous horizon ring, stretches the flat sea. The circle of it seems very apparent from the bridge or the crow's-nest. No wonder Columbus believed the world was round. On equatorial seas it seems that we are sailing the outside of an enormous bowl, sailing between a bowled sea and a bowled sky. Of course, the commoner illusion is that of an enormous waste of blue water stretched out flat and endlessly, beyond vision and beyond imagination. And over it the blue of the sky that once more stretches out into infinity. It is only in equatorial spaces that one grasps the vastness of these two immensities, only there that one gets the measure of the globe or at least a mental hint of its reach and roundness.

Islands as they appear and disappear seem only so much flotsam and jetsam, muskrat houses on an enormous lake. The crater harbor of Pago Pago, on the island of Samoa, is merely the entrance to the muskrat house, and the long shallow channel leading up to Suva on the island of Fiji is a runway of the sea. Oh, yes, they are very attractive in hills and forests and tropical foliage, but they have perhaps been overshot by exuberant writers. And the charm of the natives has rather passed out as knowledge of the white man's ways has crept in. In Captain Cook's day the women may have been lovely and the men noble, but face to face with the latter-day progeny it is hard to believe the romantic tales about their forebears.

Australia, with its fine port of Sydney, has not a scrap of romance about it. It is a bald, hard reality. Sydney harbor is capacious, well-suited for commerce, one of the finest harbors of the world, but both the harbor and the city are in continuous turmoil because of strained labor conditions. All Australia is under the labor harrow. Nothing can go on if labor turns its thumbs down. As a result, very little does go on. Trade is held up and commerce choked. Australia is a great continent of unknown, unrealizable possibilities, needing nothing so much as a huge lockout. But with a labor government in control, it is not likely to get it. And Sydney is a Victorian town that probably will always be a little dull, a little stodgy, notwithstanding its fine location and its beautiful harbor.

Ten days of that and then a steamer for Java. The first week of steaming was up the east coast, inside the Great Barrier Reef. Then to Thursday Island and Port Darwin, across to Timor, where a little scrap of land is still held by Portugal—its last holding in the Pacific—and so on through the Straits of Soembawa, skirting the north shore of that island and on to Lombok. Instead of going at once to Java, I swung off to the Celebes in a small Dutch trading steamer, went from Makassar over to Borneo, back to the northern islands, the Moluccas and the Spice Islands, and after six weeks returned to Bali and Java.

I need say little about this trip in detail because during the six months or more I was in the Dutch possessions I kept writing a travel diary which was published in January 1929 under the title *In Java*. But I may carry out a map outline here for the sake of continuity. I stopped at the island of Bali for a week and then went on to Java. Bali is a very small island compared to the Jamaica of the West Indies, but it has as many inhabitants (a million) and every one of them apparently well-fed, clothed, housed, contented, and even happy. The comparison is worth making because the million in Jamaica are far from happiness or contentment and are far from being well-fed, housed, and clothed. They are in want and know disease and death from want. The reason of the difference is not far to seek. Bali grows food for the natives to eat. Jamaica grows gamble crops to sell in the London or New York market. Bali is owned by the Balinese, but Jamaica is owned by English proprietors. Bali is administered by the Dutch, Jamaica by the English. There is a difference between races and soils in favor of Bali which must be subtracted, but there is also a difference in colonial administration which may be added. And when everything is summed up, it may be not unjustly concluded that the Dutch know more about colonial management than the English or any other overlord nation, the United States not excepted.

Java is a repetition of Bali on a larger scale. It is twelve times the size of Jamaica (about 48,000 square miles for Java and 4,000 for Jamaica) but has nearly forty times as many people (about 36,000,000 for Java and 1,000,000 for Jamaica). Once more there is the sharp contrast, with Java happy and prosperous and Jamaica in want and misery. And once more it must be said that the Jamaica black is not so good a man as the Malay nor the Jamaica land so good as that of Java. That means much but not all. When one goes about the English colonies and finds none of them prosperous, and winds up with a winter in India, he gathers an ineradicable impression that the English are not good colonizers, that they take too much out of the colony and leave not enough for those who work the land; that they care not at all for the native and are administering his country for their own profit. That is a harsh statement, and I write it reluctantly, because the English have so many admirable qualities, but it is forced on me by a rather close observation of the English colonies all around the world. Of course, it does not apply to the commonwealths and dominions, but it certainly does apply to India and the West Indies.

Java I greatly enjoyed, both the land and the people. Prosperity with the native has not been great enough to ruin him. The most decent people in the world are the poor and the lowly, the Chinaman, the West Indian black, and the Malay. Any one of them who happens to gain wealth becomes at once pretentious and unbearable, like the French, the Germans, or the Americans, but while they are poor they are gracious, kindly, generous, and polite. The Dutch in Java have never gained enough wealth to make them arrogant. They remain affable, good-natured, and courteous. From my name, I was immediately hailed as one of them. I had to explain that I was only half Dutch and that the language went out in the family two hundred years ago in America.[2] But that statement did not cool my welcome.

It was not until May of 1928 that I took a Dutch ship at Batavia, crossed to Sumatra, and eventually went over to Ceylon. The rest of the trip to England by way of Suez and Gibraltar was flat and uneventful. In London I joined the Parrs, and for several weeks we swung about among old friends or new acquaintances and early in July took ship for New York, going from there at once on our arrival to the house at Onteora for the summer.

Chapter 34

India and the Philippines

In November of 1928 I made another Sinbad-the-Sailor trip around the world, this time with India as an objective. I wanted to see how Great Britain handled India, especially from an agricultural and generally economic point of view. I had read and heard a great deal about it, but I wanted to see the country for myself, unheralded and unconducted.[1]

The Italian steamer *Augustus*, the last word in sublimated elegance and pretentious display, took me to Genoa by way of the Azores and Gibraltar. I had for company, among others, Charles R. Crane, sometime minister to China under President Wilson, and Dr. Keyser of the Rockefeller Institute. We talked, Keyser on tropical diseases, in which I was greatly interested, and Crane on Mohammedanism, of which he had been a student for thirty years. At Genoa, I transshipped to the *Aquiliae*, bound for Suez, and picked up Crane and Keyser at Naples on the way out. Crane had planned to fly from Cairo across Arabia to Busra on the Persian Gulf and asked me to join him, but I was bound for Bombay and did not care to change my plans.[2] He talked much about Arabia, about the Reformed Church missionaries in the Persian Gulf region. They were medical missionaries who were well received by the desert Arabs because of their medical skill and were fine fellows. He was to join them and go into the interior. Had I ever heard of them?

Yes, I had. The Arabian Mission had been started at the Theological Seminary at New Brunswick, with which I was connected. Some of the preliminary meetings had been held in my house, and for more than forty years I had known the missionaries who were being sent out. That intelligence was somewhat surprising to Crane but was all the more reason in his mind why I should join him on his Arabian trip. But, no, I had been promising Dr. Zwemer and others at the Seminary for years that I would visit Busra, but I could not do it this year. Sorry. Good-bye!

I went on to India, and nearly two months later I read in an Indian newspaper a finger of type to the effect that Crane, with his valet and the Rev. Henry A. Bilkert, one of our missionaries, had gone into the interior of Arabia from Busra, had been attacked by a party of warlike Wahabis, and Bilkert had been killed. Crane and his valet escaped.[3]

Down at the entrance of the Red Sea, I had a day to look over the ancient port of Aden. It is merely a rock in the sea but with a small harbor which England found convenient on the way to India and accordingly occupied. But the English occupation did not interest me so much as the Oriental trade that passed that way. Africa had been coming up to the Red Sea, opposite Aden, for centuries, crossing the Red Sea in feluccas, transferring its cargoes to camel caravans, and thence winding by desert trails hundreds of miles up into the heart of Arabia—Arabia Deserta.[4] Today, just as three thousand years ago, the slow-padding camels wind through Aden, bearing the same kind of baled goods, driven by the same kind of hooded and robed drivers, bound for the same bazaars in the same desert cities. Nothing has changed. The West and the East meet here, the very old is beside the very new, but the East goes its way unaffected.

Perhaps this is true, not of Aden alone, but of all the East. At Bombay you meet many races of men—Franks, Goths, Huns, Parsees, Hindus, Arabs, Turks, Malays, Chinese—but each goes its own way and holds by its ancient manners and customs. There is practically no mixing or blend by intermarriage of the races in India, as in America. Both English ruler and Indian subject refuse to mingle in marriage. They have no mutual point of contact. They will always be at opposing poles.

Bombay is a conglomeration architecturally as well as ethnologically. Almost every style of building under the sun is to be seen there, and the greater number of them are shockers. It is a bewildering city, not a restful or a handsome one, but the tourist loves it, and the English bosom swells with pride when it is mentioned. Of course, it is important commercially, has a fine harbor and a large trade, but perhaps you will go out of it by railway without the shedding of tears.

Everyone will tell you about your railway train and the "boy" you employ to make up your bed and all that, but no one will tell about the country you go through on the way up to Delhi. It is a country not unlike eastern Montana, has a gumbo, half alkaline soil, some isolated buttes and table mountains, few trees, few streams, sparse bunch grass, and a great deal of dust. For a hundred miles out of Bombay it seems fitted only for grazing, but goats are about the only grazers. Few native huts are seen. Some corn-stalk shelters appear in the open fields and are temporarily occupied by natives. An occasional rice paddy dried out and abandoned shows like a white check on the landscape. Then some neem trees, a corrugated iron town where the train stops for a moment. It is a Godforsaken country but for the birds. They are many, gay in plumage, but, almost without exception, songless. The small green parrots go in flocks as once the now extinct passenger pigeon of the United States, but they give out only a squawk. The myna birds come the nearest to singing of any of them.

When you reach the great valley of the Ganges, a huge, flat plain of many miles in breadth running down to Calcutta and studded with many cities, you are in the heart of India. The land here is being used for growing crops. There is some rainfall, and in addition to wells there are irrigation canals and ditches. But the water in the distributing ditches is not economically used, and no one seems to care how the native uses it or if he profits by it or not. Farming in India, in the hands of the *ryot* [peasant], is not very successful. There is not enough foodstuff raised to support the population, and half the country is always in want, is sick, diseased, or dying. Again, no one seems to care. A thousand a day dying of cholera or starvation relieves an overpopulated land. There is unending discussion of the political status of India, but no one seems to talk much about the economic status. Yet that is the weak spot in the Indian administration. It never can make a contented India while disease and starvation, waste and want, pervade the land. Calling it a dominion or a colony or an independent state will fill no stomachs.

All the way down to Calcutta you pass through a neglected, poorly worked country. A few handsome cities like Lucknow, many mud-hut villages, some native towns with filthy, disease-breeding bazaars, some pest spots like the riverfront at Benares; and everywhere a gaunt, haggard people, underfed, unhappy, hopelessly dead upon its feet. Everyone agrees about the misery of India. Everyone counts it the most depressing place in all the world. And almost every traveler shortens his schedule and gets out of the country as soon as possible, because he can do no good there and it seems a crime to eat food in a land where the native is starving.

Calcutta is just a dull English city on the Hooghly River with little to commend it. Cows and natives sleep on the sidewalks, dogs and beggars beat the streets for food, Indian clerks, government factotums, men of castes, men of different nations, men of no nation, come and go along the thoroughfares. Costumes and color, rags and silks, flowers and filth, parkways and pestholes, hotels and hovels, splendor and squalor go along together.

You drive along the river for an hour and take a steamer for Singapore. The steamer spends several days in going down the river to the sea. You pass factories—many of them—along the river bank. English factories making up something to sell in India or elsewhere. You wonder if India's hope lies in manufacture. Will industrialism put it on its feet? Is not the immediate need better agriculture and the better feeding, housing, and health of the people? And who is responsible for this indifference to death and disease, this slipshod management, this seventy-five-years-behind-the-times state of affairs? England is still engaged with Simon commissions, with Gandhi and Tagore discussions about political status, with keeping the native princes quiet, with almost everything except modern agriculture, proper sanitation, and just ordinary everyday hygiene. The Indian problem is economic, not political, but England will not look at it in that way. She prefers to argue, but you cannot argue effectively with people who have empty stomachs.

Yes, there are things worth seeing in India, some beautiful things, but you have a poor heart for them with all the misery about you. The Taj Mahal? Yes, it lives up to its very flamboyant reputation and even goes beyond expectation. It is quite a perfect piece of Mohammedan architecture (done by a Mohammedan and not an Italian, as frequently stated), and with its splendid setting, its gardens, and water approach, it is something of a wonder. From a picturesque point of view, it stands up as well as from an architectural point of view. Agra Fort with its palaces is only a trifle less grand than the Taj Mahal. Besides these there is the Akbar tomb and city and, at Delhi, dozens of fine tombs and temples crumbling to decay. And a great modern city, New Delhi, rising to take their places. The Mohammedan art of this Great Mogul period is well worth seeing. The Indian architecture is not so interesting.

There is something else to India. The English occupation has resulted in some good cities, like Lucknow and Delhi, some handsome homes and houses, even some good Georgian architecture, as witness the Governor's Palace and the more unique stables at Calcutta. There are places where for a time you forget you are in India. But eventually the misery of the inhabitants gets on your nerves. You cannot throw it off, and eventually you put on your hat and leave the country.

In the Philippines there is the same kind of political ballyhoo as in India, from native politicians like Quezon. It has always been thus and so with the Philippines, but the United States has never paid much attention. It has gone ahead with the commercial and economic development of the islands. The result is that there is magnificent prosperity, with small chance of political upheaval anywhere along the line. The Philippines are more prosperous even than the United States, and the last thing that the natives want or need is independence. Even Quezon and his friends use independence merely as a political slogan. They do not want the reality. Protected by an American army and navy, given ninety-five percent of the offices, producing with cheap Filipino labor, selling to America at American prices without import duties, furnished with good transportation to the outer world, supplied with good schools, hospitals, and sanitation, the people of the Philippines are doing exceedingly well.

Of course, the islands are not a paying investment to the United States. Mr. Coolidge in a speech made a few months before going out of office said that all our insular possessions were "a hindrance rather than a help." But that has not worried the people of the United States. They have been well disposed to help the island peoples without profit, just as they are minded to continue, and even duplicate, the Panama Canal, though it showed a balance on the wrong side of the ledger of fifty millions of dollars in the first ten years of operation.

But India, poor, miserable, starving, diseased India—pays! Some years ago an English baronet, in response to my question of whether India paid, said:

"Pay! Of course, it pays. Do you think we would bother with it if it didn't?"

I do not consider that making starving India pay is exactly a vice nor letting the prosperous Philippines go without payment a shining virtue. But it is something of a contrast, perhaps, when one thinks of how America has been shylocked by England and damned for its greed by all Europe. But let that go. My point is that there is something wrong with the colonial administrations of both England and America. One is too generous and the other not generous enough. Neither attitude has business or moral sense in it. Fairness is the happy medium. And the best example of it is right under the nose of England and the United States in the Dutch East Indies. They are prosperous, with both the native and the ruler sharing in the prosperity. What a pity that England will not drop its arrogance and the United States its conceit to learn something from little Holland.

Manila is an attractive city, with much of the picturesque about the old town and something of the stately about the new. Moreover, it is clean, free from disease, and has a good climate. It is growing rapidly and is already the center of a large trade. The other cities are of less moment. The mountain resort of Baguio, a hundred miles or more to the north, is cool and green, not unlike the foothills of the Alps in scenery, but with no great variety. The southern islands are in course of development, with inter-island steamers opening communication almost everywhere. Under the United States there is a great future ahead of the Philippines, a future for both American and Filipino. They can and probably will work together. Separation is now unthinkable. The United States is a stabilizing influence in the East, and none of the Eastern nations (save possibly Japan) but would protest her withdrawal.

I saw something of the native tribes at the north, chiefly the Igorots, and was impressed more by their physical sturdiness than their mentality. They are a bit dull, but quiet, rather good-natured, and willing workers. The Negritos are more primitive, living in the forests by hunting, and keep aloof from everyone. There are said to be about 40,000 of them, while of the Igorots there are some 400,000. The government interferes very little with the native tribes. They have their own rulers and go on with their ancient manners and customs.

China was in something of a turmoil when I reached it. The routes to Peking were practically closed. So I merely looked in on the coast cities of Hong Kong and Shanghai. Just so with Japan. I had no desire to go beyond Kyoto and Tokyo, especially in the early spring with cold and rain as a daily program. So I came across the Pacific to Honolulu and thence to San Francisco, glad enough to be back in America with the spring coming on in New Jersey. Nothing that I have seen in other lands puts me out of conceit of my own. The United States has more variety of scenery and greater natural beauty than any country under the sun.[5]

Chapter 35

Egypt

I had gone through Suez and the Red Sea several times in trips around the world, but Port Said was about all that I had seen of Egypt. That was enough. The money-changers who came on the boat at Port Said to cut the eyeteeth of the passengers in a matter of exchange were sufficient to keep people away from the land. A more sordid-looking crew never scuttled ship or cut a throat. The passengers who knew Port Said always spoke of it unsympathetically as "a robbers' roost." They disposed of all Egypt with a shrug of the shoulders or else referred to it as "a land of beggars and baksheesh."[1]

Of course, that was merely the ill-considered talk of tourists, but I had heard so much of it, hither and yon, that I came to believe there was some truth in it. At any rate, I did not go to Egypt for many years. But at last I decided to make the Nile trip, and if conditions proved unendurable, I could go to Khartoum, go out by Port Sudan, or go on up the Nile and out by Mombosa. As it turned out, I spent the whole winter on the Nile without being murdered or even robbed. The Egyptians the tourist meets with are not at all dangerous. They are just a nuisance. All the people in Egypt who live by the traveling public—dragomans, donkey boys, transportation agents, hotel keepers, shopkeepers, hawkers, and beggars—are avid, importunate, and not too scrupulous. The tourist has to watch his step, and in spite of every precaution, he will walk into small traps set for him by the cunning.

I left New York in November 1929 aboard the *Augustus* of the Italian line, walked across the dock at Naples to take the steamer for Egypt, and in four days landed at Alexandria in a cold rain. Some thoughtful person—probably an American—had taken my overcoat from my stateroom on the *Augustus* before the steamer left the New York dock, but the Atlantic and Mediterranean were not cold, and I got on very well without the coat until we reached Alexandria. There, "the wonderful climate of Egypt" and the lack of heat in the hotels set me shivering. Fortunately, Professor John Winter of the University of Michigan (with Mrs. Winter) was on the steamer and supplied me with a sweater. But in spite of many garments and basins of hot tea, we all shivered in Alexandria.

The rain followed us to Cairo, where "it never rains." The city had been having three days of it, and everything was afloat. We dragged around in the mud "doing" mosques and Pyramids and bazaars and then made a flight by automobile out of the city, out past the Pyramids, and across the desert some seventy miles to the Fayoum, an area west of the Nile River. On the eastern edge, near Lake Karun, we put in at the camp of the University of Michigan, the camp from which the diggings in the buried Greek city of Karanis have been directed for half a dozen years. Mr. Petersen, the director, welcomed us, and there we spent the Christmas week.

Following the excavations of a buried Greek city, watching the picturesque *fellahin* [peasants] digging, carrying, singing as they worked, and talking with the engineering and surveying staff proved a new and interesting experience. The expedition was not digging for pharaohs, and no sensation-producing tombs were discovered. The city was Greek and of the second, third, and fourth centuries A.D., that period of history which historians love to pass over quickly because they know so little about it. The finds were largely pottery, glass, figurines, papyri, coins, and many household articles. These were not materials to fire the fancy of tourists, but they answered their purpose with the university people by helping to reconstruct history.

I was more interested in the workers, perhaps, than the work, for here were several hundred Egyptian men, women, and children, natives of a nearby Fayoum village, who had not been corrupted by a traveling tourist public. They were simple, quiet, rather attractive people. Moreover, in their native costume, at work or resting, they greatly impressed with the resemblance to the old Egyptians of the tombs and temples. I could make nothing of it other than that these Arab-Egyptians were the lineal and actual descendants of the old Egyptians. The ingenious theories of ethnologists and the Coptic suggestions of historians went out of the window with a crash. The soil of Egypt was still producing the ancient race of the pharaohs, with some few changes to be sure, but with the type still there and recognizable.

I walked the desert, an old sea bed, rather flat, with protruding reefs and water-worn rocks here and there, but no vegetation. I motored about the populous Fayoum, saw how the native lived and worked the land, and went over to Lake Karun for no particular purpose and with no appreciable results. And then we all motored back to Cairo.

My principal work in Cairo was to check up on the contents of the famous Egyptian museum. I knew its most important things from photographic and plaster reproductions, but a chance to see the originals was not to be neglected. I spent much time there and was well rewarded. It is the most complete Egyptian collection in the world and supremely fine. The next best exhibition in Cairo was the Arabic museum, again excellent in every way. Of course, the mosques, the Pyramids, the Sphinx, were duly "done." No tourist is allowed to escape from Cairo without a visit to Mena House and a ride around the Great Pyramid on a bedizened and bedeviled camel, for which he pays enough, Heaven knows.[2] But the real collectors of tribute were yet to come. Egypt is in the hands of hotel keepers, transportation companies, guides, dragomans, donkey boys, and baksheesh howlers. That is, the Egypt that the tourist sees. He does not see the Fayoum, the Delta, or the desert, because there is lack of language, transportation, and hotels in those places. He sees only what the tourist bureaus have already mapped out for him. The system is too well established, too well grounded, to be broken up. The tourists do not attempt to break it up. They submit like docile sheep and go where they are pushed. And I, with much grumbling, went with them.

We went up the Nile on a stern-wheel steamboat that would have been out of date on the Mississippi seventy years ago. But it carried us through and was not uncomfortable. We rode miserable little donkeys, with Joseph-and-Mary saddles that never were "in date" since biblical times, but again we arrived at temple and tomb as planned in the trip. And, of course, we were pestered from Cairo to Wadi Halfi by guides, donkey boys, sellers of beads, and droves of dirty children.

Still, we beat off the hawkers, beggars, and flies from day to day and found some refuge at night in our antiquated steamboat. And the great temples and tombs proved more than interesting. I shall not describe them, for I have done that in a book just published by the Scribners, *In Egypt: Studies and Sketches along the Nile*, 1931. Nor need I speak of the desert, except comparatively, for I also wrote that down in the book. The wastes lying on either side of the Nile are lacking in interest as compared with our American deserts in Sonora and Chihuahua. They have not the interest of vegetation and wildlife, nor are the mountains, valleys, and dunes provocative of much enthusiasm.[3] The tourist raves over the desert sunsets, and undeniably they are brilliant, but I have seen others elsewhere of superior brilliancy.

Just so with the climate of Egypt. The English think it divine, but that is by comparison with the climate of northern Europe, which is about the worst imaginable. The winds and storms of England, France, and Germany come across the Alps and the Mediterranean and die out on the Upper Nile, but not before they have put a chill in the air as far south as Assouan.

The temperature of the Nile valley is variable, very uncertain. It may be fine, and then again Cairo may shiver for weeks. The finest climate in the whole world is on the west coast of Mexico. But then there is little there except climate and scenery. The comforts of civilization—hotels and something to eat, for instance—are lacking.[4]

Early in December of 1930, I again went back to the West Indies, to San Juan, Puerto Rico, as a first stop. I had on previous visits put together chapters on the Caribbean in which I had indulged in some criticism of colonial administration by the English, French, Dutch, and Americans, particularly the English. I did not care to publish this until I had seen India, Egypt, and the Sudan under English management. And even after visiting those countries, I felt it necessary to check up and verify my earlier impressions of the West Indies. So I stowed the manuscript in my kit and once more put out to open sea.

I had the great good fortune on the steamer outward bound to find Dr. Nathaniel L. Britton and Mrs. Britton, who were going to Puerto Rico for the winter. We became friends at once, and for three weeks I went with them in their car about the islands, botanizing, geologizing, and, to some extent, philosophizing. I was directly interested in the Spanish country life of the island and saw a good deal of it, but I also got from the Brittons a good deal of accurate botany, which I had never known before. They were delightful companions, and when I finally left them to go over to the Virgin Islands, it was with many regrets.

I went aboard the steamer *Catharine*, bound for St. Thomas on Christmas night. That day I had been at dinner with the Nobles in San Juan, where a group of young Englishmen and their wives lived up to the day and the dinner, and that evening, before going on the ship, I went to the old palace to keep a date that Governor Roosevelt had given me.[5] The Governor I found greatly interested in plans for the welfare of Puerto Rico and its people, particularly the schoolchildren. The island had been hit by hard times [the Great Depression], like the rest of the world, but the Governor was anxious that the schoolchildren should not suffer in consequence. And he was also interested in parceling out small farms to individuals among the Spanish peasantry. There I was sympathetic, for that had been my remedy for the want and misery of the blacks in all the islands of the Caribbean. But I had only the theory, while he was able to furnish the practice. About two thousand small farms already had been allotted. And the plan was working well.

The Virgin Islands I found much more depressed than Puerto Rico. Sugar had failed, the plantations were lying fallow, the planters were doing nothing with the lands except to pasture a few cattle, the field blacks were out of a job, out of food, and relying on a daily dole from the United States government. I went to Governor Evan's house to dinner and had several long talks with him about the situation. Commander Riefkohl, the naval commander of the port, took me over to St. Johns and Tortola and afterward sent me with letters of introduction to St. Croix. In all of these islands I was taken about and shown actual existing conditions. The causes for the depression of the West Indies and the misery of the black in those islands could not be easily determined. I had to check and countercheck. I was out to state the facts without prejudice and without sensational results. I have never cared for the spectacular utterance nor for literary "excursions and alarums."

I drifted down the islands leisurely, to St. Kitts, Antigua, Dominica, Guadeloupe, Martinique, Barbados, Grenada, and Trinidad, stopping off at places sometimes for days or, as at Trinidad, for weeks. The black problem and colonial administrations were largely side issues. My main objective was the beauty of the islands and the sea. In fact, it was something of a relief when I left Trinidad and the blacks behind me. Over in Venezuela and along the Spanish Main, I could admire the beauty of the mountains and the shore without a blessed thought of administrations, colonial or otherwise. Not even the dictatorial regime of Gómez in Venezuela caused me more than a passing thought.

Gómez has been sitting on the lid, governing Venezuela like an Oriental despot, only more despotic, for thirty years, but the people seem to be prosperous under him, and perhaps his is exactly the kind of government they need. Certainly the casual visitor in Caracas sees nothing amiss in the town. It is clean, bustling, attractive, and enough better than places like Kingston or Bridgetown. I daresay Gómez does some wholesale shooting on occasion, but he does not allow any bandits in automobiles to hold up the community. The semblance of law and order is there. And also there is the appearance of prosperity in the country. The oil wells, rather than Gómez, may be responsible for it, but it is there.

Curaçao, however, where the Dutch rule, is the one very prosperous-looking place along the Spanish Main. It is a desert island off the Venezuelan coast, with a narrow slit of a harbor at Willemstad where some thirty different lines of steamers call for oil and coal. It is the great refinery for Venezuelan oil, something of a port for local trade along the Spanish Main, and also something of a headquarters for smuggling. Out of it all the Dutch make a handsome revenue, and some of the wealth remains in Willemstad and makes of the port a picturesque and rather "smart" town.

Two enormous pipelines some four hundred miles long bring down oil from the mountains of Colombia to tidewater at Cartagena, but as yet they have not changed in any way the old Spanish of the town. It is the most colorful, the most picturesque spot along the Spanish Main or, for that matter, in the whole of the West Indies. It is very old and was originally settled by the Spanish from Seville. The stamp of southern Spain still shows upon it in the walls and forts and balconied houses—a delightful place that the tourist has not yet ruined.

I drifted on and along under the lee of the Colombian Andes to Panama. The social life of Panama, the cosmopolitan character of it, held me for nearly two months. The canal there seems to draw more ships than Suez, and Panama attracts more diverse peoples than Port Said or even Cairo. From all quarters of the earth, people in ships come through the big canal and stop off at Panama for a chat with Governor Burgess or a word with General Martin or a dance at the Union Club. The opportunity to meet these people was given me by good friends at Ancon, and that had much to do with my third long sojourn in the Canal Zone.

But when the cicada began shrilling in the trees and the summer sun began to come up red-hot out of the Bay of Panama, I began to think of the cool spring coming on up in New Jersey. I came home in March and strolled the barren meadows by the Raritan, watching the arrival of the song sparrows and overhead the northern flight of the wild geese. Ah, my own meadows are worth more than the West Indies, with all their color and splendor and their golden light. Not the grand but the lowly things are the most lasting.

And sometimes with people as with things. I would rather talk with a West Indian black in a cane field than his planter-employer in his big house on the hill. In the autumn I am thinking to go back to China, not to see the great temples and gates but to see the native Chinaman in the fields. Wherever I have met the Chinaman, he has been affable, decent, with the instincts of a gentleman. Of course, when he makes a great deal of money, which occasionally happens, he becomes as arrogant as any other rich person, but so long as he is poor he is a very good sort. Prosperity never yet lent itself to the development of the virtues. I am not sure that great riches have improved the character of my fellow American.

Chapter 36

At Home

It might be thought from the forerunning chapters that most of my life had been spent chasing around the world in ocean steamers, but that would be a false impression. The travel incidents have been thrown out of proportion because they are usually thought the more interesting. What happens at home is counted too prosaic for recital. I do not share that sentiment, though I have been forced to acknowledge its supremacy. To me:

> East or West
> Home is best.

Where one has been born and reared remains his most intimate contact, and the friends of his youth are his long, long friends. They may not be so bright or so fair as those he meets in court or camp or salon, but they are the more reliable, the more lasting.[1]

So while I make small record here of the many days and years spent in the Sage Library, my college lecture room, and my study, and no record whatever of the hundreds of professors, students, and close friends with whom I have been associated in my native town, I am not blind to the fact that the greater part of my life has been here and not there in the outer world. For more than fifty years I have been closely connected with the Sage Library and Rutgers University and in that time have seen many shifts of personnel and policy, many growths and changes, many comings and goings. The living college graduates of fifty years ago are few, and when they come back to class reunions they are old men, with a hollow mockery of their early laugh and a forced gaiety about the life that is behind them. As for the professors of fifty or even forty years ago, well, I am the last.

My first visit to the Sage Library was made with Dr. Samuel M. Woodbridge, President of the Seminary and Professor of Sacred History. Associated with him were Professors David D. Demarest, John DeWitt, and A. B. Van Zandt. They were all of them fine preachers and teachers, men of high ability and strong character. I was associated with them for many years and owed much to their friendship and their scholarship. All of them passed out long ago and were succeeded by Professors Lansing, Mabon, Riggs,

Berg, Searle, Johnson, Schenck—scholarly, companionable men with whom I struck up newer friendships. All of the second group, except Dr. Berg, have gone. And I am now living on the Seminary grounds with a third group, of which Dr. W. H. S. Demarest is president and with whom Professors Raven, Beardslee, Hoffman, Worcester, Bayles, and Weber are associated.

I have lived on terms of intimacy with all these men and have never had from them anything but unfailing kindness and courtesy. This is quite as true of the professors at Rutgers. I knew and worked with them in the Library as early as 1878 and became definitely one of them at Rutgers in 1889, serving through the administrations of Presidents Gates, Scott, and Demarest and holding over and through the administration of President Thomas. The faculty of the College was small in 1878, there being only about twelve professors and 150 students. But since then every faculty of the University has expanded enormously. There are now 357 professors and instructors, 1,600 four-year men, besides a college for women with some 1,200 students in it. All told, the University has some 5,560 students connected with it, not counting some 11,300 extension students.[2]

That means that the one-time friendships and companionships in the faculty have changed and given place to many acquaintanceships, with many who know me not at all except for a nod. And the classes, every man of which I once knew, have become a great student body, who perhaps know me, as they know the old cannon on the campus, but with whom I have nothing in common. There is no novelty about this relationship. Many men have outlived their age and generation. I happen to be one of them. But I am not sorry to have lived when I did nor do I regret being associated with the people with whom my lot has been cast.

Of course, we all have regrets. We wish we had gone the other way or done the other thing. Was it Socrates who, consulted by a young Athenian as to whether he should marry or not marry, said: "Whichever you do, you will regret it"? I regret many things and sometimes groan like a camel over the burden of my follies, but I have never been sorry about my work in the Library and College nor groaned over my associates at New Brunswick. Few of them rose to public prominence or were featured on the front page of the dailies, but perhaps they were the better and the nobler for that. They did their work truly and went their ways bravely. It is not given to everyone to live through to such an end and to pass out *sans peur et sans reproche* [without fear and without reproach]. I do not know that I shall do so, but I shall try.

Notes

Introduction

1   For complementary studies of the phenomenon, see Lears, Lutz, and Nash's two studies, *Wilderness and the American Mind* and *The Call of the Wild*. In this respect, Sayre contributes a positive definition of American sentimentalism, and he touches on an aspect important to Van Dyke, the relationship between nature writing and landscape painting.

2   In the early 1970s, Professor Lawrence Clark Powell began the modern spadework on Van Dyke scholarship. See his *Southwest Classics* (314–28). Further details of the following overview of Van Dyke's life and career are in my *John C. Van Dyke: The Desert*.

3   Given Van Dyke's penchant for privacy, he may have destroyed his papers, though the issue is by no means clear. Judging from the autobiography's rich detail in places, the letters quoted, and such, Van Dyke must have kept extensive records of his life. For material that does exist, see the section on archival sources in the bibliography.

An attempt to trace Van Dyke's papers through wills has proved fruitless. Van Dyke's will passed on most of his possessions, including manuscripts, to his closest relative, Clare Van Dyke Parr, of Yonkers, New York (1). Another Van Dyke relative, Cornelia Strong, now deceased, told me that after Van Dyke's death in 1932, Mrs. Parr arrived in New Brunswick with a truck and hauled away Van Dyke's earthly goods. The wills of Mrs. Parr and her husband, Harry L. Parr, make no mention of Van Dyke's literary materials.

However, the wills are revealing in other ways. Mrs. Parr's final testament directs that over a dozen works of art, possibly Van Dyke's personal collection, be given to Rutgers University after her death and that of her husband (1–2). The works, known as the "John C. Van Dyke Collection," are in the Jane Voorhees Zimmerli Art Museum, on the New Brunswick campus of Rutgers. Notable in the collection is *Mill Scene*, ca. 1900, a canvas by impressionist John Twachtman, one of Van Dyke's friends. Esthetically, the two men were in deep sympathy. Some of Van Dyke's lush descriptive passages of nature might be Twachtman scenes put into words. For a selection of Twachtman art, see Boyle.

4   Van Dyke's list of photographs appears at left, the editor's notations at right.

Illustrations

Frontispiece,
John C. Van Dyke . . . . .author of autobiography
John Van Dyke . . . . .author's father
Mrs. John Van Dyke . . . . .author's mother

Lincoln,
   Cooper Union Photograph. . . . . .friend of Van Dyke's father
Mrs. Schuyler Van Rensselaer,
   Saint-Gaudens bas-relief . . . . .art critic
Capt. Frank H. Mason . . . . .American consul in European capitals
Wm. M. Chase,
   Sargent portrait. . . . . .painter
Kenyon Cox. . . . . .painter and art critic
Frank Millet,
   Century bust . . . . .painter and writer
Laurence Hutton . . . . .bibliophile and writer
Brander Matthews,
   Simmons portrait . . . . .professor and writer
Mark Twain . . . . .writer
Charles Scribner. . . . . .Van Dyke's publisher
W. C. Brownell . . . . .Van Dyke's editor at Scribner's
Charles Eliot Norton . . . . .professor and writer
Frank Thomson . . . . .art connoisseur and railroad president
Andrew Carnegie. . . . . .wealthy industrialist
Edwin Booth,
   Sargent portrait . . . . .Shakespearean actor
J. A. McN. Whistler,
   portrait . . . . .painter
Joseph Pennell,
   etching . . . . .illustrator
John S. Sargent. . . . . .painter
John Muir. . . . . .writer and conservationist
Col. George B. McClellan. . . . . .mayor of New York City
Frank Chapman . . . . .writer and ornithologist
Hamlin Garland. . . . . .writer
Dr. W. H. S. Demarest,
   Smedley portrait . . .president of the New Brunswick Theological Seminary

Preface

1   Jupiter Amon, also spelled "Ammon" or "Amen," refers to the Egyptian version of the Romans' chief god, Jupiter. Ariel, of course, is the airy spirit in Shakespeare's *The Tempest*.

2   In *The Meadows* (1926), Van Dyke sees the modern age of factories, automobiles, and popular culture as hyperactive and superficial, fallen from the grace of his rural childhood into tawdry pursuits of idle entertainments and sensationalism: "The rushing world craves the novel and exotic, and in seeking to avoid the obvious it only too often falls into admiration of the merely bizarre" (125).

3   Van Dyke dates his preface October 1930, though the title page of the typescript bears a date of 1931. Apparently, Van Dyke sometimes wrote a preface before he finished a manuscript. Following suit, he dates the preface of his most famous book, *The Desert*, February 1901 (ix), though we know he did not send a completed manuscript to his publisher until May of that year. See his letter of 23 May 1901 in the

"John Charles Van Dyke Correspondence with Charles Scribner's Sons, with Related Papers," in the archives of Princeton University.

Chapter 1—Lincoln in 1861

1 Lieutenant Theodore Strong. Died in the Union Army at Belle Plain, Virginia, February 24, 1863. [Van Dyke's note.]

2 Mrs. John W. Ferdon, of Piermont, New York. [Van Dyke's note.]

3 As I recall him, none of the portraits, statues, or busts of him is quite like him. The Saint-Gaudens is too smooth and academic, and it lacks the solemn simplicity and humility of Lincoln. The French is no better, and the Barnard is grotesque in form, the Brady photograph disproving the large hands and feet. I am not sure but that the photograph which shows him seated at a table reading—the one that shows the hands and feet—is the truest representation. It may be thought too refined, but perhaps that is because we have been brought up on the tradition that he was a rail splitter and looked like a boor. He never did.

There were no small graces about him, neither were there any mean angles or features telling of low origins. He was a great gentleman, perhaps in the rough, and yet we cannot be too sure about the roughness. Carl Sandburg in his *Prairie Years* seems to emphasize the harshness of Lincoln's early surroundings, and from that the inference has been drawn that Lincoln himself must have looked harsh and coarse. When he came to New York to make the Cooper Union Speech, everyone expected to see an outlandish sort of person. The newspaper reporters played up to the idea and made him out of grotesque appearance in order to emphasize the great silence that fell, the great impression he made, when he began to speak. Sandburg reprints these reporters' descriptions, but turning his page you see a photograph of Lincoln taken the day after the speech. That is a document that knocks all the reporters' tales into a cocked hat. There he stands quietly in his very nice-fitting clothes, looking for all the world like some "swell" of the Henry Clay type. The photograph was taken in 1860. The next year—a hundred chances to one wearing similar, if not the same, clothes— he passed through New Jersey, and I saw him. I appeal from Sandburg and the reporters to the photograph. Lincoln looked like a great gentleman who had been born and bred in a rough land and yet in essence always remained the gentleman. [Van Dyke's note.]

4 Reported in the *New York Tribune* of that date and at some length but not in full. [Van Dyke's note.]

5 Published in Nicolay and Hay, *Abraham Lincoln: A History*. Vol. II, p. 36. [Van Dyke's note.] The Lincoln letter, as other quoted correspondence to follow, is printed without emendations of Van Dyke's text.

6 *Century Magazine*. Vol. 76, p. 189. [Van Dyke's note.]

7 See the frontispiece portrait of Lincoln in Frederick Trevor Hill's *Lincoln the Emancipator* where he appears at thirty-five with a face almost like that of Poe. [Van Dyke's note.]

8 The poem was not unknown to my mother, for she copied it in her Washington diary of 1847. [Van Dyke's note.]

9 Wallace Stegner, historian of the American West, agrees with Van Dyke that books and education on the frontier often were far more available than is popularly imagined (8–15). Of Lincoln's frontier, Stegner observes that "often, somebody in

town or within reach turned out to have some sort of intellectual or professional or scientific interest or capacity . . . and that when it showed was a very bright star to tell direction by" (12).

10   Yearning for a treasured past is a common theme in romantic Van Dyke. In *The Raritan* he says, "Nothing lasts for long in America—not even the graves" (20).

Chapter 2—The Family in the Revolution

1   Van Dyke's often charming genealogy, *The Raritan*, tells the story of his family in greater detail. The little book was privately printed, and in its brief preface Van Dyke states that he intends the work "for the use of the Family." Otherwise, the volume "calls for no public attention or recognition" (1). Aitken and Dwight provide more extensive studies of the Van Dyke and Strong clans.

2   *The Raritan* emphasizes that the love of the wild was a chief trait of the Van Dykes. Even the Old World ancestors lived in a wild country, on the north shore of what is now the Netherlands, in a vast forest inhabited by wolves, where "only the boar hunters penetrated" (15). Van Dyke views his own love of wildness as inherited, as in the "old Dutch blood" (83).

3   The area bore an earlier and more poetic name, Prigmore's Swamp. At the head of navigation on the Raritan River, New Brunswick became a prominent link in transportation routes, especially between New York City and Trenton and Philadelphia. During the Revolutionary War, the town served as a base for naval raiders attacking British shipping in nearby New York Bay. Today's New Brunswick is the home of Rutgers University, founded in 1766, and the headquarters of the pharmaceutical giant Johnson and Johnson.

Michael Moffatt's *The Rutgers Picture Book* provides illustrations showing the town's transformation over the centuries from a pioneer outpost, through a leafy town of college spires, to its present industrial importance. The standard historical reference, the bible of New Brunswick history, is John P. Wall's *Chronicles of New Brunswick, New Jersey*.

4   See Stryker's *Battle of Trenton and Princeton*, p. 87 et seq. [Van Dyke's note.]

5   *The Raritan* depicts the Dutch side of Van Dyke's family as hard-working, rural people. They were lovers of wilderness satisfied with their lot. With the infusion of blood from outside the stable ethnic group come humor, sentiment, and the desire for success—in other words, worldliness. The result of the blend is confusion of purpose, a longing for the wilds and the old, innocent ways at war with ambition—a welter which romantic Van Dyke feels he embodies.

Chapter 3—Green Oaks

1   Something less than a mile from downtown New Brunswick and the Rutgers campus, the old Van Dyke home is the first house on the right as one leaves New Brunswick via Hamilton Street and crosses Mile Run, the stream forming the boundary between New Brunswick and Somerset. Saints Peter and Paul Catholic Church (Eastern Orthodox) now owns the mansion. Though its exterior appears to have undergone some renovation and much of the rural countryside of Van Dyke's childhood has been suburbanized, the house, still set back in stately oaks, retains a good deal of its former dignity.

In Van Dyke's day, a number of relatives lived in other mansions nearby.

2 Some years ago, the huge, ornate mansion of Professor Theodore Strong was cut into sections and moved to several different places. Assisted by Mr. Philip L. Strong, I was able to locate one large part, likely the central and largest section of the building. It now houses the Somerset Inn Pizzeria, on Hamilton Street, a few blocks from its original location. For a contemporary photograph, see "Painting the Town."

3   GUINEA HENS

The guinea hens would run each day
Into the field of clover,
Pattering, chattering on their way
Up the hill and over,
And those behind with warning clack
Called out ahead: Come back! Come back!

The guinea hens ran on and on
Into the barley stubble;
They crossed the buckwheat and the corn
And never thought of trouble,
But those that followed in the track
Kept calling out: Come back! Come back!

The guinea hens ran on all day
And then came home at nightfall,
Pattering, chattering on their way,
Not thinking of what might fall,
But still behind there was no lack
Of ones to call: Come back! Come back!
                    [Van Dyke's note.]

In this and other examples below, Van Dyke demonstrates that he was an adequate, at times creditable and even moving, but certainly not a brilliant, poet. Despite his lifelong efforts, he seems to have known his limits. Besides the few poems included in his autobiography and his verses introducing the chapters of *The Meadows*, I have found only one complete Van Dyke poem, "Change," appearing in print. For more on his sometimes surprising use of poetry, see my "Van Dyke's Little Trick."

4 At the bottom of a deep dingle thick with trees and vines, Mile Run retains the aura of a wild childhood place, a refuge from the urbanization surrounding it today. Several yards wide as it passes the old Van Dyke mansion, the stream meanders for another mile or so before flowing into the broad Raritan River.

From the Midland dialect of England, the word "run" is used locally to refer to what elsewhere in the United States would be called a brook or a creek.

Chapter 4—Trenton

1 Here the spelling changes from "Onderdonk" to "Ouderdonk."
2   WILD GEESE

In Spring one day
When snow still lay
And grass was not yet growing,
I heard a cry
Far up the sky,

A cry far northward going.
A-honk! A-honk! the notes
Blown from the long gray throats.

Oh where, oh where,
Through that thin air
Could those strong wings be flying!
Had fellows they
Along the way
To signal with their crying?
A-honk! A-honk! they blew
Far northward as they flew.

I watched their flight
Till out of sight
Faded the last gray flier,
Yet still that cry
Came from the sky
From somewhere farther, higher:
A-honk! A-honk! the notes
Blown from the long gray throats.

[Van Dyke's note.]

3   Theodore Strong Van Dyke, author of *The Still Hunter* and other books on hunting, one of them, *The Deer Family*, written in collaboration with Theodore Roosevelt. [Van Dyke's note.] For more on Theodore, see especially chapter 28, note 2.

4   A number of Van Dyke's relatives already lived in the region. William Duncan Van Dyke, for instance, was born in Milwaukee in 1856. Typical of many of the Van Dykes, he was a lawyer, and also typically, he prospered. He was the president of the Northwestern Mutual Life Insurance Company, a director of a railroad and of a mining company, and had real estate interests. See "Van Dyke, William Duncan."

5   Whatever the youthful rejoicing, this was an abrupt change for a family long established in the East. At the time, Van Dyke's father was in his sixty-first year, hardly an age to throw over a career and start anew in the West.

Van Dyke gives little motive for the uprooting. His *The Open Spaces* claims that the move was for the benefit of brother Theodore's health (143). However, by 1868 Theodore was an independent young man, physically active, and in no apparent need of the presence of the entire family. *The Raritan* casts a darker light on the Minnesota adventure. It notes the "discontent" of Van Dyke's father in his later years and his wish to "turn his back on courts and cities and civilization" (79). Family tradition has it that political reverses lay behind the elder Van Dyke's flight.

Chapter 5—Minnesota in 1868

1   Pronounced Wá-ba-sha. A resident told me that Wabasha is an Indian word meaning "red leaf." Several Sioux chiefs over the years also bore the name (Meyer 18–19, map opposite 42, 169). The 1980 Census lists Wabasha as having a population of 2,372, the 1990 Census, 19,744.

The little town is approximately 400 miles upstream from St. Louis, Missouri, as the crow flies, and much farther, of course, if one follows the twisting Mississippi River, as teenage Van Dyke did.

2   Van Dyke refers to the recent "big Sioux massacre." In 1862, the power of the Minnesota Sioux was broken when an uprising resulted in "many . . . killed and hundreds imprisoned or exiled" (Chaput and Stone 609).

3   There were Indians in the Wabasha area but not as Van Dyke describes. In a telephone conversation of 9 March 1992, Alan R. Woolworth, an anthropologist at the Minnesota Historical Society who has devoted his life to studying the Indians of the state, told me the following.

With the possible exception of poor, individual families scattered here and there, the only concentration of Indians in the area was the Prairie Island Dakota. The band lived on Prairie Island, in the Mississippi River, about sixteen miles south (downriver) of Wabasha. The little community consisted of perhaps a hundred people, mostly women and old men. Dr. Woolworth described them as "a pathetic remnant" of the eastern Dakota, survivors of the bloodshed of the early 1860s. The island's soil was poor, and the Indians subsisted on welfare and local hunting. Because of their poverty, the Indians had few horses.

Meyer states that "information on the Sioux in Minnesota during the seventies is scarce indeed" (271). However, his picture of the situation in the Wabasha area also shows a small Indian population of poverty-stricken and dispirited people (271–72).

4   Dakota and the buffalo I have described in *The Mountain*, chapter 1 (New York, 1916), and the Mississippi has also been dealt with in my *Open Spaces*. [Van Dyke's note.] The Indians Van Dyke would have encountered in Minnesota likely were poor and nearly horseless. Dr. Woolworth characterized the account of the buffalo hunt detailed in *The Mountain* (1–19), an excursion from eastern Minnesota clear to the Rocky Mountains and back, as "fanciful." In addition to the lack of horses, during this period the U.S. Army was coming down hard on the Indians of the northern Great Plains, which the hunters would have crossed. The plains Indians had been forced onto reservations and needed permits from their agents to travel beyond reservation boundaries. A band of Indians traveling hundreds of miles from its home, as Van Dyke describes, surely would have been noticed and pursued by the authorities, according to Woolworth. Nonetheless, Van Dyke's passages in *The Mountain* (1–19) and *The Open Spaces* (143–95), though colored with romantic exaggeration, are among his brightest, liveliest writing.

5   Was Van Dyke at once the clerk of both steamboats? Here his meaning is unclear.

6   *The Open Spaces* offers a more dramatic version of the incident (174–76).

7   Van Dyke read widely and practically "everything." I gather that eventually he had at least a working knowledge of French, German, Italian, Spanish, and possibly other languages.

8   For more on Theodore Strong Van Dyke, see chapter 28, note 2. His eventual settlement in Southern California would have an unexpected impact on John C. Van Dyke. Many years later, when he, too, sought relief from respiratory problems, he joined his brother Theodore, an event leading to the writing of *The Desert*. One of the large factors in the settlement of America's desert regions was the curative powers of its climate. See Jones.

9   Van Dyke's financial matters are something of a mystery. Here, as elsewhere,

he implies that he was not a man of great means, yet throughout his life he moved in elegant social circles, traveling widely and often around the world, even in the depths of the Great Depression.

10   Through their many generations in America, the Van Dykes had been a close, fairly stable family of the Northeast. The sudden breakup of the family struck Van Dyke with pathos. See *The Raritan* (74–89, especially 82).

Chapter 6—New York in 1876

1   The city was changing rapidly. Thirty years later, Van Dyke was singing its praises in *The New New York*.

2   From a close and powerful family, Van Dyke was blessed by numerous "contacts" with relatives and friends. People such as the Ferdons and the Lamberts keep weaving in and out of his life in intricate ways not entirely understood. His aunt's house in Piermont was about twelve miles north of Manhattan Island, an easy commute by train into the city.

3   Van Dyke, then, shows himself capable of criticizing the "older generation," and he will defend his own times against upstarts Van Wyck Brooks and H. L. Mencken. There's a difference, however, both in Van Dyke's tone and substance. Van Dyke's comments on his forebears are far more understanding and sometimes tempered by humor. He does not here attack personal beliefs with claws bared, as does Mencken. But when it comes to art, writing, and environmental issues, Van Dyke proves himself a more vehement critic.

4   This is an early mention of Van Dyke's groping toward two major aspects of his thinking about esthetics. He will reject realism in art, the story a picture tells, replacing it with appreciation of abstract forms and colors. As regards art history, Van Dyke's doubts about the attributions of famous paintings will lead to eventual publication of *Rembrandt and His School* (1923), a book that upset the apple cart of the art world. In such things, Van Dyke was something of an iconoclast.

5   Van Dyke's drive, opposed by a sense of being hopelessly overwhelmed, owes much to the Protestant ethic then holding sway, his family background, his own personal bent, and, according to Lutz, the temper of Van Dyke's time. Lutz argues that such frustration was endemic among the late, upper-class Victorians, who indeed felt overwhelmed by the societal changes outpacing their ability to adjust. In such a welter, notes Hoffer, "The individual's most vital need is to prove his worth, and this usually means an insatiable hunger for action. For it is only the few who can acquire a sense of worth by developing and employing their capacities and talents" (25).

6   To offer a context for events to come, as the family was breaking up and scattering, an idealistic and youthful Van Dyke flounders to get his sea legs in the "real world." In 1878, in the midst of his confusion, Van Dyke seeks refuge in the security of his childhood New Brunswick. There, he had numerous relatives, and his family's reputation bore considerable weight.

The oldest institution of its kind in the United States, the venerable New Brunswick Theological Seminary perches on what to this day is fondly called "Holy Hill," overlooking the Rutgers campus. It was a focus of the Reformed Church in America. Called "An Ark of Rare Books," the elegant Gardner A. Sage Library was dedicated in 1875 and served as a repository for valuable theological manuscripts and many records of the early Dutch in America.

Promoted in 1886 from assistant to head librarian, Van Dyke occupied a prestigious position, and he took his work seriously. He shows himself perfectly capable, whatever the romantic *Sturm und Drang* he was going through, to take a practical job in hand. It's a comment on his dual nature. The young Van Dyke, not much older than the students around him, began expanding the library's holdings—up until then concentrated on theology, Dutch history, and related subjects—into literature, art, and the sciences. Soliciting donations from wealthy Dutch families, Van Dyke became the most successful fund-raiser the Sage ever had. Eventually, he completed construction of the library's original Romanesque plan. In the overview, Van Dyke turned his library into the airy place of paintings, stained glass, and statuary that it remains to this day. What he did, and the library's background, Van Dyke explains in the "Sage Library" number of the *New Brunswick Theological Seminary Bulletin*. However, as the Reverend Daniel James Meeter shows in "The Gardner A. Sage Theological Library," not everyone has applauded Van Dyke's changes (72–73).

In 1889, Van Dyke also began lecturing across the street at Rutgers, and in a few years he became its first professor of the history of art. Add to his duties at Rutgers and the Sage his travels abroad and throughout the American West and the writing of nearly fifty books. Van Dyke's energy is little short of amazing.

That may have a good deal to do with Van Dyke's fortunate circumstances in New Brunswick. The Church was theologically conservative but intellectually generous, and as he expresses in the final chapter of his autobiography, Van Dyke enjoyed the camaraderie of his colleagues and the perquisites of a college and a seminary both graced with aristocratic timbre. In Van Dyke's day, the Seminary provided housing for its faculty members and families—some of it elegant, if one judges from the multi-storied Victorian houses on campus, since turned into student dormitories. The Seminary was so pleased with Van Dyke that it eventually built a house specifically for him.

Seeing Van Dyke in his comfortable campus home once again brings his dual nature into play, and not without certain irony. For here we see the sophisticated critic, capable of holding his own amidst the cuts and slashes of the *haute monde*, periodically retreating to a small college town. There, within earshot of mooing cows and at peace with himself, the world traveler overlooked the broad Raritan River and the woods and meadows beyond, where he often strolled. His house offered an idyllic prospect, and New Brunswick a comfortable "home base," as he puts it, a familiar refuge from the turmoil of the world beyond. Van Dyke's *The Meadows* glows with his love for his rural environs. See also Garland, *Afternoon Neighbors* (117–18).

The best I can make of it, the Van Dyke house, located at 564 George Street, perched on the grassy knoll behind what is now the Seminary's married-student housing. Prof. John W. Beardslee, who grew up on the campus, took me to the spot and assured me that two houses once stood between the Van Dyke residence and Bishop Place, a nearby street. This is important, because I have been unable to find any certain pictures of the Van Dyke house, and the information may help with tentative identification of the residence in old photographs. For example, Moffatt's *The Rutgers Picture Book* reproduces a two-page, bird's-eye lithograph of the Rutgers-Seminary neighborhood, done in 1910 (42–43). Counting from the corner of George Street and Bishop Place, I believe the Van Dyke house may be the third structure to the left, on George Street (43). The book prints an aerial photograph of the area taken in 1931 from a different perspective (106–107). Again, the third house from the same corner, this time counting to the right, should be Van Dyke's (107). Though Garland's *Afternoon Neighbors* describes the house as a "cottage" (117), the residence in question appears to be at least two stories and a fairly substantial affair for the needs of one man who enjoyed the services of a housekeeper. In another aerial view, taken in the late 1940s from yet a third perspective, the foliage of trees partially obscures the site, but it appears that the house is gone (180), confirming Prof. Beardslee's memory that the house was torn down sometime in the 1940s.

There are still rabbits and squirrels on this out-of-the-way portion of the campus, as there were in Van Dyke's day. For the wildlife about his house, see *The Meadows* (37–38, 53, 59–60). My *Interviews and Notes* contains further comment on the present site (143–45, 166–68, 178).

Chapter 7—Reading

1   In the light of the literary allusions and outright quotes sprinkled throughout much of Van Dyke's work, this paragraph is puzzling. Given the sense of the next paragraph, by his "first two publications" Van Dyke apparently means his first two articles. Their identity is unknown.

2   *Books and How to Use Them* (1883) was Van Dyke's first full-length volume. That Van Dyke's advice on how to use books drips with the pomposity of earnest youth is illustrated by the first sentence: "The true philosopher's stone, that by its magical touch converts existence into a golden success, is Knowledge" (7).

3   Mrs. Schuyler Van Rensselaer (Mariana Griswold, 1851–1934) was an author, art critic, and historian, married to an engineer. Her broad cultural interests typify Van Dyke's circles. Unfortunately, Van Dyke doesn't say what directions Mrs. Van Rensselaer gave to the young enthusiast's art fancies. Hamlin suggests some clues.

4   Perhaps an understatement. Intellectually flexible in some areas, Van Dyke could be independent to the point of bullheadedness in others. Frank Jewett Mather, Jr., friend of Van Dyke and professor of art history at Princeton University, remarks of Van Dyke that "in the literature of art criticism, he intentionally read little, preferring to stand on his own vivid impressions" (189). To judge from the books Van Dyke mentions early in his autobiography, it seems that especially in his younger years Van Dyke went through periods of reading art criticism. However, once he had formulated his own ideas, he plunged on largely unassisted, fueled by his own feelings of rectitude.

5   Van Dyke took his first trip to Europe in the early 1880s. The 1889 biographical article on Van Dyke in *Appletons' Cyclopaedia* notes that "He studied art in Europe in 1883, 1887, and 1888. . . ."

6   This is Van Dyke's first mention of "natural appearances," the Art for Art's Sake movement's appreciation of the forms and colors of nature, without regard to human meaning other than their beauty. This would become the theme for six of Van Dyke's books.

Van Dyke does not explain how he arrived at the concept of "natural appearances," whether he got it from Ruskin or Pater or some other writer. Van Dyke may not have known himself, since in the closing decades of the nineteenth century the idea was "in the air" and easily absorbed without knowing it by a young man searching for direction. In chapter 11, Van Dyke is nearly "bowled . . . over" when he finds someone else with a similar view of nature. Perhaps Van Dyke thought the concept self-generated, and there's at least the possibility that it was.

7   This is Van Dyke's big breakthrough in esthetics, the "aha! experience" psychologists talk about. Van Dyke already has shown his fascination for natural appear-

ances, for the effects of light on lakes and rivers and other features of nature. Now the scales fall from the young man's eyes, and he sees that paintings, too, can be appreciated solely for their decorative attractions. Thus, in this sense, nature and art are the same. Surprising himself, Van Dyke has forged the essential link of his artistic outlook.

It's difficult to pin down the precise date of the lightning stroke. Van Dyke doesn't say whether or not this is his first trip to Europe. However, considering the context and Van Dyke's reference to himself as a novice in this paragraph, as well as his wide-eyed wonder expressed in the next, it's fair to speculate that the event occurred on his first venture across the Atlantic, in 1883 or thereabouts.

8   Van Dyke may be referring to the strains resulting from the aftermath of World War I, such as the resentment in Germany over the huge reparation payments demanded by the Allies. He also hints at what probably bothered him more. Mass tourism was turning travel into a pedestrian affair. Gentlemen such as Van Dyke were losing their exclusive sheen as they got jostled in the tourist shuffle.

9   Newstead Abbey is the history-steeped ancestral home of the Byrons, located in Sherwood Forest, Nottinghamshire.

Chapter 8—Art and Artists

1   The holdings of the Sage Library contain a few rare copies of the magazine. See the New Brunswick Theological Seminary, in the archival sources section of the bibliography, below.

2   The list is revealing, a credit to Van Dyke's openness at this stage, for it contains artists with a wide spread of talents and approaches. La Farge, for instance, was a muralist also known for his work in stained glass. An early disciple of the Hudson River School, landscapist Inness, a Swedenborgian, saw the mystical in nature. Van Dyke's inclusion of the well-known Weir and Twachtman reflects his interest in American impressionism.

3   In Van Dyke's time, as now, New Brunswick was linked to New York City by rail, and to participate in the activities just discussed, Van Dyke would have made the thirty-mile trip regularly.

4   This is a good place to pause and consider the results of Van Dyke's artistic flounderings in the late 1870s and on into the 1880s. In a youthful welter, Van Dyke was trying to get his balance and form his own opinions amid the bewildering bombardment of ideas about art; he has been straining to find the "truth" about art, as if art had an essential core awaiting discovery by the determined searcher.

The consequence of his search was a fundamental shift in his esthetic perception of the world. The change would influence his way of seeing paintings as well as shape the prose of his nature/travel books, which largely are his way of seeing put into words. Van Dyke rejected realism, the story a picture tells. He replaced it with appreciation of a picture's forms and colors, without regard to its literal content. Though Van Dyke doesn't tell us the particulars of his slow "conversion," he became a devotee of the Art for Art's Sake movement, popular among the upper classes in the closing decades of the last century. Basically, such people held that the enjoyment of beauty is life's highest good, and along with some other followers Van Dyke arrived at the opinion that the greatest beauty is to be found not in paintings hanging on museum walls but in the forms and colors of wild nature. Wherever he traveled, the esthetician saw nature in terms of huge canvases which he described for his readers. Thus, in Van

Dyke we have a unifying feature, the essential link between art and nature confirmed by Sayre (114). A link, too, between the man's life and his art. No effete theorizer of the exclusive salon set, Van Dyke was a practical man toughened by his stolid Dutch upbringing and balanced by his genuine love of nature.

In terms of cultural history, the Art for Art's Sake movement may be seen as an escape. Frightened by the immense social problems caused by rapid industrialization, disgusted by the resultant slums, noise, and pollution—problems so huge they defied solution—many intellectuals fled in the opposite direction, into the idealization of nature, much as, perhaps, we do today. The danger here is sentimentality, hazy yearnings from comfortable living rooms and country estates for the pleasures of a nature created in the mind. It's a pitfall Van Dyke often avoided, again thanks to his interest in the outdoors and in science. On the last point, see my "The Handmaiden of Science."

Art for Art's Sake was a romantic movement treasuring individual feelings. It rejected authority and advocated a variety of often gauzy approaches. As Van Dyke thumps in *Art for Art's Sake*, great art can be recognized, but its greatness "cannot be reduced to rule" (50). You cannot "pin Nature to a board," he cautions in *The Desert*, "and chart her beauties with square and compasses . . ." (viii–ix).

As one might gather from this, Van Dyke, along with other romantics, places little value on consistency; indeed, he often violates his own dicta. What counts is the "impression" that he passes on, an impression so valid for him that he cares not one whit (or so he says) what the public thinks. This hardly is logically satisfying, but we can give thanks that he saw so well esthetically and had the talent to put his impressions into memorable prose. For more on Van Dyke's often wayward esthetics, see my *John C. Van Dyke: The Desert* (25–35) and "Van Dyke's Shoes."

But Van Dyke was a dualist, and he balanced his enthusiasm for the changing art scene about him with appreciation of the old masters. In this, the critic showed a stereotypically Dutch attraction, not only to tradition, but to a Leeuwenhoekian fascination for detail. Van Dyke bases his groundbreaking *Rembrandt and His School*, for instance, on a thirty-year study heavily emphasizing the master's brush strokes, a "signature" Van Dyke uses to identify Rembrandt's canvases. This is the classical, the scientific, side of Van Dyke. It's helpful to think of this as complementing, rather than opposing, his romanticism. As a romantic approaching nature, Van Dyke can wax rhapsodic over the drama of the panoramas before him, while as a classicist he doesn't fail to catch their details. To go the other way, as a classicist, as a scientist and a realist, he understands the physical forces producing such grand effects, but the romantic in him appreciates their intimate delicacy.

5   I have written about the cowboy and Montana in *The Open Spaces*, chapter 4. [Van Dyke's note.] This is "The Cowboy" (59–77), but don't miss "Riding the Open" (22–40) and "Riding the Ranges" (41–58). Van Dyke says, "I had one summer for a partner a boy who had killed two men, been a gambler, served a term for stealing . . ." (62). His "I had one summer" leaves one wondering how many summers and exactly when he worked as a cowboy.

6   Van Dyke reflected a common prejudice of the day, that wolves were "bad" animals and such creatures as deer were "good." At the time, the essential role of predators in nature's scheme of things was little understood.

7   Following custom, Van Dyke refers to the ranch by the brand it used on its cattle. However, what he remembers, both here and in *The Open Spaces* (55), as the 70L was the ⌐○⌐ . The brand can be read variously, but one way of putting it into

words would be "Reverse Seven, O (the letter, not zero), Reverse L." I have also seen it written simply "Reverse 70L." The large, unpaged map in *Faded Hoof Prints* shows the ranch as location Number 8, six miles upriver from Powderville and about midway between Powderville and Broadus.

As further concerns the ranch, we are dealing with two men, Van Dyke's cousin, William Ferdon, and his ranching partner, S. F. B. Biddle, both from well-off, Eastern families. In the *Annual Report of the Auditor and Treasurer of the Territory of Montana for the Fiscal Year 1885*, I could find no reference to either man or to the ranch brand in question. However, the report lacks an index, is somewhat unwieldy in its listing of brands, and may not be complete on the score, given the "rawhide" nature of ranching at the time.

In a further effort to establish a time frame for this chapter, I consulted volumes of the annual *Brand Book of the Montana Stock Growers' Association*. These proved more illuminating. The volume for 1886, the *Brand Book*'s first edition, lists Ferdon and Biddle as owners of the ⌐ O ⌐ and gives their post office address as "Powderville, Custer Co., Mont.," in the southeastern part of the state (70) (and since 1919 part of Powder River County). The 1888 volume repeats the information (50), and the unpaged front matter lists William Ferdon on the executive committee of the Association. See also the volume for 1890, with similar information (54).

Change comes with the volume of 1894. Both men still receive their mail in Powderville, but the partnership has broken up. Biddle now runs the Biddle Cattle Company, using the + brand (29), while Ferdon shows a new brand ⊟ (58). Ferdon appears for the last time in the 1899 volume (59). He is not mentioned in the brand books for 1900, 1903, or 1908. His ranching enterprise, along with many others, may have been a slowly dying casualty of the disastrous winters of the late 1880s.

That could place Van Dyke on his cousin's ranch in 1886, or perhaps somewhat earlier. The year of 1886 or thereabouts jibes with Van Dyke's mention of completing his first art book, *Principles of Art* (1887). The date holds well, too, in light of the reference below to Theodore Roosevelt, who ranched in the adjacent Dakota Territory between 1884 and 1886. A note in *The Mountain* concerning Van Dyke's first experience of Montana, his prolonged, boyhood hunt after buffalo with the Sioux Indians, refers to "a later trip across Montana, in the early eighties" (15). Van Dyke's dating can often be fuzzy.

However, I think we are on fairly sure ground to place the events under question as occurring roughly between 1884 and 1886. Following this sequence, the next chapter opens in 1887, with the publication of *Principles of Art*.

8   Though Van Dyke often discounts dangers as foolish imaginings, the cowboy had good reason to be nervous. Bounded by the Yellowstone River to the north, the Big Horn Mountains to the southwest, and the Black Hills to the east, the Powder River country had been the bloody focus of the Indian Wars of 1876. Though by the 1880s the threat of a large-scale menace by the Plains Indians had diminished considerably, memories, such as of Custer's obliteration in 1876, kept the white newcomers on edge. For their part, the Indians remained discontented and jittery.

9   Theodore Roosevelt ranched in the Dakota Territory during 1884–1886. Here, Van Dyke's original sentence reads, in part: ". . . of Theodore Roosevelt who had in 1883 taken up a ranch down there." At some time, Van Dyke struck out "in 1883," as if unsure of the date.

10   The nature of the relationship between Roosevelt and Van Dyke remains uncertain. Both men were associated with the Reformed Church in America, and

both were from prominent Republican families living not many miles apart. With this in mind, it's not surprising that Van Dyke states, "I had met him." Indeed, as earlier noted, Roosevelt coauthored a book with Van Dyke's elder brother. Furthermore, Roosevelt appears in the next chapter as a fellow member of one of Van Dyke's New York clubs.

Hinting at the possibility of a closer connection, someone later donated Roosevelt's communion beaker, a vessel of some monetary value, to Van Dyke's Sage Library, a gesture in keeping with tradition for the substantial number of well-off families in the church. See my *Interviews and Notes* (35–36).

Chapter 9—Authors and Painters

1   In the last chapter, Van Dyke was out in Montana, leaving his cowboy outfit and riding off "just to be alone and to feel for a time that I was the only human on the globe." Now he's a habitué of New York's private clubs, associating closely and often with people. Was he a loner or a joiner?

Keeping in mind the double nature running through much of his character, the reply is that he represented himself as both. He enjoyed close company, but at times he also yearned to wander off on his own. This parallels what people who remember him told me throughout my *Interviews and Notes*. According to the interviewees, Van Dyke was a dignified and aloof person with an idiosyncrasy or two, capable of a sharp tongue. But he was also a superb fund-raiser, popular lecturer, and a long-time member of the New Jersey State Board of Education who obviously could adjust his "loner" tendencies when the need arose to the social situation at hand. Mather's portrait:

> He was a man of magnificent stature, easily carried, with large gray-blue eyes that belied the habitual fixity of his fine olive mask. He wore his clothes well, said the right word and never too much, and exhibited a native dignity and kindliness. He had the gift of companionship, a perfect rectitude, an elevation of character entirely without pretentiousness. In any group of gentlemen he was a moral and physical ornament. (189)

See my reconstruction in "Curmudgeon or Campus Ornament?"

2   In rubbing shoulders with Twain, Howells, Henry James, and Roosevelt, Van Dyke was at the very center of a largely Northeastern, mostly white male, well-educated literary establishment. In their gatherings, openness and intellectual litheness were admired. Mark Twain, a man quick to sniff out pretention, was delighted by his first visit to New York City's Century Club, where Van Dyke later would be a member. Twain notes the liberal atmosphere, the "tendency to exclude parties who have bank accounts and pedigree, but no brains." And he was gladdened that the Club nourished both mind and body, for "Conversation there is instructive and entertaining, and the brandy punches are good, and so are the lunches" (Clemens, *Mark Twain's Travels with Mr. Brown* 89).

3   In those days, the thousand dollars offered must have seemed a handsome sum. Yet as things turned out, Van Dyke's instincts were right in preferring a royalty over the one-time payment. *How to Judge of a Picture* sold steadily over the years, and a royalty rather than a lump sum probably would have earned Van Dyke a far larger return. However, Van Dyke was quick on the uptake in business affairs. Once his growing reputation gave him leverage, he became a sharp negotiator with publishers.

On another matter, there is a problem surrounding the book that bears some explanation. In this case, there is a danger of confusion. The *National Union Catalog* lists an earlier edition of the book, supposedly published in New York by Hunt and Eaton in 1880 (629: 309). A number of libraries across the country also claim to possess an 1880 edition. This would make *How to Judge of a Picture* Van Dyke's first book-length publication, and its date would throw our chronology off by eight years. Van Dyke also muddies the issue when, as in chapter 8, he refers to "my first art book" but omits the title.

To state the matter clearly, there was no 1880 edition of *How to Judge of a Picture*. *Books and How to Use Them* (1883) was Van Dyke's first book. *Principles of Art* (1887) was his second book but his first book about art. *How to Judge of a Picture* (1888) was his third book and his second book on art.

The confusion arises from a problem in printing the date in a reprint of *How to Judge of a Picture*. After Chautauqua first released the book in 1888, reprints from several publishers followed. I have examined two copies of the supposed 1880 edition, one from the library of North Carolina State University at Chapel Hill, the second from the library of Central State University in Edmond, Oklahoma. Both bear imperfectly printed dates on the copyright page. The "9" in 1889 is lower than it should be, and its tail is only partially printed. The number easily could be misread "0" instead of "9," as some of my colleagues did when put to the test. I suggest, then, that this is an 1889 reprint mistaken for a nonexistent 1880 edition.

Further complicating the issue, the entry in the *National Union Catalog* for the supposed 1880 edition takes the publisher, Hunt and Eaton, as it appears on the book's copyright page (629: 309). The entry for the 1889 listing (629: 310) cites the publisher, Eaton and Maines, as it appears on the same book's title page. From this, one might wrongly suppose these to be two separate printings, at different dates and by different publishers. Again, I pursue the issue here only because establishing the correct date, 1888, for the book's first edition is vital to arriving at a proper time period for this chapter.

4 Van Dyke's slip-in of the date, 1928, may tell us something about the writing of the autobiography. Van Dyke dates his manuscript's preface in 1930. The typescript of the title page bears the date of 1931. Van Dyke's last three books were *In Java* (1929), *In Egypt* (1931), and *In the West Indies* (1932). One assumes, then, that he wrote his autobiography over the last few years of his life, turning to it in between other projects. Again, his energy, even in later years when illness plagued him, is impressive.

5 The relationship with Scribner's was long, lasting well over forty years, and Van Dyke's exchange of letters with Brownell revealing. See "John Charles Van Dyke Correspondence with Charles Scribner's Sons, with Related Papers," in the Princeton University archives.

To judge from the correspondence, the writer felt so at ease with his Scribner's editor that he let down his guard on his private life and showed himself a man of wide emotional swings (letters of 10 January 1916, 29 June 1911 [?], and 7 January 1926). On the other hand, Brownell was a man of more stable emotional constitution, wary of romanticism and "excessive individualism" (Bates 173). Van Dyke clung to Brownell for literary stability in the midst of his own, sometimes roiled, romantic impulses. Thus, he pleads with his editor to save him from banalities creeping into his prose (10 January 1916)—a huge admission for a man of Van Dyke's self-assured exterior.

Just how valid Van Dyke's concerns were regarding his own excessive emotion can be judged when he's left to his own literary devices, as in his *The Story of the Pine* (1893), not published by Scribner's. It's a tale about the love affair between two trees. All his life Van Dyke struggled against the huge reservoir of sentiment that lay beneath his granitic appearance (*The Raritan* 59), and he was fortunate to have Brownell as a literary rescuer. I am unaware of any further record documenting how Brownell guided Van Dyke or in what directions, but the letters indicate that the influence was large.

Among lesser matters revealed by the letters is Van Dyke's keen business sense. Today's readers of *The Desert* who like to think of Van Dyke as a romantic riding off into the wilderness with not a care for the practical aspects of the life left behind might be surprised by his strict attention to the business side of writing (letters of 20 January 1892, 20 September 1923, 2 September 1926, 4 July 1928)—to the extent of calling Scribner's on an error of $1.65 in a royalty statement (2 September 1915 and 3 September 1915)!

The correspondence receives more thorough treatment in my " 'My Dear Van Dyke'; 'My Dear Brownell.' "

Chapter 10—Lecturing in 1890

1   Throughout *The Raritan*, Van Dyke makes much of inheritance as a determiner of character, going so far as to call the little volume "a study in heredity" (1). As to the nervousness, sadness, and other negative qualities he assigns to himself, they result from the mating of the old Dutch with the Puritan strains in his background (87). On this, one recalls Lutz's study on the nervousness of the age.

Van Dyke's hesitancy to mount a platform seems a little strange, since in 1890 he was lecturing on art at Rutgers. I can remember but one other reference to Van Dyke's voice, and this information is not particularly helpful, since it refers to Van Dyke at the age of sixty-seven. Visiting the aging professor in his home, novelist Hamlin Garland refers to Van Dyke's voice as "husky" and "feeble" (*Afternoon Neighbors* 117). Whatever the case, as the chapter develops, another aspect of Van Dyke's dualism emerges. He belittles his lecture audiences, while also fretting about his successes with them.

Finally, as Van Dyke punishes himself over his public performances, one begins to wonder why he went to the trouble of joining the lecture circuit in the first place, though he explains the activity in terms of missionary zeal about art.

2   There is some uncertainty surrounding the dates here. The title of this chapter bears an 1890 date. The best I can tell, this is the year after Van Dyke began lecturing at Rutgers. Mather puts the issue this way: "In 1889 [Van Dyke] became a lecturer upon modern art at Rutgers College and from 1891 to 1929 was professor of the history of art" (188–89).

3   I have heard rumors that in his final years Van Dyke suffered from cancer.

4   Edwin Booth (1833–1893), a famous Shakespearean actor of the day and brother of John Wilkes Booth, Lincoln's assassin.

5   *Life and Letters of W. D. Howells.* 2 vols. [Van Dyke's note.]

6   There may be a touch of the defensive in the statement. Van Dyke held no earned degrees.

7   Besides serving as mayor of New York City, George B. McClellan (1865–1940) was, variously, an attorney, congressman, and patron of the arts. In light of Van Dyke's

admiration of Abraham Lincoln, there is an unintended irony here. McClellan was the son of General George Brinton McClellan, a controversial commander of the Union Army in the Civil War who unsuccessfully challenged President Lincoln in the bitter election of 1864.

Chapter 11—Friendships

1   Here and elsewhere in references to James McNeill Whistler (1834–1903), Van Dyke omits the details of the friendship with the flamboyant artist. When he does write about Whistler at length, he keeps his focus on the man's art (*American Painting and Its Tradition* 147–83).

2   This is Van Dyke's first book with a dedication. Laurence Hutton (1843–1904) knew how to enjoy his father's wealth through the pursuits of the bibliophile, the litterateur, and the traveler (Buck). There seems no essential link between the dedicatee and the content of the book, other than the friendship of the two men and their shared sympathy for the subject. In other cases, the choice of dedicatee may serve a larger purpose.

3   Henry Clay Frick (1849–1919), the steel, coal, and railroad magnate. His will left his mansion and art collection to New York City.

4   On May 31, 1889, a flood swept through Johnstown, a small city deep in a valley in the mountains of southwestern Pennsylvania. In a matter of minutes, the sudden deluge killed about 2,200 people.

5   The dedication reads: "To Frank Thomson, who knows and loves nature."

Frank Thomson (1841–1899) spent his entire career with the Pennsylvania Railroad. Through the years, he oversaw a wide range of functions, from improving brake devices to beautifying railway stations, and eventually became the railroad's president (Dixon).

Van Dyke often praises his friends but never as heartfully as when he mentions Thomson. In *The Open Spaces*, Van Dyke repeats the eulogy: Frank Thomson "taught me how to cast a fly, how to strike, how to play a fish. He was the most expert fisherman (and the best companion) I ever knew. I shall never look upon his like again, either as man or fisherman" (198).

Nature for Its Own Sake launched the "natural appearances" series of six similar volumes written over nearly three decades. After the general introduction of the first volume, each book thereafter examined a specific feature of nature from the esthetic viewpoint. The titles are *Nature for Its Own Sake* (1898), *The Desert* (1901), *The Opal Sea* (1906), *The Mountain* (1916), *The Grand Canyon* (1920), and *The Meadows* (1926). See my "A Western Sun Sets in the East" for further discussion of the series.

6   To judge from the many, favorable notices reviewers gave Van Dyke's books, the writer's oft-repeated complaints that the public misunderstood the purposes of his volumes, and that readers pigeonholed him, are exaggerated. Still, Van Dyke had his just gripes. The *Dial* thought the esthetically refined *The Desert*, his paean to arid-land beauty, such a handy item for sightseers that the book "should be in the travelling-bag of every transcontinental tourist by Central and Southwestern routes" ("In the Western Wastes" 23).

7   The long friendship between Van Dyke and Andrew Carnegie must come as another shock to readers who think of Van Dyke as an early forerunner of "Earth First!"

Throughout his books on nature, Van Dyke storms over the mindless destruction of the planet by the rapid industrialization of his age. To ask moneygrubbing developers busily "flaying the fair face" of the continent (*The Desert* 61) to spare nature for the sake of her loveliness is useless, a sentiment "to suckle fools withal" (60), and he rails against vandals spewing trash across his beloved land in hordes of automobiles "worse than the plagues of Egypt" (*The Open Spaces* 138). In his pained life, nature has been his balm, his succor, "the most lasting love of all" (*The Raritan* 86), but now he must watch as she's raped before his very eyes.

Then what is Van Dyke doing hobnobbing with Scottish-born Andrew Carnegie (1835–1919), one of the greatest developers America has ever seen? Even as Van Dyke wrote, Carnegie's railroads, steel complexes, and iron mines were polluting the pristine air and tearing up primeval landscapes.

I would be careful not to read blatant hypocrisy into the situation. Those were different times. Not yet radicalized, conservationists often enlisted wealthy people in their causes. John Muir was warmest friends with railroad magnate E. H. Harriman, and George Burroughs accepted a Model T from bird-lover Henry Ford. Whatever their varying opinions on some matters, there seemed plenty of nature to go around, and it was thought that gentlemen could sit down and work out their differences for the betterment of all.

Van Dyke could shift into different value systems as need occurred. After all, the man who proclaimed that the desert "should never be reclaimed" but "be preserved forever" (*The Desert* 59) often stayed at the desert ranch of his much-admired, elder brother Theodore, a developer of the desert. Then, too, Van Dyke was a thoroughly urban man, living most of his life in and around cities. His escapes into nature were just that, escapes ending in returns to civilization. Van Dyke, for all his poetic rantings, was not a Luddite. Practical Van Dyke was not against the cutting of trees and the mining of minerals. He *was* against waste, development that didn't take mind for the future.

Just how he brought this to bear when it came to Carnegie's spreading empire of steel mills and iron mines can't be said with certainty, though his view of Carnegie had its own logic. Carnegie, like Thomson, also was a nature lover, a man who enjoyed the outdoors. More than this, dualist Van Dyke divided millionaires into two types: good and bad. While the bad trustees of wealth were legion, interested only in profits regardless of the costs to nature and humanity, Carnegie was of the good sort, using his money to benefit mankind (*The Money God* 126–35). However one might agree or disagree with this line of reasoning, on the latter point Van Dyke was correct. Philanthropist Carnegie donated millions upon millions of dollars to schools, scientific institutions, and libraries—areas, we might point out, dear to the heart of educator and librarian Van Dyke (Ingham and Wild, "The Preface as Illumination" 335–37).

8   Note Van Dyke's view of himself as an "uplifter," as a teacher, a missionary, if you will. In the late nineteenth century the Reformed Church emphasized foreign missionary work. Quoted in the "John Charles Van Dyke Memorial Number" of the *New Brunswick Seminary Bulletin*, a former student at the Seminary recalls a young Van Dyke's "joy in the establishment of the new mission to Arabia in 1889" (10). Add to that Van Dyke's inborn rectitude and his Calvinistic sense of "being right," and you might view in Van Dyke the later writer and art connoisseur the secularization of the missionary spirit.

9   Carnegie's castles in Scotland.

Chapter 12—Fairs

1   At this point, a lacuna appears, for page 123 of the typescript ends about two-thirds of the way down the page. The first words on the top of page 124 of the typescript read, ". . . of date and out of countenance—mine with the others." They are crossed out. A new paragraph continues the text reproduced here, beginning, "John G. Moore, head of. . . ."

2   This is one of Van Dyke's few references to music in all his writings, and here it is sarcastic. Another mention occurs in "Green Oaks," chapter 3 of the autobiography. However, this seems more a backward glance through aureate glasses on childhood than genuine musical appreciation. Van Dyke fairly regularly notes aural phenomena in his books. He doesn't like noise, and as an amateur ornithologist he listens keenly for the calls of birds (though somewhat strangely complaining about the dearth of birdsong in places he travels). But as to human music, the man who saw so richly seems not to have heard richly. At least, that's the impression he leaves.

3   "The Lotto Portrait of Columbus" displays Van Dyke's persistent detective work in identifying a canvas. The article foreshadows Van Dyke's larger and far more controversial achievement, *Rembrandt and His School*. Apparently, feisty Van Dyke enjoyed sailing into a row and being shot at.

4   Despite Van Dyke's applause for captains of industry, note his own aristocratic disdain for making money. On his desert travels in chapter 19, he chances upon gold while digging for water in stream beds: "Occasionally, I found particles of gold at the bottom (seen through a microscope), but that did not greatly interest me." Then he adds, "I was not seeking gold," implying his was a higher calling, a search for beauty. He chuckles over men's cupidity, contrasted with his own indifference, in *The Open Spaces* (79, 92–96). His *The Money God* calls "ambition for mere wealth" the "evil of these American days" (vi). Despite Van Dyke's sharp business sense and his enjoyment of civilized comforts, making money for its own sake—or at least, talking publicly about making money for its own sake—was far beneath him.

5   For reasons unknown, Van Dyke could get his prose rolling into just such an occasional storm. Another example occurs in *The Open Spaces*: "In Greece, Turkey, Asia Minor, and the Balkans I never saw anything shootable, except some of the hotel people and a few camels that had been recommended for tourist travel" (241). This contrasts, however, with his sympathy for mankind, as shown in the outrage he felt over the treatment of the Yaqui Indians by the Mexican government (96–99).

6. American illustrator Joseph Pennell (1857–1926) was a long-time friend of both Van Dyke and artist James McNeill Whistler. Pennell did the drawings for Van Dyke's *The New New York*. For his tribute to the man, see Van Dyke's "Joseph Pennell."

Chapter 13—The Players

1   Van Dyke is a little miffed by Twain's humorous handling of him. But, once again, he has not told all. Rather than give an address, Twain's article wrongly identifies Van Dyke as "Professor Van Dyke, of Princeton" (446). Twain knew Van Dyke mainly through New York City connections, and it's possible that the humorist was fuzzy about Van Dyke's academic whereabouts. Or he could be confusing Van Dyke with his cousin, poet Henry van Dyke, who indeed was connected with Princeton. Or perhaps he confused the two men on purpose, as a further tweak.

2   We're left wondering who was pulling whose leg. Scholars propose a number of sources for Twain's celebrated frog story. This incident tells us much about Van Dyke, in that most of the anecdotes he passes on are positive, compliments to the people concerned. With his autobiography, Van Dyke had his chance to settle scores and fire parting shots, but as a gentleman he took a more gracious course.

A few further words about Twain and Van Dyke. One can argue that Twain made overly much of the "frontier" background of his early years, as perhaps did Van Dyke. Still, Hamlin Garland knew Van Dyke for years before he learned of Van Dyke's life in Minnesota (*Afternoon Neighbors* 117; *Commemorative Tributes* 291–92). Many writers shape their public images to their advantage. Twain knew what the public wanted, and he delivered it. A number of Van Dyke's books project a romantic image of their writer as an intellectual maverick and a lone wanderer, but beyond that Van Dyke mostly guards his privacy. Closer to home, Twain was notorious in his blustering dislike of Van Dyke's beloved painters, the old masters. But Twain's art "criticism" often is so unschooled and preposterous that we can imagine Van Dyke forgiving his friend with a chuckle.

Whatever their differences, Van Dyke and Twain had much in common: a genuine dreaminess and a sense of social justice. Add to that a love of wild nature and nostalgia for childhoods spent in nature's bosom. Both men shared a widespread malaise of the time, a feeling that in the rush of industrialization the nation had gone off the track from its bright promise, and the thought pained both men deeply.

3   James Brander Matthews (1852–1929), another man of "wealth and fine taste" (Odell 414), professor of literature at Columbia and for a time president of the Modern Language Association (416).

Chapter 14—In England and Scotland

1   This is Van Dyke's friend, the flamboyant Art for Art's Sake painter James Abbott McNeill Whistler. For a somewhat different, but more lively, version of the dispute, in which Van Dyke is the object of a Whistler joke, see Pennell and Pennell, *The Life of James McNeill Whistler* (335). For more on Van Dyke and Whistler, see the Pennells' *The Whistler Journal* (30–31).

2   Photographs in Carnegie's autobiography, edited by Van Dyke, give some idea of the lavish enormity of the Skibo castle (opposite 326, 356, and 370). For further anecdotes about visits with the Carnegies, see Van Dyke's *The Open Spaces* (203–9).

3   Van Dyke is here referring to English writer and statesman Sir John Morley (1838–1923). Further admiring words about Morley, as well as photographs of him, are found in Carnegie's autobiography (21–22, 188, 293, 311, 314, and 322–27). Carnegie also gives the background of the Acton library gift to Morley (325).

4   The Homestead Strike (1892) took place in Homestead, Pennsylvania, near Pittsburgh, while Carnegie was vacationing in Scotland. The violence resulted in the deaths of at least seven Pinkerton guards and of eleven strikers and bystanders, with many other people wounded on both sides. Because of the confusion during and after the mêlée, the exact numbers never will be known. Quelling the long disturbance required thousands of troops of the Pennsylvania militia.

Van Dyke's version emphasizes Carnegie's lasting pain over the situation and his refusal to hold a grudge. Carnegie's sentiments on the strike in his autobiography (228–38) quote Van Dyke on the McLuckie story (235–37) and conclude with a note by Van Dyke on the steel magnate's generosity (238–39). The separate studies of

Burgoyne and Wolff, along with others, give less buoyant accounts of the bloody mess and document Carnegie's involvement in the sordid company policies leading up to it. In his afterword to Burgoyne, Demarest concludes that Carnegie cared passionately about "his public image, which he was willing to maintain through duplicity, if necessary" (314). Hacker, however, presents a view kindlier to Carnegie (373–84).

Concerning long-term consequences of Homestead to Carnegie, both public and personal, the incident badly damaged his image and its barbed aftermath lingered long in his flesh. Following the strike, Carnegie and Frick parted ways and as time passed became bitter opponents. Years after the breach, an aging Carnegie sent an emissary to his former partner with an offer of friendship and a handshake. Wolff reports that "The response was, 'Tell your friend Carnegie that I will see him in hell where we are both going'" (249).

That Mrs. Carnegie asked Van Dyke to arrange her husband's notes into the book (vi), and that Van Dyke enthusiastically accepted the task (vii–viii), indicates the closeness of the two men.

5 I find the meeting in Mexico between John McLuckie and Van Dyke an extraordinary "chance" encounter but have been unable to unravel this curious happenstance. Wolff summarizes the little information we have about the hounded striker, once the mayor of Homestead, but unfortunately the historian offers no sources other than the Van Dyke account cited above (244–45). Wolff does offer that McLuckie's reply to Carnegie's generosity may have been sarcastic, since Carnegie had ruined him (245). Joseph Frazier Wall gives three sentences to McLuckie's Mexican adventure (579) and cites Carnegie's quote of Van Dyke (1084. n. 81). Burgoyne's contemporary account (297) and Demarest's afterword (312–13) shed little light on the issue. So we are left with Van Dyke as the sole source for locating McLuckie in Mexico.

Chapter 15—Of Many Things

1 Van Dyke took extensive notes and organized them thoroughly, but I suspect he wrote *alla prima*, as the painters say. That is, he worked quickly and with few changes. He wrote his autobiography in his vigorous, serrated, but hard-to-read longhand on twenty-two booklets, now in the archives of the Sage Library. Most of them are Blue Books, of the kind students still bring to college examinations. If I'm piecing this together accurately, he revised his first draft lightly, then handed the manuscript on to a typist. I believe he used a typist because many of the mistakes at this stage— misspellings of friends' names and of place names—are not the sort a writer likely would make himself. But such would be the errors someone trying to puzzle out Van Dyke's difficult hand would make. He next corrected the typescript, editing the text lightly and almost never changing the thrust of a passage. At least this was the method apparently used for the autobiography, and he may have followed a similar one for other books. I know of no other extant Van Dyke book manuscript in holograph, although the library of the American Academy and Institute of Arts and Letters in New York City preserves a trove of Van Dyke manuscripts along with other material. Perhaps most valuable among this is the corrected typescript of *The Desert*.

People in New Brunswick still recall that Van Dyke often worked at his desk in the Sage Library (Wild, *Interviews and Notes* 10, 22–23). Photographs in a scrapbook of Van Dyke material in the library show him seated at his desk beneath a large statue of Hagar and Ishmael. The significance of this I leave up to the reader (see Genesis 16).

The "John Charles Van Dyke" number of the *New Brunswick Seminary Bulletin* also suggests that he wrote in the Sage (10–11).

Though how and where a writer writes is of far less import than what he writes, I go into the matter at further length because at the end of it a small insight opens on Van Dyke's personality, one of irony and humor regarding the difference between the private man and his public face.

In the bulletin mentioned above, a former student at the Seminary remembers Van Dyke as "a cheerful, helpful guide" (10), another as a man "glad to turn" from "his own writing" to answer questions (9). However, "The Sage Library" number of the same bulletin, written by Van Dyke and published a year before his death, shows a different picture. After all those thousands of interruptions to his writing, his most important work, the forbearing librarian finally has his say. He urges that, rather than disturb the person at the library desk, patrons first should use their own brains and consult the card catalog. Yet, alas, a "great many callers have not [the] 'remotest idea'" of what they're after "but strangely enough fancy the librarian a mind reader who can tell them what they want by looking at them" (34). It's vintage Van Dyke.

2   Points to keep in mind when in chapter 23 Van Dyke complains over Scribner's reasons for rejecting the only novel he wrote.

3   I have rewritten this sentence. The original reads: "It was frankly material and in its elementary phase was nothing more than the examination of the painting for its technical and decorative qualities."

4   Born in Lithuania, American Bernard Berenson (1865–1959) was an acknowledged connoisseur of Italian Renaissance art. Today many of his conclusions are looked upon as unreliable.

5   Van Dyke's methods of determining the attributions of paintings contain much wisdom. However, he oversimplifies a complex task. It is true, as he observes, that the old masters tended to stay with a technique, but the particular technique of any one painter can vary greatly over the years as the artist matures. Studying the brushwork is only one tool among many, and it is by no means infallible.

Chapter 16—Play and Work

1   The original reads: "Wherever he went for recreation there were people to be met, sometimes about business but more often on recreation bent like himself."

2   American impressionist painter, John Twachtman (1853–1902). For a good sampling of his work, see Boyle. Twachtman was unable to adjust the intimacy of his impressionism to the expanse and power of the American West (62–63). Similar troubles dogged him when confronting the enormity of Niagara Falls (60–61). However, he could handle powerful seascapes (56–59).

Van Dyke praises the delicacy of Twachtman in *The Meadows* (32–33, 67) and likely had a Twachtman in his private art collection. Van Dyke's nature prose often seems Twachtman's impressionism put into words.

3   A three-quarter-length portrait, from the knees up. The term is not often used.

4   This may be the same dinner Wagenknecht describes in his *Mark Twain* (145).

5   Van Dyke's "cottage" hardly was small. The Onteora Club consisted of mansions scattered about a wooded mountainside, with a guard at the gate to turn back curiosity seekers. It was one of the most exclusive summer hideaways of the day.

Onteora offers the pleasures of a lake, golf course, field club, tennis, a library, and such, as well as hiking and fine views of the Catskills. Gaillard reviews the history of

Onteora and prints photos of the Parr house where Van Dyke stayed (17, 22) and a location map for the residences (21). For further notes on Onteora and other first-class amenities Van Dyke often enjoyed when away from New Brunswick, see my " 'My Dear Van Dyke'; 'My Dear Brownell' " (133–36).

There is evidence that even in his later years Van Dyke took part in the activities at Onteora. The legend on Harry L. Parr's *Map of Onteora Trails* states that the work is based "upon the map of the Trails Committee of 1930, John G. Evans, John C. Van Dyke."

Chapter 17—More Books

1   Van Dyke could show a keen business sense on the one hand and a disdain for mere moneymaking on the other. Here he is taking pride in a job well done—quite another matter. But he remains a Calvinist and has to josh himself for the "conceit" the success brought him.

2   The last edition of Isham has an introduction and additions by Royal Cortissoz. [Van Dyke's note.]

3   This is an early reference to Van Dyke's physical illness and bouts of moroseness. When assaulted by conflict, Van Dyke, like Twain's Huckleberry Finn or Hemingway's Nick Adams, follows the typical route for an American romantic—he flees toward the wilds.

Chapter 18—Montana

1   Theodore Strong (1863–1928) served as a New Jersey state senator and was a longtime Republican leader in the state. He was the father of Philip L. Strong, Esq., who preserved the manuscript of Van Dyke's autobiography.

2   Van Dyke frequently laments the passing of the wilderness, often with great bitterness (*The Desert* v–vi, 57–61; *The Open Spaces* vi–vii; *The Raritan* 8, 12). The nation that had recently conquered a wild continent next waxed nostalgic for what it had destroyed. Nash studies the phenomenon in both his books. However, more is going on with Van Dyke than participation in a general sentiment. Personally, Van Dyke disliked change. He sees an idealized past shouldered aside by a brash and rapid modern world, and he longs for what he perceives as the simpler, more stable ways of old (*The Raritan* 8, 12, 19–20, 74, 85).

3   At the time, cavalry troops of the United States Army administered Yellowstone, trying to bring an end to rampant vandalism by tourists.

The distance between Deadwood, South Dakota, and Yellowstone is about three hundred miles as the crow flies. The route lay across a largely roadless country of plains, mountains, and rivers. Such a trip would have been a rugged adventure, though a mere frolic when compared to Van Dyke's account of desert wanderings.

4   Murray's dictionary describes a Spanish windlass as "a wooden roller having a rope wound about it, through the bight of which rope an iron bolt is inserted as a lever for heaving it round" (9:508).

5   A measure Van Dyke claims he took in Mexico (*The Open Spaces* 95). Van Dyke could both romanticize and depreciate Indians (*The Desert* 6–22; *The Mountain* 1–19). However, at other times he showed deep sympathy for Indians (*The Open Spaces* 96–99).

6   Van Dyke is referring to his long, boyhood buffalo hunt with the Sioux, which

he says took him from Minnesota to the foot of Montana's Rocky Mountains. See *The Mountain* (14–19).

7   Van Dyke also possessed these qualities, whence his admiration for the renegade.

Van Dyke wasn't an easy sentimentalist when it came to animals. As a realist and a Darwinist, he knew that nature is "red in tooth and claw," as Tennyson put it. In *The Desert* Van Dyke says that nature "cares nothing for the individual" (230). Yet he also had his soft spot when it came to animals. In *The Meadows* Van Dyke chuckles over the antics of a squirrel living under his bathroom (53), enjoys romps with his dogs (59–60, 135), rescues a bird (31), and on autumn nights feels pity for "the little screech-owls that call at this time of year—call perhaps for the mother that has turned them adrift" and "have a chill whimper in their note" (236). Which is to say that with nature, as with so many other aspects of his life, Van Dyke brings to bear a wide range of emotions.

8   The passing reference to English critic John Ruskin (1819–1900) leads to some revelations about Van Dyke. In his essay "John Ruskin," Van Dyke acknowledges the influence of the English esthetician: "his great service to mankind has been his revelation of the beauties of nature" (12509). Van Dyke also shows that he understands his own esthetic provenance, for Ruskin "was a part of the romantic, poetic, and Catholic revival in this century" (12515). Lears details the phenomenon.

9   This is a rare mention of Van Dyke's involvement in politics, though he came from a politically active family. He also served on the New Jersey State Board of Education, perhaps more as an educator than as a politico. It is difficult to determine how politically active Van Dyke was. His writings at some times reveal decidedly conservative sentiments, at others decidedly liberal views. I find it a bit strange that for the most part he remains silent on major political events, even when, for instance, World War I breaks out. However, it would be in character for Van Dyke to stay aloof from the everyday throes of politicians but, as here, speak his mind when a clear, moral issue arose.

10   Van Dyke's abrupt and multiple resignations indicate a crisis in his life and a determination to make a sharp break with his past. This leads one to wonder if perhaps much more was involved in his unusual leave-taking than a trip for his physical health.

Neither the College nor the Seminary accepted Van Dyke's precipitous resignations. He had become something of an institution on the two campuses, and over the decades, College and Seminary were highly flexible in accommodating Van Dyke's absences for illness and travel.

Chapter 19—The Desert

1   This begins the journey that resulted in Van Dyke's most important contribution to literature, publication of *The Desert* (1901). The little book was the first to celebrate the beauty of the nation's vast, arid sweeps and remains the most moving work of its kind, the grandfather of almost all desert writing since, from that by Mary Austin to Joseph Wood Krutch to today's Edward Abbey. Yet as a work of "pure" esthetics, *The Desert* says almost nothing about Van Dyke's personal experiences on his journeys. Van Dyke's account needs to be read in the context of the doubts raised in my introduction, where I strongly suggest that Van Dyke was not a toughened

frontiersman striking out on his own into a feared land, but likely saw the desert through the windows of trains and hotels.

In his latter years Van Dyke published three pieces on his Southwestern experiences. The account in Van Dyke's *The Open Spaces* (1922), though unclear on the sequence of his travels, is the earliest and the most polished as literature (78–142). In 1924 he published "The American Desert" in *The Mentor* magazine, an article revealing that he took photographs (14) and made watercolors (9, 11) while he traveled— important references to the art critic's efforts in the visual arts. Unascribed desert photographs accompany the article, but I have been unable to identify them as Van Dyke's work, and this holds true for some of the watercolors and photographs in the archives of the Sage Library. Anyone interested in this aspect might consult the Sage's holdings as well as those at the Alexander Library of Rutgers University, a few blocks down the street from the Sage. Finally, most of the present chapter appeared as "My Experiences on the Desert," in the pages of *Progressive Arizona* (1931).

Readers with a geographical bent interested in tracing Van Dyke's route through the Southwest and Mexico are in for a wild ride. Though both Powell (Introduction 6–12) and Shelton (Introduction xix–xxv) have attempted it, they come to somewhat different conclusions. From Van Dyke's account here it seems clear that the route of the first stage of the trip, beginning in Southern California, led out into the desert through San Gorgonio Pass, where a freeway runs today, then down the Coachella Valley in a southeasterly direction. South of Yuma, Arizona, Van Dyke says he followed the marked, international boundary, probably to the Tinajas Altas Mountains, just over the border in Arizona. This was a well-known oasis for travelers, for the mountains contain Tinajas Altas (Spanish for "High Tanks"), deep plunge pools worn in rock by the heavy runoff careening down a mountain canyon after cloudbursts. The pools are the first reliable source of water east of the Colorado River. Then, discouraged by the land's dryness, Van Dyke struck north across thirty or so miles of desert for the railroad. There, as he hoped, he found the shade and water of idle tank cars.

Or so he claims. But the itinerary Van Dyke presents here is so scrambled, so shot through with inconsistencies and gaps, that we simply don't have enough information to follow Van Dyke with other than general accuracy. Because of the vagaries, much of the account strikes me as fabrication, spun from the stories Van Dyke heard from Southwesterners as he traveled about by train and visited his brother's ranch in Southern California.

And that brings up the related issue of exactly when Van Dyke made his series of desert travels resulting in *The Desert*. He writes his preface for the book in Mexico, at La Noria Verde (ix) (Noria Verde, an alternate name for Noria del Verde), approximately twenty-five miles north of Hermosillo, Sonora, in northern Mexico. Van Dyke dates the preface February 1901 (*The Desert* ix), though he did further desert wandering after that. From the "John Charles Van Dyke Correspondence with Charles Scribner's Sons, with Related Papers," we know that he mailed the manuscript of his book to his publisher from Del Rio, Texas, in the spring of 1901 (letter of 23 May 1901). Correspondence seems to indicate that Van Dyke returned to New Brunswick by July of 1901, his first excursion into the arid lands ended.

However, it is much more difficult to determine when Van Dyke began his famed desert travels. It is possible that Van Dyke may have earlier visited his brother in Southern California. But as to the particular travels under discussion, both Powell (Introduction 6–7) and Shelton (Introduction xi, xxiv–xxv) state the year was 1898.

My " 'My Dear Van Dyke'; 'My Dear Brownell' " reviews the where and when of Van Dyke's desert period (note 1, 139–42) and proposes 1899 as the correct date for the onset of Van Dyke's desert journeys. Let me sum up the issue. Van Dyke's 1901 preface to *The Desert* mentions his "two years of wandering," which by simple subtraction makes the beginning of his travels 1899 (ix). But Van Dyke isn't always accurate when he gives dates. His trip to Montana occurred in 1898, and I think the date for the Montana trip is the more reliable, as Van Dyke makes several references to the Spanish-American War of that year. Closing that chapter, after he returns to New Brunswick from Montana, Van Dyke notes that "the cold of February" is driving him to seek out the desert. That would make it February of 1899.

However one might wrangle over such evidence, rainfall records seem to clinch 1899 for the beginning of his desert experiences. In discussing the beginning of his trip and the difficulty of finding water in that dry land, Van Dyke notes that "it was a year of fierce drought," a point to keep in mind. A few paragraphs later, he's over on the "Colorado River near the Mexican border." Both Powell (Introduction 6, 8; *Southwest Classics* 323) and Shelton (Introduction xx) indicate that this occurred during the first year of Van Dyke's travels. I agree. So this locates Van Dyke in the early part of the journey a few miles from Yuma, Arizona, near where the Colorado River enters Mexico.

Something interesting jumps to light when one consults the annual precipitation chart, compiled at Yuma, for the years around this time:

Year	Inches
1897	4.12
1898	2.38
1899	0.60
1900	0.85
1901	3.65 (Sellers n. pag.)

From 1898 to 1899, then, the rainfall dropped off dramatically, from 2.38 inches to a meager 0.60 inches. In other words, in 1899 the desert received approximately one-fourth the rain of the previous year, a "fierce drought" indeed for that normally arid country. In 1900 the rainfall remains low, then it bounces back in 1901.

So we have two successive dry years, 1899 and 1900. I think we can eliminate 1900 as the first year of Van Dyke's travels. It simply would not give him time to visit all the places he did. And it would rudely violate the general time frame he states for his travels ("The American Desert" 3; *The Desert* ix). I know of no one who suggests 1900.

That makes 1899, the year marking the onset of the severe drought he mentions, the year Van Dyke first traveled in the desert. That is, at least to judge from the information he gives us.

Last, we might deal with a number of other puzzles surrounding the trip and Van Dyke's account. As seen from his text here, and contrary to the impression one might get from reading *The Desert*, the next two years did not consist of a solid period of desert exploration. Rather, Van Dyke traveled intermittently into the arid lands. Furthermore, both here and in *The Desert* Van Dyke treats the several distinct deserts he explored as one generic unit, often with little or no regard for their differences in landforms, flora, and fauna. Thus, in this chapter Van Dyke mentions the saguaro cactus even though readers may have the impression that he is in a place where there definitely are no saguaros. Perhaps Van Dyke used this telescoping of time and events for esthetic unity, or, perhaps, he was unaware of the distinctions.

Experienced desert travelers through the regions Van Dyke describes arch their eyebrows over the professor's rendition of how and where he went. My notes on this and the following chapter don't seize on every questionable issue possible, but they do discuss some of the major problems. To cite one, portions of the deserts Van Dyke crossed were so wild and waterless that, at least on parts of his trip as he tells it, even a man of considerable abilities in the outdoors almost certainly would need someone to guide him from water hole to isolated water hole and perhaps to steer him clear of local bandits. More than this, Van Dyke's statement that he traveled "for weeks without seeing a soul" simply doesn't ring true. Dry as some of that country is, it hardly was unexplored. Men since Spanish colonial times had searched it for minerals. In Van Dyke's day the region had its share of permanent settlements, Mexican ranches, and Indian villages. By necessity, these were located near the scarce sources of water. Thus, all but inevitably, a wanderer would come across such places and the people traveling among them, as indeed Van Dyke mentions in his version of the trip recounted in *The Open Spaces*, cited at the beginning of this note. In this regard, it's again worth bearing in mind that Van Dyke's *The Desert* is an esthetic rendering of his experiences, not a journalistic account of them. In the pages of his autobiography concerning the trip, Van Dyke is writing in a similar vein, blowing smoke for literary effect by leaving out the guides and the people he met—if indeed he ever ventured out into the desert on horseback for more than day trips. One cannot help but note that in chapter 23 Van Dyke states that he used his one novel, *The Jaws of the Desert*, to tell the "truth" about his desert forays—implying that the factual version of his desert travels appears nowhere else.

I could locate only one photograph of Van Dyke taken during his first Southwestern forays. Significantly, it shows Van Dyke, not in the dress of a vagabond, but of a gentleman. Given his interest in photography, the technology of the times, and the position of his hands in the picture, I suggest the possibility that Van Dyke took the picture himself, by remote means.

In any case, with his arrival back in New Brunswick in 1901, Van Dyke was not done with the West. It was one of his favorite places, and my sense of it is that over the years he returned a number of times—perhaps a good number. A family member has a number of snapshots of Van Dyke taken at Theodore's ranch. Two include John Muir, and others clearly show Van Dyke as older in the years after Muir's death in 1914. Besides Theodore, Van Dyke likely visited other relatives scattered about the West, and, as the coming chapters reflect, he also traveled about the region for his own pleasure and curiosity. In this, however, he left a blurred trail, and I've been unable to trace the exact where and when of his Western travels through the decades.

2   I take this to mean that Van Dyke had free railroad passes and perhaps enjoyed other courtesies from the railroads.

3   Van Dyke fails to mention that by the time he wrote his autobiography, he had a personal link to Hollywood. One of his nephews, Woodbridge Strong (Woody) Van Dyke, II (1889–1942), became a well-known movie maker of the 1920s–1940s (Cannom).

4   Popular, lightweight, maneuverable, the .30-.30 made a handy rifle for use in brush or from horseback. It was fine for deer in chaparral country, but considering its limited range and stopping power, one would have to be an optimist or in extremis to use it on the powerful grizzly bear.

Although it is remotely possible that Van Dyke saw a grizzly bear in the San Jacinto Mountains in 1899, the last grizzly known to have lived in Riverside County reportedly was killed about 1895 (Storer and Tevis 28). There were no gray wolves in California (Brown 19).

5   Van Dyke wrings too much horror out of the public's fear of the desert. Many people avoided the forbidding arid stretches. Others didn't. By the time Van Dyke arrived, the railroad crossed the expanse, and ranches and tiny settlements were pushing out into it. Furthermore, artists were beginning to appreciate the esthetic attractions of Southern California's deserts. For instance, German-born Carl Eytel had preceded Van Dyke into the area (Roy F. Hudson 2).

6   Grinding together all his food, including coffee, would have made a strange concoction.

Van Dyke's figure for the total weight of such equipment and supplies could be accurate, though I'm a bit skeptical. The rifle and pistol, along with their ammunition, would make up a good part of the weight, say, about ten pounds, depending on how much ammunition was carried. Add to that the gallon of water, at somewhat over eight pounds. Throw on the scales the hatchet, blankets, shovel, etc., and we haven't much room left for food that would last "for weeks." A horse, even a scrappy one as mentioned, can't carry a man, plus a large load, for long, particularly in the desert heat.

Van Dyke does not give the name of his horse, either here or in any other place he writes about his desert trips. The dog, Cappy, presents a conundrum. *The Open Spaces* describes Cappy as "a large fox-terrier" (87). This is confusing. Ranging in weight from fifteen to nineteen pounds, fox terriers hardly can be described as large, and in the next chapter we'll see Van Dyke carrying the dog under one arm, presumably onto a train. Possibly Van Dyke meant that Cappy was on the large size for a fox terrier. Though Van Dyke was a dog lover, I have been unable to locate a photograph of Cappy.

7   The saguaro is the giant cactus, emblem of the Southwest. The bisnaga, or barrel cactus, is a stout cactus much shorter than the saguaro. It is possible to get moisture from the barrel cactus (but, due to its woody interior, not much from the saguaro) in the way Van Dyke describes but not a great deal, and what it yields is bitter—nasty, sickening stuff. This contrary to old tales about desert wanderers tapping into cactuses for life-sustaining liquid. Hal Coss, a naturalist retired from the National Park Service, reacted to this passage by telling me that years ago he tested the myth. He drank about a half cup of cactus fluid. Within a few hours he was ill and sorely regretting his experiment.

Depending on a person's size, the weather conditions, the amount of exertion, and such, a man needs at least a gallon of water a day in hot weather. With similar variables in mind, a horse requires about ten to twenty gallons. This is a considerable amount to eke from slowly filling seeps.

It's hard to believe that Van Dyke or anyone else chewed creosote leaves to stave off thirst. Another example of literary smoke. Other than insects, few creatures can tolerate the chemical cocktail of the creosote plant. A lizard, the desert iguana, eats creosote as a staple, and jackrabbits will nibble small amounts. If Van Dyke followed the regimen he outlines, he would have been in terrible shape and probably dead— from dehydration, the poisons of the cactus juice and creosote leaves, and from the bacteria-laden water of some fetid pools.

8   Again, it's hard to take this paragraph at face value. Up in the mountains, the calls of doves gathered around water in canyons may lead a person to water. But out on

the flats, how does one know when birds are flying toward, or away from, water? Doves are not "the only desert birds that would drink at all." Some desert birds seem to go for long periods on the moisture they obtain from the insects, lizards, and snakes they eat, but in dry times few birds seem disposed to pass up a good drink if they can get it.

9   To repeat, there were no wolves in California. Even if there were, wolves are hard enough to distinguish from coyotes or wild dogs in daylight, let alone at night.

10   On this or some other stopover in Tucson, Van Dyke discussed the natural history of the desert with professors at the University of Arizona (*The Desert* 32, note; 134, note).

11   He is referring to the Baboquivari Mountains, or Baboquivari, the soaring main peak of the range, southwest of Tucson. This portion of the trip inspired one of the most vivid passages Van Dyke ever wrote:

> I have seen at sunset, looking north from Sonora some twenty miles, the whole tower-like shaft of Baboquivari change from blue to topaz and from topaz to glowing red in the course of half an hour. I do not mean edgings or rims or spots of these colors upon the peak, but the whole upper half of the mountain completely changed by them. The red color gave the peak the appearance of hot iron, and when it finally died out the dark dull hue that came after was like that of a clouded garnet. (*The Desert* 91)

12   Having left the United States, Van Dyke now is on or near the sparsely settled desert seacoast of Sonora, a state in northwestern Mexico.

13   Why did there seem "no alternative"? There's no apparent reason why Van Dyke couldn't have boarded the train in Mexico and been back at his Sage Library in a matter of days. Something of the loner's pose, of the abandon of Pierre Loti's books, and of the romantic morbidity of the times that Lutz studies in *American Nervousness*, may come into play here. Possibly Van Dyke may not be telling all at this point, and some other, personal factor besides physical illness or wanderlust may have driven him into the desert.

Chapter 20—Mexico

1   For a note on the publishing history of *The Desert* see Powell's *Southwest Classics* (326). Though Scribner's eventually stopped reissuing the book, it has been available since 1976, perhaps a comment on the contemporary interest in desert writing and ecology.

Powell's quote from Van Dyke's letter of 23 May 1901 to Scribner's at once reveals Van Dyke's high-minded attitude toward esthetics and his low opinion of popular taste. *The Desert* "is a whole lot better than the swash which today is being turned out as 'literature,'" thumps Van Dyke to editor Brownell, "and it will sell too, but not up in the hundreds of thousands. It is not so bad as that. My audience is only a few thousand, thank God" (*Southwest Classics* 325). It's a typical Van Dykeian comment when he is in his mode of toploftiness edged with sardonic humor. Ironically, the book sold well but for the "wrong" reasons.

The book was dedicated to A. M. C. In "The Preface as Illumination," Zita Ingham and I suggest that the dedicatee is Van Dyke's wealthy friend Andrew Carnegie and further that the choice serves a rhetorical purpose. We argue that the refined coterie of readers which would recognize Carnegie from his initials would read the book as a work of esthetics, as Van Dyke intended, rather than perceive it as a book about desert travel, as was largely the case with the mass audience. Van Dyke was wont to insert such little "tricks" into his writing.

In 1903, two years after publication of *The Desert*, the Carnegie Institution founded the Desert Laboratory in Tucson, Arizona. The Laboratory's purpose was to study desert ecology. However, I have not come upon any direct link between Carnegie and Van Dyke and the opening of the Desert Laboratory.

The saguaro cactus, symbol of the Southwest, bears Carnegie's name in its scientific designation, *Carnegiea gigantea*. Some scientists also refer to the cactus as *Cereus giganteus*.

2   Somewhat contradicting these last statements, Van Dyke inserts this note into the manuscript:

When *The Desert* first appeared, Dr. R. L. Woodward, the geologist, writing from Washington about other matters, at the end of his letter wrote that he had: ". . . read with interest and pleasure your book on the desert. Perhaps you will not feel flattered by my conclusion that you have just missed becoming an eminent geologist or geophysicist. There is room, however, in our small planet for all classes of men who write so clearly and plainly as you have done in *The Desert*." I refrained from answering that he had "just missed" comprehending my book, which set out to describe the desert from an esthetic, not a scientific, point of view. But I gladly accepted the compliment and let the comment go.

3   To trace Van Dyke's journeyings on a map during this period shows that he was traveling erratically, perhaps a reflection of his mental and/or physical condition.

In May of 1901, Van Dyke mailed the manuscript of *The Desert* from Del Rio, Texas, to Scribner's (see letter of 23 May 1901 in the "John Charles Van Dyke Correspondence with Charles Scribner's Sons"; also Powell, *Southwest Classics* 325–26).

4   The statement may come as a surprise to readers who form their impressions of the arid lands—and of Van Dyke as a heroic figure wandering through them—mainly from *The Desert*. Indeed, Van Dyke encourages just such colorful views in his book's preface-dedication. But *The Desert*, and his other works like it, are not travel journals, not true accounts of Van Dyke's journeys, but renderings of them through his painter's eye into esthetic experiences in print. The result is an idealized desert, attractive to Van Dyke's audience, as it remains to today's. This calls to mind David Muench's lush and popular (and technically excellent but, to me, overly chromatic and perhaps misleading) photographs of Southwestern deserts. In one of Muench's collections, editor Bernard L. Fontana comments: "It's almost as if Muench carried a copy of Van Dyke with him when he took his pictures" (Waters, "Editor's note" n. pag.). The photographs are captioned by quotations from *The Desert*. Such is the heavy sway of Van Dyke on our way of seeing deserts.

5   I have trouble reconciling Van Dyke's sense of sluggishness with his production. From 1901 to 1904, while continuing his duties in library and classroom, Van Dyke published four, full-sized books—an average of one a year—plus a number of shorter pieces. In any case, I find the dolefulness of the two paragraphs above curious in light of the following paragraphs' brightness.

Chapter 21—Art for the Public

1   It's interesting that Van Dyke recognizes "the missionary spirit" in himself and curious that he treats it with some humor here. Perhaps from the perspective of

later years he realized that the trait could swing over into a haughty self-righteousness. It seems to me that much of the frustration voiced in the following paragraphs arises because Van Dyke wouldn't accept the fact that the elitist writer isn't often popular.

Of pertinence to Van Dyke's view of himself as a leader in taste, among the four offices of the Reformed Church in America is the teaching office. Ministers are ordained into this category not simply to perform classroom work and oversee the spiritual development of their students. Clergy ordained into the teaching office also are teachers in the much larger sense. They take on the role of conscience of the public, as were the prophets of old, setting the community aright when it wanders. See my *Interviews and Notes* (17–18). Van Dyke was not ordained, but he worked among professors who were so charged in the teaching office, and something of the authority they bore may have rubbed off on him.

Add that his father was a judge, his grandfather on his mother's side an august professor of mathematics, and that the families on both sides had produced community leaders for many generations. As a missionary "carrying the gospel of art and nature to the heathen," Van Dyke bent a long tradition to his own artistic ends.

2   Van Dyke dedicated *What Is Art?* to James Brander Matthews (1852–1929), a professor of literature at Columbia University.

3   Dedicated to A. T., identity unknown.

Chapter 22—Adventures

1   The following events, as well as Van Dyke's presentation of them, are unusual. Typically, Van Dyke handles out-of-the-ordinary incidents—an attack by wolves or an encounter with bandits—by making them part of the larger story at hand. Here, however, the events are so bizarre that he passes them on for themselves.

One guesses the suspicions cast on the two travelers were part of the complex of intrigues building in the region before World War I.

2   Coleridge, "The Rime of the Ancient Mariner," part 2, lines 117–18. Van Dyke quotes from the poem in *The Mountain* (13).

3   Abdul-Hamid II (1842–1918) was the sultan of Turkey from 1876 to 1909.

4   The typescript curiously crosses out the parenthesis.

5   The penned revision substitutes "a friend" for "someone" and deletes all words through "Constantinople."

Chapter 23—To and Fro

1   Some of Van Dyke's imagery echoes George Perkins Marsh's in *Man and Nature* (1864). The first scholarly overview of man's often unintentional destruction of nature documented, for instance, that floods in river valleys may be caused by excessive logging far upstream. Marsh warned: "We are, even now, breaking up the floor and wainscoting and doors and window frames of our dwelling" (52). Van Dyke likely was familiar with the book that became the fountainhead of the conservation movement.

2   At first glance, *The Money God* seems an intemperate outburst about the nation's chief ill, greed (vi). As Van Dyke storms through chapter after chapter, he takes off after businessmen, labor unions, professors, and other groups. By book's end, he's had just about everyone in his sights, except Andrew Carnegie and men like

him. They should become society's models, Van Dyke argues, because they use their wealth not for private gain but for public good (129). For the rest, the nation is sliding on greased skids toward Hades, and the only hope, a slim one at best, is a return to "the Ten Commandments and the gospel of love and faith" (vii). It's worth remembering that many years earlier Van Dyke's friend Mark Twain had teamed up with Charles Dudley Warner to coauthor *The Gilded Age.* Unlike Van Dyke's humorless blast, however, the rollicking novel entertained readers with a sardonic view of avarice.

3   As observed, Van Dyke's trust of Brownell's literary judgment is extraordinary for a man otherwise wedded to his own rectitude, so he was all the more hurt at Brownell's rejection of his sole novel.

It's difficult to imagine a Van Dyke book with "no 'pep,'" though see his comments on the art of writing novels in chapter 15. And it's worth pondering that Van Dyke's supposedly nonfiction *The Desert* is a string of beautiful illusions, while he reserves the fictive novel for telling the "truth" about his desert wanderings. An illustration, perhaps, of the blurred boundaries in some of Van Dyke's writings.

No amount of opening table drawers in New Brunswick and elsewhere has yielded *The Jaws of the Desert.* I fear that it has disappeared along with most of Van Dyke's personal papers.

4   As in art, so in nature. Note the parallel here with Van Dyke's view of nature: "She cares nothing for the individual man or bird or beast; can it be thought that she cares any more for the individual world? She continues the earth-life by the death of the old and the birth of the new . . ." (*The Desert* 230).

5   See Poe's *The Raven.* The second line reads, "Over many a quaint and curious volume of forgotten lore. . . ."

Both the prose and Pennell's delicate illustrations in *The New New York* offer a pleasing transformation of an urban landscape into esthetic appreciation. But what an incredible irony with the book! The man who has spent much of his career praising nature and condemning civilization, who has just published a volume railing against commercialism and "the exhaustion of our natural resources" (*The Money God* vii), next reverses himself. He praises the handiwork of man and the businessmen whose wealth makes art possible (*The New New York* 147, 374). One suspects, especially from Van Dyke's note on the contradiction (147), that one of his motives with the volume was to mend fences with wealthy acquaintances who took umbrage at his attack in *The Money God.*

6   William M. Chase's (1849–1916) oil portrait of Van Dyke hangs in the Sage Library. My *Interviews and Notes* expands on the inscription on the back of the canvas (53–56, 98–103, 117–21, 128–35, 146–47, 217–26).

7   Another member of the international set, American painter John Singer Sargent (1856–1925) was born in Italy but settled in London. A virtuoso with his brush strokes, he did lavish portraits of socialites as well as impressionistic landscapes in watercolor.

Chapter 24—Glacier Park and Alaska

1   James J. Hill (1838–1916) was a financier whose Great Northern Railway crossed Montana.

2   Compare with his similar exhilaration over flowers in *The Open Spaces* (130). See also my "John C. Van Dyke: The Flora-Loving Frontiersman."

3   Van Dyke's use of "before" is not accidental. The opening sentences of *The Desert* read: "After the making of Eden came a serpent, and after the gorgeous furnishing of the world, a human being. Why the existence of the destroyers? What monstrous folly, think you, ever led Nature to create her one great enemy—man" (v).

4   If this was indeed a traditional Sun Dance, Van Dyke was watching a forbidden ceremony. Partly because of the human mutilation involved in the complex Sun Dance celebration and partly because the federal government wished to discourage Indian religions, in 1904 the United States outlawed the Sun Dance. Judging from Van Dyke's comments, the year is approximately 1909, the year before the official creation of Glacier National Park. Why would the Indians admit three white intruders to their outlawed ceremony? Such a large assembly of thousands of Indians would be remarkable. And where would they get the "huge tent"? For more on the time frame of the trip, see *The Open Spaces* (209–10).

Van Dyke's account shows that he was not always rigid in applying his artistic dicta. Theoretically, he rejected the meaning and the human context of art. They are irrelevant to the appreciation of the pure form and color. Here, however, the anthropological aspects of the ceremony have a large bearing on his esthetic excitement. Van Dyke assures us that this was "not a performance prepared for tourists" but a genuine religious event, an issue he makes much of elsewhere (*In Egypt* 15–22). In their distrust of technological society, romantics idealized primitive nature and the ways of "primitive" peoples, valuing such "authentic" experiences as Van Dyke here describes. See Lears (xiii–xiv).

5   Van Dyke's intelligent perceptions balanced by childlike appreciation tends to make him a man of superlatives for whatever happens to excite him at the moment. While celebrating the visual delights of the East Indies, on at least nineteen separate occasions he proclaims different aspects the most wonderful he's ever beheld. The irony is that he condemns the same trait in others.

6   Frederick W. Van Dyke (1852–1911). This is a rare reference to any of Van Dyke's brothers besides Theodore and the only one, the best I can recall, named in Van Dyke's extant writings. See *The Raritan* (83–89, and the unpaged family tree at the end).

7   It's hard to know how much sarcasm Van Dyke intends in this passage about his "cure" by the three-fingered doctor who was looking for gold where there was no gold. In *The Open Spaces*, Van Dyke testifies that years earlier, out on the range as a cowboy, he had treated a case of appendicitis with "heroic doses" of castor oil (72). Van Dyke claims his patient finally came around, for "he was too tough even for ignorance and malpractice to kill" (73). In light of Van Dyke's own nagging physical ills, it certainly would be understandable if he cast a jaundiced eye on the efficacy of doctors.

However, if Van Dyke indeed contracted the malaria mentioned earlier, that might well account for the recurrent bouts of fever which are typical of the persistent infection.

Chapter 25—Happenings

1   Dublin-born portraitist William Orpen (1878–1931) was a founding member of England's National Portrait Society. Knighted in 1918, by 1920 he had become the country's most fashionable portrait painter.

2   The painting likely is *On the Yacht* Namouna, *Venice*, 1890, by Julius L. Ste-

wart. It also is known as *The Yacht* Namouna *in Venetian Waters*. Van Dyke may be the man to the extreme right, reading to the lady in the striped blouse. Stewart did another painting of the *Namouna*, the less dramatic *Yachting in the Mediterranean*, 1896. However, none of the figures in this second piece is as readily identifiable as Van Dyke states he was in the painting he describes.

Born in Philadelphia to a well-off family, Julius L. Stewart (1855–1919) spent most of his life in Paris. A devotee of the opera and an accomplished pianist, Stewart captured the leisured class on lush canvases, sometimes, as here, with striking perspectives. Thompson quotes a wry connoisseur of the day on Stewart's tastes for subjects: "He never paints a woman who appears to be of lower rank than that of baroness . . . " (1047). As to the painting, the catalog for an exhibition of works by Stewart and other artists of his time throws light on the Van Dyke milieu:

> The *Namouma* was the largest and the most luxurious private yacht in existence when it was built in 1881 by the publisher and editor of the New York *Herald*, James Gordon Bennett. A floating palace nearly 227 feet in length, the ship boasted nine staterooms, a main dining hall, a ladies' salon, a number of offices, and a stairway of carved wood befitting a royal chateau. As the ne plus ultra of Aesthetic Movement exoticism and elegance, the general scheme of the interior decorations was directed by McKim, Mead and White, while Louis C. Tiffany, representing Associated Artists, carried out the mantelpiece mosaics and all the glass in the ship.
>
> Bennett had been an enthusiastic yachtsman since youth. One of the most picturesque, dashing figures of his time in France and America, his name was often associated with balloon, airplane, and yacht racing. He maintained three homes in the States as well as three homes in France and entertained on a lavish scale. . . . (*The Quest for Unity* 244–45)

Bennett is the second figure from the left.

The commentary continues by identifying the seated lady in the striped blouse to the right as the renowned English actress Lillie Langtry. The man reading to her is not identified as Van Dyke but as American playboy-sportsman Freddie Gebhard. However, the author admits some doubt in the matter, basing his statement on the oral tradition surrounding the work. Furthermore, he remarks that neither Langtry nor Gebhard likely were in Europe at the time (245). This, together with other evidence, such as Van Dyke's description, the centrality of the blond in the painting, and the fact that no other figure in the painting so immediately resembles Van Dyke, strengthens, but does not prove, the case for Van Dyke over Gebhard. Both men had similar, thin and athletic physiques. If Gebhard was absent, possibly the artist used his friend Van Dyke as a model for Gebhard, since, as Van Dyke says, "Models in Venice at that time were not easy to find."

For more on Stewart, his milieu, and the painting in question, see Thompson.

3   Born in Spain, Martin Rico (1835–1908) studied at the Madrid Academy but moved on to France in 1862. There, he fell under the sway of the Barbizon School of landscape painting and later showed the influence of Fortuny. I was unable to identify the infamous Carlotta.

4   *The Opal Sea* opens with a paean to "this Dalmatian coast" (v). The Ragusa of the setting is the Italian name for Dubrovnik, in what formerly was southwestern Yugoslavia—not the Ragusa in Sicily.

5 The poem and the two sentences before it are crossed out in the typescript. The poem strikes me as one of Van Dyke's more successful efforts in verse because here he uses his painter's eye to catch specific details enriching the sentiment of the piece. Poetic tastes aside, "The Piazetta" shows how deep genuine longings ran in the publicly dignified Van Dyke, and it reveals how lonely the world traveler—something of a loner to begin with—could feel in his later years.

Judging from the last line of stanza one and the date of the poem bracketing the events of this chapter, Van Dyke frequented Venice from the early 1880s through the early 1920s.

Chapter 26—New Undertakings

1 Van Dyke may have known Woodrow Wilson (1856–1924) from Wilson's days as president of Princeton, about fifteen miles southwest of New Brunswick. Wilson, of course, was a Democrat and Van Dyke from a long Republican tradition. Why, then, would a Democratic governor appoint a Republican to his Board of Education? To make himself look good is the suggestion of a person familiar with New Jersey politics of the time. With the Van Dyke appointment, Wilson could take credit for ecumenical generosity. Van Dyke's answering the call to put the state's school system "on a high plane" is in line with his family's tradition of public service. Van Dyke served on the New Jersey State Board of Education from 1911 to 1924.

2 Individual volumes in the "New Guides to Old Masters" series take their titles from the places they cover, for instance, the book on the Netherlands, *Amsterdam, the Hague, Haarlem: Critical Notes on the Rijks Museum, the Hague Museum, Hals Museum*. The volumes appeared in a pocket-sized format offering brief, picture-by-picture commentaries on the museums' holdings.

Besides the volume on the Netherlands, in 1914 Scribner's published guides on the museums of Berlin, Brussels, London, Madrid, Munich, Paris, St. Petersburg, and Vienna. After the war, Scribner's issued further guides on Rome (1924), Venice (1924), and Florence (1927).

Chapter 27—Work and War

1 Governor Wilson had launched a reform movement in the politically corrupt state, and the educational changes Van Dyke mentions were part of the state's forward-looking "fresh start."

Van Dyke's paragraphs summarizing his career on the Board of Education are more than usually telling. Perhaps Van Dyke's admirers too often think of him as a man of varying moods, in the romantic terms of melancholy and manic flights many of his books project. However, the writing here shows yet another aspect. He could roll up his sleeves, get involved in an argumentative fray, yet emerge friends with his other gentlemanly combatants. This is his realistic and positive side. Here, he cooperates with others in a common cause, handles dissension firmly yet graciously, takes pride in working like a wheel horse, and looks to the future with hope. The chapter's first paragraph contains the sole reference in the body of Van Dyke's extant writings to making use of his legal training.

2 Along with much of the world, Van Dyke and his friends refused to believe that a conflagration would break out. Then the people in Van Dyke's party began to realize they were in a trap quickly closing around them. The Carlsbad Van Dyke

mentions is the former name of Karlovy Vary, a spa in the western part of the present-day Czech Republic, in a region then ruled by Austria-Hungary. The vacationing Americans were deep within mobilizing Europe. Van Dyke makes his narrow escape through Austria-Hungary, Italy, Switzerland, France, England, and on home across the Atlantic. The crisis brings out several of Van Dyke's characteristics: his stubbornness, his shrewdness under fire, his loyalty to family, and his sympathy for people suffering around him.

3   This is "Devonshire" in the typescript, changed with pen to "Derbyshire." The "Devonshire" of the paragraph's second sentence is uncorrected.

Chapter 28—Mountain, Desert, and Grand Canyon

1   A study of the esthetics of mountains around the world, the book is the fourth volume in Van Dyke's "natural appearances" series. For further comment on the book, see my foreword to the reprint. I have been unable to identify B. R. C., the dedicatee of *The Mountain*.

2   The ranch of Theodore Strong Van Dyke was located in the Mojave desert, near the town of Daggett, California, east of Barstow. John C. Van Dyke often visited the place. Lest there be any confusion over its name, Silver Valley was a term applied to the entire area, not to this ranch specifically. Perhaps Van Dyke's "Silver Valley Ranch" actually is a shortening for the meaning of "the ranch that was in the Silver Valley." In any event, local people assure me that even in Van Dyke's time the place was called the Van Dyke Ranch, and to this day it is known as that or as the Old Van Dyke Ranch. According to Chambers (33), it may once have been called the Cold Water Ranch; there is a Silver Valley Ranch in the area, though it is not the old Van Dyke place. Or Van Dyke may have used the Silver Valley designation because his brother was associated with a land development company of that name. Fletcher reproduces a letter to him dated 8 June 1919, signed "T. S. Van Dyke," and bearing on its letterhead "The Van Dyke Ranch." Beneath it in smaller print appears "Located in the Silver Valley on the Main Lines of the Salt Lake and Santa Fe Railroads." The letterhead continues by informing us that "We make a specialty of fine alfalfa for horse feed" (152).

The Van Dyke Ranch is owned at the present time by Mr. Gordon Stricler (no "k"), a local historian of Daggett.

Keeling gives the general history of the area. For a brief account of a visit to the ranch, a photograph of the Van Dyke family, and another of the ranch, see 41–43. For a photograph of Helen Muir Funk, John Muir's daughter, at the ranch, see 192. For some colorful stories about Daggett and further photographs of the ranch, see two articles, "Law on the Desert" and "Old Times in Daggett," both by Theodore's son, desert explorer and historian Dix Van Dyke.

Theodore Strong Van Dyke was a journalist, land and water developer, outdoors writer, and a long resident of Southern California. He also has a niche in literature. His ironic novel about the land boom of the 1880s, *Millionaires of a Day* (1890), "initiates the tradition of life in the [Los Angeles] basin as a fantasy of development gone wrong" (Wyatt 158).

There is no full-length study of Theodore Strong Van Dyke. For further information and photographs, see Fletcher (151–61); "Pioneer of Desert Dies"; Smythe (414–17); Stone; "Van Dyke, Theodore Strong"; and John C. Van Dyke's *The Raritan* (83–89). In a letter dated 22 December 1949, written by Dix Van Dyke to a person identified only as Alice, Dix describes his father. For comments on Theodore's literary contributions, see Walker (115–17, 186) and Wyatt (158). Daggett was a rip-roaring mining town of the day, and Theodore was the area's justice of the peace, a man still colorfully remembered in local oral tradition. He conveniently kept the local jail at his ranch. It's still there.

Some haze surrounds the date Theodore first arrived in the Daggett area. This is a matter of importance concerning Theodore's influence on brother John's writing of *The Desert*. Stone says that Theodore bought some acreage near Daggett in 1903, a date two years after John C. Van Dyke published *The Desert*. Chambers says the family moved into the area in 1901 (33). However, in the above-cited letter of Dix Van Dyke to Alice, Dix states that his father "first came to Daggett in 1893."

Some of the personal papers of Theodore Strong and Dix Van Dyke are in the archives of the San Diego Historical Society and of the San Bernardino Public Library. The Mojave River Valley Museum contains related material and is rich in documenting the history of Daggett, surrounding ranches, and local personalities, as is the Daggett Museum.

3   See my "Van Dyke's Little Trick."

4   Generally, this is an accurate sketch of Scottish-born John Muir (1838–1914). Muir was an early explorer of California's Sierra Nevada. A founder of the Sierra Club, one of the nation's early conservation groups, Muir was famous for his abstemious habits while on the trail. When he was out in the wilds, nature was his food.

Given Van Dyke's wide acquaintance with literature, it is likely that he had read Muir long before he met him. For more on the possible influence of Muir on Van Dyke, see my "Viewing America's Deserts, Part 1" (64), and Ingham and Wild, "Viewing America's Deserts, Part 2" (314–15). Van Dyke mentions Muir briefly in *The Open Spaces* (131).

There was no contradiction in Muir's dislike of sheep. He realized that their massive overgrazing degraded the ecological diversity of fragile mountain meadows, a fault, of course, of men, not of the sheep. However, Muir is better known for calling sheep "hoofed locusts" rather than "four-footed locusts" (Wolfe 271).

In 1907 Muir brought his daughter Helen to live "near the town of Daggett on the Mohave Desert," says Muir biographer Wolfe (309). Muir hoped the dry desert air would cure Helen's chronic respiratory problems. Helen later married Buel A. Funk, a local rancher's son, and she continued living in the area. So again in Van Dyke we're adrift in time, here somewhere between 1907 and Muir's death in 1914.

For more on Muir and the possible connection to the Van Dyke ranch, see Wolfe (309–10, 327, 347). My "Months of Sorrow and Renewal" is a less happy portrait of Muir around the time Van Dyke knew him.

5   Pierre Loti, pseudonym of Julien Viaud (1850–1923), was a wildly popular French novelist of the Decadent school. His influence is difficult to overestimate. The exoticism of one of his novels so gripped frothy Paul Gauguin (1848–1903), for example, that it helped persuade the artist to select Tahiti as a paradisiacal refuge (Danielsson 29). Rushing madly into the darker side of romanticism, Loti attempted to lose himself in a life of debauchery, then thrilled his vast, international audience by writing about his experiences. In this respect, he hardly could be more different from self-disciplined and socially proper Van Dyke. But there are close similarities in the two men's abandon when they write about nature—so close that at times their writing is indistinguishable. My "Viewing America's Deserts, Part 1" develops the case that Loti may have been a major shaper of Van Dyke's *The Desert*.

6   *The Raritan* is dedicated "To C. V. D. P., With Much Love," that is, to Van Dyke's daughter, Clare Van Dyke Parr.

7   Originally called Queen's College, Rutgers was founded in 1766 by a charter granted by King George III of England. The school's early history owes much to the zeal for learning on the part of New Jersey's Dutch settlers. Queen's College became Rutgers College in 1825, renamed for Henry Rutgers, an elder in the Dutch Reformed Church. The college became a university in 1924.

Rutgers celebrated its sesquicentennial in October of 1916.

8   Van Dyke draws a sharp distinction between the scientific causes and the esthetic effects of nature. To him, when in his absolutist mode, the facts of nature are one thing, perhaps interesting as scientific curiosities, but of little import by comparison to the beauty they generate. As he states in *The Mountain*, the things of nature are but "the bases of form and color" (vii). See my "The Handmaiden of Science."

9   German-born artist William Ritschel (1864–1949) settled in California and spent much of his career painting nature in the American West. Van Dyke's spelling in the manuscript leaves the "e" out of Ritschel's name.

10   William Bass (1841–1933) is a central character in early Grand Canyon history. A hunter and a miner, colorful Bass also accommodated guests—many of them famous—in tent houses he set up at Bass Camp, then regaled them with tales of his exploits. A number of Canyon places, such as Bass Canyon, Bass Rapids, and Bass Tomb, where Bass's ashes were scattered, continue his name.

11   Once again, Van Dyke's version of his physical prowess needs to be considered in the light of my comments in the introduction about the disparity between reality and literary fantasy in Van Dyke. He's already advised hikers not to carry water (*The Grand Canyon* 110). Walking thirty miles in the Canyon, without water and in summer temperatures often soaring well beyond the century mark, is a feat defying credibility.

12   The book is *The Grand Canyon* (1920), the fifth in his "natural appearances" series. Details of dedicatee Marie Edgar are unknown. During Van Dyke's lifetime, *The Grand Canyon* went through three printings, and it remains a favorite among Canyon buffs. For further analysis of the work, see my foreword to the reprint.

Van Dyke's pride in *The Grand Canyon* shows between the lines of this chapter, but he often comments negatively on the book, here stating that "the shaft fell short of the mark." How could it not, when according to Van Dyke's esthetics, nature is the greatest art, irreplicable by man? In addition, a common theme in Van Dyke is that such natural wonders as the Grand Canyon simply are too vast to be captured by paint or in words. As he says in *The Desert*, "The desert is not more paintable than the Alps. Both are too big" (202). Knowing that he was doomed from the start of a literary work may have given Van Dyke solace as the romantic striving for the unachievable (see Van Dyke's admiration in chapter 16 for three noble but defeated artists). Nevertheless, in his valuable Grand Canyon anthology, Bruce Babbitt, former governor of Arizona, praises Van Dyke: "More than anyone, John C. Van Dyke was responsible for bringing canyon writing back to reality, to style and imagination built upon the bedrock of good observation and knowledge of real places and real rock formations" (59). Babbitt also notes that in objecting to such Canyon names as Cheops Pyramid and Hindu Amphitheater as "pseudo-poetry," Van Dyke began the continuing debate over the alien architectural and mythological nomenclature imposed on the wonder (58–59). See Van Dyke's *The Grand Canyon* (13–17).

Ironically, the Van Dyke who early in this chapter rakes scientists for their haughtiness ends by mentioning that he submitted the manuscript of *The Grand Canyon* to a scientist for his imprimatur.

Chapter 29—Concerning Rembrandt

1   Van Dyke devoted considerable attention to the Revolutionary War and the Civil War. He protested the Spanish-American War and gave a cliffhanger account of his escape from the onset of World War I. Strangely, then, he has little in addition to say about the latter conflict, at the time the greatest military upheaval the world had suffered.

2   *The Open Spaces* stands second only to the autobiography in revelations of Van Dyke's life. As he describes the book here, *The Open Spaces* relates his adventures in the outdoors. Concentrating on the American West, chapters show Van Dyke's boyhood on the Minnesota frontier, his days as a cowboy in Montana and Wyoming, and most importantly discuss his forays leading to publication of *The Desert*. Portions of the book also touch on trout fishing in the Eastern United States with Frank Thomson and on life in Carnegie's vacation castles on the moors of Scotland.

Structurally, the book consists of a string of episodes, with some near escapes thrown in for excitement—close calls with bears and bandits—and it captures the thrill of riding alone across the unsettled plains. All is delivered with the grace and humor of a man at his ease and at his literary peak. Contrary to what Van Dyke says here, however, the book is not formally part of the series "concerned with the beauty of natural appearances." The work contains much appreciation of natural beauty. Yet, as the subtitle, *Incidents of Nights and Days Under the Blue Sky*, indicates, the volume also presents a number of colorful people and discusses its writer's personal adventures. This contrasts with the esthetic stance of the "natural appearances" series. Here, relieved of an esthetic burden, Van Dyke looks back on his life and tells good stories about roaming freely in nature.

The personal features of *The Open Spaces* mark the book as uncharacteristic, and one puzzles why a Van Dyke who usually prides himself in keeping "the door barred" on his privacy lets the door open for this moment. His comments on the book in this chapter suggest an answer. Andrew Carnegie, one of Van Dyke's best friends, had recently died, and Van Dyke's editing of Carnegie's autobiography made him reflect on his own life. Van Dyke was well into his sixth decade by then, and perhaps the feel of the years moved him to ease his autobiographical proscriptions and leave something of his own personal record, as his friend had done. The sentiment had been working on him for some years, as can be seen in his preface to *The Raritan* (l).

Though there is some overlap of events in *The Open Spaces* and Van Dyke's autobiography, the two are companion works, the former discussing Van Dyke's outdoor life, the latter concentrating on his life among people, most often, urban people. Yet material in two further books fills in other gaps. As noted earlier, the first chapter of *The Mountain* (1–19) describes Van Dyke's story of his boyhood excursion with the Sioux after buffalo. His later *The Meadows* tells about wandering his rural haunts around New Brunswick and gives some glimpses of the idyllic college town.

I have been unable to track down Muriel Moore, the dedicatee of *The Open Spaces*. My foreword to the reprint offers additional context for the book.

3   In his heat, Van Dyke forgets to give the title of his first Rembrandt book, *Rembrandt and His School* (1923). If *The Desert* is the crowning work of Van Dyke the

romantic, *Rembrandt and His School* occupies a similar position for the classical Van Dyke. A meticulously assembled piece of detective work, the book culminates forty years of studying Rembrandt (vii).

The autobiography hardly exaggerates the howls that went up when the Rembrandt book appeared. Van Dyke's revisionist treatise stung critics and collectors where it hurt, in their reputations and, perhaps more painfully, in their pocketbooks. Royal Cortissoz's essay emerges from among the vitriolic attacks as one of the most thorough and evenhanded analyses of the book. How correct Van Dyke was in his judgments remains open to debate. For years the Rembrandt Research Project has been trying to determine the definitive catalog of the old master's work, and one sometimes wonders if any such project ever will settle the issue. In reviewing the current state of Rembrandt scholarship, Bailey credits Van Dyke with having "pioneered" the century's "effort to disentangle" the canvases of Rembrandt from those of his students (58).

No doubt anticipating the book's landmark nature, Van Dyke dedicates the volume to Clare Van Dyke Parr, the same relative so recognized by the dedication of his family history, *The Raritan*. She is the only person so honored twice by Van Dyke.

4   The book is dedicated to Georgiana L. McClellan, wife of George B. McClellan, to whom Van Dyke dedicated *The New New York*. Van Dyke sometimes traveled abroad with the couple.

5   See Matthew 22:21. Van Dyke's childhood was steeped in religion, and in later life the professor often caught the swing of Biblical language to make a point forceful. Ingham and Wild explore this aspect of Van Dyke's writing in "Viewing America's Deserts, Part 2" (309–10). The piece argues that, in certain passages, "With Van Dyke we have nothing less than nature writing as Scripture" (310).

Chapter 30—Compensations

1   The two institutions, intertwined as Van Dyke describes, are now known when referred to together as the American Academy and Institute of Arts and Letters. Van Dyke was elected a member of the National Institute of Arts and Letters in 1908 and served as its president in 1924–1925. He was elected to the more prestigious American Institute of Arts and Letters in 1923. "John Charles Van Dyke," an item in the obituary notes of *Publishers Weekly*, states that Van Dyke was "elected president of the American Academy of Arts and Letters on December 6, 1923." This is in error. Van Dyke never was president of the American Academy, and the date likely refers to his election as a member of that body.

Van Dyke's admission to the American Academy, coming so soon after the uproar caused by his first Rembrandt book, was perceived as an endorsement of a man whose "critical status remained unimpaired" in the eyes of the august American Academy ("John Charles Van Dyke"), though here we see Van Dyke chuckling that the decision to admit him occurred before the Rembrandt book appeared.

Geoffrey Hellman's "Some Splendid and Admirable People" gives a valuable overview of the two institutions, how they work, how they have dealt with squabbles over the years, and how they have changed. The conservative tastes in art and literature prevailing in the two institutions during Van Dyke's time must have offered a comfortable atmosphere for Van Dyke (57, 60, 61, 63, 72).

2   In the last two paragraphs, Van Dyke shows himself wading through a swamp of contradictions of his own creation. The man who prides himself as an independent

thinker also desires the approval of his peers; he looks down his nose at the opinion of "the general public" but glows when "the man in the street" shouts his praise. It's a measure of the man that in his later years he recognizes the inconsistencies in himself and accepts his own humanness. As he will in the next paragraph concerning his physical condition.

3   Another indication of Van Dyke's esteem in the eyes of Rutgers and the Seminary. He continued to reside in his house on the Seminary campus. Whether or not he received further remuneration from the institutions is not known.

4   See Hamlin Garland's sketch of Van Dyke sitting like "a gray old eagle" on his porch in Onteora ("John Charles Van Dyke" 293). Yet Van Dyke couldn't stop working. In the seven years remaining him he wrote seven books.

5   In his later years, busy as he was, Van Dyke shows himself mellowing from a hard-driving reformer into a more contemplative and accepting man. *The Meadows*, the sixth and final book in his "natural appearances" series, reflects the change.

His own poetry preceding each chapter of the book is pretty much, as he says, purple patch, but Van Dyke is overly apologetic in applying the term to his prose. *The Meadows* turns to the quieter joys of strolling the woods and fields around New Brunswick, familiar for so long that Van Dyke knew them "by heart." With only an occasional slip into sentimentality, he writes a tender and moving tribute to a man's home turf. Yet he hasn't lost his evocative powers, only channeled them differently. His memorable description of a snowstorm concludes the book (242–45). Even in old age, Van Dyke had the flexibility to change. For an expansion of the above, see my "A Western Sun Sets in the East," especially 227–28.

I have been unable to identify the dedicatee of *The Meadows*, Antoinette Devereux Andrews.

6   As discussed above, this was in the exclusive Onteora Club in the Catskills. For general background, see Gaillard. Also my "'My Dear Van Dyke'; 'My Dear Brownell'" (134–35). To this day, residents of Onteora refer to their mansions as "cottages."

Van Dyke says "we bought" the cottage. Whatever the financial arrangement, Clare Van Dyke Parr is the buyer listed on the deed of sale.

7   Despite his questioning of Winslow Homer's palette, Van Dyke used Homer's *The Cocoanut Palm* as a frontispiece for his book on the Caribbean, *In the West Indies* (1932), his final book-length publication.

Chapter 31—South America

1   Born in Argentina of American parents, naturalist William Henry Hudson (1841–1922) offers lush sketches of his boyhood and youth on the pampas in *Far Away and Long Ago*. When it comes to nature, both Hudson and Van Dyke share a similar excitement and dreaminess.

2   Here, as in other of his books, Van Dyke celebrates both wild nature and its conquest through development. As he states in the next chapter, nature seems so vast to him that it is "limitless." It was a misapprehension in the common wisdom of the day. However, in other places Van Dyke storms until he exhausts himself to depression over man's "monstrous folly" in his brash, mindless treatment of the earth (*The Desert* v). Here, man is the "great annihilator" (vi; see also 57–61). The conflicting attitudes again illustrate that philosophical issues rarely are cut and dried in Van Dyke.

3   This is *In the West Indies*, published in 1932, the year of his death.

Chapter 32—The West Indies

1   *In The West Indies* expands on Van Dyke's happy days at Barro Colorado (179–211).

2   Carl Posey reflects on the halcyon days of the setting in "The Bittersweet Memory that was the Canal Zone." Van Dyke's letter of 7 January 1926 in the "John Charles Van Dyke Correspondence with Charles Scribner's Sons" gives a hint of the racier entertainments available.

3   The United States military occupied Haiti from 1915 through 1934.

Van Dyke elsewhere applauds colonialism when it improves the lot of native peoples. *In Java* states: "The Dutch are indirectly making money out of Java, but they are letting the natives make money, too. . . . [The Dutch] are trying to establish a just and equable government and a prosperous colony. To that end they are confirming the land rights of the natives, introducing improved methods of irrigation and husbandry, conserving the forests . . . ," etc. (297). By contrast, *In the West Indies* is quick to criticize exploitation primarily for the white man's gain (39–41; 90–92).

4   Naturalist, writer, and oceanographer Charles William Beebe (1877–1962) won public attention in the 1930s when exploring the ocean in a bathysphere, a spherical apparatus for descending deep into the sea.

Chapter 33—Malay Archipelago

1   Possibly, ministerial office in the Church.

2   Actually, Van Dyke was less than half Dutch, though his sense of Dutch heritage certainly was strong. For the intricacies of his genealogy, the infusion of "alien" blood, and the effects Van Dyke perceives on the family, see his *The Raritan* (63, 66, 69–73, 74–76, 83–89, and the unpaged family tree printed at the end).

For well over a century, the line of Van Dykes in America married within its ethnic group and continued to speak Dutch. If I'm piecing the situation together correctly, around the Revolutionary War the old language finally "went out" in favor of English (71). This does not jibe particularly well with Van Dyke's rounded figure here for the family shifting languages "two hundred years ago."

Chapter 34—India and the Philippines

1   Van Dyke is seventy-two years old, suffering from bouts of illness, but still curious, still independent, still pressing to find and report "the truth."

2   I have not come across any evidence that Van Dyke ever flew in an airplane. This touches on his acerb attitude toward automobiles in *The Open Spaces* (138), though Van Dyke's own words didn't keep him from making use of automobiles and other technological conveniences when they suited his purposes (*In Java* 161, 232–33). Still, he manages to get in his dig: "The tourist and the automobile were sent forth by some avenging angel to destroy the earth" (239).

3   It is difficult to pin down Van Dyke's religious beliefs. Here, while giving no solid reason why, Van Dyke makes clear that he doesn't wish to visit the missionaries, and his words verge on the caustic. Was he simply offended by the man's insistence, or is something else being hidden? That Van Dyke ends the passage with an unemotional statement on the disaster of Crane's venture into the desert seems to have a bearing on Van Dyke's meaning. But all this by inference. The "John Charles Van

Dyke" issue of the *New Brunswick Seminary Bulletin* comments on Van Dyke's earlier "joy in the establishment of the new mission to Arabia in 1889" (10). This seems to be out of character with his attitude here. Once more, Van Dyke has kept the door barred.

4 The last two words echo Charles M. Doughty's *Travels in Arabia Deserta* (1888). Englishman Doughty had wandered through the Arabian desert, and the resulting book awakened the imagination of the English-speaking public to the romance and intrigue of desert travels. The widely read Van Dyke must have been familiar with Doughty's work and it probably influenced his perceptions during his early travels through Southwestern deserts.

5 After surveying conditions in Asia, Van Dyke doesn't hesitate to express his patriotism. Yet readers may be little short of amazed that the renowned travel writer dismisses China and Japan with a few listless sentences. Much of this chapter lacks Van Dyke's usual color and energy. Perhaps the aging professor was not feeling well, for he notes his discouragement at the "cold and rain" driving him from Japan toward the coming spring in home-town New Brunswick.

Chapter 35—Egypt

1 Van Dyke's trip resulted in his title *In Egypt* (1931), his penultimate book. His spirits have improved, and he is now curious about the people and antiquities around him. Even when he's griping about the exploitation of tourists, there's a happy edge to his words, a sign of life and hope rather than of weariness. *In Egypt* opens with Van Dyke on a steamer crossing the Mediterranean in a storm. Yet rather than complain about the weather, here he dwells on the visual delights of the rain and waves (3–4).

Van Dyke mentions leaving New York City in November of 1929. *In Egypt* refers to the winter of 1930 (161), the months of January (137), February (158), and March of 1930 (29). Van Dyke dates the preface of his book July 1, 1931, from the Sage Library. So the Egyptian venture lasted a good while, from November 1929 to at least March 1930. Once again, Van Dyke was avoiding the rawness of a New Jersey winter.

In Egypt is Van Dyke's "other" desert book, published exactly thirty years after *The Desert*. Wisely, the writer didn't try to top this masterpiece with *In Egypt*. Because of the different and more various approach to a desert land, *In Egypt* makes a good contrast with the earlier desert volume. Paralleling *The Desert*, it offers a series of impressions of what Van Dyke sees, but here, if his end is not as lofty, it is more entertaining. *In Egypt* is full of humor—probably Van Dyke's most humorous book— as he pillories not only the scheming Egyptians (171) but the tourists who "sit and watch the traffic and suck the paint off the handles of their canes and umbrellas" (15). But Van Dyke varies both his tone and technique. He insists with some heat that his travel journal "is not a guide book" (92), yet it is that, too, for he instructs readers about which antiquities should be on their "must" list and which to avoid as not worth their time in their boat trip up the Nile River.

Further varying the pace, *In Egypt* also is a book of visions—at least, an occasional vision creeps in. Romance, wonder, and the disparity between illusion and reality still lie at the core of the much older man. As his paddle-wheeler winds up the Nile:

> A native town perched on the river bank appears. At a distance it looks very romantic as well as picturesque. The pink and yellow houses overhang the Nile from terraces. There are glimpses of balconies, screens, latticed windows, as in Old Cairo, with gardens, trees and flowers. Laborers are loading stone into

felukas at the water's edge. A troop of cavalry is moving out of the town, along the river bank, its bright reflection in the stream moving with it. Seen through the palms are the exquisite rose and violet of the hills and above them the serene blue of the sky. Here again is an illustration out of *The Thousand and One Nights*. We might be under the walls of Bagdad. But no. It is just a squalid Egyptian town where a convict colony is kept at work. The convicts are loading the stone into the *felukas* for shipment to Cairo and the cavalry is presumably the guard that keeps an eye on the convicts. (70)

So *In Egypt*, too, is a book of appearances, the intermingling of the landscape with what's in the willful viewer's head. For further analysis of the volume, see my "John C. Van Dyke's 'Other' Desert Book."

2   Van Dyke despised camels as "evil-minded." There was a physical reason for the antipathy. The swaying gait of camels gave Van Dyke motion sickness (*In Egypt* 195).

3   The meager rainfall, far less than found in the arid Southwestern United States and Mexico, supports little flora and fauna.

4   The portion of the country to which Van Dyke refers probably is the coastline of Sonora, a state in northwestern Mexico. Its arid coast has fierce summers, but the winters for the most part are mild and sunny.

Warm, dry air—balm for his respiratory problems—was what Van Dyke sought all his life. He'd found relief on the deserts of the Southwestern United States, which he proclaimed "are the breathing-spaces of the west and should be preserved forever" (*The Desert* 59).

5   Theodore Roosevelt (1887–1944), the eldest son of former President Theodore Roosevelt, served as the governor of Puerto Rico from 1929 to 1932.

Chapter 36—At Home

1   By ending the story of his life at home, Van Dyke confirms the basic conservatism of the heritage underlying his ebullient romanticism. Though readers familiar with the ways of academe may doubt that Van Dyke's years at college and seminary were as idyllic as he portrays them below, nonetheless Van Dyke takes the gracious stance and at the last shows himself at peace with the world he'll soon leave.

2   Van Dyke's numbers do not add up to a total of 5,560 students. At this point, the manuscript shows an unusual doubt in purpose, with blanks left for numbers later inserted by hand, places crossed out, and words added, as if Van Dyke hesitates whether to count students only or all people associated with the university community.

Selected Bibliography

Part 1: Articles, Books, and Manuscripts

Aitken, William Benford. *Distinguished Families in America Descended from Wilhelmus Beekman and Jan Thomasse Van Dyke*. New York: Knickerbocker, 1912.

Almada, Francisco R. *Diccionario de Historia, Geografía y Biografía Sonorenses*. 1952. Hermosillo: Instituto Sonorense de Cultura, 1990.

Annual Report of the Auditor and Treasurer of the Territory of Montana for the Fiscal Year 1885. Helena: Territory of Montana, 1886.

Archibald, Raymond Clarke. "Strong, Theodore." *Dictionary of American Biography*. Ed. Dumas Malone. New York: Scribner's, 1936. 9, part 2: 152.

Ayer, Edward Everett. "Second Part of Mr. Ayer's Journal for 1918." Manuscript in Special Collections, Newberry Library, Chicago.

Babbitt, Bruce, ed. *Grand Canyon: An Anthology*. Flagstaff: Northland Press, 1978. 58–60.

Bailey, Anthony. "The Art World: A Young Man on Horseback." *New Yorker* 5 Mar. 1990: 45–48, 50–53, 56–77.

Banham, Peter Reyner. *Scenes in America Deserta*. Salt Lake City: Gibbs M. Smith, 1982. 152–69, 222–23.

Bates, Ernest Sutherland. "Brownell, William Crary." *Dictionary of American Biography*. Ed. Dumas Malone. New York: Scribner's, 1946. 3: 172–74.

Baylor, Byrd. "One of Tucson's Hottest." *Tucson Weekly*. 25 Sep.–1 Oct. 1991: 78.

"Bolshevism in Art Criticism." Rev. of *Rembrandt and His School*, by John C. Van Dyke. *New Republic* 24 Oct. 1923: 218–19.

Boyle, Richard J. *John Twachtman*. New York: Watson-Guptill, 1979.

Brand Book of the Montana Stock Growers' Association. Helena: Montana Stock Growers' Association, 1886, 1888, 1890, 1894, 1899, 1900, 1903, 1908.

Brooks, Van Wyck. "The Critics and Young America." *Criticism in America: Its Function and Status*. 1917. New York: Harcourt, 1924. 116–51.

Brown, David E., ed. *The Wolf in the Southwest: The Making of an Endangered Species*. Tucson: University of Arizona Press, 1983.

Buck, Paul H. "Hutton, Laurence." *Dictionary of American Biography*. Ed. Dumas Malone. New York: Scribner's, 1933. 5, part 1: 445.

Burgoyne, Arthur G. *The Homestead Strike of 1893*. 1893. Afterword David P. Demarest, Jr. Pittsburgh: University of Pittsburgh Press, 1979.

Cannom, Robert C. *Van Dyke and the Mythical City, Hollywood*. Culver City: Murray and Gee, 1948.

Carmony, Neil. Letter to this editor. 9 March 1992.

Carnegie, Andrew. *Autobiography of Andrew Carnegie*. Ed. John C. Van Dyke. Boston: Houghton Mifflin, 1920.

Carta Topográfica. Index Map. México, D.F. [Mexico]: Comisión de Estudios del Territorio Nacional, 1977.

Chambers, Wes, ed. "The Van Dyke Papers: Historic Routes in the Mojave Desert, Compiled from the Notes of Dix Van Dyke." *Quarterly* [of the San Bernardino County Museum Association] 38.1 (1991): 33–45.

Chaput, Donald, and Lyle M. Stone. "History of the Upper Great Lakes Area." *Handbook of North American Indians.* Ed. William C. Sturtevant. Washington, D. C.: Smithsonian, 1978. 602–9.

Clemens, Samuel Langhorne. *Mark Twain's Travels with Mr. Brown.* Ed. Franklin Walker and G. Ezra Dane. New York: Knopf, 1940.

————. "Private History of the 'Jumping Frog' Story." *North American Review* 158 (1894): 446–53.

Clemens, Samuel Langhorne, and Charles Dudley Warner. *The Gilded Age: A Tale of Today.* Hartford: American, 1873.

Cortissoz, Royal. *Personalities in Art.* New York: Scribner's, 1925. 17–43.

Danielsson, Bengt. *Gauguin in the South Seas.* Trans. Reginald Spink. London: George Allen and Unwin, 1965.

"Deed of Sale." Between Elizabeth A. Alexander and Clare Van Dyke Parr. 15 Oct. 1925. Book 242, page 79. Office of the Clerk of Greene County, Catskill, New York.

De Jong, Gerald F. *The Dutch in America: 1609–1974.* Boston: Twayne, 1975.

Dixon, Frank Haigh. "Thomson, Frank." *Dictionary of American Biography.* Ed. Dumas Malone. New York: Scribner's, 1936. 9, part 2: 483–84.

Doughty, Charles M. *Travels in Arabia Deserta.* 1888. New preface by the author and introduction by T. E. Lawrence. New York: Boni and Liverright, 1923.

"Dr. John C. Van Dyke, Rutgers Art Critic, Dies after Operation." *Daily Home News* [New Brunswick, N.J.] 6 Dec. 1932: 1, 3.

"Dr. Van Dyke Dead." *Art Digest* 7.6 (1932): 4.

"Dr. Van Dyke's Attack on the Rembrandt Tradition." Rev. of *Rembrandt and His School,* by John C. Van Dyke. *Current Opinion* 75 (1923): 689–91.

Dwight, Benjamin Woodbridge. *The History of the Descendents of Elder John Strong, of Northampton, Mass..* 2 vols. Albany: Munsell, 1871.

Edwards, E. I. *The Enduring Desert: A Descriptive Bibliography.* Los Angeles: Ward Ritchie, 1969. 241.

Faded Hoof Prints: Bygone Days. Broadus, Mont.: Powder River Historical Society, 1989.

Fletcher, Ed. *Memoirs of Ed Fletcher.* San Diego: privately printed, 1952.

Gaillard, E. Davis. *Onteora: Hills of the Sky, 1887–1987.* [Tannersville, N.Y.: Onteora Club], 1987.

Garland, Hamlin. *Afternoon Neighbors: Further Excerpts from a Literary Log.* New York: Macmillan, 1934. 117–18.

————. *Hamlin Garland's Diaries.* Ed. Donald Pizer. San Marino: Huntington Library, 1968. 62, 227–28.

————. "John Charles Van Dyke." *Commemorative Tributes of the American Academy of Arts and Letters: 1905–1941.* 1936. New York: American Academy of Arts and Letters, 1942. 291–93.

Graham, Frank. *Man's Dominion: The Story of Conservation in America.* New York: Evans, 1971.

Hacker, Louis M. *The World of Andrew Carnegie, 1865–1901*. Philadelphia: Lippincott, 1968.

Hamlin, Talbot Faulkner. "Van Rensselaer, Mariana Griswold." *Dictionary of American Biography*. Ed. Dumas Malone. New York: Scribner's, 1936. 10: 207–8.

Hays, Samuel P. *Conservation and the Gospel of Efficiency: The Progressive Conservation Movement, 1890–1920*. Cambridge: Harvard University Press, 1959.

Hellman, Geoffrey T. "Some Splendid and Admirable People." *New Yorker* 23 Feb. 1976: 43–48, 52–54, 56–57, 60–64, 68–81.

Hendrick, Burton J. *The Life of Andrew Carnegie*. 2 vols. Garden City: Doubleday, 1932.

Hoffer, Eric. *The Ordeal of Change*. 1963. New York: Harper, 1967.

Hubert, P. G., Jr. "Travels Far and Wide." Rev. of *The Desert*, by John C. Van Dyke. *Book Buyer* 24 (1902): 39–41.

Hudson, Roy F. *Forgotten Desert Artist: The Journals and Field Sketches of Carl Eytel, an Early-Day Painter of the Southwest*. Palm Springs: The Desert Museum, 1979.

Hudson, William Henry. *Far Away and Long Ago: A History of My Early Life*. London: Dent, 1918.

"In the Western Wastes." Rev. of *The Desert*, by John C. Van Dyke. *Dial* 1 Jan. 1902: 22–23.

Ingham, Zita. "Reading and Writing a Landscape: A Rhetoric of Southwest Desert Literature." Diss. University of Arizona, 1991.

Ingham, Zita, and Peter Wild. "The Preface as Illumination: The Curious (If Not Tricky) Case of John C. Van Dyke's *The Desert*." *Rhetoric Review* 9 (1991): 328–39.

————. "Viewing America's Deserts, Part 2." *Puerto del Sol*. 27.1 (1992): 303–21.

"John Charles Van Dyke." *New Jersey's First Citizen's and State Guide*. Ed. John James Scannell. Paterson: J. J. Scannell, 1919. 460–63.

"John Charles Van Dyke." *Publishers Weekly* 17 Dec. 1932: 2253.

John Charles Van Dyke Memorial Number. Spec. issue of *New Brunswick Seminary Bulletin* 8.1 (1933): 1–11.

Jones, Billy M. *Health-Seekers in the Southwest: 1817–1900*. Norman: University of Oklahoma Press, 1967.

Keeling, Patricia Jernigan, ed. *Once Upon a Desert: A Bicentennial Project*. Barstow: Mojave River Valley Museum Association, 1976.

Lears, T. J. Jackson. *No Place of Grace: Antimodernism and the Transformation of American Culture, 1880–1920*. New York: Pantheon, 1981.

Limerick, Patricia Nelson. *Desert Passages: Encounters with the American Deserts*. Albuquerque: University of New Mexico Press, 1985. 91–111.

Lopez, Barry. *Of Wolves and Men*. New York: Scribner's, 1978.

Loti, Pierre. *The Desert*. 1895. Trans. Jay Paul Minn. Salt Lake City: University of Utah Press, 1993. Forthcoming.

————. *La Galilée*. Paris: Calmann-Lévy, 1896.

Lutz, Tom. *American Nervousness, 1903: An Anecdotal History*. Ithaca: Cornell University Press, 1991.

Lyon, Thomas J. "The Nature Essay in the West." *A Literary History of the American West*. Ed. J. Golden Taylor, Thomas J. Lyon, et al. Fort Worth: Texas Christian University Press, 1987. 221–65.

————, ed. *This Incomperable Lande: A Book of American Nature Writing*. Boston: Houghton Mifflin, 1989. 69–70, 73.

Marsh, George Perkins. *Man and Nature: Or, Physical Geography as Modified by Human Action*. 1864. Ed. and introd. David Lowenthal. Cambridge: Harvard University Press, 1965.

Mather, Frank Jewett, Jr. "Van Dyke, John Charles." *Dictionary of American Biography*. Ed. Dumas Malone. New York: Scribner's, 1946. 19: 188–89.

Meeter, Daniel James. "The Gardner A. Sage Theological Library." *Journal of the Rutgers University Libraries* 45 (1983): 65–81.

Mencken, H. L. *Prejudices: Second Series*. New York: Knopf, 1920.

Mexico: Official Standard Names. Washington, D.C.: Office of Geography, Department of the Interior, 1956.

Meyer, Roy W. *History of the Santee Sioux: United States Indian Policy on Trial*. Lincoln: University of Nebraska Press, 1967.

Moffatt, Michael. *The Rutgers Picture Book*. New Brunswick: Rutgers University Press, 1985.

Murray, James A. H., et al., eds. *A New English Dictionary on Historical Principles*. Oxford: Clarendon, 1919.

Nash, Roderick. *The Call of the Wild: 1900–1916*. New York: Braziller, 1970.

————. *Wilderness and the American Mind*. 3rd ed. New Haven: Yale University Press, 1982.

Novak, Barbara. *American Painting of the Nineteenth Century: Realism, Idealism, and the American Experience*. New York: Praeger, 1969.

Odell, George C. D. "Matthews, James Brander." *Dictionary of American Biography*. Ed. Dumas Malone. New York: Scribner's, 1933. 6, part 2: 414–16.

"Painting the Town." *Daily Home News* [New Brunswick, N.J.] 16 Dec. 1988, sec. A: 1.

Parr, Clare Van Dyke. "Last Will and Testament of Clare Van Dyke Lambert Parr." Dated 5 May 1952. Proved 10 Dec. 1963. Surrogate's Court of Westchester County, White Plains, New York.

Parr, Harry L. "Last Will and Testament of Harry L. Parr." Dated 12 May 1964. Proved 18 Jun. 1964. Surrogate's Court of Westchester County, White Plains, New York.

————. *Map of Onteora Trails*. Map. [Tannersville, N.Y.]: The Park Committee [of the Onteora Club], 1933.

Pennell, Elizabeth Robins, ed. *The Life and Letters of Joseph Pennell*. 2 vols. Boston: Little, Brown, 1929.

————. *Nights: Rome-Venice in the Aesthetic Eighties; London-Paris in the Fighting Nineties*. Philadelphia: Lippincott, 1916.

Pennell, Elizabeth Robins, and Joseph Pennell. *The Life of James McNeill Whistler*. Philadelphia: Lippincott, 1911.

————. *The Whistler Journal*. Philadephia: Lippincott, 1921.

Pennell, Joseph. *The Adventures of an Illustrator*. Boston: Little, Brown, 1925.

"Pioneer of Desert Dies." *Los Angeles Times* 30 Jun. 1923, part I: 6.

Porter, Joseph C. *Paper Medicine Man: John Gregory Bourke and His American West*. Norman: University of Oklahoma Press, 1986.

Posey, Carl. "The Bittersweet Memory That Was the Canal Zone." *Smithsonian* 22.8 (1991): 156–58, 160, 162–64, 166, 168, 170–76, 178–79.

Powell, Lawrence Clark. "According to LCP." *Anchor & Bull: An Occasional Newsletter of the Friends of the University of Arizona Library* 5 (1985): 1.

_____. "The Desert Odyssey of John C. Van Dyke." *Arizona Highways* 58.10 (1982): 5–29.

_____. "Henry Van Dyke." *Anchor & Bull: An Occasional Newsletter of the Friends of the University of Arizona Library* 6 (1985): 3.

_____. Introduction. *The Desert*. By John C. Van Dyke. Tucson: Arizona Historical Society, 1976. 1–16.

_____. *Southwest Classics: The Creative Literature of the Arid Lands*. 1974. Tucson: University of Arizona Press, 1982. 314–28.

"Prof. J. C. Van Dyke, Art Authority, Dies." *New York Times* 6 Dec. 1932: 21.

The Quest for Unity: American Art between World's Fairs, 1876–1893. Detroit: Detroit Institute of Arts, 1983.

Rev. of *The Desert*, by John C. Van Dyke. *Athenaeum* [UK] 28 Dec. 1901: 869.

Rev. of *The Desert*, by John C. Van Dyke. *Critic* 39 (1901): 475.

Rev. of *The Desert*, by John C. Van Dyke. 1918 ed. Photographs by J. Smeaton Chase. *Dial* 19 Sep. 1918: 216.

Rev. of *The Money God*, by John C. Van Dyke. *Outlook* 20 Jun. 1908: 389–90.

Roosevelt, Theodore, Theodore Strong Van Dyke, et al. *The Deer Family*. New York: Grosset and Dunlap, 1902.

San Miguel de Horcacitas, H 12, D 31, Sonora. Map. México, D.F. [Mexico]: Comisión de Estudios del Territorio Nacional, 1973.

Sayre, Robert F. "Aldo Leopold's Sentimentalism: 'A Refined Taste in Natural Objects.'" *North Dakota Quarterly* 59.2 (1991): 112–25.

Schiff, Bennett. "Let's Go Get Drunk on the Light Once More." *Smithsonian* 22.7 (1991): 100–104, 106–11.

Sellers, William D., ed. "Total Precipitation (Inches) for Yuma, Arizona." *Arizona Climate*. Tucson: University of Arizona Press, 1960. n. pag.

Shelton, Richard. "Creeping Up on *Desert Solitaire*." *Resist Much, Obey Little: Some Notes on Edward Abbey*. Ed. James Hepworth and Gregory McNamee. Salt Lake City: Dream Garden Press, 1985. 66–78.

_____. Introduction. *The Desert*. By John C. Van Dyke. Salt Lake City: Peregrine Smith, 1980. xi-xxix.

Smythe, William E. *History of San Diego: 1542–1907*. San Diego: History, 1907. 414–17.

Stegner, Wallace. *Beyond the Hundredth Meridian: John Wesley Powell and the Second Opening of the West*. Boston: Houghton Mifflin, 1954.

Stone, Joe. "T. S. Van Dyke Paved Way for San Diego Water." *San Diego Union* 13 Aug. 1973, sec. B: 3.

Storer, T. I., and L. P. Tevis, Jr. *The California Grizzly*. 1955. Lincoln: University of Nebraska Press, 1978.

"Strong, Theodore." *National Cyclopaedia of American Biography*. New York: James T. White, 1907. 9: 288.

Sudol, David. "Perspective and Purpose: Person in John C. Van Dyke's *The Desert*." *Southwestern American Literature* 16.2 (1991): 14–22.

Swieringa, Robert P. "Dutch." *Harvard Encyclopedia of American Ethnic Groups*. Ed. Stephan Thernstrom. Cambridge: Harvard University Press, 1980. 284–95.

Thompson, D. Dodge. "Julius L. Stewart, a 'Parisian from Philadelphia.'" *Magazine Antiques* 130 (1986): 1046–57.

Van Dyke, Dix. "Law on the Desert." *Westways* 29.11 (1937): 14–16.

————. Letter to Alice. 22 Dec. 1949. Mojave River Valley Museum, Barstow, Calif.

————. "Old Times in Daggett." *Westways* 35.2, part 1 (1943): 16–17.

Van Dyke, John. *"Slaveholding Not Sinful": A Reply to the Argument of Rev. Dr. How.* New Brunswick: Fredonian and Daily New Brunswicker Office, 1856.

"Van Dyke, John." *Twentieth Century Biographical Dictionary of Notable Americans.* Ed. Rossiter Johnson. Boston: Biographical Society, 1904. 10: n. pag.

Van Dyke, John C. "The American Desert." *Mentor* 12.6 (1924): 1–22.

————. *American Painting and Its Tradition.* New York: Scribner's, 1919.

————. *Amsterdam, The Hague, Haarlem: Critical Notes on the Rijks Museum, The Hague Museum, Hals Museum.* New York: Scribner's, 1914.

————. *Art for Art's Sake: Seven University Lectures on the Technical Beauties of Painting.* New York: Scribner's, 1893.

————. *Books and How to Use Them: Some Hints to Readers and Students.* New York: Fords, Howard and Hulbert, 1883.

————. "Change" [Poem]. *Poems of New Jersey.* Ed. Eugene R. Musgrove. New York: Gregg, 1923. 45–46.

————. *The Desert: Further Studies in Natural Appearances.* New York: Scribner's, 1901.

————. *The Desert: Further Studies in Natural Appearances.* Photographs by J. Smeaton Chase. Notes by Dix Van Dyke. New York: Scribner's, 1930 ed.

————. *The Grand Canyon of the Colorado: Recurrent Studies in Impressions and Appearances.* New York: Scribner's, 1920.

————. *How to Judge of a Picture: Familiar Talks in the Gallery with Uncritical Lovers of Art.* New York: Chautauqua, 1888.

————. *In Egypt: Studies and Sketches along the Nile.* New York: Scribner's, 1931.

————. *In Java: And the Neighboring Islands of the Dutch East Indies.* New York: Scribner's, 1929.

————. *In the West Indies: Sketches and Studies in Tropic Seas and Islands.* New York: Scribner's, 1932.

————. *Italian Painting.* Boston: A. W. Elson, 1902.

————. "John Charles Van Dyke Correspondence with Charles Scribner's Sons, with Related Papers." Manuscript in Special Collections, Princeton University Library, Princeton.

————. "John Ruskin." *Library of the World's Best Literature.* Ed. Charles Dudley Warner. New York: International Society, 1897. 32: 12509–16.

————. "Joseph Pennell." *Commemorative Tributes of the American Academy of Arts and Letters: 1905–1941.* New York: American Academy of Arts and Letters, 1942. 200–207.

————. "The Last Will and Testament of John C. Van Dyke." Dated 8 Apr. 1932. Proved 12 Dec. 1932. Surrogate Court of Middlesex County, New Brunswick, New Jersey.

————. "The Lotto Portrait of Columbus." *Century Magazine* 44 (1892): 802, 818–22.

————. *The Meadows: Familiar Studies of the Commonplace.* New York: Scribner's, 1926.

————. *The Meaning of Pictures: Six Lectures Given for Columbia University at the Metropolitan Museum of Art.* New York: Scribner's, 1903.

————. *The Money God: Chapters of Heresy and Dissent Concerning Business Methods and Mercenary Ideals in American Life.* New York: Scribner's, 1908.

————. *The Mountain: Renewed Studies in Impressions and Appearances.* New York: Scribner's, 1916.

————. "My Experiences on the Desert." *Progressive Arizona* 11.11 (1931): 3–5, 18, 19.

————. *Nature for Its Own Sake: First Studies in Natural Appearances.* New York: Scribner's, 1898.

————. *The New New York: A Commentary on the Place and the People.* Illustrated by Joseph Pennell. New York: Macmillan, 1909.

————. *Old Dutch and Flemish Masters, Engraved by Timothy Cole.* New York: Century, 1895.

————. *Old English Masters, Engraved by Timothy Cole.* New York: Century, 1902.

————. *The Opal Sea: Continued Studies in Impressions and Appearances.* New York: Scribner's, 1906.

————. *The Open Spaces: Incidents of Nights and Days Under the Blue Sky.* New York: Scribner's, 1922.

————. *Principles of Art.* New York: Fords, Howard, and Hulbert, 1887.

————. *The Raritan: Notes on a River and a Family.* New Brunswick: privately printed, 1915.

————. *Rembrandt and His School: A Critical Study of the Master and His Pupils with a New Assignment of Their Pictures.* New York: Scribner's, 1923.

————. *The Rembrandt Drawings and Etchings, with Critical Reassignments to Pupils and Followers.* New York: Scribner's, 1927.

————. *The Sage Library: Its Books, Manuscripts and Portraits.* Spec. issue of *New Brunswick Seminary Bulletin* 6.1 (1931): 1–34.

————. *The Story of the Pine.* New York: Authors Club, 1893.

————. *Studies in Pictures: An Introduction to the Famous Galleries.* New York: Scribner's, 1907.

————. *A Text-Book of the History of Painting.* New York: Longmans, 1894.

————. *What Is Art? Studies in the Technique and Criticism of Painting.* New York: Scribner's, 1910.

————, ed. *Autobiography of Andrew Carnegie.* Boston: Houghton Mifflin, 1920.

————, ed. *Modern French Masters: A Series of Biographical and Critical Reviews by American Artists.* New York: Century, 1896.

"Van Dyke, John Charles." *Appletons' Cyclopaedia of American Biography.* Ed. James Grant Wilson and John Fiske. New York: D. Appleton, 1889. 6: 246.

"Van Dyke, John Charles." *Concise Dictionary of American Biography.* 3rd. ed. New York: Scribner's, 1980. 1078.

"Van Dyke, John Charles." *The National Cyclopaedia of American Biography.* New York: James T. White, 1930. C: 489–90.

"Van Dyke, John Charles." *Who's Who in America.* 1932 ed. 2331.

Van Dyke, Theodore Strong. *Millionaires of a Day: An Inside History of the Great Southern California "Boom."* New York: Fords, Howard and Hulbert, 1890.

————. *The Still-Hunter.* New York: Fords, Howard and Hulbert, 1883.

"Van Dyke, Theodore Strong." *Appletons' Cyclopaedia of American Biography.* Ed. James Grant Wilson and John Fiske. New York: D. Appleton, 1889. 6: 246.

"Van Dyke, William Duncan." *The National Cyclopaedia of American Biography.* New York: James T. White, 1933. 23: 66.

Wagenknecht, Edward. *Mark Twain: The Man and His Work.* New Haven: Yale University Press, 1935.

Walker, Franklin. *A Literary History of Southern California*. Berkeley: University of California Press, 1950. 115–17, 185–89, 200.

Wall, John P. *Chronicles of New Brunswick, New Jersey: 1667–1931*. New Brunswick: privately printed, 1931.

Wall, Joseph Frazier. *Andrew Carnegie*. New York: Oxford, 1970.

Waters, Frank. *Eternal Desert*. Ed. Bernard L. Fontana. Photographs by David Muench. Phoenix: Arizona Highways Books, 1990.

"Western Scenes and Problems." Rev. of *The Desert*, by John C. Van Dyke. Photographs by J. Smeaton Chase. 1918 ed. *Nation* 10 Aug. 1918: 148–49.

Wild, Peter. "Curmudgeon or Campus Ornament? Focusing the Images of John C. Van Dyke, Librarian/Professor." *New Jersey History* 108.1–2 (1990): 31–45.

————. Foreword. *The Grand Canyon of the Colorado*. By John C. Van Dyke. Salt Lake City: University of Utah Press, 1992. vii–xix.

————. Foreword. *The Mountain*. By John C. Van Dyke. Salt Lake City: University of Utah Press, 1992. vii–xiv.

————. Foreword. *The Open Spaces*. By John C. Van Dyke. Salt Lake City: University of Utah Press, 1991. vii–xxi.

————. "The Fox of Piscataway." *Sierra* 75.5 (1990): 68–71.

————. "The Handmaiden of Science in the Romance of John C. Van Dyke's *The Desert*." *North Dakota Quarterly* 59.2 (1991): 80–91.

————. *Interviews and Notes Regarding John C. Van Dyke*. Archives of the Alexander Library, Rutgers University; the Gardner A. Sage Library, New Brunswick Theological Seminary; and the University of Arizona Library. Sealed until 2009.

————. "John C. Van Dyke: A Western Esthetician as His Own Outlier." *South Dakota Review* 29.1 (1991): 7–23.

————. "John C. Van Dyke: Desert Days and Indians." *Onaway* [UK] 47 (1990): 3.

————. "John C. Van Dyke: Desert Saint or Flimflam Man?" *Valley Guide Quarterly* 4.1 (1993): 62–65.

————. *John C. Van Dyke:* The Desert. Boise: Boise State University, 1988.

————. "John C. Van Dyke: The Flora-Loving Frontiersman." *Wildflower* [Canada] 7.4 (1991): 38–41.

————. "John C. Van Dyke's 'Other' Desert Book." *North Dakota Quarterly*. Forthcoming.

————. "Months of Sorrow and Renewal: John Muir in Arizona, 1905–1906." *Journal of the Southwest* 29 (1987): 20–40.

————. " 'My Dear Van Dyke'; 'My Dear Brownell': New Perspectives on Our Foremost (and Most Coy) Desert Writer." *New Mexico Humanities Review* 35 (1991): 131–48.

————. *The Saguaro Forest*. Photographs by Hal Coss. Flagstaff: Northland Press, 1986.

————. "Seeing and Believing in the Southwest: John C. Van Dyke's Unwitting Conspiracy." *Sonora Review* 17 (1989): 49–57.

————. "Sentimentalism in the American Southwest: John C. Van Dyke, Mary Austin, and Edward Abbey." *Reading the West: Essays on the Literature of the American West*. Ed. Michael Kowalewski. New York: Cambridge University Press. Forthcoming.

————. " 'Sheilaism,' Words, and John C. Van Dyke." *Life on the Line: Selections on Words and Healing*. Ed. Sue Brannan Walker and Rosaly Demaios Roffman. Mobile: Negative Capability Press, 1992. 493–97.

————. "Van Dyke's Little Trick: Catching the Wily Esthetician in a Net of Poetry—Some of It (Probably) His Own." *New Mexico Humanities Review* 32 (1989): 116–28.

————. "Van Dyke's Shoes: Tracking the Aesthetician behind the Desert Wanderer." *Journal of the Southwest* 29 (1987): 401–17.

————. "Viewing America's Deserts, Part 1: John C. Van Dyke and the French Connection." *Puerto del Sol* 26.2 (1991): 58–78.

————. "Viewing America's Deserts, Part 2." See Ingham, Zita, and Peter Wild.

————. "Viewing America's Deserts, Part 3." *Puerto del Sol.*

————. "Viewing America's Deserts, Part 3: John C. Van Dyke's Literary Offenses, and Those Who Tried to Mend Them." *Puerto del Sol* 28.1 (1993): 147–61.

————. "Viewing America's Deserts, Part 4." *Puerto del Sol.* Forthcoming.

————. "A Western Sun Sets in the East: The Five 'Appearances' Surrounding John C. Van Dyke's *The Desert.*" *Western American Literature* 25 (1990): 218–31.

————, ed. *The Desert Reader: Descriptions of America's Arid Regions.* Salt Lake City: University of Utah Press, 1991. 111–20.

Wild, Peter, and Neil Carmony. "The Trip Not Taken." *Journal of Arizona History.* 34.1 (1993). Forthcoming.

Wolfe, Linnie Marsh. *Son of the Wilderness: The Life of John Muir.* New York: Knopf, 1945.

Wolff, Leon. *Lockout: The Story of the Homestead Strike of 1892.* New York: Harper, 1965.

Wyatt, David. *The Fall into Eden: Landscape and Imagination in California.* Cambridge: Cambridge University Press, 1986. 93–94, 158.

Part 2: Archival Sources

Most of Van Dyke's personal papers have disappeared. Much of what is left is dispersed. For example, one finds his letters scattered through many collections. The following lists the archives known to contain substantial Van Dyke material and material related to Van Dyke, both published and unpublished.

American Academy and Institute of Arts and Letters. New York, New York. A miscellany of approximately 300 items, business correspondence, press clippings, articles, and tributes, by, to, and about Van Dyke. Both Van Dyke and Clare Van Dyke Parr donated typescripts of some of Van Dyke's books, notably that of *The Desert*, to the holdings.

Daggett Museum. Daggett, California. Material on local history and some concerning Theodore Strong Van Dyke, his son Dix, and their ranch.

Mojave River Valley Museum. Barstow, California. Contains a variety of material relating to the history of Daggett, California, some pertaining to Theodore Strong Van Dyke, his son Dix Van Dyke, and to their ranch.

Montana Historical Society. Helena, Montana. This rich source should be the starting place for anyone interested in the state's old ranches. The archives contain numerous books, articles, and records with references to the Montana ranch of William Ferdon, where his cousin, John C. Van Dyke, worked, and the good people at the Society will guide the researcher toward local museums and libraries containing further material.

New Brunswick Theological Seminary. Gardner A. Sage Library. New Brunswick, New Jersey. A large number of items, including two oil paintings of Van Dyke; a scrapbook with coats of arms, letters, photographs, etc.; the holograph manuscript of Van Dyke's autobiography; a collection of photographs, watercolors, and drawings, some possibly by Van Dyke; a copy of Wild, Peter, *Interviews and Notes Regarding John C. Van Dyke*, sealed until 2009. Circulating holdings contain a large number of Van Dyke's books, including the rare *The Raritan*.

New Jersey Historical Society. Newark, New Jersey. A copy of Van Dyke's *The Meadows* and *The Raritan*. Photocopy of the typescript of Van Dyke's autobiography.

Princeton University. Special Collections, Princeton University Library. Princeton, New Jersey. Charles Scribner's Sons Archives contains the "John Charles Van Dyke Correspondence with Charles Scribner's Sons, with Related Papers," over 200 letters between Van Dyke and his editors at Scribner's, William C. Brownell and Maxwell E. Perkins. Also some miscellaneous papers, such as book contracts.

Rutgers University. Special Collections, Alexander Library. New Brunswick, New Jersey. Twenty manila envelopes in the Biographical Files, Faculty (Dead Files), hold newspaper clippings, articles, and monographs by Van Dyke, in addition to photographs, various articles about Van Dyke, and a notebook with two holograph poems and drawings likely by Van Dyke. Wild, Peter, *Interviews and Notes Regarding John C. Van Dyke*, sealed until 2009. Circulating holdings include perhaps the most extensive set of Van Dyke's published books available in one place.

San Bernardino Public Library. California Room. San Bernardino, California. "Dix Van Dyke Papers," a miscellany of letters, articles, clippings, notes, and typescripts, some of them concerning Dix's father, Theodore Strong Van Dyke. In the circulating holdings are the books formerly in Dix's personal library.

San Diego Historical Society. San Diego, California. Archives contain miscellaneous material, books and manuscripts of Theodore Strong Van Dyke, donated by his son, Dix Van Dyke. Manuscript of "Recollections of Boyhood Days in San Diego, 1880–1895," by Dix Van Dyke.

University of Arizona. Special Collections, University of Arizona Library. Tucson, Arizona. Photocopy of Van Dyke autobiography in holograph manuscript; partial typescript from holograph manuscript includes chapters 1, 2, 19, 20, 28. Wild, Peter, *Interviews and Notes Regarding John C. Van Dyke*, sealed until 2009. Circulating holdings include a large number of Van Dyke's books, notably *The Raritan*.

Index